Concrete Technology

Concrete Technology

Kiran Bhaskar
Assistant Professor
School of Engineering
NICMAR University
Pune, Maharashtra, India

CBS Publishers & Distributors Pvt Ltd

New Delhi • Bengaluru • Chennai • Kochi • Kolkata • Lucknow • Mumbai
Hyderabad • Jharkhand • Nagpur • Patna • Pune • Uttarakhand

ISBN: 978-93-5466-803-6

First Edition: 2025

Published by Satish Kumar Jain and produced by Varun Jain for
CBS Publishers & Distributors Pvt Ltd
4819/XI Prahlad Street, 24 Ansari Road, Daryaganj, New Delhi 110 002, India.
Ph: 011-23289259, 23266838 Website: www.cbspd.com
e-mail: delhi@cbspd.com

Corporate Office: 204 FIE, Industrial Area, Patparganj, Delhi-110092
Ph: 011-4934 4934 Fax: 011-4934 4935 e-mail: publishing@cbspd.com
publicity@cbspd.com

Branches

- **Bengaluru:** Seema House 2975, 17th Cross, K.R. Road, Banasankari 2nd Stage, Bengaluru 560 070, Karnataka, India
  Ph: +91-80-26771678/79 Fax: +91-80-26771680 e-mail: bangalore@cbspd.com
- **Chennai:** 18/8B, Subbarayan Street, Shenoy Nagar, Chennai 600 030, Tamil Nadu, India
  Ph: +91-044-42032115, 26681266 e-mail: chennai@cbspd.com
- **Kochi:** 42/1325, 1326, Power House Road, Opp KSEB, Power House, Ernakulam 682 018, Kochi, Kerala, India
  Ph: +91-484-4059061-65 Fax: +91-484-4059065 e-mail: kochi@cbspd.com
- **Kolkata:** 147, Hind Ceramics Compound, 1st Floor, Nilgunj Road, Belghoria, Kolkata 700 056, West Bengal, India
  Ph: +91-033-25633055, 033-25633056 e-mail: kolkata@cbspd.com
- **Lucknow:** Basement, Khushnuma Complex, 7-Meerabai Marg (behind Jawahar Bhawan), Lucknow 226 001, UP, India
  Ph: +91-522-400043, 9919002738 e-mail: tiwari.lucknow@cbspd.com
- **Mumbai:** PWD Shed, Gala no. 25/26, Ramchandra Bhatt Marg, Next to JJ Hospital Gate no. 2
  Opp. Union Bank of India, Noorbaug, Mumbai-400009, Maharashtra, India
  Ph: 022-60061880/89 e-mail: mumbai@cbspd.com

Representatives

- **Hyderabad** 0-9885175004
- **Jharkhand** 0-9811541605
- **Nagpur** 0-8692091830
- **Patna** 0-9334159340
- **Pune** 0-9664372571
- **Uttarakhand** 0-9716462459

Printed at: SRK Graphics, Delhi, India

Preface

Cement concrete is the most widely used building material in the world. It plays an important role in infrastructure and buildings construction. Due to the fast development of construction worldwide over the past decade, concrete technology has advanced significantly. This title reflects the frontier development of concrete technology.

Concrete technology delivers a state-of-the-art exploration of contemporary and advanced concrete technologies developed over the last decade. It emphasizes the fundamental and scientific exploration of materials structures of concrete, and clarifies the essential concepts of concrete. The book combines the theories of concrete with practical examples of material design, explains the correlations among the composition, processing, characterization, properties, and performance of concrete and stresses the constraint of end-users on materials development.

This book is divided into thirteen chapters, including chapters on descriptions of the most recent advances in concrete technology. Chapter 1 gives a thorough introduction to concrete, including definition and historical evolution, as a material used in engineering and construction. Chapter 2 provides an in-depth insight into the materials for making concrete with detailed explanations on cement, aggregates, mineral admixtures, and water. Chapter 3 deals with the chemical and mineral admixtures. The impact of accelerators, superplasticizers, waterproofers to mineral additives on concrete properties is understood. Chapter 4 discusses the properties of fresh concrete, including its workability and rheology. Chapter 5 discusses the methods for manufacturing, delivery, placing, compaction, finishing, and curing of concrete. Chapter 6 presents rheological models for fresh concrete, offering insights into its flow and deformation characteristics. Chapter 7 covers the properties of hardened concrete, including its strength, the stress-strain relationship, dimension stability, and durability. Chapter 8 deals with concrete mix design, understanding the proportioning of concrete mixtures to achieve desired properties. Chapter 9 focuses on the durability of concrete, addressing factors influencing durability and methods for enhancing resistance to deterioration. Chapter 10 deals with the ready-mixed concrete, gaining insights into its production, quality control, and applications in construction projects. Chapter 11 introduces nondestructive testing techniques for assessing concrete integrity without causing damage, ensuring structural safety and longevity. Chapter 12 discusses about the machinery and equipment integral to concrete production and placement processes. Chapter 13 discusses the future and development trends of concrete technology including applications of nanotechnology, data science and artificial intelligence in concrete technology.

This book perfectly fits the teaching needs of undergraduate and postgraduate students studying civil or materials engineering—especially those taking classes in the disciplines of properties of concrete or concrete technologies. It also provides the necessary knowledge and sufficient guidelines for practical engineers in the concrete industry.

During the process of writing the book, I have received enthusiastic help and invaluable assistance from the management of NICMAR University, Pune, Maharashtra, India, which is deeply appreciated. I am grateful to CBS Publishers & Distributors, for their cooperation in publishing this book.

Finally, I would like to thank my family for their love, understanding and support.

Kiran Bhaskar

Contents

Preface v

1. Introduction to Concrete 1

1.1 Concrete Definition and Historical Development *1*
1.2 Concrete as a Structural Material *6*
1.3 Characteristics of Concrete *7*
1.3.1 Advantages of Concrete *7*
1.3.2 Limitations *8*
1.4 Types of Concrete *9*
1.4.1 Classification in Accordance with Unit Weight *9*
1.4.2 Classification in Accordance with Compressive Strength *10*
1.4.3 Classification in Accordance with Additives *11*
1.4.4 Classification in Accordance with Construction Methods *11*
1.4.5 Classification in Accordance with Non-structural Functionality *12*
1.5 Factors Influencing Concrete Properties *13*
1.5.1 w/c Ratio or (w/b or w/p Ratio) *13*
1.5.2 Cement Content *13*
1.5.3 Aggregate *14*
1.5.4 Admixtures *14*
1.5.5 Mixing Procedures *15*
1.5.6 Curing *15*

2. Components of Concrete 17

2.1 Cement *17*
2.1.1 Manufacturing Process of Cement *17*
2.1.2 Chemical Composition of Portland Cement *20*
2.1.3 Hydration of Cement *22*
2.1.4 Types of Cement *25*
2.1.5 Storage of Cement *27*
2.1.6 Testing of Cement *28*
2.2 Aggregates *33*
2.2.1 Classification of Aggregates *33*
2.2.2 Characteristics of Aggregates *34*
2.2.3 Alternatives to Aggregates *36*
2.2.4 Tests on Aggregates *37*
2.3 Mineral Admixtures *39*
2.3.1 Fly Ash *39*
2.3.2 Ground Granulated Blast Furnace Slag (GGBFS) *39*
2.3.3 Silica Fume *39*
2.3.4 Metakaolin *39*
2.3.5 Natural Pozzolans *40*
2.3.6 Rice Husk Ash (RHA) *40*
2.4 Water *40*
2.4.1 Quantity of Water *41*
2.4.2 Water-Cement Ratio *42*
2.4.3 Sources of Water *44*
2.4.4 Indirect Water—Bulking Quantity Test *45*
2.4.5 Water Quality *46*

3. Chemical and Mineral Admixtures 48

Chemical Admixture
3.1 Accelerators *48*

3.1.1 Set Accelerators *49*
3.1.2 Hardening Accelerators *51*
3.2 Retarders *51*
3.2.1 Dosage of Retarders *53*
3.3 Plasticizers *54*
3.3.1 Finely Divided Minerals *55*
3.3.2 Air-entraining Agents *56*
3.3.3 Synthetic Derivatives *57*
3.4 Superplasticizers *58*
3.5 Viscosity Modifying Admixtures *59*
3.6 Waterproofers *60*
3.7 Miscellaneous Admixtures *62*
3.7.1 Gas-forming and Expansive Chemicals *62*
3.7.2 Corrosion-inhibiting Chemicals *63*
3.7.3 Pigments *64*
3.7.4 Antifungal Admixtures *65*
3.7.5 Curing Compounds *66*
3.7.6 Sealants *68*

Mineral Admixture

3.8 Fly Ash *68*
3.8.1 Characteristics of Fly Ash *70*
3.9 Silica Fume *71*
3.9.1 Characteristics of Silica Fume *71*
3.10 Ground Granulated Blast Furnace Slag *73*
3.10.1 Characteristics of GGBFS *73*

4. Properties of Fresh Concrete 76

4.1 Workability of Fresh Concrete *76*
4.1.1 Factors Affecting Workability *77*
4.1.2 Methods to Measure Workability *77*
4.2 Compactability *83*
4.3 Mobility *84*
4.4 Stability *84*
4.5 Consistency *85*
4.6 Segregation *86*
4.7 Bleeding *87*
4.7.1 Test for Bleeding *88*
4.8 Factors Affecting Workability *89*
4.9 Rheology *90*
4.10 Factors Affecting Rheology *90*
4.11 Analysis of Fresh Concrete *91*

5. Stages in Concrete Manufacturing 93

5.1 Batching of Concrete *93*
5.1.1 Volume Batching Method *94*
5.1.2 Weigh Batching Method *97*
5.2 Mixing Concrete *97*
5.2.1 Methods of Mixing *98*
5.2.2 Mixing Time *99*
5.2.3 Performance Attributes of Mixed Concrete *99*
5.2.4 Re-tempering of Concrete *100*
5.3 Transporting Concrete *100*
5.4 Placing Concrete *100*
5.4.1 Site Preparation *101*
5.4.2 Conveying Concrete *103*

5.5 Compacting Concrete *105*
5.6 Curing of Concrete *108*
5.6.1 Methods of Curing Concrete *108*
5.6.2 Importance of Concrete Curing *109*
5.7 Finishing the Concrete Surface *110*
5.8 Autogenous Healing of Concrete *111*

6. Rheology of Concrete 112
6.1 Introduction *112*
6.2 Representation of Rheological Behavior *113*
6.3 Measurement of Rheology by the Modified Slump Test *116*
6.3.1 Procedure for Measuring the Slump Time *116*
6.3.2 A Semi-empirical Model for Evaluation of the Plastic Viscosity *119*
6.4 Factors Affecting Rheological Properties *120*
6.4.1 Mix Proportions *120*
6.4.2 Consistency *121*
6.4.3 Hardening and Stiffening *121*
6.4.4 Aggregate Shape and Texture *121*
6.4.5 Aggregate Grading *121*
6.4.6 Maximum Aggregate Size *121*
6.4.7 Admixtures *122*
6.5 Mixture Adjustments *123*
6.6 Rheology Models of Concrete *123*

7. Properties of Hardened Concrete 125
7.1 Uniaxial and Multiaxial Strength of Concrete *126*
7.1.1 Uniaxial Strength of Concrete *126*
7.1.2 Multiaxial Strength of Concrete *127*
7.2 Compressive Strength *127*
7.2.1 Specimens for Compression *128*
7.3 Flexural Strength *129*
7.4 Tensile Strength *131*
7.5 Factors Impacting the Strength of Concrete *132*
7.5.1 Aggregate *134*
7.5.2 Hardened Cement Paste or Mortar Matrix *134*
7.5.3 Transition Zone *134*
7.6 Stress-strain Relationship *137*
7.7 Modulus of Elasticity *140*
7.8 Dimensional Stability—Shrinkage and Creep *141*
7.8.1 Aggregate *141*
7.8.2 Autogenous Shrinkage *142*
7.8.3 Drying Shrinkage *144*
7.8.4 Shrinkage Control *148*
7.8.5 Creep of Concrete *149*
7.9 Durability *150*
7.9.1 Factors Influencing Durability *150*
7.9.2 Role of Water-Cement Ratio *150*
7.9.3 Permeability *151*
7.9.4 Factors Contributing to Durability Issues *152*

8. Concrete Mix Design 157
8.1 Mix Design *157*
8.2 Principal Requirements for Concrete *157*
8.3 Weight Method and Absolute Volume Method *158*

8.4 Factors to be Considered in Concrete Mix Design *158*
8.4.1 Water/Cement Ratio *159*
8.4.2 Durability *160*
8.4.3 Workability *161*
8.4.4 Cement Type and Content *162*
8.4.5 Major Aggregate Properties and Aggregate Content *163*
8.5 Approaches for Concrete Mix Design *166*
8.5.1 Prescriptive Method *166*
8.5.2 Statistical Method *172*
8.6 Concrete Mix Proportioning—IS Guidelines *175*
8.6.1 Mix Design Procedure *176*

9. Durability of Concrete 188
9.1 Why Durability? *188*
9.2 Factors Influencing Durability *189*
9.3 Transport Properties *189*
9.4 Measurement of Transport Properties *191*
9.5 Cracking in Concrete *196*
9.6 Major Durability Problems *198*
9.6.1 Corrosion of Reinforcing Steel *198*
9.6.2 Corrosion Mechanisms *201*
9.7 Prevention of Steel Corrosion *203*
9.8 Deterioration Caused by Freeze-Thaw Cycling *205*
9.9 Durability in a Marine Environment *206*
9.10 General Methods to Enhance the Durability of Concrete *208*

10. Ready-mixed Concrete 210
10.1 Historical Development *210*
10.2 Advantages of Ready-mixed Concrete *211*
10.3 Production Methods *212*
10.3.1 Material Types *212*
10.3.2 Storage Capacity *212*
10.3.3 Processing Sequence *213*
10.3.4 Truck Mixer Capacity and Throughput *214*
10.3.5 Planning Requirements *214*
10.3.6 Quality Control Requirements *214*
10.3.7 Duration of Operations *215*
10.3.8 Health and Safety *215*
10.4 Organizing Production and Delivery *216*
10.5 Delivery *216*
10.5.1 Truck Mixers *216*
10.5.2 Mixing *216*
10.5.3 Delivery *217*
10.5.4 Distribution *217*
10.5.5 Types of Vehicles *217*
10.5.6 Tippers *218*
10.5.7 Conveyors *218*
10.6 Quality Assurance *219*

11. Nondestructive Testing of Concrete 220
11.1 Introduction *220*
11.2 Principles and Classifications *222*
11.2.1 Direct Measurement NDT Techniques *223*
11.2.2 Load-induced Reaction Measurement NDT Techniques *224*
11.2.3 Measurement through Inquiring Agent NDT Techniques *224*

11.3 Components of NDT *224*
11.3.1 Testing Objects *224*
11.3.2 Testing Problems *225*
11.3.3 Testing Methods *225*
11.4 Commonly Used NDT Techniques *231*
11.4.1 Ultrasonic Technique *231*
11.4.2 Acoustic Emission Technique *238*
11.4.3 Impact-echo *240*
11.4.4 Penetrative Radar Technique *245*
11.4.5 Optical Techniques *247*

12. Concreting Machinery and Equipment 250
12.1 Concrete Mixers *250*
12.1.1 Freefall Mixers *250*
12.1.2 Power Mixers *252*
12.2 Placing Concrete *254*
12.2.1 Buckets *254*
12.2.2 Chutes and Drop Pipes *255*
12.2.3 Bell Conveyors *255*
12.2.4 Concrete Pumps *255*
12.3 Finishing Concrete *257*
12.3.1 Floating *258*
12.3.2 Troweling *258*

13. Future Trends in Concrete Technology 260
13.1 Sustainability of Concrete *260*
13.2 Utilizing Eco-friendly Resources in a Scientific Manner *261*
13.3 Low Energy and Low CO_2 Emission Binders *265*
13.4 Efficiently Utilizing Materials: HSC and UHSC Applications *268*
13.5 Deep Understanding of the Nature of Hydration *268*
13.6 Integrated Materials and Structural Design *273*
13.6.1 Load-carrying Capability: Durability Unified Service Life Design Theory *274*
13.7 High-tensile-strength and High-toughness Cement-based Materials *276*
13.8 Application of Nanotechnology in Concrete *279*
13.9 Data Science and Artificial Intelligence in Concrete Technology *282*

Index 283

Introduction to Concrete

1.1 CONCRETE DEFINITION AND HISTORICAL DEVELOPMENT

Concrete is a man-made construction material resembling natural stone, its name originating from the Latin word "concretus," meaning "to grow together." It comprises coarse granular components, known as aggregate or filler, enmeshed within a solid matrix, typically cement or binder, which fills the gaps between the aggregate particles, creating cohesion. In essence, concrete can be defined as a composite substance primarily constituted of a binding agent wherein aggregate particles or fragments are incorporated. The simplest definition of concrete can be written as:

$$\text{Concrete} = \text{Filler} + \text{Binder}$$

Different types of concrete are classified based on the binder used in their composition. For example, concrete made with nonhydraulic cement is referred to as nonhydraulic cement concrete, while that made with hydraulic cement is called hydraulic cement concrete. When asphalt is used as the binder, it is termed asphalt concrete, and when polymer serves as the binder, it becomes polymer concrete. Both nonhydraulic and hydraulic cement require water for mixing and reaction, but they vary in their ability to gain strength in water, with nonhydraulic cement lacking this capacity.

Nonhydraulic cement concretes have a rich historical background, dating back to approximately 6500 BC when they were utilized by the Syrians. This technology spread across regions such as Egypt, the Middle East, Crete, Cyprus, and ancient Greece, with the Romans notably refining its use. The primary ingredients of early nonhydraulic cement concrete included gravel, coarse sand, hot lime, and water, with occasional additions like animal blood. The Romans extensively employed concrete in road construction, erecting an impressive 5300 miles of roads using this material. They also experimented with various admixtures such as pozzolana, animal fat, milk, blood, and horsehair to improve concrete properties and reduce shrinkage. Additionally, historical evidence suggests that Assyrians and Babylonians utilized clay as a bonding material, while lime was obtained by calcining limestone through a specific chemical reaction:

$$CaCO_3 \xrightarrow{1000°C} CaO + CO_2$$

When CaO is mixed with water, it can react with water to form:

$$CaO + H_2O \xrightarrow{\text{ambient temperature}} Ca(OH)_2$$

and is then further reacted with CO_2 to form limestone again:

$$Ca(OH)_2 + CO_2 + H_2O \xrightarrow{\text{ambient temperature}} CaCO_3 + 2H_2O$$

The Egyptians used gypsum mortar in construction, and the half-water gypsum was obtained by calcining two-water gypsum with a reaction of:

$$2CaSO_4 \cdot 2H_2O \xrightarrow{107-130°C} 2CaSO_4 \cdot \tfrac{1}{2}H_2O + 3H_2O$$

When mixed with water, half-water gypsum could turn into two-water gypsum and gain strength:

$$2CaSO_4 \cdot \tfrac{1}{2}H_2O + 3H_2O \xrightarrow{\text{ambient temperature}} 2CaSO_4 \cdot H_2O$$

The Egyptians opted for gypsum over lime due to its ability to be calcined at lower temperatures. Around 3000 BC, gypsum mortar was utilized in constructing the Pyramid of Cheops, although the pyramid was plundered long before archaeologists could study its building materials. Figure 1.1 shows a pyramid in Giza. Chinese engineers in the Qin dynasty (220 BC) employed lime mortar in constructing the Great Wall, as depicted in Fig. 1.2.

Fig. 1.1: Pyramid built with gypsum mortar, Giza, Egypt

Hydraulic lime, a development by the Greeks and Romans, was derived from limestone containing clayey impurities. The Greeks utilized volcanic ash from Santorini, while the Romans sourced volcanic ash from the Bay of Naples to create hydraulic lime by mixing it with lime. This hydraulic lime mortar proved resistant to water, hence its widespread use in hydraulic structures from the first century BC to the second century AD. However, the quality of cementitious materials declined during the Middle Ages due to a loss of expertise in lime burning and a lack of siliceous impurities, leading to a scarcity of high-quality mortars.

Fig. 1.2: The Great Wall built in the Qin dynasty

In 1756, John Smeaton undertook the reconstruction of the Eddystone Lighthouse off the coast of Cornwall, England. Recognizing the importance of siliceous impurities in water resistance, Smeaton conducted extensive experiments with various limes and pozzolans. He discovered that limestone with a high clay content produced superior hydraulic lime for mortar. Smeaton ultimately used a mortar composed of hydraulic lime mixed with imported pozzolan from Italy. This mixture, combined with coarse aggregate and powdered brick, closely resembled the proportions of modern concrete. The reconstructed Eddystone Lighthouse stood for 126 years until it was replaced with a modern structure.

Following Smeaton's pioneering work, the development of hydraulic cement progressed rapidly. In 1796, James Parker of England patented a natural hydraulic cement produced by calcining nodules of impure limestone containing clay. Meanwhile, Vicat of France developed artificial hydraulic lime by calcining synthetic blends of limestone and clay. Joseph Aspdin of England patented Portland cement in 1824, naming it after the limestone quarried in Portland, southern England, due to its similar color post-hydration. However, Aspdin's claimed temperature in his invention wasn't sufficient to create true Portland cement. It was Isaac Johnson who achieved this milestone in 1845 by burning the raw materials to the necessary clinkering temperature. Consequently, the use of Portland cement spread rapidly throughout Europe and North America, primarily in concrete production.

Germany conducted the first systematic testing of concrete in 1836, measuring its tensile and compressive strength. Aggregates, including sand, crushed stone, clay, gravel, slag, and shale, are integral components of concrete. The term "first generation of concrete" typically refers to plain concrete comprising Portland cement and aggregates. The advent of reinforced concrete marked the second generation, pioneered by François Coignet in France. Coignet began experimenting with iron-reinforced concrete in 1852 and, in 1853, constructed the world's first iron-reinforced concrete structure: a four-story house in St. Denis, near his family's cement plant. This house, designed by local architect Theodore Lachez, served as a promotional endeavor for Coignet's cement business.

At the 1855 Paris Exposition, Coignet showcased his reinforced concrete technique, confidently predicting its eventual displacement of stone as a primary construction material. He proceeded to patent a method employing iron tirants for reinforced concrete in 1856, followed by the publication of his techniques in 1861.

Further advancements in reinforced concrete were made by Hennebique towards the end of the 19th century. It was recognized that performance could be enhanced by placing bars under tension, thereby keeping the concrete under compression. While early attempts at tension reinforcement showed promise by reducing cracking, these cracks tended to reopen after a few months, as documented in Leonhardt (1964). The first reinforced concrete bridge was erected in 1889 in San Francisco's Golden Gate Park.

To address cracking issues in reinforced concrete, prestressed concrete emerged, with engineer P.H. Jackson patenting the concept as early as 1886 in San Francisco. Prestressing involves applying stress to a structural member before it bears the service load. Prestressed concrete was hailed as the third generation of concrete. This stress is typically induced by stretching reinforcing steel within the member. Prestressing methods are categorized as pretensioning or post-tensioning based on the sequence of concrete casting. Pretensioning involves stretching the reinforcing steel before concrete casting, with prestress achieved through the bond between the stretched steel and hardened concrete. In contrast, post-tensioning involves stretching the steel after casting and attaining sufficient strength. In post-tensioning, steel tendons are inserted into preformed holes in the concrete specimen, and prestress is applied through end anchorage. Figure 1.3 illustrates the sequence of the pretensioning technique for prestressed concrete.

Following World War II, prestressed concrete gained widespread acceptance in Europe, partly driven by steel shortages. North America's inaugural prestressed concrete structure, the Walnut Lane Memorial Bridge in Philadelphia, Pennsylvania, was completed in 1951. Today, the advancement of prestressed concrete technology has facilitated the construction of long-span bridges, tall buildings, and marine structures. The Barrios de Lura Bridge in Spain currently holds the record as the world's longest-span prestressed concrete cable-stayed bridge, boasting a main span of 440 meters. Additionally, the Shibanpo Yangtze Bridge stands as the world's longest prestressed concrete girder bridge, featuring a main span of 330 meters. Notably, in Canada, the prestressed Toronto CN Tower stands at a towering height of 553 meters.

In concrete design, the compressive strength at 28 days is a primary consideration. This choice is based on several factors, including concrete's principal function of bearing compression loads and the relatively straightforward measurement of compressive strength. Moreover, it is believed that other concrete properties correlate with its

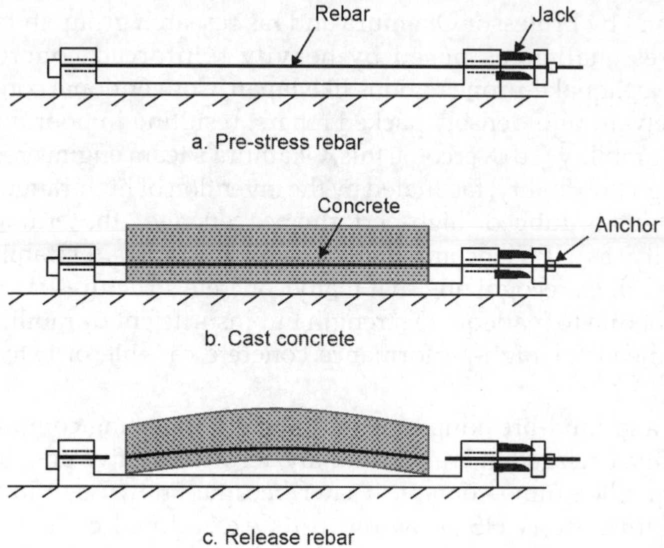

Fig. 1.3: Pretensioning sequence for prestressed concrete

compressive strength. Efforts to enhance compressive strength date back to 1918 when Duff Adams discovered its inverse relationship with the water-to-cement (w/c) ratio. Despite this, progress in achieving high compressive strength was slow until the 1960s, with concrete exceeding 30MPa considered high-strength.

Since the 1960s, advancements in high-strength concrete have accelerated, driven primarily by the invention of water-reducing admixtures and the incorporation of mineral additives like silica fume, fly ash, and slag. Water-reducing admixtures enhance workability under low w/c ratios, while mineral additives densify the concrete's microstructure, improving its properties. Notable milestones include the production of 52MPa concrete for the 52-story Mid-Continental Plaza in Chicago in 1972 and 62MPa concrete for Water Tower Place, a 74-story building, also in Chicago. By the 1980s, the industry achieved a remarkable 95MPa concrete for the 225 West Wacker Drive building project. The pinnacle was reached with Union Plaza in Seattle, Washington, boasting a compressive strength of 130MPa in its construction.

Since the 1980s, contemporary concrete production has typically involved the inclusion of fly ash, slag, or silica fume, along with various chemical admixtures. Consequently, the hydration mechanism, hydration products, and microstructure characteristics of such concrete differ significantly from those produced without these additives. Additionally, their mechanical properties diverge from traditional concrete, leading to their classification as contemporary concretes.

Two notable innovations in contemporary concrete are self-compacting concrete (SCC) and ultra-high-performance concrete (UHPC). SCC, a type of high-performance concrete (HPC), emerged as a concept in the 1980s, aiming to meet specialized performance and uniformity requirements that conventional materials and practices couldn't consistently achieve. These requirements include improved placement and compaction without segregation, enhanced long-term mechanical properties, early-age strength, toughness, volume stability, and durability in harsh environments.

SCC, developed by Professor Okamura and his research group in Japan in the late 1980s, addresses challenges posed by heavily reinforced concrete structures, particularly in earthquake-prone regions like Japan. Conventional concrete struggled to flow effectively around densely packed rebars, resulting in poor-quality casts and compromised durability. To overcome this, Okamura's team engineered concrete with exceptionally high flowability, facilitated by the invention of high-range water reducers or plasticizers. Initially dubbed "high-performance concrete," the term was later refined to SCC for clarity, as HPC encompasses broader meanings. Durability stands as a primary focus of HPC, recognizing that many concrete structures fail to meet service requirements not due to inadequate strength but insufficient durability. Hence, there arose a critical need for high-performance concrete capable of extending concrete service life.

In the 1990s, a ground-breaking type of "concrete" boasting compressive strength exceeding 200MPa emerged in France. Initially, termed reactive powder concrete due to its significant silica fume content, it later became known as ultra-high-strength (performance) concrete (UHSC) owing to its exceptional compressive strength. Researchers Richard and Cheyrezy introduced this material in 1995. Ultra-high-strength concrete has achieved compressive strengths of up to 800MPa with thermal treatment. However, its inherent brittleness necessitates the incorporation of fibers. By integrating fine steel fibers, UHSC can attain flexural strength of up to 50MPa. The first practical application of UHSC was witnessed in Sherbrooke, Canada, where a footbridge was constructed in 1998.

1.2 CONCRETE AS A STRUCTURAL MATERIAL

In this book, the term concrete usually refers to Portland cement concrete, if not otherwise specified. For this kind of concrete, the compositions can be listed as follows:

$$\text{Portland cement + Water (and admixtures)} \rightarrow \text{Cement paste +}$$
$$\text{Fine aggregate} \rightarrow \text{Mortar + Coarse aggregate} \rightarrow \text{Concrete}$$

It is worth noting that admixtures have become indispensable in modern concrete practices, being incorporated into nearly all concrete mixes. Admixtures, defined as materials added to concrete batches just before or during mixing, offer various benefits. Chemical admixtures, for instance, can alter the setting and hardening properties of cement paste by influencing hydration rates. Water-reducing admixtures enhance the workability of fresh concrete by lowering water surface tension. Air-entraining admixtures enhance concrete durability, while mineral admixtures like pozzolans can mitigate thermal cracking.

Concrete stands as the most prevalent construction material globally, owing to two primary factors. Firstly, its versatility allows for its application in a myriad of structures such as dams, pavements, building frames, and bridges, surpassing other construction materials. Secondly, concrete's usage surpasses that of any other material by a considerable margin, with global production exceeding that of steel by a factor of 10 in tonnage and over 30 in volume.

In concrete structures, two main structural materials are commonly employed: concrete and steel. A structural material not only supports its own weight but also bears the load from other components.

Steel undergoes precise manufacturing under controlled conditions in sophisticated facilities. The properties of each steel type are meticulously determined in laboratories and documented in manufacturer certificates. Consequently, for a steel structure, designers need only specify compliant steel, while constructors must ensure correct usage and proper connections between steel members.

Contrastingly, concrete production is less refined, resulting in variable quality. While cement quality is assured by manufacturers akin to steel, concrete quality lacks such assurance due to numerous factors like aggregates, mixing techniques, and the expertise of personnel involved in production, placement, and consolidation.

Attaining concrete of specified quality from a ready-mix supplier is feasible, but even in this scenario, only the raw materials are procured for a construction project. The quality of a cast concrete structure is significantly influenced by transportation, placement, and especially compaction. Unlike steel, where choices are relatively limited, the array of concrete mixes is virtually endless, demanding a thorough understanding of concrete properties and behavior for proper selection. Consequently, the designer and specifier's expertise determines potential concrete qualities, while the supplier and contractor's proficiency ensures actual quality in the finished structure. This underscores the importance of their familiarity with concrete properties, production, and placement.

Within a concrete structural element, concrete primarily bears compressive and shear stresses, while steel handles tension stresses. Additionally, concrete typically contributes stiffness to structures, aiding in their stability.

1.3 CHARACTERISTICS OF CONCRETE

1.3.1 Advantages of Concrete

(a) **Cost-effectiveness:** Concrete stands as the most economical and abundantly available material worldwide. Its production costs are comparatively low when contrasted with other engineered construction materials. Water, aggregate, and cement, the three primary components of concrete, are readily accessible and inexpensive globally. This allows for concrete to be manufactured at minimal expenses for local markets across the globe, mitigating transport costs and associated carbon emissions associated with alternative materials.

(b) **Ambient temperature strength development:** Cement, as a low-temperature bonded inorganic material, undergoes its reaction at room temperature, enabling concrete to achieve strength without necessitating high-temperature curing procedures.

(c) **Ability to be cast:** Fresh concrete possesses fluid-like properties, facilitating its pouring into various moulds to create diverse shapes and sizes directly on-site or within precast facilities.

(d) **Energy efficiency:** Concrete production consumes less energy compared to steel. The energy requirement for plain concrete production ranges from 450 to 750 kWh/ton, while reinforced concrete production consumes 800 to 3200 kWh/ton. In contrast, structural steel demands 8000 kWh/ton or more for manufacturing.

(e) **Superior water resistance:** Unlike wood and steel, concrete can cure underwater and withstand water action without significant deterioration. This feature makes it an ideal material for water-related structures like pipelines and dams. For instance, the Central Arizona Project utilizes concrete pipelines for water transportation. Contrary to common belief, water itself is not detrimental to concrete; rather, chemicals dissolved in water, such as chlorides, sulfates, and carbon dioxide, lead to concrete deterioration.

(f) **High-temperature resilience:** Concrete has a slow heat conduction rate and can retain substantial heat from its surroundings. Moreover, the primary hydrate responsible for binding aggregates in concrete, calcium silicate hydrate (C–S–H), remains partially hydrated until temperatures reach 910°C. Consequently, concrete exhibits superior resistance to high temperatures compared to wood and steel, withstanding fire for 2 to 6 hours, allowing ample time for rescue operations. Hence, concrete is frequently used to provide protective layers for steel structures.

(g) **Waste utilization capability:** With industrial development, the generation of by-products and waste has escalated, posing environmental challenges. To address this issue, many industrial wastes can be repurposed as substitutes for cement or aggregate in concrete production, such as fly ash, slag (GGBFS), waste glass, and ground vehicle tires. Incorporating industrial waste in concrete production not only aids environmental preservation but also enhances concrete structure performance. Given the significant global concrete production, there exists potential to utilize a substantial portion of industrial waste worldwide, provided suitable techniques for waste integration are available.

(h) **Compatibility with reinforcing steel:** Concrete exhibits a coefficient of thermal expansion similar to steel, providing excellent protection to steel due to the presence of calcium hydroxide (CH) and other alkalis under normal conditions. Concrete serves as a physical barrier against aggressive agents while offering chemical protection in a highly alkaline environment (pH approximately 13.5), effectively passivating black steel.

(i) **Reduced maintenance requirements:** Under typical conditions, concrete structures do not necessitate coating or painting for weatherproofing, unlike steel or wooden structures, which require protective layers. Furthermore, coatings and paints on steel or wooden structures need periodic replacement, resulting in higher maintenance costs compared to concrete structures.

1.3.2 Limitations

(a) **Quasi-brittle failure mode:** Material failure modes are typically categorized as brittle, quasi-brittle, or ductile, as shown in Fig. 1.4 . Brittle materials, exemplified by glass, fracture abruptly upon reaching their tensile strength. Quasi-brittle

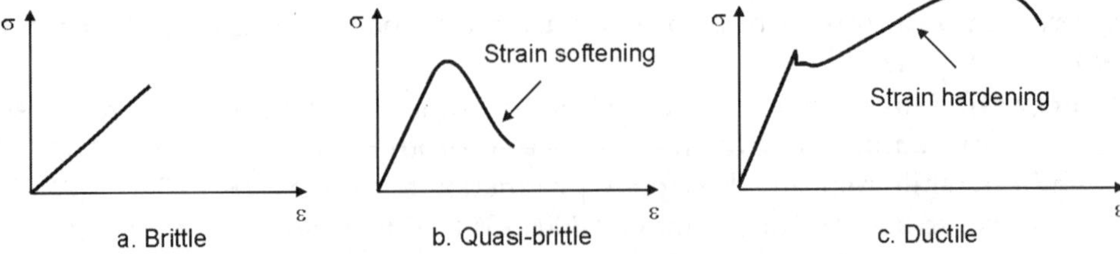

Fig. 1.4: Three failure modes of materials

materials exhibit strain-softening behavior, characterized by a lack of significant deformation before failure. Concrete falls into the category of quasi-brittle materials due to its low fracture toughness. To enhance its structural performance, concrete is often reinforced with steel bars, forming reinforced concrete, which offers improved stability.

(b) **Low tensile strength:** Concrete demonstrates significant discrepancy between its compression and tension strengths, with its tensile strength typically only about one-tenth of its compressive strength for normal-strength concrete. This ratio is even lower for high-strength concrete. To address this limitation, techniques such as fiber-reinforced concrete and polymer concrete have been developed to augment concrete's tensile strength.

(c) **Low toughness (ductility):** Toughness, denoting a material's capacity to absorb energy, is evaluated by the area under a load-displacement curve. Concrete exhibits notably low toughness compared to steel, typically ranging from 1/50 to 1/100 of steel's toughness, as shown in Fig. 1.5. Incorporating fibers into concrete is an effective method to enhance its toughness.

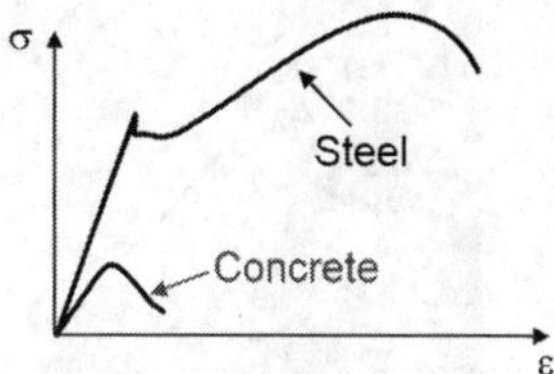

Fig. 1.5: Stress-strain curves of steel and concrete

(d) **Low specific strength (strength/density ratio):** Concrete generally has a specific strength lower than 20, whereas steel boasts a value of about 40. Increasing concrete's specific strength can be achieved by either reducing its density or enhancing its strength. Consequently, lightweight concrete and high-strength concrete have been developed to address this issue.

(e) **Requirement for formwork:** Fresh concrete, in its liquid state, necessitates formwork to maintain its shape and support its weight until it sets. Formwork construction, typically using steel or wood, is labor-intensive and time-consuming, contributing to its costliness, as shown in Fig. 1.6. To streamline this process, methods such as precast concrete, extrusion, and 3D printing have been introduced to enhance efficiency.

(f) **Lengthy curing time:** Concrete's strength development is typically assessed based on its 28-day compression strength, requiring a month for full strength development at ambient temperature. Measures such as steam curing or microwave curing have been introduced to expedite the curing period.

(g) **Management of cracks:** Despite reinforcement, concrete structures often develop cracks, particularly on the tension side due to concrete's low tensile strength. To address this issue, prestressed concrete has been developed, representing a third-generation concrete solution. Many reinforced concrete structures exhibit existing cracks on their tension sides while under service load.

1.4 TYPES OF CONCRETE

1.4.1 Classification in Accordance with Unit Weight

According to the unit weight of concrete, it can be categorized into four types, as outlined in Table 1.1. Ultra-lightweight concrete is suitable only for non-structural

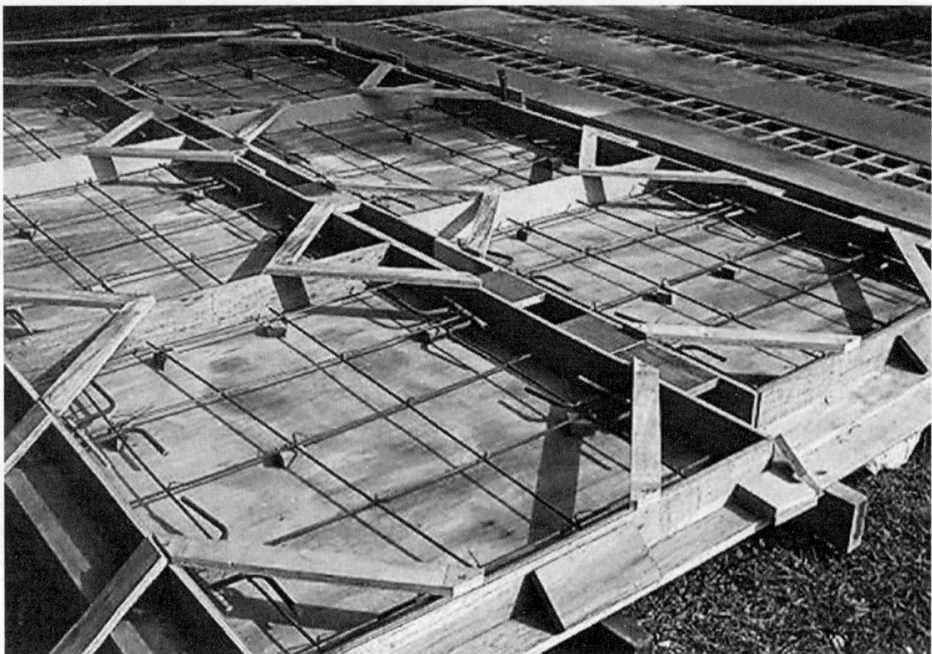

Fig. 1.6: Formwork for concrete casting

components. Lightweight concrete can be employed for both structural and non-structural elements, contingent upon its specified composition. Normal weight concrete is widely used in infrastructure and building construction. Heavyweight concrete finds application in specialized structures such as laboratories, hospital examination rooms, and nuclear plants, where protection against radiation is imperative for public health.

Table 1.1: Classification of concrete in accordance with unit weight

Classification	*Unit weight (kg/m³)*
Ultra-lightweight concrete	<1200
Lightweight concrete	1200 < UW < 1800
Normal weight concrete	≈ 2400
Heavyweight concrete	>3200

The primary factor influencing the unit weight of concrete is the aggregate used. The distinctions in unit weight correspond to different types of aggregates utilized: ultra-lightweight aggregates for ultra-lightweight concrete, lightweight aggregates for lightweight concrete, normal weight aggregates for normal weight concrete, and heavyweight aggregates for heavyweight concrete.

1.4.2 Classification in Accordance with Compressive Strength

In accordance with its compressive strength, concrete can be categorized into four classes, as outlined in Table 1.2. Low-strength concrete finds application in mass concrete structures, road subgrades, and partitions. Moderate-strength concrete stands as the most commonly utilized type in building construction, bridges, and similar infrastructure. High-strength concrete is suitable for constructing tall building columns, bridge towers, and shear walls. Ultra-high-strength concrete, although not extensively employed in structural projects, has been utilized in select footbridges and specific structural elements such as girders.

Table 1.2: Concrete classified in accordance to compressive strength

Classification	*Compressive strength (MPa)*
Low-strength concrete	< 20
Moderate-strength concrete	20~50
High-strength concrete	50~150
Ultra-high-strength concrete	> 150

1.4.3 Classification in Accordance with Additives

Concrete can be categorized into various types based on additives other than cement, aggregate, and water. Table 1.3 presents four examples of such classifications. Fiber-reinforced concrete (FRC) incorporates various fibers like steel, glass, polymers, and carbon to enhance toughness, tensile properties, shrinkage control, and decorative aspects. Macro-defect-free (MDF) is a cement-based composite enriched with a water-soluble polymer, manufactured via a twin-roll mixing process to boost tensile and flexural properties. DSP concrete, densified with small particles, integrates a significant amount of silica fume, offering excellent abrasion resistance, primarily used in manufacturing machine tools and industrial molds. Polymer incorporation into concrete is facilitated through three methods: utilizing the polymer as a binder, impregnating normal Portland cement concrete members with the polymer, or employing the polymer as an admixture in normal Portland concrete.

Table 1.3: Concrete classifications in accordance to additives

Classification	*Additives*
MDF	Polymers
Fiber reinforced concrete	Different fibers
DSP concrete	Large amount silica fume
Polymer concrete	Polymers

1.4.4 Classification in Accordance with Construction Methods

Within the realm of concrete construction methods, aside from traditional casting, there exist specialized approaches yielding concretes with distinct properties, necessitating tailored designs. Notable methods include 3D printable concrete, sprayable concrete (also known as shotcrete), and roller-compacting concrete.

3D concrete printing (3DCP) (Fig. 1.7) is a recent technological advancement, employing a layer-by-layer deposition technique guided by computer-aided design. This method offers several advantages over conventional casting, including reduced

Fig. 1.7: 3D printing technology

waste (due to formwork-free construction), decreased labor requirements, and heightened construction efficiency. Moreover, it enables the fabrication of structures with intricate geometries through customized designs and automated printing, thereby lowering construction costs. Successful formulation of 3D printable concrete demands a multi-level material design, addressing mixture composition, rheology, printing process intricacies, and composite structure requirements. Achieving optimal pumpability for delivery and buildability for deposition is crucial, emphasizing meticulous tailoring of fresh concrete's flow characteristics, with rheological properties being of paramount importance.

Spray concrete technology, also known as shotcrete, employs the pneumatic projection of sprayable concrete through a hose onto a substrate at high velocity to construct desired structures. This method is commonly utilized for vertical and overhead surfaces, where conventional casting is impractical, as well as for reinforcing caves or tunnels and repairing defective structures. Compared to castable concrete, sprayable concrete exhibits enhanced cohesion to resist pressure-induced bleeding during pumping and improved adhesion to ensure strong bonding with the substrate. Furthermore, it must demonstrate good pumpability for efficient material delivery.

Roller-compacting concrete represents another conventional method primarily employed in road pavement construction. This approach offers superior resistance to abrasion compared to castable concrete. Fresh roller-compacting concrete exhibits high stiffness and low flowability, necessitating compaction by road rollers to ensure uniform distribution and leveling to the desired height.

1.4.5 Classification in Accordance with Non-structural Functionality

Concrete, primarily known for its structural capabilities, is traditionally engineered to optimize mechanical properties like compressive and flexural strength, and elastic modulus. However, with advancements in concrete technology, there has been a shift towards developing new types of concrete, such as high-strength and ultra-high-strength varieties. Moreover, the emergence of multi-functional concretes highlights the importance of non-structural functionalities in certain scenarios.

(a) **Decoration function:** Transforming plain concrete structures into visually appealing decorative elements has gained significance due to their ubiquitous presence in daily environments. Specialized concretes designed for decorative purposes include architectural, colored, polished, stained, and stamped variants.

(b) **Abrasion-resistant function:** Resistance to abrasion is critical in various applications like dams, water channels, floors, and pavements. Specific binder selections (e.g. high calcium aluminate ferrite phase), stronger aggregates, and meticulous mix proportioning ensure enhanced abrasion resistance.

(c) **Shielding function:** Ensuring protection from microwaves, radiation, acoustic noises, and heat is crucial for maintaining a safe living environment. Concrete structures endowed with shielding capabilities are engineered through unique designs involving density, pore structures, and compositions.

The advent of nanotechnology has facilitated innovative approaches in realizing multi-functionalities in concrete structures. Leveraging nanomaterials like nanoTiO_2, nanoSiO_2, nano$CaCO_3$, nanoclay, carbon nanotubes, and graphene has led to the development of novel functionalities such as photocatalysis, self-cleaning properties, rheology modification, and improved heat conduction. These innovations aim to enhance specific features and overall performance of traditional concrete.

1.5 FACTORS INFLUENCING CONCRETE PROPERTIES

1.5.1 w/c Ratio (or w/b or w/p Ratio)

In determining the properties of concrete, a critical factor is the water/cement (w/c) ratio. In modern concrete practices, this ratio is often substituted with the water/binder (w/b) or water/powder (w/p) ratio, acknowledging that Portland cement isn't the sole binding material. The w/c or w/b ratio significantly impacts concrete properties such as compressive strength, permeability, and diffusivity. Generally, a lower w/c ratio results in stronger and more durable concrete. This relationship between w/c and concrete compressive strength has been recognized since the early 1900s, leading to Abrams's law.

1.5.2 Cement Content

When water is introduced to a concrete mix, it combines with cement to form cement paste, which serves three primary functions: binding, coating, and lubricating. Cement paste binds individual aggregates, reinforcing bars, and fibers together, creating a cohesive material. Additionally, it coats the surfaces of aggregates and fibers during the fresh stage of concrete, while the remaining paste acts as a lubricant, facilitating the movement of aggregates or fibers. Cement content plays a pivotal role in concrete workability during the fresh stage, heat release rate during rapid hydration, and volume stability in the hardened stage. Typically, cement content ranges from 160 to 200 kg/m^3 in mass concrete, less than 400 kg/m^3 in normal strength concrete, and between 400 and 600 kg/m^3 in high-strength concrete.

1.5.3 Aggregate

(a) **Maximum aggregate size:** The largest coarse aggregate size significantly affects the cement paste requirement in concrete. With larger aggregate sizes, there is less total surface area requiring cement paste coating. Consequently, concrete with larger maximum aggregate sizes, when using the same amount of cement, retains more cement paste as a lubricant, enhancing fluidity compared to concrete with smaller maximum aggregate sizes. For normal-strength concrete, at equivalent water/cement ratios and cement content, larger maximum sizes improve workability; conversely, at consistent workability, larger maximum sizes yield higher strength. However, larger aggregate sizes may introduce non-homogeneity and affect concrete transport and mechanical properties. Generally, the maximum aggregate size should be the largest economically viable size compatible with structural dimensions, ensuring it doesn't exceed specified proportions relative to form dimensions, slab depth, or reinforcing bar spacing.

(b) **Aggregate grading:** Aggregate grading, defining the size distribution of aggregates, primarily impacts particle packing. Optimal grading reduces voids in concrete, hence decreasing cement content. Given aggregate costs are typically one-tenth that of cement, well-defined grading not only enhances compressive strength and reduces permeability but also proves more cost-effective.

(c) **Aggregate shape and texture:** Shape and texture influence concrete workability, bonding, and compressive strength. Angular, rough-surfaced aggregates enhance bond and mechanical properties but reduce workability, while spherical, smooth-surfaced aggregates offer higher workability at the expense of bond strength and mechanical properties.

(d) **Sand/Coarse aggregate ratio:** The ratio impacts concrete packing and fresh-stage workability. Increasing sand to coarse aggregate ratio enhances cohesiveness but diminishes consistency, being a proven measure for improving concrete cohesiveness.

(e) **Aggregate/Cement ratio:** This ratio affects concrete cost, workability, mechanical properties, and volume stability. Increasing the ratio decreases concrete cost but lowers consistency due to reduced cement paste lubrication. While higher ratios yield greater stiffness and compressive strength with proper compaction, they also enhance dimensional stability by reducing shrinkage and creep.

1.5.4 Admixtures

Chemical and mineral admixtures play crucial roles in modern concrete technology, offering essential means to modify or enhance concrete properties, both when fresh and hardened. For instance, air-entraining agents, water reducers, and fly ash can influence concrete workability, while silica fume is known to enhance concrete strength.

1.5.5 Mixing Procedures

Mixing procedures encompass the arrangement of adding raw materials into a mixer and the duration required for each step. These procedures have a direct impact on the workability of fresh concrete and indirectly affect certain mature concrete properties.

Currently, ready-mixed concrete (RMC) is gaining popularity and can be produced through three methods:

(a) **Central mixing:** Concrete is thoroughly mixed in a stationary mixer before being discharged into transporting equipment such as a truck agitator, a truck mixer operating at agitation speed, or a no-agitating truck.

(b) **Shrink mixing:** Concrete undergoes partial mixing in a stationary mixer and completes mixing in a concrete truck mixer during transportation to the work site.

(c) **Truck mixing:** Concrete is entirely mixed in a concrete truck mixer. Mixing constituents are batched at a plant, loaded into the transporting truck, and mixed as the truck travels to the work site.

The duration of mixing depends on mixer power, slump requirements, and properties of raw materials, typically ranging from 30 seconds to several minutes.

A specialized mixing procedure can achieve excellent workability with proper coating on coarse aggregates to prevent alkali-aggregate reaction:

- **Step 1:** Coarse aggregate + 50% water + 50% cement: Mix for 30 seconds to 1 minute.
- **Step 2:** Add 50% cement + 25% water + superplasticizer + fine aggregate: Mix for 2 minutes.
- **Step 3:** Add 25% water: Mix for 3 minutes.

1.5.6 Curing

Curing refers to the practices implemented immediately after the casting of fresh concrete. The primary objective of curing is to maintain favorable moisture levels within an appropriate temperature range during the rapid hydration process of concrete. This stage is pivotal for the development of concrete strength and for regulating early volume changes. Proper care during curing is essential, akin to nurturing a newborn. Diligent curing ensures that concrete undergoes proper hydration, resulting in a sound microstructure, adequate strength, and dimensional stability. Conversely, negligent curing often leads to inadequate hydration, resulting in microstructural defects, insufficient strength, and unstable dimensions. One common consequence of improper curing is plastic shrinkage, which can cause early-age cracking, providing pathways for harmful agents to penetrate the concrete and compromise its durability. Despite its simplicity, curing is frequently overlooked on construction sites.

Various methods can aid in curing:

(a) Moistening the subgrade and forms.

(b) Sprinkling water on aggregates.

(c) Installing windbreaks and sunshades.

(d) Cooling aggregates and mixing water.
(e) Employing fog spray.
(f) Using covers.
(g) Implementing high-temperature (70–80°C) steam curing.
(h) Utilizing shrinkage-compensating admixtures.

Recently, a novel technique known as internal curing has emerged, leveraging saturated porous aggregates to create a reservoir within concrete, supplying water internally for curing purposes.

Components of Concrete

Concrete, as a construction material, is composed of various constituent materials that work together to create its unique properties and characteristics. Understanding the components of concrete is essential for designing and producing high-quality and durable structures. Let's explore the constituent materials that make up concrete and their roles in the construction process.

2.1 CEMENT

Cement is a fine powder that acts as the binding agent in concrete. It is primarily composed of limestone, clay, and other minerals that are processed at high temperatures to form a hydraulic binder. When mixed with water, cement undergoes a chemical reaction known as hydration, which results in the hardening and solidification of the concrete mixture. Different types of cement, such as Portland cement, blended cement, and specialty cements, are available to meet specific project requirements.

2.1.1 Manufacturing Process of Cement

Cement manufacturing is a complex process that involves several stages and precise control to produce high-quality cement. Understanding the manufacturing process is essential for ensuring consistent quality and meeting the demands of the construction industry (Fig. 2.1). The step-by-step manufacturing process of cement is detailed in the following:

Quarrying and Raw Material Preparation

The manufacturing process begins with the extraction of raw materials from quarries. The most common raw materials used in cement production are limestone, clay, shale, sand, and iron ore. These raw materials are typically obtained from mines or quarries located near the cement plant.

The extracted raw materials are then crushed, dried, and finely ground into a powder. This process is known as raw material preparation or milling. The purpose of milling is to create a homogenous mixture called raw meal, which has the desired chemical composition for cement production.

Fig. 2.1: Cement factory—production line

Clinker Production

The next stage is the production of clinker, which is the key ingredient in cement [Fig. 2.2(a)]. Raw meal is fed into a rotary kiln, a large cylindrical furnace, where it is heated to extremely high temperatures [Fig. 2.2(b)]. The rotary kiln operates at temperatures up to 1450°C (2642°F), causing the raw materials to undergo chemical reactions.

(a)

(b)

Fig. 2.2: (a) Cement clinker; (b) Rotary kiln

During this process, the raw materials fuse together and form small, marble-sized nodules called **Clinker**. The chemical reactions result in the formation of compounds like tricalcium silicate, dicalcium silicate, tricalcium aluminate, and tetracalcium aluminoferrite, which are responsible for the cement's binding properties.

Grinding and Blending

The clinker produced in the rotary kiln is cooled and then ground into a fine powder through a ball mill (Fig. 2.3) or a roller mill (Fig. 2.4). This grinding process enhances the surface area of the clinker particles, allowing for better reactivity when mixed with water.

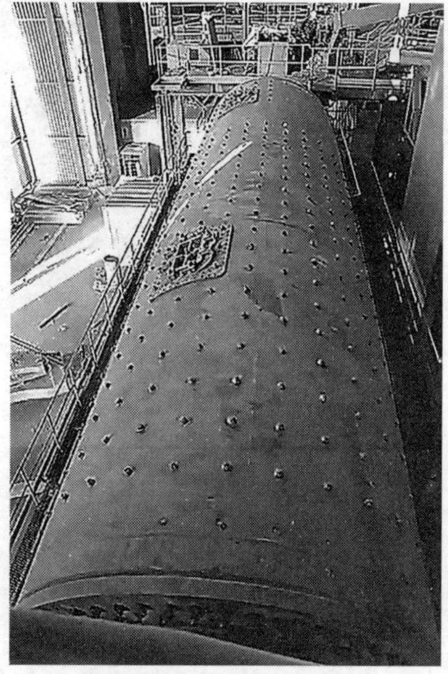

Fig. 2.3: Ball mill

Fig. 2.4: Roller mill

To control the cement's properties, other materials like gypsum or anhydrite are added during the grinding process. These materials regulate the setting time and provide the desired workability and strength characteristics.

Cement Storage and Distribution

Once the cement is ground to the required fineness, it is stored in silos or storage tanks to prevent moisture absorption and maintain quality. From the storage facilities, the cement is transported to distribution terminals or directly to construction sites in bulk trucks, railcars, or bags, depending on the market requirements [Fig. 2.5(a) and (b)].

Quality Control and Testing

Throughout the manufacturing process, quality control measures are implemented to ensure the cement meets the desired standards. Sampling and testing are conducted to monitor chemical composition, fineness, setting time, strength development, and other crucial parameters.

(a) (b)

Fig. 2.5: (a) Cement bunker; (b) Cement silo

Advanced analytical techniques, such as X-ray fluorescence (XRF) and X-ray diffraction (XRD), are used to analyze and verify the quality of the cement.

Cement Applications

The final cement product is used in various applications within the construction industry. It serves as the primary binding agent in the production of concrete, mortar, and grout. Concrete, made by mixing cement with aggregates and water, is used in the construction of buildings, bridges, roads, and infrastructure projects world-wide.

The manufacturing process of cement involves quarrying and preparing the raw materials, producing clinker through high-temperature heating, grinding the clinker to a fine powder, and conducting quality control measures. The resulting cement is a versatile and essential material used in a wide range of construction applications.

2.1.2 Chemical Composition of Portland Cement

The chemical composition of Portland cement reveals the precise combination of elements and compounds that form this widely used construction material. Understanding the chemical composition is crucial for comprehending the properties, behavior, and performance of Portland cement in various applications. The following gives us the intricacies of the chemical composition of Portland cement and the significance of its constituent elements.

Portland cement consists primarily of the following key elements:

Calcium (Ca)

Calcium is a fundamental element in Portland cement, present in various compounds. It forms the backbone of the cement's chemical composition and contributes to its strength and durability.

Silicon (Si)

Silicon is another significant element found in Portland cement. It plays a crucial role in the formation of silicate compounds, which contribute to the cement's strength and early hydration characteristics.

Aluminum (Al)

Aluminum is present in smaller quantities but still holds importance in the chemical composition of Portland cement. It contributes to the cement's sulfate resistance and influences the setting time and early strength development.

Iron (Fe)

Iron, though present in lesser amounts, is a vital element in Portland cement. It contributes to the cement's color and can influence its reactivity and durability.

The usual composition limits of Portland cement in India, as per the Bureau of Indian Standards (BIS), are given in Table 2.1.

Table 2.1: Chemical composition of ordinary Portland cement

Chemical	*Percentage amount*
Lime (CaO)	60–67%
Silica (SiO_2)	17–25%
Alumina (Al_2O_3)	3–8%
Iron oxide (Fe_2O_3)	0.5–6%
Magnesia (MgO)	0.1–4%
Sulfur trioxide (SO_3)	1–3%
Loss on ignition	0.5–4%

These composition limits represent the typical ranges for the major chemical constituents in Portland cement used in India. However, it is important to note that specific cement compositions may vary depending on the manufacturer and the intended application. It is always recommended to refer to the specific standards and specifications provided by the BIS for accurate and up-to-date information.

The chemical composition of Portland cement can be categorized into four main components, known as **"Bogue Compounds"**:

Tricalcium Silicate (C_3S)

Tricalcium silicate is the primary compound responsible for the early strength development in cement. It comprises approximately 50% of the cement's chemical composition. C_3S reacts with water during hydration, forming calcium silicate hydrate (C-S-H) gel, which provides strength and rigidity to the cement matrix.

Dicalcium Silicate (C_2S)

Dicalcium silicate makes up around 25% of the chemical composition of Portland cement. It hydrates slower than tricalcium silicate but contributes to the long-term strength development. C_2S also forms C-S-H gel, reinforcing the structure and enhancing the durability of the cement.

Tricalcium Aluminate (C_3A)

Tricalcium aluminate comprises approximately 10% of the chemical composition of Portland cement. It reacts rapidly with water during the initial stages of hydration, contributing to the early setting and hardening of cement. C_3A is responsible for the early strength gain but can also cause the generation of heat, which needs to be controlled in certain applications.

Tetracalcium Aluminoferrite (C_4AF)

Tetracalcium aluminoferrite makes up about 10% of the chemical composition of Portland cement. It has a minor contribution to the strength development of cement. C_4AF is responsible for the gray color of ordinary Portland cement and can enhance the cement's sulfate resistance.

In addition to these primary compounds, Portland cement may contain minor constituents that influence its properties and performance. These include gypsum (calcium sulfate), which is added during the grinding process to regulate the setting time, and various mineral admixtures like fly ash, slag, and silica fume, which can be used to enhance specific properties of the cement, such as workability, durability, and sustainability.

Understanding the chemical composition of Portland cement allows engineers and construction professionals to tailor the cement to meet specific project requirements. By adjusting the proportions of the primary compounds and incorporating suitable admixtures, it is possible to optimize the cement's performance and ensure its suitability for diverse construction applications.

2.1.3 Hydration of Cement

The hydration of cement is a chemical process that occurs when cement comes into contact with water, resulting in the formation of hydration products. This process is fundamental to the development of concrete, as it imparts the strength, durability, and other essential properties to the material. Understanding the elaborate process of hydration in cement is crucial for designing and producing high-quality concrete. The detailed explanation of the hydration of cement is narrated in the following sections:

Activation

The hydration process begins as soon as water is added to the cement. Water molecules penetrate the surface of the cement particles, initiating the dissolution of various cement compounds, primarily tricalcium silicate (C_3S) and dicalcium silicate (C_2S). These compounds react with water to release calcium ions (Ca^{2+}) and hydroxide ions (OH^-) into the solution. The presence of these ions activates the subsequent chemical reactions.

Nucleation

During the nucleation stage, the dissolved ions in the water solution begin to form clusters or nuclei. These nuclei serve as the starting points for the formation of hydration products. The most important product that forms during nucleation is the calcium silicate hydrate (C-S-H) gel, which is the primary binding agent in concrete. Additionally, other compounds such as calcium hydroxide (CH) and ettringite may also begin to nucleate.

Growth

As the hydration process progresses, the nuclei grow and develop into larger hydration products. The calcium silicate hydrate (C-S-H) gel grows and fills the void spaces between cement particles and aggregates, providing the strength and cohesion to the concrete matrix. Simultaneously, calcium hydroxide (CH) and ettringite crystals also continue to grow. These crystals contribute to the overall structure and properties of the hydrated cement paste.

Structural Development

During the hydration process, the calcium silicate hydrate (C-S-H) gel undergoes structural development. It forms a network of interconnected particles, resulting in the development of a solid and cohesive structure within the cement paste. This network contributes significantly to the strength and durability of the concrete.

Water Consumption and Setting

As the hydration reactions progress, the cement paste consumes water. This water consumption is an essential aspect of the hydration process and is crucial for the setting of concrete. As the cement paste hardens, it goes through the initial setting and final setting stages, where the material transitions from a plastic state to a solid state. The setting process is influenced by factors, such as temperature, water-cement ratio, and the presence of chemical admixtures.

Long-term Reactions

Hydration is an ongoing process that continues even after the initial setting and hardening of concrete. Long-term reactions, such as pozzolanic reactions, continue to take place between unhydrated cement particles and any supplementary cementitious materials present in the mix, such as fly ash or slag. These reactions contribute to the continued strength development and improve the durability of concrete over time.

The hydration reaction is a heat-releasing chemical reaction that occurs between water and the key components of cement. The primary components involved in the reaction are:

$$(C_3S, C_2S) + H_2O \rightarrow C\text{–}H\text{–}S + Ca(OH)_2$$

This reaction takes place between C_3S and C_2S when they come into contact with water, resulting in the formation of C-H-S and $Ca(OH)_2$ over a period of time. The reaction can continue for up to 90 days or even longer, but the most crucial period is the 28-day mark after concrete production. The C–H–S compound is essential for the mechanical properties and durability of concrete, whereas $Ca(OH)_2$ does not contribute significantly on its own. In the subsequent section, we will explore how we can utilize calcium hydroxide in conjunction with mineral additives to enhance the quality of concrete.

While the other components of cement also react with water, the products of the reaction between C_3A and C_4AF are not as influential as those formed by C_3S and C_2S when it comes to the properties of concrete. Table 2.2 illustrates the hydration reaction products for various compositions of Portland cement.

Table 2.2: Hydration process of Portland cement

Cement composition	*Reaction*
C_3S	Tricalcium silicate + Water = Calcium silicate hydrate + Calcium hydroxide
C_2S	Dicalcium silicate + Water = Calcium silicate hydrate + Calcium hydroxide
C_3A	Tricalcium aluminate + Gypsum + Water = Ettringite
	Tricalcium aluminate + Ettringite + Water = Calcium monosulfoaluminate
	Tricalcium aluminate + Calcium hydroxide + Water = Tricalcium aluminate hydrate
C_4AF	Tetracalcium aluminoferrite + Calcium hydroxide + Water = Calcium aluminoferrite hydrate

The inclusion of mineral additives in concrete technology holds significant importance. The primary component in these materials is active SiO_2. As mentioned earlier, the hydration reaction between C_3S and C_2S with water results in the formation of C–H–S and calcium hydroxide. While C–H–S contributes to the strength and quality of concrete, calcium hydroxide alone does not have any significant effect.

Mineral additives can be employed along with calcium hydroxide. The active SiO_2 in these additives can react with calcium hydroxide, leading to the production of more C-H-S. Consequently, the utilization of mineral additives helps to consume the calcium hydroxide. The reaction can be expressed as:

$$Ca(OH)_2 + \text{Mineral additives } (SiO_2) \rightarrow \text{more C–H–S}$$

The most notable mineral additives are as follows:

- **Silica fume:** It is obtained as a by-product from ferro-silica alloy factories, often collected from their chimneys. Silica fume is known for its exceptional pozzolanic properties, containing over 90% active SiO_2.
- **Fly ash:** This by-product is derived from coal-fired power plants. The quantity of active SiO_2 in fly ash can vary depending on the type of coal and the power plant system used, but it typically exceeds 50%.
- **Ground granulated blast furnace slag (GGBS):** GGBS is obtained as a by-product from steel factories during the extraction of iron from minerals. By rapidly cooling down the slag, high-quality GGBS suitable for concrete applications can be obtained. The SiO_2 content in GGBS varies depending on the steel production process but is generally less than 40%.
- **Natural pozzolans:** These materials occur naturally and possess pozzolanic activity. The SiO_2 content and activity levels of natural pozzolans vary based on their mineralogy. However, high-quality natural pozzolans can be found in different regions worldwide.

The hydration of cement is a complex and time-dependent process that is influenced by several factors, including water-cement ratio, temperature, curing conditions, and cement composition. By understanding the detailed mechanisms of hydration, engineers and concrete technologists can optimize mix designs, select appropriate curing methods, and predict the long-term performance of concrete structures. The hydration of cement is a chemical process that involves the dissolution of cement compounds, the formation of hydration products, and the development of a solid and cohesive structure within the concrete matrix. The resulting products, such as the calcium silicate hydrate (C–S–H) gel, contribute to the strength, durability, and overall quality of concrete. The hydration of cement is influenced by various factors, including:

Water-Cement Ratio

The water-cement ratio is the ratio of the weight of water to the weight of cement in a concrete mix. The amount of water added affects the hydration process, and a lower water-cement ratio can lead to higher strength and durability.

Temperature

The temperature of the environment affects the rate of hydration. Higher temperatures can accelerate the hydration process, but excessive heat can cause cracks in concrete.

Cement Composition

The chemical composition of cement, including the type and proportion of compounds, influences the rate and extent of hydration. The presence of additives, such as fly ash, slag, or silica fume can also affect the hydration process.

Curing

Proper curing of concrete is essential for the hydration process to proceed effectively. Adequate moisture and temperature levels need to be maintained for an extended period to ensure the complete hydration of cement compounds and the development of desired strength and durability.

2.1.4 Types of Cement

There are several types of cement available, each designed to meet specific requirements and applications. Let's explore in detail the different types of cement and their characteristics:

Ordinary Portland Cement (OPC)

OPC is the most commonly used type of cement and serves as the foundation for various construction projects. It is produced by grinding clinker, gypsum, and a small amount of other materials. OPC is available in different grades, such as OPC 33, OPC 43, and OPC 53, indicating their respective compressive strength in megapascal (MPa). OPC offers good workability, moderate setting time, and satisfactory durability for general construction purposes.

Portland Pozzolana Cement (PPC)

PPC is a blend of OPC and pozzolanic materials, such as fly ash, volcanic ash, or silica fume. These pozzolanic materials enhance the cement's properties by improving workability, reducing heat generation during hydration, and increasing the long-term strength of concrete. PPC is known for its low heat of hydration, improved resistance to sulfates, and reduced permeability, making it suitable for structures exposed to harsh environmental conditions.

Rapid Hardening Cement (RHC)

RHC, also known as high early strength cement, is manufactured by finely grinding clinker with increased proportions of calcium sulfate. It is designed to achieve higher early strength development compared to OPC. RHC is particularly useful in situations where quick formwork removal or early loading of structures is required. It finds applications in precast concrete elements, repair works, and cold weather concreting.

Sulfate Resistant Cement (SRC)

SRC is specifically formulated to resist the damaging effects of sulfate attacks, which can occur when concrete is exposed to sulfates in soil or water. It contains a low percentage of tricalcium aluminate (C_3A) and higher amounts of dicalcium silicate (C_2S) and tricalcium silicate (C_3S). SRC is commonly used in construction projects where concrete is in contact with sulfate-rich environments, such as marine structures, sewage treatment plants, and foundations in sulfate-bearing soils.

Low Heat Cement (LHC)

LHC is produced by reducing the percentage of C_3A and C_3S in OPC clinker, which results in less heat generation during the hydration process. It is suitable for mass concrete constructions, such as dams, foundations, and large structural elements.

High Alumina Cement (HAC)

HAC is produced by fusing bauxite and limestone at high temperatures. It contains around 35–50% alumina and is highly resistant to chemical attack, making it suitable for the construction of chemical plants, blast furnaces, and sewage treatment plants.

White Cement

White cement is made from raw materials that have low iron oxide content, resulting in its distinctive white color. It is primarily used for architectural and decorative purposes where the aesthetic appearance is essential. White cement is often used in facades, sculptures, terrazzo, and decorative concrete applications.

Colored Cement

Colored cement is produced by adding pigments to ordinary Portland cement. It offers a wide range of colors, allowing for creative and decorative applications in flooring, tiles, stucco, and precast elements. Colored cement provides an attractive alternative to traditional gray cement, enhancing the visual appeal of concrete surfaces.

Oil Well Cement (OWC)

OWC is specifically formulated for cementing oil wells. It has properties that enable it to withstand high temperatures and pressures encountered in oil well environments. OWC is designed to provide zonal isolation, preventing the migration of fluids between different layers of rock formations.

The different types of cement have unique properties that make them suitable for specific applications in the construction industry. It is important to select the appropriate type of cement based on the desired properties and the environment in which it will be used.

2.1.5 Storage of Cement

The storage of cement is a crucial aspect to ensure its quality and usability in construction projects. Proper storage conditions help prevent moisture absorption, reduce the risk of caking or hardening, and maintain the chemical properties of cement. In this section, we will discuss the detailed guidelines for the storage of cement.

Storage Area

Cement should be stored in a dedicated storage area that is clean, dry, and well-ventilated. The storage area should be free from any sources of moisture, such as leaky roofs or walls. It should also be protected from direct sunlight, extreme temperatures, and humidity fluctuations.

Packaging

Cement is typically supplied in bags, which should be intact and properly sealed to prevent the entry of moisture. Any damaged or torn bags should be discarded or repaired immediately. The bags should be stacked in a neat and orderly manner, away from walls and floors, to allow proper air circulation.

Elevation and Flooring

The storage area should have an elevated floor to prevent water seepage from the ground. If the floor is not elevated, a moisture barrier, such as plastic sheeting, should be installed to create a barrier between the cement bags and the ground.

Protection from Moisture

To safeguard against moisture absorption, the storage area should be equipped with appropriate measures. This may include moisture-proofing the walls, using dehumidifiers or air- conditioning units to control humidity levels, and ensuring proper ventilation to prevent condensation.

FIFO System

Adopting a "first in, first out (FIFO)" system is essential to prevent cement from being stored for prolonged periods. This ensures that older stock is used first, reducing the risk of cement deterioration and maintaining freshness. The storage area should be organized in a way that allows easy access to older stock.

Handling and Transportation

When handling cement bags, it is important to avoid rough handling, dropping, or throwing them, as this can lead to damage and the entry of moisture. Cement bags should be transported using appropriate equipment, such as pallets or forklifts, to minimize the risk of damage.

Regular Inspections

Regular inspections of the storage area should be conducted to identify any signs of moisture, caking, or other forms of damage. Any issues should be addressed promptly to prevent further deterioration and maintain the quality of the cement.

Shelf Life

While cement does not have an expiration date, it is recommended to use it within three months from the date of manufacture. Beyond this period, the cement's quality and performance may start to decline. Therefore, it is important to manage inventory and avoid stockpiling excessive amounts of cement.

By following these detailed guidelines for the storage of cement, construction professionals can ensure the preservation of its quality and performance. Proper storage conditions contribute to the production of durable and reliable concrete, leading to successful construction projects.

2.1.6 Testing of Cement

Cement testing is a critical process carried out to assess the quality, performance, and conformity of cement to specific standards and requirements. It involves a series of tests that evaluate various properties and characteristics of cement. Detailed below are the key aspects of cement testing.

Fineness

The fineness test measures the particle size distribution of cement. It is typically performed using the Blaine air permeability method or the sieve analysis method. The results of this test indicate the surface area of cement particles, which affects its reactivity and hydration rate. As previously mentioned, the final step in the production of Portland cement involves grinding the clinker with calcium sulfate.

The fineness of particles is a crucial characteristic of Portland cement and significantly impacts its quality. The following points outline the effects of cement fineness on cement and concrete properties:

- Finer cement exhibits greater activity.
- Finer cement generates more heat during the hydration reaction.
- Finer cement results in higher early age strength and a smaller increase in strength between 7 and 28 days.
- Finer cement requires more water for hydration.
- Finer cement necessitates a higher dosage of plasticizer and super-plasticizer to achieve the same workability.
- Finer cement leads to a reduced slump retention effect during concrete transportation.

As evident from the above, understanding the fineness of Portland cement is crucial for project applications, and maintaining uniformity in fineness is essential for quality control of concrete. Varying fineness from one part to another can have a significant impact on concrete properties, ranging from early age compressive strength to water requirements and final compressive strength, as well as the dosage of plasticizer and super-plasticizer and the slump retention effect during concrete transportation.

The Blaine test (Fig. 2.6) is the most important test for assessing fineness. It measures the area of cement particles per unit mass, thus indicating the finer cement will have a higher area per unit mass. The unit for the Blaine test is cm^2/g. Typically, a common cement would yield results ranging from approximately 2800 to 3300 cm^2/g when subjected to the Blaine test.

Fig. 2.6: Blaine's test apparatus

Particle Size Distribution

In the preceding section, we emphasized the significance of fineness as a critical property of cement. Now, we turn our attention to another equally crucial property of cement that is also influenced by the grinding process: particle size distribution.

Particle size distribution holds greater importance than the Blaine fineness of cement, as it is possible for two cements to possess the same Blaine value but exhibit different particle size distributions. Consequently, their behavior in the concrete production process would vary. Therefore, the impact of particle size distribution on concrete properties surpasses that of Blaine fineness. The optimal size range for cement particles is between 5 and 45 μm. Particles finer than 5 μm exhibit extremely high activity and can lead to issues, such as a drastic reduction in setting time, increased slump loss, and excessive heat generation during early-age hydration.

Conversely, particles coarser than 45 μm display minimal activity and contribute to a lower reaction rate in the formation of C–H–S. Therefore, it is essential to limit the presence of particles coarser than 45 μm.

Currently, we lack a highly accurate test method to determine the percentage of very coarse particles in cement. One approach involves using sieves with sizes of 45, 75, or 90 μm to separate and wash the cement, allowing the quantification of the amount of cement remaining on the sieve. This indicates the presence of non-active or low-active cement particles. The standard test method for wet washing of cement is IS 4031: Part 1 (Fig. 2.7).

Fig. 2.7: Sieve used for testing the particle size of cement

However, the most precise test for determining the particle size distribution of cement is conducted using the laser diffraction method. This method requires expensive and accurate instruments, which are commonly employed for analyzing particle size

Fig. 2.8: Analyzer for determining the distribution of particle sizes

distribution in various powder types. Researchers are actively exploring the best practices for utilizing this instrument, particularly for cement particles. Figure 2.8 depicts an image of the instrument used for the laser diffraction method test, while Fig. 2.9 illustrates a sample particle size distribution curve for cement.

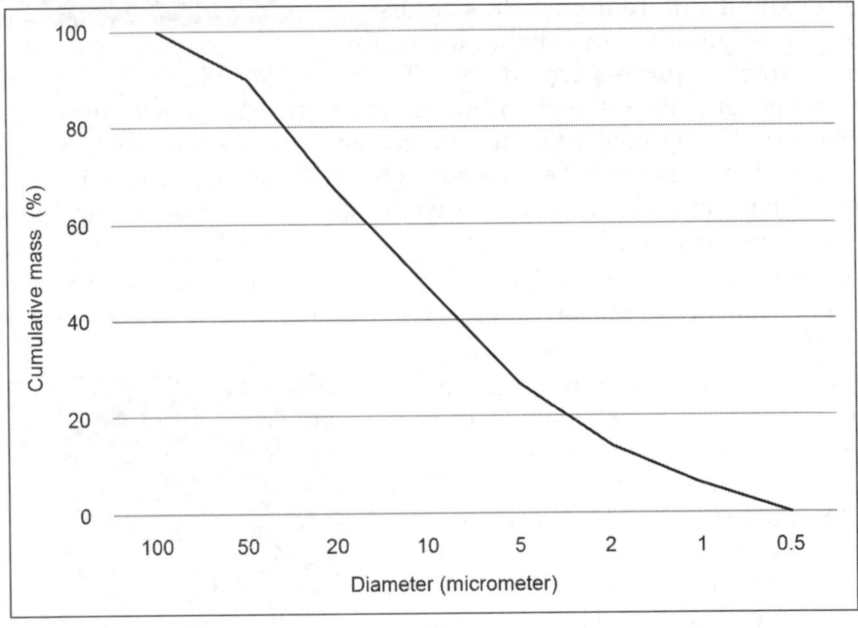

Fig. 2.9: A typical particle size distribution curve for cement

Cement Stability

One of the crucial characteristics of Portland cement is its ability to maintain volume stability in concrete or mortar. When certain materials, such as free CaO, are present in high amounts in cement, it can lead to expansion of the cement mortar or concrete. This expansion can result in significant cracks on the surface and within the concrete structure. Hence, a cement that exhibits controlled expansion is considered to be a healthy cement.

To assess and control cement health and expansion, the autoclave expansion test specified is utilized. The detailed procedure for this test can be found in the standard documentation. In summary, a cement mortar is prepared using specific sand, cement, and water. Special prisms are then cast from this mortar. These prisms are subjected to an autoclave, and their dimensional changes are monitored. If the dimensional changes fall within the defined range, the cement is deemed suitable for concrete production. Figure 2.10 illustrates cement prism molds, and Fig. 2.11 shows an autoclave used in the expansion test.

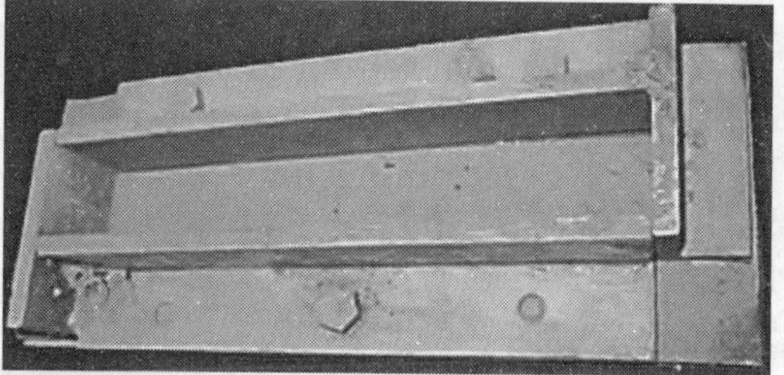

Fig. 2.10: Mold for cement prisms

Fig. 2.11: Image of autoclave

Cement Setting Time

During the concrete production process, we can observe three distinct phases:

Phase 1: This phase corresponds to the fresh concrete stage. Concrete in this phase is fluid and can be molded into various structural elements. It allows for shaping, working, pumping, and mixing of the concrete. At this stage, the hydration reaction of cement has either not started or is in its initial stages. The time from the first contact of cement and water to the end of the fresh concrete phase is known as the initial setting time. For ordinary Portland cement without any admixture or additive and under normal temperature conditions (approximately 20°C), the typical range for the initial setting time is 70 to 110 minutes.

Phase 2: The second phase can be compared to the consistency of jelly. While it is still possible to mix the concrete during this phase, it becomes more challenging than in the previous phase. The concrete is not yet sufficiently hard to bear loads but not soft enough for easy workability. Attempting to mix the concrete in this phase can weaken its overall strength by disrupting the hydration reaction bonds. The time from the first contact of cement and water to the end of the jelly-like concrete phase is referred to as the final setting time. For ordinary Portland cement without any admixture or additive and under normal temperature conditions, the typical range for the final setting time is 150 to 200 minutes.

Phase 3: This phase marks the hardened concrete stage. It begins at the final setting time when the concrete becomes sufficiently hard to bear loads. During this phase, the compressive strength of the concrete gradually increases over time. The most critical time for measuring compressive strength is typically 28 days after the final setting time.

Understanding the initial setting time of cement is crucial for determining the working time of concrete made with a specific cement type. Similarly, knowledge of the final setting time is essential for the demoulding of certain concrete elements and precast segments.

Various setting time tests exist based on different global standards. However, one of the most significant and widely used tests is the Vicat needle test, conducted in accordance with IS 4031: Part 5.

Fig. 2.12: Vicat apparatus

In this test, a cement paste with a predetermined normal consistency is prepared. The paste is then placed in the cone of the Vicat test instrument (Fig. 2.12). At different time intervals, the 1 mm needle is released from the Vicat test instrument, and its penetration into the cement paste is measured. The initial setting time is defined as the time when the 1 mm needle penetration reaches 25 mm, while the final setting time is identified when the needle sink becomes invisible in the paste.

Soundness Test

The soundness test evaluates the ability of cement to retain its volume after setting and hardening. It measures the potential expansion caused by unsoundness, such as the presence of excessive amounts of free lime or unsuitable constituents. The most common test method for soundness is the Le-Chatelier test, where the expansion of a cement briquette is measured after autoclaving.

Compressive Strength Test

The compressive strength test is one of the most crucial tests for cement. It determines the ability of cement to withstand loads and resist deformation under compression. The test involves preparing cement mortar cubes or cylinders, curing them under specified conditions, and subjecting them to compressive forces until failure. The results indicate the strength development of cement over time.

Heat of Hydration Test

The heat of hydration test measures the heat generated during the chemical reaction between cement and water. This test helps evaluate the potential temperature rise in large concrete structures, as excessive heat can lead to cracking and reduced durability. It is typically performed using specialized calorimeters.

Chemical Analysis

Chemical analysis involves determining the chemical composition of cement, including the percentages of major and minor constituents. This analysis helps ensure that the cement meets the required specifications and does not contain excessive amounts of impurities that may affect its performance.

Other Tests

Additional tests may be conducted to evaluate specific properties of cement, such as sulfate resistance, alkali-silica reactivity, shrinkage, and workability. These tests provide insights into the suitability of cement for specific applications and its compatibility with other materials.

Cement testing is typically carried out in accredited laboratories using standardized test methods, such as those outlined by organizations like ASTM International and EN standards. The test results help manufacturers, engineers, and construction professionals ensure the quality and performance of cement, leading to the production of safe and durable concrete structures. In India, cement testing is conducted according to the standards set by the Bureau of Indian Standards (BIS). BIS has established specific guidelines and procedures for testing cement to ensure its quality and adherence to Indian standards. The testing methods and requirements are outlined in the Indian Standard IS 4031:1988 (Part 1 to 13)—Methods of Physical Tests for Hydraulic Cement.

2.2 AGGREGATES

Aggregates are granular materials that form the skeleton of the concrete mixture. They can be classified into two types: fine aggregates and coarse aggregates. Fine aggregates consist of natural sand or crushed stone particles smaller than 5 millimeters in diameter. Coarse aggregates, on the other hand, are larger particles, typically ranging from 5 to 20 millimeters in diameter, such as gravel or crushed stone. Aggregates provide bulk, stability, and strength to the concrete mixture.

2.2.1 Classification of Aggregates

Aggregates used in concrete can be classified into two main categories: fine aggregates and coarse aggregates. This classification is based on the size of the particles comprising the aggregates. Here is a breakdown of the classification:

Fine Aggregates

Definition

Fine aggregates consist of small-sized particles, typically smaller than 4.75 mm (0.187 inches) in diameter.

Examples

Fine aggregates are commonly represented by natural sand, crushed stone sand, or a combination of both.

Characteristics

Fine aggregates have a smaller particle size and a smoother texture compared to coarse aggregates. They are often used to fill the voids between larger particles in the concrete mix, improving workability and cohesiveness.

Functions

Fine aggregates enhance the workability, bonding, and finish ability of concrete. They help in achieving a dense and compact concrete matrix.

Coarse Aggregates

Definition

Coarse aggregates are larger-sized particles, typically ranging from 4.75 mm (0.187 inches) to 20 mm (0.75 inches) in diameter.

Examples

Coarse aggregates can include natural gravel, crushed stone, or a combination of both.

Characteristics

Coarse aggregates have a larger particle size and a rougher texture compared to fine aggregates. They provide bulk and stability to the concrete mix.

Functions

Coarse aggregates contribute to the strength and durability of concrete. They help in achieving a strong interlocking structure and provide resistance against applied loads.

It is important to note that there is some overlap in particle sizes between fine and coarse aggregates. The specific size limits to classify an aggregate as either fine or coarse may vary based on regional standards or project requirements. In some cases, aggregates falling within the borderline size range may be classified based on their intended purpose in the concrete mix. The combination of fine and coarse aggregates in appropriate proportions is essential to achieve a well-balanced and workable concrete mixture. The selection of the right types and gradation of aggregates depends on factors, such as the desired strength, workability, and project specifications.

2.2.2 Characteristics of Aggregates

Aggregates used in concrete possess various characteristics that significantly influence the properties and performance of the final concrete product. Understanding these characteristics is crucial for selecting suitable aggregates and designing concrete mixes. Here, we'll discuss in detail some key characteristics of aggregates used in concrete:

Particle Shape

Aggregates can have different shapes, such as rounded, angular, or irregular. Rounded aggregates, like river gravel, result from natural weathering and erosion processes, and they offer good workability and lower water demand in concrete. Angular or rough-textured aggregates, like crushed stone, provide better interlocking and contribute to higher concrete strength. Irregular-shaped aggregates may have a mixture of rounded and angular particles.

Particle Size Distribution

The gradation or distribution of particle sizes in aggregates is an essential characteristic. Well-graded aggregates have a balanced distribution of various sizes, ranging from fine to coarse. They provide better workability, reduced voids, and improved strength. Gap-graded or poorly-graded aggregates have an uneven distribution of particle sizes, resulting in higher void content and potential segregation.

Surface Texture

The surface texture of aggregates influences the bond between the aggregates and the cement paste. Aggregates with rough and textured surfaces, such as crushed stone, enhance the bond strength and overall mechanical properties of concrete. Smooth or polished aggregates may reduce the bond strength and require surface treatments to improve adhesion.

Absorption and Moisture Content

Aggregates have the ability to absorb moisture, and their moisture content affects the water-cement ratio in concrete mixes. Highly absorptive aggregates can increase the water demand of concrete, affecting its workability, strength, and durability. It is important to account for the moisture content of aggregates when proportioning concrete mixes to achieve the desired water-cement ratio.

Specific Gravity

Specific gravity is the ratio of the density of aggregates to the density of water. The specific gravity of aggregates influences the overall density, volume, and weight of concrete. Aggregates with higher specific gravity contribute to higher concrete density and strength. Lower specific gravity aggregates may result in lightweight concrete with reduced strength.

Aggregate Crushing Value (ACV)

ACV is a measure of the resistance of aggregates to crushing under compressive loads. It indicates the durability and strength of aggregates used in concrete. Higher ACV values suggest weaker aggregates that may affect the overall strength and durability of concrete.

Aggregate Impact Value (AIV)

AIV is a measure of the toughness of aggregates when subjected to impact loads. It helps assess the suitability of aggregates for concrete construction, especially in areas prone to impact or dynamic loads. Lower AIV values indicate tougher aggregates that can withstand impact stresses.

Chemical Composition

The chemical composition of aggregates, particularly in the case of recycled aggregates, can influence the behavior of concrete. Aggregates containing harmful substances or contaminants may adversely affect the setting time, strength, and durability of concrete. Proper testing and analysis are necessary to ensure the suitability of aggregates from a chemical perspective.

Gradation Limits and Specifications

Aggregates used in concrete must comply with specific gradation limits and specifications defined by industry standards or project requirements. These limits ensure that the aggregate mix provides the desired workability, strength, and durability for the intended application. It is important to consider these aggregate characteristics when selecting and proportioning aggregates for concrete mixes. Proper understanding and evaluation of these characteristics allow engineers and concrete producers to design mixes that meet the required performance criteria for specific applications.

2.2.3 Alternatives to Aggregates

Concrete is a ubiquitous construction material widely used for its strength, durability, and versatility. One of the key components of concrete is aggregates, which typically consist of sand, gravel, or crushed stone. However, due to growing environmental concerns and the need for sustainable construction practices, researchers and concrete specialists have been exploring alternative materials that can replace or supplement traditional aggregates. In this section, we will delve into some of these alternatives, their properties, and their potential impact on the future of concrete construction.

Recycled Aggregates

One of the most widely adopted alternatives to natural aggregates is the use of recycled materials. Construction and demolition waste, such as crushed concrete, asphalt, and masonry rubble, can be processed and reused as aggregates in new concrete production. Recycling these materials not only reduces the strain on natural resources but also helps divert waste from landfills. Recycled aggregates can exhibit comparable mechanical properties to natural aggregates, making them a viable option for sustainable concrete construction.

Industrial By-products

Certain industrial by-products have also shown promise as alternatives to traditional aggregates. For example, fly ash and ground granulated blast furnace slag (GGBFS) are by-products of coal-fired power plants and iron-making processes, respectively. When used as partial replacements for cement in concrete, these materials enhance the strength, durability, and workability of the resulting concrete while reducing carbon emissions associated with cement production. Additionally, silica fume, a by-product of silicon and ferrosilicon alloy production, can be utilized as a supplementary cementitious material, further improving the properties of concrete.

Lightweight Aggregates

In applications where weight reduction is desired, lightweight aggregates offer a compelling alternative. These aggregates, typically derived from expanded clay, shale, or slate, are lightweight, insulating, and can improve the thermal properties of concrete. Lightweight concrete made with such aggregates provides benefits, such as reduced dead loads, improved seismic resistance, and enhanced energy efficiency in buildings.

Bio-based Aggregates

With a growing emphasis on sustainability and the desire to reduce reliance on non-renewable resources, bio-based aggregates have gained attention. These aggregates are made from renewable resources, such as agricultural waste, straw, bamboo, or recycled materials like cellulose fibers. While still in the early stages of development and research, bio-based aggregates show potential in reducing the environmental impact of concrete production and improving the overall sustainability of construction.

Nanomaterials

In recent years, nanotechnology has opened up new possibilities in concrete technology. Nanoscale additives, such as nanoparticles of silica, titanium dioxide, or carbon nanotubes, can modify the properties of concrete at the molecular level. These additives can enhance the strength, durability, and self-cleaning properties of concrete while reducing cracking and improving its resistance to environmental factors. Although the commercial application of nanomaterials in concrete is still evolving, their potential to revolutionize the industry is substantial.

2.2.4 Tests on Aggregates

Aggregates play a vital role in the performance and durability of concrete. As a concrete specialist, it is crucial to understand the properties of aggregates and how they can impact the overall quality of concrete. This article focuses on various tests conducted on aggregates to assess their physical, mechanical, and chemical characteristics. By conducting these tests, engineers and concrete specialists can make informed decisions regarding aggregate selection and optimize concrete mix designs for specific applications.

Particle Size Distribution

The particle size distribution of aggregates significantly affects the workability, strength, and durability of concrete. The sieve analysis test is commonly used to determine the gradation of aggregates (Fig. 2.13). It involves passing the aggregate sample through a series of sieves with different mesh sizes and measuring the weight retained on each sieve. The resulting gradation curve provides valuable information about the distribution of particle sizes, enabling engineers to fine-tune the concrete mix proportions.

Fig. 2.13: Series of sieves for coarse aggregate

Moisture Content

The moisture content of aggregates directly influences the water-cement ratio and, consequently, the workability and strength of concrete. Moisture content can be determined using the oven-drying method, where a sample of aggregates is heated to remove the moisture content. This test is crucial in ensuring that the correct amount of water is added to achieve the desired consistency and strength of concrete.

Specific Gravity and Absorption

The specific gravity and absorption capacity of aggregates are vital parameters in concrete mix design. The specific gravity test measures the density of aggregates relative to the density of water. Higher specific gravity indicates higher density and quality. Absorption capacity, on the other hand, determines the amount of water absorbed by the aggregates. It affects the water content in the concrete mix, potentially leading to changes in workability and strength. These tests are typically performed using the pycnometer and immersion methods, respectively.

Aggregate Crushing Value (ACV)

The ACV test evaluates the strength of aggregates by measuring their resistance to crushing under a compressive load. It provides an indication of the aggregate's ability to withstand heavy loads and is crucial in determining the suitability of aggregates for road construction and other load-bearing applications. The test involves applying a gradually increasing load to a sample aggregate and measuring the percentage of fines produced.

Los Angeles Abrasion Test

The Los Angeles abrasion test (Fig. 2.14) assesses the resistance of aggregates to abrasion and degradation caused by mechanical actions, such as impact and rubbing. This test helps evaluate the durability and quality of aggregates for road construction and other applications subjected to wear and tear. The test involves subjecting a sample aggregate to repeated impacts in a rotating drum and measuring the percentage of material lost due to abrasion.

Fig. 2.14: Los Angeles abrasion testing machine

Chemical Tests

Chemical tests on aggregates determine their reactivity and potential deleterious effects on concrete. The alkali-silica reaction (ASR) test, for instance, assesses the susceptibility of aggregates to react with the alkalis present in cement, leading to the formation of expansive gel and subsequent concrete cracking. Other chemical tests evaluate the presence of harmful substances, such as organic impurities, chlorides, sulfates, and carbonates that can adversely affect concrete durability.

Conducting comprehensive tests on aggregates is essential for ensuring the quality, strength, and durability of concrete. By evaluating particle size distribution, moisture content, specific gravity, absorption, crushing value, abrasion resistance, and potential chemical reactivity, concrete specialists can select aggregates that meet the specific requirements of each project. These tests enable engineers to optimize concrete mix designs, improve workability, enhance structural performance, and ensure long-term durability. By incorporating thorough aggregate testing protocols, we can advance the quality and reliability of concrete in construction projects worldwide.

2.3 MINERAL ADMIXTURES

In the realm of concrete technology, mineral admixtures play a crucial role in improving the performance, durability, and sustainability of concrete. These finely ground materials, often by-products of industrial processes, are added to concrete mixes to enhance specific properties. This article provides a comprehensive understanding of the various mineral admixtures used in concrete, their benefits, and their impact on concrete performance.

2.3.1 Fly Ash

Fly ash is a by-product of coal combustion in power plants and is one of the most commonly used mineral admixtures. It consists of fine particles that improve the workability, strength, and long-term durability of concrete. Fly ash acts as a pozzolan, reacting with calcium hydroxide in the presence of moisture to form additional cementitious compounds. This reaction increases the strength and reduces the permeability of concrete, making it less susceptible to chemical attacks and improving its resistance to sulfate and chloride ingress.

2.3.2 Ground Granulated Blast Furnace Slag (GGBFS)

GGBFS is a by-product of the iron-making process in blast furnaces. When finely ground and activated, it exhibits pozzolanic properties similar to fly ash. GGBFS improves concrete workability, reduces heat of hydration, enhances long-term strength development, and enhances resistance to sulfates and alkalis. Additionally, it provides improved resistance to alkali-silica reaction (ASR) and mitigates the potential for thermal cracking.

2.3.3 Silica Fume

Silica fume is an ultrafine amorphous material obtained as a by-product of silicon metal and ferrosilicon alloy production. Its high silica content contributes to its pozzolanic properties. Silica fume is highly reactive and fills the voids between cement particles, resulting in denser and more impermeable concrete. It improves the compressive and flexural strength, enhances durability by reducing chloride ion penetration, and increases resistance to chemical attacks, such as sulfate and acid attacks.

2.3.4 Metakaolin

Metakaolin is a highly reactive pozzolan produced by calcining kaolin clay at high temperatures. Its fine particle size and high reactivity contribute to improved concrete strength, durability, and workability. Metakaolin reduces the calcium hydroxide content in concrete, resulting in denser microstructure and enhanced resistance to chemical attacks, including sulfates and acids. It also improves the resistance to alkali-aggregate reactions and mitigates the potential for efflorescence.

2.3.5 Natural Pozzolans

Natural pozzolans, such as volcanic ash, calcined clays, and diatomaceous earth, have been used in concrete for centuries. These materials contain reactive silica and alumina, which contribute to the pozzolanic properties. Natural pozzolans enhance the strength, durability, and workability of concrete. They reduce the heat of hydration, improve long-term strength development, and provide resistance to sulfate and chloride attacks.

2.3.6 Rice Husk Ash (RHA)

Rice husk ash is a by-product of the rice milling industry. It is rich in amorphous silica and possesses pozzolanic properties. RHA improves concrete workability, reduces bleeding and segregation, enhances compressive strength, and improves resistance to sulfate and chloride attacks. Additionally, RHA contributes to the reduction of CO_2 emissions and promotes the utilization of agricultural waste.

Mineral admixtures are essential ingredients in modern concrete technology. Incorporating fly ash, GGBFS, silica fume, metakaolin, natural pozzolans, and rice husk ash into concrete mixes enhances properties, such as workability, strength, durability, and sustainability. These mineral admixtures act as supplementary cementitious materials, improving the overall performance of concrete and reducing its environmental impact. By understanding the unique characteristics and benefits of each mineral admixture, concrete specialists can optimize mix designs and create high-performance, durable, and sustainable concrete structures.

2.4 WATER

Water is a fundamental ingredient in concrete, playing a critical role in the mixing, hydration, and overall performance of the material. Its presence and proper management are essential for achieving desired workability, strength development, and durability of concrete. This comprehensive section explores the significance of water in concrete, including its functions, requirements, and potential challenges in its application.

Functions of Water in Concrete

a. **Hydration:** Water is essential for the chemical reaction between cement and other cementitious materials, known as hydration. It activates the cement particles, leading to the formation of calcium silicate hydrate (C-S-H) gel, responsible for the strength and binding properties of concrete.

b. **Workability:** Water provides the necessary lubrication and fluidity to facilitate the mixing, placing, and compaction of concrete. Proper workability ensures easy placement and compaction, allowing for the desired shape, finish, and consolidation of the concrete.

c. **Chemical reactions:** Water participates in various chemical reactions during concrete curing. It enables the dissolution of cement particles, which subsequently react to form calcium hydroxide and other compounds that contribute to concrete strength and durability.

Challenges and Considerations

a. **Loss of moisture:** Concrete is susceptible to moisture loss through evaporation, especially in hot and dry conditions. It is important to minimize water evaporation by covering freshly placed concrete with curing blankets, plastic sheets, or using evaporation retardants.

b. **Overwatering:** Excessive water added during mixing can lead to lower strength, increased porosity, and decreased durability. Care should be taken to avoid overwatering, which can compromise the integrity and long-term performance of concrete.

c. **Freezing and thawing:** In cold climates, water trapped in the concrete pores can freeze and expand, causing internal stresses and potential damage. Proper air entrainment and use of low permeability concrete can mitigate the effects of freeze-thaw cycles.

2.4.1 Quantity of Water

The quantity of water used in concrete is a critical factor that significantly influences the workability, strength, durability, and overall performance of the material. Achieving the appropriate water content is essential to ensure optimal hydration of cement particles while avoiding potential issues associated with excessive or insufficient water. The following sections provides a understanding of the quantity of water to be used in concrete, including factors affecting water content, methods of determining water requirements, and considerations for achieving the desired water-cement ratio.

Factors Affecting Water Content

a. **Workability:** The desired workability of concrete, which depends on the placement method and specific application, influences the amount of water required. Higher workability typically requires a higher water content to achieve the desired flow and ease of placement.

b. **Aggregate characteristics:** The characteristics of aggregates, such as their particle shape, surface texture, grading, and moisture content, affect the water demand. Angular or rough-textured aggregates generally require more water than smooth and rounded aggregates to achieve adequate workability.

c. **Admixtures and supplementary cementitious materials (SCMs):** The use of chemical admixtures or SCMs, such as fly ash or silica fume, can modify the water demand of concrete. These materials may increase or decrease the water requirement depending on their specific properties and dosage.

d. **Environmental conditions:** Ambient temperature, humidity, and wind speed can significantly influence the rate of evaporation, affecting the water content needed to maintain workability. In hot and dry conditions, additional water may be necessary to compensate for increased evaporation rates.

Methods for Determining Water Requirements

a. **Prescriptive methods:** Prescriptive methods, such as empirical guidelines and standardized tables, provide general recommendations for water content based on the desired concrete strength, slump, and aggregate characteristics. These methods offer a quick estimation but may not consider specific project requirements.

b. **Trial batches:** Conducting trial batches involves testing various water-cement ratios and evaluating the resulting concrete properties to determine the optimal water content. This method allows for customization based on specific project requirements and helps achieve the desired balance between workability and strength.

c. **Water-cement ratio (w/c ratio):** The water-cement ratio is a crucial parameter used to determine the water content in concrete. By specifying the desired w/c ratio based on project requirements, the corresponding water content can be calculated using the weight or volume of cementitious materials in the mix.

Achieving the Desired Water-Cement Ratio

a. **Adjusting water content:** Once the desired water-cement ratio is determined, the water content can be adjusted by considering the moisture content of aggregates and the amount of water carried by admixtures. Care should be taken to ensure accurate measurement and uniform distribution of water throughout the mix.

b. **Consistency control:** Regular testing of the fresh concrete's consistency using slump tests or other appropriate methods allows for on-site adjustments to the water content. This ensures the desired workability is achieved without compromising the strength and durability of the concrete.

c. **Quality of water:** The quality of water used in concrete mixing is crucial. Potable water or water from approved sources should be used to avoid any adverse effects on the hydration process and long-term durability of the concrete.

2.4.2 Water-Cement Ratio

The water-cement ratio is a fundamental parameter in concrete mix design that plays a crucial role in determining the strength, durability, workability, and overall performance of the hardened concrete. This comprehensive comprehension provides a detailed understanding of the water-cement ratio, its significance, factors influencing its selection, and the effects of different ratios on concrete properties.

Definition and Significance

The water-cement ratio (w/c ratio) is defined as the ratio of the weight or volume of water to the weight or volume of cementitious materials (cement and supplementary cementitious materials) in a concrete mixture. It represents the amount of water available for cement hydration, which is necessary for the development of strength and durability.

The water-cement ratio is a critical parameter as it directly affects various properties of concrete, including strength, permeability, workability, shrinkage, and durability. Balancing the water-cement ratio is essential to achieve the desired concrete performance while ensuring sufficient hydration and minimizing potential issues associated with excessive or inadequate water content.

Factors Influencing the Selection

a. **Strength requirements:** The desired compressive strength of concrete is an important factor in determining the water-cement ratio. Higher strength requirements typically require lower water-cement ratios to optimize the cement paste's strength and minimize porosity.

b. **Durability considerations:** The exposure conditions and intended service life of the concrete structure influence the selection of the water-cement ratio. For aggressive environments, such as marine or chemical exposure, a lower water-cement ratio is typically recommended to enhance durability and reduce the potential for deterioration.

c. **Workability requirements:** The workability or consistency of fresh concrete affects its ease of placement and compaction. Different applications may require varying degrees of workability, and the water-cement ratio is adjusted accordingly to achieve the desired flowability without sacrificing strength and durability.

d. **Aggregate characteristics:** The properties of aggregates, including shape, size, and surface texture, influence the water-cement ratio. Rough-textured and angular aggregates require more water to achieve workability compared to smooth and rounded aggregates.

e. **Admixtures and supplementary cementitious materials (SCMs):** The use of chemical admixtures, such as water reducers or superplasticizers, can significantly influence the water-cement ratio. Admixtures can enhance workability, reduce water demand, and improve the overall performance of concrete. The incorporation of SCMs, such as fly ash or silica fume, may also impact the water-cement ratio due to their pozzolanic or cementitious properties.

Effects of Different Water-Cement Ratios

a. **Strength and durability:** The water-cement ratio directly influences the compressive strength and durability of concrete. A lower water-cement ratio generally leads to higher strength and improved resistance to permeability, chemical attack, and freeze-thaw cycles.

b. **Workability and finishability:** Increasing the water-cement ratio enhances the workability and ease of concrete placement and finishing. However, excessive water can lead to segregation, bleeding, and reduced long-term strength and durability.

c. **Shrinkage and cracking:** Higher water-cement ratios can result in increased drying shrinkage and potential cracking due to excessive moisture loss during curing.

d. **Porosity and permeability:** The water-cement ratio affects the porosity and permeability of concrete. Lower ratios reduce the interconnected voids, enhancing the concrete's resistance to water penetration and chemical ingress.

The water-cement ratio is a crucial factor in concrete design and has a significant impact on the strength, durability, workability, and other properties of hardened concrete. By carefully selecting an appropriate water-cement ratio based on specific project requirements, engineers can optimize the mixture to achieve the desired performance while considering factors, such as strength, durability, workability, and aggregate characteristics. Maintaining a proper balance in the water-cement ratio is essential to ensure the long-term durability and sustainability of concrete structures.

2.4.3 Sources of Water

Water is a critical component in the production of concrete, playing a vital role in the hydration process of cement and the workability of the fresh mix. The quality and suitability of the water used in concrete construction have a direct impact on the strength, durability, and overall performance of the hardened concrete. This comprehensive discussion explores various sources of water commonly used in concreting, their characteristics, and considerations for ensuring high-quality concrete.

Potable Water

Potable water, also known as drinking water, is the most commonly used source for concrete production. It is sourced from municipal water supplies, wells, or treated surface water. Potable water generally meets the drinking water standards set by regulatory authorities, ensuring its safety for human consumption. It is typically suitable for use in concrete without any adverse effects on the hydration process or the properties of the hardened concrete.

Well Water

Well water is sourced from underground aquifers and is commonly used for concrete production, particularly in rural areas. The quality of well water can vary depending on the geological characteristics of the region. It is important to assess the well water for potential contaminants, such as high mineral content, organic matter, or dissolved solids, which may affect the concrete's performance. Water testing and analysis should be conducted to ensure its suitability for concrete production.

River Water

River water is another source commonly used for concrete production, particularly in large construction projects. It is readily available and easily accessible in many areas. However, river water may contain impurities, such as suspended solids, organic matter, silt, and clay particles. These impurities can adversely affect the concrete's workability, setting time, and strength development. Proper treatment and filtration may be necessary to remove or minimize these impurities before using river water in concrete.

Recycled Water

In certain cases, recycled water from various sources, such as wastewater treatment plants or water reclamation systems, may be used for concrete production. However, the use of recycled water requires careful consideration and adherence to regulatory guidelines. Recycled water may contain contaminants or high levels of dissolved salts that can affect the concrete's properties. Proper treatment, testing, and quality control measures should be implemented to ensure the recycled water's compatibility with concrete production.

Sea Water

In coastal regions or marine construction projects, sea water may be used for concrete production. However, the high salt content in sea water can be detrimental to the durability of concrete due to its corrosive nature. The chloride ions present in sea water can initiate the corrosion of reinforcing steel, leading to structural deterioration. If sea water is used, it is crucial to take appropriate measures to mitigate the effects of chloride attack, such as using corrosion inhibitors or special concrete mixes designed for marine environments.

2.4.4 Indirect Water—Bulking Quantity Test

In concrete production, it is crucial to accurately determine the moisture content of fine aggregates to ensure the proper water-cement ratio and achieve desired concrete properties. The Indirect Water—Bulking Quantity Test, also known as the bulking test, is a widely used method to assess the effect of moisture on fine aggregates. This comprehensive comprehension explores the significance of the bulking test, its procedure, and the interpretation of test results.

Significance of the Bulking Test

Fine aggregates, such as sand, have the tendency to absorb and retain moisture when exposed to humid conditions. This moisture absorption causes the particles to swell or 'bulk,' resulting in an increase in the volume of the aggregate. The bulking effect can significantly impact the workability and yield of the concrete mix, affecting its overall quality. By determining the bulking factor of fine aggregates, the appropriate adjustments can be made to the water content, ensuring accurate proportioning and consistent concrete performance.

Procedure

The indirect water—bulking quantity test involves the following steps:

a. **Sample collection:** Obtain a representative sample of fine aggregates from the source. Ensure the sample is free from contaminants and thoroughly dried to eliminate any pre-existing moisture.

b. **Container preparation:** Take a cylindrical container (typically a graduated glass cylinder) and clean it thoroughly. The container should be dry and free from any residue or moisture.

c. **Initial volume measurement:** Fill the container to a known volume with the dry sample of fine aggregates. The volume can be measured by pouring a specific weight of aggregates into the container and observing the resulting volume. Record this as the initial volume.

d. **Moistening the sample:** Gradually add a controlled amount of water to the sample while gently mixing it. Ensure the water is evenly distributed throughout the aggregates. The quantity of water added should be sufficient to achieve the desired moisture content but not excessive.

e. **Final volume measurement:** After the aggregates have absorbed the moisture, allow the sample to settle and recompact. Carefully measure the volume occupied by the moistened sample. Record this as the final volume.

f. **Calculation of bulking factor:** Calculate the bulking factor using the formula: Bulking Factor = (Final Volume/Initial Volume)*100.

g. **Interpretation of test results:** The bulking factor obtained from the test indicates the percentage increase in volume of the fine aggregates due to the presence of moisture. The higher the bulking factor, the greater the potential for the aggregates to exhibit bulking and require adjustments in the water content of the concrete mix. Test results can be interpreted as follows:

   Bulking factor less than 10%: Negligible or no bulking effect. The moisture content of the aggregates can be ignored for water-cement ratio calculations.

   Bulking factor between 10% and 20%: Moderate bulking effect. Adjustments in the water content may be necessary to maintain the desired workability and consistency of the concrete mix.

   Bulking factor greater than 20%: Significant bulking effect. Considerable adjustments in the water content are required to compensate for the increase in volume caused by moisture absorption.

It is important to note that the bulking factor can vary depending on the specific characteristics of the fine aggregates, such as particle shape, surface texture, and grading. Therefore, conducting the test with aggregates from the actual source being used in concrete production provides the most accurate results.

The Indirect Water—Bulking Quantity Test is a valuable tool for assessing the bulking effect of moisture on fine aggregates in concrete production. By determining the bulking factor, appropriate adjustments can be made to the water content, ensuring optimal workability, and consistent concrete quality. Regular testing and consideration of the test results enable concrete producers to achieve the desired water-cement ratio and deliver durable, high-quality concrete structures.

2.4.5 Water Quality

Water is a crucial ingredient in the production of concrete, and its quality plays a significant role in determining the strength, durability, and overall performance of the concrete structure. This section explores the importance of water quality in concrete production, the key factors to consider, and the potential impacts of poor water quality.

Importance of Water Quality

Water serves multiple functions in concrete production, including hydration of cement particles, workability control, and chemical reactions. The quality of water used can directly influence the properties and behavior of concrete. It is important to consider the following aspects of water quality:

a. **Chemical composition:** The chemical composition of water, particularly the presence of impurities and dissolved substances, can impact the hydration process and the long-term durability of concrete. Certain chemicals, such as sulfates and chlorides, can cause concrete deterioration, including corrosion of reinforcement.
b. **pH level:** The pH level of water affects the hydration process and the stability of concrete. Ideally, water with a neutral pH (around 7) is preferred. Highly acidic or alkaline water can lead to adverse chemical reactions and affect the setting time and strength development of concrete.
c. **Impurities and contaminants:** Water may contain impurities, such as organic matter, silt, clay, dissolved solids, and microorganisms. These impurities can

interfere with the cement hydration process, reduce the strength of concrete, and cause issues with workability and finishing.

d. **Salt content:** Water with a high salt content, particularly chlorides, can lead to corrosion of reinforcement in concrete. It is important to ensure that the water used in concrete production has a low chloride content to prevent long-term durability issues.

To maintain good water quality in concrete production, the following considerations should be taken into account:

a. **Source of water:** The source of water should be carefully evaluated. It can be from various sources, such as municipal supply, wells, rivers, or groundwater. Assessing the quality of the water source is essential to determine its suitability for concrete production.
b. **Testing and analysis:** Regular testing and analysis of water quality parameters should be conducted to ensure compliance with relevant standards and specifications. This includes testing for pH, chemical composition, chloride content, and other impurities. Laboratory testing or on-site water quality meters can be used for this purpose.
c. **Water treatment:** If the water quality is found to be unsatisfactory, appropriate treatment measures should be employed. Treatment methods, such as filtration, sedimentation, disinfection, and chemical dosing can be used to remove impurities, control pH, and reduce the chloride content.
d. **Adherence to standards:** It is essential to follow the guidelines and standards set by regulatory bodies or concrete industry associations regarding water quality in concrete production. These standards provide specific limits and requirements for various water quality parameters.

Poor water quality in concrete production can have several detrimental effects:

a. **Reduced strength and durability:** High chloride content, chemical impurities, or improper pH levels can compromise the strength and durability of concrete, leading to early deterioration and decreased service life.
b. **Poor workability:** Water with excessive impurities can affect the workability of concrete, making it difficult to achieve the desired consistency and finish.
c. **Corrosion of reinforcement:** Elevated chloride levels in water can initiate corrosion of steel reinforcement, weakening the structural integrity of the concrete.
d. **Aesthetic issues:** Water containing organic matter, sediments, or other impurities may cause discoloration or staining on the concrete surface, affecting its aesthetic appeal.

Chapter 3

Chemical and Mineral Admixtures

Chemical admixtures play a crucial role in enhancing the properties and performance of concrete. These admixtures are substances that are added to the concrete mix in small quantities during the mixing process. They can modify the fresh or hardened properties of concrete, offering benefits, such as improved workability, strength, durability, and setting time control. Chemical admixtures are a valuable tool for concrete producers and engineers, allowing them to tailor concrete mixes to meet specific project requirements and optimize performance.

Mineral admixtures are powdered materials added to concrete mixes to enhance performance. Types include fly ash, silica fume, GGBFS, and metakaolin. Mineral admixtures offer several advantages, including reduced cement consumption, improved workability, increased strength, and enhanced resistance to harsh environmental conditions. They also contribute to sustainable construction practices by utilizing industrial by-products and reducing the carbon footprint of concrete production.

CHEMICAL ADMIXTURES

3.1 ACCELERATORS

Accelerators play a vital role in concrete technology by significantly influencing the setting time and early strength development of concrete. They are chemical admixtures that are added to concrete mixtures to expedite the hydration process, leading to faster curing and early strength gain. This comprehension will delve into the importance of accelerators in concrete, their types, working mechanisms, dosage considerations, and their impact on the overall performance of concrete structures.

Accelerators are primarily used in situations where rapid setting and early strength development are desired. These conditions can arise in various construction scenarios, such as cold weather concreting, emergency repairs, fast-track projects, or when early formwork removal is necessary. By accelerating the chemical reactions within the concrete matrix, these admixtures enable the concrete to achieve sufficient strength earlier than conventional concrete mixtures.

There are different types of accelerators available in the market, including calcium chloride, non-chloride accelerators, and accelerating admixtures based on different chemical compounds. Calcium chloride, the most commonly used accelerator, has been used for decades due to its effectiveness and cost-efficiency. However, it is important to note that calcium chloride can accelerate corrosion of steel reinforcement, limiting its usage in reinforced concrete structures. Non-chloride accelerators have been developed as alternatives that provide similar performance without the detrimental effects of chloride ions.

The working mechanism of accelerators involves several processes that enhance the early hydration of cementitious materials. They increase the solubility of cement particles, resulting in the formation of more reactive compounds. This leads to the acceleration of chemical reactions, primarily the hydration of tricalcium silicate (C_3S) and dicalcium silicate (C_2S) in cement. The increased rate of hydration leads to the formation of additional hydration products, resulting in faster setting and early strength gain.

The dosage of accelerators in concrete mixtures is a critical factor that needs to be carefully determined. Insufficient dosage may not provide the desired acceleration effect, while excessive dosage can lead to excessive heat generation and potential negative impacts on the long-term durability of the concrete. The dosage depends on various factors such as the type and dosage rate of the accelerator, cement type, ambient temperature, and desired setting time and early strength requirements. Proper testing and evaluation should be conducted to determine the optimal dosage for specific project conditions.

The use of accelerators in concrete has both advantages and limitations. The main advantage is the ability to expedite construction schedules, allowing for faster completion of projects. It enables early formwork removal, reducing construction time and increasing productivity. Additionally, accelerated concrete gains sufficient early strength to withstand early loads and expedite subsequent construction activities. However, it is essential to consider potential limitations, such as increased cost, potential corrosion risks with certain accelerators, and careful handling to ensure optimal performance.

There are two main types of accelerators—set accelerators and hardening accelerators.

3.1.1 Set Accelerators

Set accelerators, also known as initial or flash set accelerators, are used to speed up the initial setting time of concrete (Fig. 3.1). They are typically employed when early strength gain is desired or to counteract the effects of cold weather on concrete placement and curing. Some common types of set accelerators include:

a. **Calcium chloride ($CaCl_2$):** This is the most commonly used set accelerator. It is highly effective and economical. Calcium chloride accelerates the early hydration reactions of cement, reducing the setting time and promoting early strength development. However, it may cause corrosion of reinforcing steel if used in excessive amounts or in the presence of high moisture and oxygen levels.
b. **Calcium nitrate [$Ca(NO_3)_2$]:** This accelerator is commonly used in cold weather concreting. It provides a controlled acceleration of the setting time, allowing concrete to gain strength quickly even in low temperatures. Calcium nitrate also

Fig. 3.1: Production of concrete in cold weather (cement concrete mixer truck)

acts as an anti-freeze agent, preventing freezing and thawing damage during curing.

c. **Sodium nitrite ($NaNO_2$):** This accelerator is primarily used in concrete exposed to deicing salts or other harsh environments. It enhances the setting time and provides early strength gain. Sodium nitrite also provides corrosion protection to reinforcing steel by forming a protective film.

On certain occasions, it becomes necessary to apply concrete as shotcrete (Fig. 3.2). This technique is commonly used for stabilizing excavated walls or tunnel walls, where concrete is sprayed onto the surfaces (Fig. 3.3). It is crucial that the shotcrete adheres to the walls and attains sufficient strength within a short timeframe to stabilize the soil. To achieve this, powerful set accelerators are employed. When using shotcrete admixtures, it is essential to introduce them at the nozzle's inception, as they can

Fig. 3.2: Shotcrete application

Fig. 3.3: Device for tunnel shotcreting (Putzmeister Wetkret 5)

cause the concrete to set rapidly within approximately one minute. Shotcrete admixtures are available in both liquid and powder forms in the market.

3.1.2 Hardening Accelerators

Hardening accelerators, also known as strength accelerators, are used to expedite the development of concrete strength beyond the initial setting stage. They are typically added to concrete mixtures when early strength gain is crucial, such as in fast-track construction projects or in applications where the concrete needs to be put into service quickly. Some common types of hardening accelerators include:

a. **Alkali hydroxides (e.g. sodium hydroxide, potassium hydroxide):** These accelerators promote the rapid development of concrete strength by accelerating the chemical reactions during the hydration process. They are effective in achieving early strength gain, but their use should be carefully controlled as they can cause alkali-silica reaction (ASR) in certain aggregates.

b. **Triethanolamine (TEA):** TEA is a commonly used organic hardening accelerator. It enhances the rate of cement hydration, resulting in early strength development. TEA is particularly effective in low-temperature conditions.

c. **Sodium silicate (water glass):** This accelerator reacts with calcium hydroxide in cement to form calcium silicate hydrate, which contributes to the strength development. Sodium silicate is used in applications where early strength gain and improved durability are desired.

3.2 RETARDERS

Retarders are chemical additives used in concrete to delay the setting time of the material. They play a crucial role in construction projects that require extended workability, transportation of ready-mix concrete over long distances (Fig. 3.4), or when weather conditions are unfavorable for rapid setting. Let us understand the significance of retarders in concrete, their working mechanisms, types, dosage considerations, and their impact on the overall performance of concrete structures.

Fig. 3.4: Concrete ready-mix plant

Retarders are particularly useful in situations where the extended workability of concrete is required, such as mass concreting or large-scale construction projects (Fig. 3.5), hot weather concreting, or projects with long transportation distances. By slowing down the hydration process, retarders allow for more time to place, compact, and finish the concrete, ensuring proper consolidation and reducing the risk of premature setting.

Fig. 3.5: Large-scale concreting project

There are various types of retarders available, including lignosulfonates, gluconates, sugars, and organic acids. These chemicals work by adsorbing onto the surface of cement particles, hindering the contact between water and cement and thus delaying the chemical reactions involved in the hydration process. The retarder molecules act as a barrier, preventing the formation of hydration products and prolonging the setting time of the concrete.

The working mechanism of retarders involves the modification of the cement-water interaction. They inhibit the early hydration reactions, particularly the formation of calcium silicate hydrate (C-S-H) gel, which is responsible for the setting and hardening of concrete. By delaying the formation of C-S-H gel, retarders provide additional time for concrete placement, compaction, and finishing.

Dosage considerations are crucial when using retarders in concrete. The optimal dosage depends on various factors, including the type and dosage rate of the retarder, cement type, ambient temperature, and desired setting time and workability requirements. Insufficient dosage may not achieve the desired retardation effect, while excessive dosage can lead to excessive retardation or even loss of setting. Proper testing and evaluation are essential to determine the appropriate dosage for specific project conditions.

The use of retarders offers several advantages in concrete construction. By extending the setting time, they improve the workability of concrete, allowing for better placement and compaction. This is particularly beneficial in large-scale projects where a considerable amount of concrete needs to be placed and finished within a specific time frame. Retarders also help in reducing the risk of cold joints or honeycombing caused by premature setting, especially in hot weather conditions.

However, it is important to consider potential limitations when using retarders. Extended setting time can result in longer construction schedules, and special precautions may be required to protect the concrete during the extended period. In addition, excessive use of retarders can affect the ultimate strength development of the concrete and may require adjustments to the mix design to compensate for the delayed strength gain.

3.2.1 Dosage of Retarders

Optimum dosage is a crucial aspect to consider when using retarder admixtures. Determining the correct dosage is more complex compared to other types of admixtures due to several factors influencing the retarding effect on concrete:

- **Cement type:** Different cement types have varying degrees of acceleration or retardation. For instance, cement type V requires less retarder admixture compared to cement type I.
- **Ambient temperature:** Higher temperatures accelerate cement activity, necessitating increased retarder admixture dosage. Temperature fluctuations throughout the day in summer may require different dosages.
- **Type of retarder:** Numerous chemicals possess retarding properties, resulting in a variety of retarder types with different strengths. The exact chemical composition of admixtures may not be disclosed, so referring to technical data sheets is crucial for determining starting dosages.
- **Duration of retarding effect:** The purpose of using retarder admixture influences the dosage required. For instance, using a retarder to enhance slump retention with a superplasticizer may necessitate a lower dosage, while achieving seamless pours in multilayered foundations may require a higher dosage.
- **Other admixtures:** When combining multiple types of admixtures, consulting the manufacturers and conducting trials is essential. Interaction between retarder admixtures and other types of admixtures should be assessed. For example, a plasticizer with lignosulfonate as a base may already possess retarding properties, reducing the need for additional retarder dosage.
- **Use of supplementary cementitious materials:** Incorporating supplementary cementitious materials alongside Portland cement may decrease the required

retarder dosage. These materials exhibit lower reactivity than pure Portland cement and initiate their reaction after sufficient $Ca(OH)_2$ is produced.

Determining the optimal retarder admixture dosage for specific purposes proves more challenging compared to other admixture types. Therefore, conducting trials under conditions simulating the actual project is highly recommended before finalizing the dosage.

In the event of using a higher dosage of retarder than necessary, the concrete may not set within the defined timeframe. In such cases, appropriate curing techniques should be applied based on weather conditions until the concrete sets. For example, if the expected setting time is 24 hours but the concrete remains unset, curing for an additional 24 hours is advised. Typically, the concrete will eventually set within two to three times the expected setting time. At 28 days, the mechanical properties of the concrete should be evaluated. Although lower mechanical properties may be observed at early ages, the 28-day properties generally align with the desired concrete specifications.

3.3 PLASTICIZERS

Plasticizers, also known as water reducers or dispersants, are chemical additives used in concrete to improve its workability and performance. These additives are primarily used to increase the flowability of concrete without compromising its strength or durability. The following will delve into the significant role of plasticizers in concrete, their working mechanisms, types, dosage considerations, and their impact on the overall performance of concrete structures.

The primary function of plasticizers in concrete is to reduce the amount of water required to achieve a desired level of workability. By dispersing the cement particles and lubricating the mix, plasticizers enable better particle dispersion and reduce interparticle friction. This results in improved flowability and ease of concrete placement, compaction, and finishing. Slump retention ability is a highly significant characteristic of plasticizers and superplasticizers, particularly when it comes to the transportation of concrete from a ready mixed plant (Fig. 3.6).

Fig. 3.6: Long-distance transportation of concrete using truck mixers

There are different types of plasticizers available, including lignosulfonates, sulfonated naphthalene formaldehyde condensates, polycarboxylates, and melamine-based superplasticizers. Each type of plasticizer has its own unique chemical composition and characteristics, influencing the specific effects it imparts on the concrete mix. These additives work by adsorbing onto the surface of cement particles, creating a repulsive force between particles and allowing them to disperse more easily.

The working mechanism of plasticizers involves three main aspects: dispersion, deflocculation, and water reduction. Dispersion refers to the ability of plasticizers to separate and disperse the cement particles, reducing their agglomeration and promoting better particle distribution within the mix. Deflocculation occurs when plasticizers provide a repulsive force between particles, minimizing the attractive forces and allowing for better flowability. Water reduction is achieved by the lubricating effect of plasticizers, which reduces the water-cement ratio without compromising the workability or strength of the concrete.

Dosage considerations are crucial when using plasticizers in concrete. The optimal dosage depends on factors, such as the type of plasticizer, cement type, aggregate characteristics, ambient temperature, desired workability, and project specifications. The dosage should be carefully determined through laboratory testing or trial mixes to achieve the desired flowability and performance while minimizing the risk of segregation or excessive air entrainment.

The use of plasticizers offers several advantages in concrete construction. By reducing the water-cement ratio, plasticizers improve the strength, durability, and density of concrete. They enhance workability, allowing for easier placement, compaction, and finishing, even in congested reinforcement areas or complex formwork. Plasticizers can also improve the resistance of concrete to segregation and bleeding, resulting in a more uniform and consistent mix.

However, it is important to note that excessive use of plasticizers can lead to potential issues, including extended setting time, increased shrinkage, or reduced early-age strength gain. Therefore, careful consideration of the specific project requirements, mix design, and dosage is essential to achieve the desired balance between workability and performance.

3.3.1 Finely Divided Minerals

Finely divided minerals, also known as mineral admixtures or mineral fillers, are a type of additive used as plasticizers in concrete. These minerals are finely ground and added to the concrete mix to improve its workability, enhance certain properties, and optimize the overall performance of the concrete.

There are several types of finely divided minerals commonly used as plasticizers in concrete:

a. **Silica fume:** Silica fume, also known as microsilica, is a by-product of the production of silicon metal or ferrosilicon alloys. It consists of very fine particles, typically with a high silica content. When added to concrete, silica fume acts as a highly effective plasticizer, improving the flowability and reducing the water demand of the mix. It also enhances the strength, durability, and resistance to chemical attack of the resulting concrete.

b. **Fly ash:** Fly ash is a by-product of coal combustion in thermal power plants. It is composed of fine particles that are predominantly spherical in shape. When used as a plasticizer in concrete, fly ash enhances workability and improves the cohesiveness of the mix. It also contributes to the long-term strength development, reduces heat generation during hydration, and enhances the resistance to sulfate attack and alkali-silica reaction.

c. **Ground granulated blast furnace slag (GGBFS):** GGBFS is a by-product of the iron and steel industry. It is produced by quenching molten slag from a blast furnace with water and then grinding it into a fine powder. GGBFS acts as a plasticizer in concrete by improving workability and reducing the heat of hydration. It also enhances the long-term strength, reduces permeability, and provides better resistance to sulfate attack and alkali-silica reaction.

d. **Metakaolin:** Metakaolin is a calcined form of kaolin clay. It is produced by heating kaolin clay at high temperatures, causing the clay to undergo a phase transformation. Metakaolin acts as a plasticizer by improving the workability and reducing the water demand of the concrete mix. It also enhances the early-age strength development, reduces shrinkage, and improves durability properties such as resistance to sulfate attack and carbonation.

These finely divided minerals are typically added to concrete in varying proportions, depending on the desired effect and specific project requirements. They are often used in combination with other plasticizers or chemical admixtures to optimize the overall performance of the concrete mix.

3.3.2 Air-entraining Agents

Air-entraining agents are a type of additive used as plasticizers in concrete. These agents are chemical compounds that are added to the concrete mix to introduce a controlled amount of microscopic air bubbles into the hardened concrete. These air bubbles improve the durability and workability of the concrete, especially in harsh weather conditions or freeze-thaw environments.

There are two main types of air-entraining agents commonly used as plasticizers in concrete:

a. **Surfactant-based agents:** Surfactant-based air-entraining agents are typically organic compounds that contain surface-active substances. These agents work by reducing the surface tension of water, allowing it to form stable air bubbles within the concrete mix. Surfactant-based agents are usually available as liquid formulations and are added to the concrete mix during the mixing process. They help in creating a network of air voids within the concrete, which improves its resistance to freezing and thawing cycles.

b. **Vinsol-based agents:** Vinsol-based air-entraining agents are derived from the resinous extract of pine trees, known as vinsol resin. These agents are natural and renewable and have been used in concrete for many years. Vinsol-based agents are typically in powdered form and are added to the concrete mix during the mixing process. They work by improving the stability of the air bubbles, providing increased durability and workability to the concrete.

Both types of air-entraining agents act as plasticizers by reducing the water content required for a given workability, thereby increasing the strength and reducing the permeability of the concrete. The microscopic air bubbles introduced by these agents provide several benefits, including:

- **Improved freeze-thaw resistance:** The air bubbles act as pressure relief zones, allowing water to expand when it freezes and preventing internal pressure build-up that can cause cracking and damage to the concrete.

- **Increased durability:** The air voids provide internal lubrication within the concrete, reducing internal friction and enhancing its resistance to abrasion, scaling, and chemical attack.
- **Enhanced workability:** The presence of air bubbles improves the workability and cohesiveness of the concrete mix, making it easier to handle, place, and finish.

3.3.3 Synthetic Derivatives

Synthetic derivatives are a type of plasticizers commonly used in concrete to improve its workability and performance. These plasticizers are chemical compounds that are added to the concrete mix to enhance its flowability, reduce water content, and increase its strength and durability.

There are different types of synthetic derivatives used as plasticizers in concrete:

a. **Polycarboxylate ether (PCE):** PCE-based plasticizers are widely used in modern concrete technology. They are highly efficient and offer excellent water-reducing capabilities. PCE molecules have a unique structure that allows them to disperse cement particles more effectively, resulting in improved workability and flow of the concrete mix. PCE-based plasticizers provide high slump retention, which means that the concrete maintains its desired consistency for a longer period, allowing for better placement and finishing.

b. **Lignosulfonates:** Lignosulfonate-based plasticizers are derived from wood pulp or other lignocellulosic materials. These plasticizers have been used in concrete for many years. They work by dispersing the cement particles and reducing the water content needed for a given workability. Lignosulfonates also provide some air-entraining properties, enhancing the freeze-thaw resistance of the concrete. However, compared to newer plasticizers like PCE, lignosulfonates may have limitations in terms of their water-reducing efficiency and slump retention.

c. **Melamine-based superplasticizers:** Melamine-based plasticizers are another type of synthetic derivative used in concrete. They offer excellent water reduction capabilities and have good slump retention properties. Melamine-based plasticizers are particularly effective in high-temperature environments, where they help maintain the workability and delay the initial setting time of the concrete.

d. **Naphthalene-based superplasticizers:** Naphthalene-based plasticizers have been widely used in the past but are now less commonly used due to their environmental concerns. They provide significant water reduction and improve workability, making them suitable for a variety of concrete applications. However, naphthalene-based plasticizers may have a higher potential for air entrainment and can cause a slight delay in setting time.

These synthetic derivatives act as dispersants and water reducers in concrete, allowing for a lower water-to-cement ratio while maintaining workability. By reducing the water content, they enhance the strength, durability, and overall performance of the hardened concrete. They also contribute to reducing the drying shrinkage and permeability of the concrete, resulting in more durable and long-lasting structures.

3.4 SUPERPLASTICIZERS

Superplasticizers, also known as high-range water reducers (HRWRs), are a type of chemical admixture used in concrete to significantly improve its workability without compromising its strength. They are powerful water-reducing agents that enable the production of highly flowable and cohesive concrete mixes.

Superplasticizers work by dispersing cement particles and reducing the surface tension of water, allowing for better lubrication and flow within the concrete mix. This increased flowability is achieved by reducing the amount of water needed to maintain the desired consistency, resulting in a higher solids content and improved particle packing. As a result, superplasticizers can greatly reduce the water-to-cement ratio, leading to increased strength, improved durability, and enhanced workability.

There are two main types of superplasticizers commonly used in concrete:

a. **Sulfonate-based superplasticizers:** Sulfonate-based superplasticizers are typically derived from lignosulfonates or naphthalene sulfonates. These superplasticizers work by dispersing the cement particles and providing a more uniform distribution throughout the concrete mix. They improve the flowability and workability of the concrete, allowing for easier placement and compaction. Sulfonate-based superplasticizers are generally effective at reducing the water content by 15-25% while maintaining the desired workability.

b. **Polycarboxylate ether (PCE)-based superplasticizers:** PCE-based superplasticizers are a more recent and advanced development in concrete technology. They offer superior water-reducing capabilities and have become widely used in the construction industry. PCE molecules have a unique structure that provides excellent dispersing and water-reducing properties. They have a higher efficiency in reducing water content and can achieve water reductions of 30–40% or more. PCE-based superplasticizers also provide excellent slump retention, allowing the concrete to maintain its desired consistency for an extended period, even in hot weather conditions. This gives workers more time for placing and finishing operations.

The benefits of using superplasticizers in concrete include:

- **Improved workability:** Superplasticizers greatly enhance the flowability and workability of concrete, making it easier to place, compact, and finish. This results in improved construction efficiency and better-quality finishes.
- **Increased strength:** By reducing the water-to-cement ratio, superplasticizers promote higher cementitious content and improved hydration, leading to increased compressive strength and overall durability of the hardened concrete.
- **Enhanced durability:** Superplasticizers help in producing dense and well-compacted concrete, reducing porosity and permeability. This results in improved resistance to aggressive chemicals, water penetration, and freeze-thaw cycles.
- **Better cohesion and segregation resistance:** Superplasticizers improve the cohesion of the concrete mix, preventing segregation and bleeding. This ensures a more uniform distribution of the ingredients and homogeneity in the final hardened concrete.

- **Reduced shrinkage and cracking:** The reduced water content achieved with superplasticizers helps minimize drying shrinkage, leading to fewer cracks and improved long-term durability of the concrete.

Superplasticizers are commonly used in a wide range of concrete applications, including high-strength concrete, self-consolidating concrete (SCC), precast concrete, pumped concrete, and underwater concrete. The dosage of superplasticizers varies depending on factors, such as the desired workability, cement type, ambient conditions, and specific project requirements. It is crucial to follow manufacturer recommendations and conduct proper testing to determine the optimal dosage for a particular concrete mix.

3.5 VISCOSITY MODIFYING ADMIXTURES

Viscosity modifying admixtures (VMAs) play a crucial role in enhancing the performance and workability of concrete mixes. These chemical additives are specifically designed to modify the viscosity and rheological properties of concrete, resulting in improved flow, stability, and cohesion.

VMAs are primarily used to address the challenges associated with highly flowable concrete mixes, such as self-consolidating concrete (SCC) or high-performance concrete (HPC). These types of concrete often have a high water content, which can lead to issues like excessive bleeding, segregation (Fig. 3.7), and poor stability. VMAs help mitigate these problems by controlling the viscosity and flow characteristics of the mix, allowing for better control during placement and reducing the risk of defects.

Fig. 3.7: Segregated concrete

The key functions and benefits of viscosity modifying admixtures are as follows:

- **Enhanced workability:** VMAs improve the workability of concrete by increasing its resistance to segregation and improving its flow properties. This is particularly important in applications where the concrete needs to flow easily into intricate formwork or congested reinforcement.

- **Reduced bleeding and segregation:** Bleeding is the phenomenon of water separation from the concrete mix, resulting in the accumulation of water at the surface. VMAs help to reduce bleeding by increasing the viscosity of the mix, preventing excessive water movement. This leads to improved surface finish and reduced potential for defects.
- **Improved cohesion and stability:** VMAs promote cohesion within the concrete mix, ensuring that the aggregates and other components remain uniformly distributed. This enhances the stability of the mix, preventing segregation and improving its overall homogeneity.
- **Controlled setting time:** VMAs can help control the setting time of concrete, allowing for better coordination during construction activities. By adjusting the rheological properties of the mix, VMAs can delay or accelerate the initial and final setting times as required.
- **Enhanced pumpability and placement:** VMAs improve the pumpability of concrete, making it easier to transport and place in challenging locations or through long pipelines. The modified viscosity allows the mix to flow smoothly, reducing the risk of blockages and ensuring efficient pumping operations.
- **Improved finish and surface quality:** By reducing the likelihood of bleeding, segregation, and surface defects, VMAs contribute to a better finish and improved surface quality of the hardened concrete. This is especially important for architectural concrete applications where aesthetics are a key consideration.
- **Compatibility with other admixtures:** VMAs are generally compatible with other admixtures used in concrete, such as water reducers, superplasticizers, and air-entraining agents. They can be combined with these admixtures to achieve specific performance objectives and tailor the concrete mix to the project requirements.

There are different types of VMAs available in the market, including cellulose ethers, hydroxyethyl methyl cellulose (HEMC), hydroxypropyl methylcellulose (HPMC), and polymeric-based admixtures. These admixtures function by modifying the rheological properties of the concrete, influencing its viscosity, flow, and stability.

3.6 WATERPROOFERS

Waterproofers in concrete are chemical additives specifically designed to enhance the water resistance and impermeability of concrete structures. These additives work by reducing the capillary porosity of concrete, preventing the penetration of water and other liquids into the material.

The role of waterproofers in concrete is crucial in various construction applications where protection against water ingress is essential, such as basements, swimming pools, tunnels, and foundations. The following points highlight the key aspects and benefits of using waterproofers in concrete:

- **Water resistance:** The primary function of waterproofers is to make concrete structures resistant to water penetration. They form a barrier that prevents water molecules from entering the concrete matrix, thus protecting it from potential damage caused by moisture, freeze-thaw cycles, and chemical reactions.

- **Durability enhancement:** By reducing water permeability, waterproofers contribute to the long-term durability of concrete. They help prevent the ingress of harmful substances, such as chloride ions, sulfates, and aggressive chemicals, which can cause corrosion of reinforcing steel and deterioration of concrete over time.
- **Increased service life:** Concrete structures treated with waterproofers have an extended service life due to their improved resistance to water-related deterioration. This is particularly important in areas with high moisture levels or exposure to harsh environmental conditions.
- **Reduced cracking and efflorescence:** Waterproofers can help minimize cracking in concrete by reducing the absorption of water. By limiting the amount of water that enters the concrete, they decrease the potential for internal pressure build-up and subsequent cracking. Additionally, they can help prevent efflorescence, which is the formation of white salt deposits on the concrete surface due to water migration and evaporation.
- **Improved aesthetic appearance:** Waterproofers can contribute to the aesthetic appeal of concrete structures. By reducing water absorption, they help maintain the color, texture, and overall appearance of the surface, preventing discoloration and staining caused by waterborne contaminants.
- **Ease of application:** Waterproofing additives can be easily incorporated into the concrete mix during the batching process. They are typically available as liquid or powder forms, and their dosage can be adjusted to meet the specific project requirements.
- **Compatibility with other admixtures:** Waterproofers are generally compatible with other concrete admixtures, such as plasticizers, superplasticizers, and air-entraining agents. They can be used in combination with these additives to achieve multiple performance objectives, ensuring a customized approach to concrete mix design.

It is important to note that waterproofers should be used in conjunction with proper construction practices, including adequate joint design, proper surface preparation, and application of appropriate sealants. These practices help create a comprehensive waterproofing system that ensures the best performance and longevity of concrete structures.

There are several types of waterproofers available for use in concrete, each with its own specific properties and application methods. Here are some common types of waterproofers used in concrete:

a. **Integral waterproofers:** These are additives that are mixed directly into the concrete during the batching process. Integral waterproofers work by reducing the water permeability of the concrete matrix from within. They typically consist of hydrophobic materials that create a barrier against water penetration. Integral waterproofers provide long-lasting protection throughout the entire thickness of the concrete.

b. **Surface applied waterproofers:** These are coatings or membranes that are applied to the surface of cured concrete to create a waterproof barrier. Surface applied waterproofers include products, such as liquid-applied membranes, cementitious coatings, and epoxy-based coatings. They form a protective layer on the concrete surface, preventing water ingress and offering additional benefits, such as UV resistance and chemical resistance.
c. **Crystalline waterproofers:** Crystalline waterproofing products work by reacting with moisture in the concrete to form insoluble crystals. These crystals fill the capillary pores and microcracks in the concrete, effectively blocking water penetration. Crystalline waterproofers can be applied as coatings, admixtures, or as a dry-shake material on freshly placed concrete.
d. **Silane/siloxane waterproofers:** Silane and siloxane waterproofers are penetrating sealers that are applied to the surface of concrete. These products chemically react with the concrete to form a hydrophobic barrier that repels water. Silane/siloxane waterproofers penetrate into the pores of the concrete, providing protection against water intrusion while allowing the concrete to breathe and release moisture vapor.
e. **Bentonite waterproofers:** Bentonite is a clay-based material that can be used as a waterproofing agent. Bentonite waterproofers are typically available as sheets or panels that are applied to the exterior of below-grade concrete structures. When hydrated, bentonite forms a waterproofing gel-like substance that seals against water penetration.
f. **Rubberized waterproofers:** Rubberized waterproofers are typically liquid-applied coatings that contain rubber polymers. These waterproofers form a flexible and elastic membrane on the surface of concrete, providing protection against water intrusion and accommodating minor substrate movements. Rubberized waterproofers are commonly used in areas where there may be structural movement or cracking.
g. **Cementitious waterproofers:** Cementitious waterproofers are coating materials that contain cement or cementitious binders. These waterproofers are applied as a slurry or thin coating to the concrete surface. They work by filling the capillary pores and creating a barrier against water penetration. Cementitious waterproofers can also provide additional benefits, such as enhanced bonding strength and resistance to chemical attack.

It is important to note that the choice of waterproofing material depends on various factors, including the specific application, the condition of the concrete, and the desired level of waterproofing. Consulting with a waterproofing professional or manufacturer can help determine the most suitable type of waterproofing product for a specific project.

3.7 MISCELLANEOUS ADMIXTURES

3.7.1 Gas-forming and Expansive Chemicals

Gas-forming and expansive chemicals are additives used in concrete to introduce controlled expansion or generate gas bubbles within the concrete matrix. These additives serve various purposes and offer specific benefits in different concrete applications.

Gas-forming agents: Gas-forming agents are materials that release gases when mixed with water or react with other components in the concrete. The gas generated creates voids or bubbles within the concrete, which can provide benefits, such as improved workability, reduced density, and enhanced freeze-thaw resistance. Common gas-forming agents include aluminum powder, calcium carbide, and hydrogen peroxide. These additives are typically used in lightweight concrete, foam concrete, and certain types of concrete blocks to reduce weight and increase insulation properties.

Expansive chemicals: Expansive chemicals are materials that cause controlled expansion in the concrete as they react with moisture. This expansion helps compensate for shrinkage or cracking that may occur during the drying and hardening process of concrete. Expansive chemicals can be particularly useful in concrete applications where the risk of cracking due to restrained shrinkage is high. One commonly used expansive chemical is calcium sulfoaluminate. It reacts with water to form ettringite, which creates internal pressure and causes the concrete to expand. This expansion helps to minimize cracking and improve the long-term durability of the concrete.

Gas-forming and expansive chemicals are typically added to the concrete mix during the batching process. The dosage and timing of their addition depend on the specific product and application requirements. It is important to follow the manufacturer's instructions and guidelines to achieve the desired results.

Gas-forming and expansive chemicals should be used judiciously and with proper consideration of the overall concrete mix design, as excessive amounts or improper usage can lead to unwanted effects, such as excessive expansion, reduced strength, or compromised durability. It is advisable to consult with concrete experts or manufacturers to determine the appropriate dosage and application method for specific projects.

3.7.2 Corrosion-inhibiting Chemicals

Corrosion-inhibiting chemicals are additives used in concrete to prevent or reduce the corrosion of reinforcing steel within the concrete structure. Corrosion of steel in concrete can lead to significant structural damage and deterioration. Corrosion-inhibiting chemicals work by either passivating the steel surface or creating a protective barrier that prevents or slows down the corrosion process. Here are some common types of corrosion-inhibiting chemicals used in concrete:

a. **Calcium nitrite:** Calcium nitrite is a commonly used corrosion inhibitor in concrete. It works by forming a protective layer on the surface of the reinforcing steel, preventing the corrosive action of chloride ions. Calcium nitrite also provides temporary cathodic protection to the steel, reducing the risk of corrosion.

b. **Calcium nitrate:** Calcium nitrate is another corrosion inhibitor that functions by reducing the penetration of chloride ions into the concrete. It helps to mitigate the risk of chloride-induced corrosion in structures exposed to chloride-rich environments, such as coastal areas or structures in contact with deicing salts.

c. **Organic corrosion inhibitors:** Organic corrosion inhibitors are chemical compounds that are typically added to the concrete mix. These inhibitors adsorb onto the steel surface, forming a protective film that hinders the corrosion process. Organic inhibitors can be effective in reducing corrosion caused by chloride ions and other aggressive substances.

d. **Migrating corrosion inhibitors:** Migrating corrosion inhibitors are chemicals that are added to the concrete mix or applied as surface treatments. These inhibitors migrate through the concrete matrix and form a protective layer on the reinforcing steel. They offer long-term corrosion protection by continuously releasing corrosion inhibitors over time.

e. **Silicates and silanes:** Silicate and silane-based corrosion inhibitors work by penetrating the concrete pores and chemically reacting with the reinforcing steel surface. They form a barrier that prevents the ingress of corrosive agents and inhibits the corrosion process.

Corrosion-inhibiting chemicals should be used in accordance with manufacturer guidelines and recommended dosages. It is important to consider factors, such as the exposure conditions, concrete mix design, and the specific corrosion risks associated with the project. Regular inspection and maintenance of the concrete structure are also crucial to ensure the long-term effectiveness of corrosion inhibitors.

3.7.3 Pigments

Pigments are often used as admixtures in concrete to add color and enhance the aesthetic appeal of concrete surfaces. These pigments are available in various forms and can be classified into two main categories: inorganic pigments and organic pigments. Here is an overview of each type:

Inorganic Pigments

Iron oxide pigments: Iron oxide pigments are commonly used in concrete due to their excellent color stability and resistance to UV radiation. They are available in red, yellow, brown, and black shades. Iron oxide pigments are highly durable and can withstand harsh weather conditions.

Titanium dioxide pigments: Titanium dioxide pigments are primarily used as white pigments in concrete. They offer excellent opacity and brightness, making them suitable for producing lighter shades of concrete.

Chromium oxide pigments: Chromium oxide pigments are used to create green-colored concrete. They are known for their high heat stability and lightfastness.

Organic Pigments

Carbon black pigments: Carbon black pigments are used to achieve black or gray shades in concrete. They are derived from the incomplete combustion of hydrocarbons and provide good color intensity.

Phthalocyanine pigments: Phthalocyanine pigments are organic pigments that offer a wide range of colors, including blue and green. They provide high color strength and good resistance to fading.

Azo pigments: Azo pigments are organic pigments that offer a wide spectrum of colors, including red, yellow, orange, and brown. They are highly versatile and can be used to achieve various shades in concrete.

Pigments are typically added to the concrete mix during the batching process. The dosage of pigment depends on the desired color intensity and the specific pigment being used. It is important to follow the manufacturer's recommendations for the correct dosage to achieve consistent and uniform color throughout the concrete.

In addition to providing color, pigments in concrete may also have some influence on the concrete's properties. They can affect the workability, setting time, and strength development of the concrete to some extent. Therefore, it is essential to consider the compatibility of the chosen pigment with the concrete mix and conduct necessary trials to ensure the desired color and performance are achieved.

3.7.4 Antifungal Admixtures

Antifungal admixtures are additives used in concrete to inhibit the growth and proliferation of fungi and molds on the concrete surface. These admixtures are particularly useful in environments where moisture, humidity, and organic matter are present, as these conditions can promote fungal growth.

Mechanism of Action

Antifungal admixtures work by releasing fungicidal or fungistatic compounds into the concrete mix. These compounds act by disrupting the cellular structure and metabolic processes of fungi, preventing their growth and reproduction. The admixtures are designed to provide long-lasting protection against fungal colonization on the concrete surface.

Benefits

- **Prevention of fungal growth:** The primary benefit of antifungal admixtures is the prevention of fungal growth on the concrete surface. Fungi and molds cannot only mar the appearance of concrete but also lead to degradation and structural damage over time.
- **Improved aesthetics:** By inhibiting fungal growth, antifungal admixtures help maintain the appearance of the concrete, preventing discoloration, staining, and the formation of unsightly patches or biofilms.
- **Enhanced durability:** Fungal growth can contribute to the deterioration of concrete, including surface degradation, cracking, and loss of strength. Antifungal admixtures can help preserve the structural integrity and longevity of the concrete.
- **Health and safety:** Fungi and molds can produce allergens, toxins, and volatile organic compounds (VOCs), posing health risks to occupants. Antifungal admixtures help create a healthier indoor environment by reducing the presence of these microorganisms.

Types of Antifungal Admixtures

a. **Organic compounds:** Some antifungal admixtures contain organic compounds, such as quaternary ammonium compounds (QACs) or organic acids. These compounds exhibit fungicidal or fungistatic properties and are effective against a wide range of fungi.

b. **Metallic compounds:** Certain metallic compounds, including copper-based additives, are effective in inhibiting fungal growth. Copper ions released by these additives disrupt fungal cell membranes and metabolic processes.
c. **Combination products:** Some antifungal admixtures combine different active ingredients to provide broader-spectrum protection against a variety of fungal species.

It is important to note that antifungal admixtures are not a substitute for proper construction practices and moisture control measures. Adequate ventilation, moisture management, and good surface drainage are essential to minimize the conditions that favor fungal growth.

When using antifungal admixtures, it is crucial to follow the manufacturer's instructions regarding dosage, compatibility with other admixtures, and mixing procedures. Additionally, periodic maintenance and cleaning of the concrete surface may be required to remove accumulated dirt or organic matter that could provide a substrate for fungal growth.

3.7.5 Curing Compounds

Curing compounds are a type of chemical admixture used in concrete construction to enhance and control the curing process. Curing is a critical step in concrete placement and involves providing optimal conditions for the hydration of cement, which leads to the development of strength, durability, and overall performance of the concrete. Curing compounds are applied to the concrete surface to retain moisture, regulate temperature, and promote proper curing (Fig. 3.8).

Fig. 3.8: Applying the curing compound

Purposes of Curing Compounds

- **Moisture retention:** Curing compounds form a thin film or membrane on the concrete surface, preventing the loss of moisture through evaporation. This helps to maintain a moist environment necessary for the complete hydration of cement and the development of strength.

- **Temperature regulation:** Curing compounds can also help regulate the temperature of the concrete during the early stages of curing. By reducing rapid temperature fluctuations, these compounds minimize the risk of thermal cracking and ensure uniform curing.
- **Improved curing efficiency:** Curing compounds provide a more controlled and efficient curing process compared to traditional curing methods, such as water curing or covering the concrete with wet burlap or plastic sheets. They eliminate the need for manual watering or covering, saving time and labor costs.

Types of Curing Compounds

- **Film-forming curing compounds:** These compounds form a thin, continuous film or membrane on the concrete surface. The film acts as a barrier, preventing moisture evaporation and protecting the concrete from external factors that could hinder proper curing. Film-forming curing compounds can be further classified into:
  - **Solvent-based compounds:** These compounds consist of a solvent (such as water or mineral spirits) and a film-forming material (such as waxes, resins, or polymers). They are easy to apply and provide excellent moisture retention.
  - **Water-based compounds:** These compounds are formulated with water as the carrier and can contain film-forming agents like acrylics or styrene-butadiene. Water-based compounds are environmentally friendly and offer good curing performance.
- **Non-film-forming curing compounds:** Unlike film-forming compounds, non-film-forming curing compounds do not create a physical barrier on the concrete surface. Instead, they penetrate the concrete pores and react with the hydration products to provide moisture retention. Non-film-forming curing compounds can be classified into:
  - **Reactive silicates:** These compounds contain alkali silicates that react with the calcium hydroxide in concrete to form a gel-like substance, sealing the surface and reducing moisture loss.
  - **Membrane-forming resins:** These compounds penetrate the concrete surface and form a breathable membrane that allows moisture to escape while retaining sufficient moisture for proper curing.

Benefits of Curing Compounds

- **Improved strength and durability:** Curing compounds promote the complete hydration of cement, leading to increased strength, durability, and resistance to cracking, shrinkage, and surface defects.
- **Uniform curing:** Curing compounds provide a more uniform and controlled curing environment, ensuring consistent properties throughout the concrete.
- **Reduced surface drying:** By minimizing moisture evaporation, curing compounds prevent surface drying, which can result in premature cracking and reduced bond strength with subsequent layers or toppings.
- **Time and labor savings:** Curing compounds eliminate the need for manual watering or covering of the concrete, saving time and labor costs during the curing process.

- **Enhanced aesthetics:** Curing compounds can contribute to improved aesthetics by reducing surface discoloration, efflorescence, and dusting.

It is crucial to follow the manufacturer's instructions when applying curing compounds to concrete. These compounds are typically applied immediately after finishing and before the concrete reaches its initial set. Prior to application, it is essential to prepare the surface properly by cleaning it and removing any contaminants that may hinder proper curing. By adhering to these guidelines, the curing compound can effectively protect the concrete and promote optimal curing and strength development.

3.7.6 Sealants

Sealants play a vital role in concrete applications by providing a protective barrier against moisture, chemicals, and other external factors that can potentially damage the concrete surface. These materials are specifically designed to fill and seal joints, cracks, and gaps in concrete structures, preventing the ingress of water, air, and contaminants.

Sealants enhance the durability and longevity of concrete by reducing the risk of moisture infiltration, which can lead to corrosion of reinforcement, freeze-thaw damage, and deterioration of the concrete matrix. They also help in maintaining the structural integrity of the concrete by preventing the penetration of harmful substances, such as chemicals, oils, and salts. Furthermore, sealants contribute to the aesthetic appeal of concrete surfaces by providing a smooth and uniform appearance. They can be color-matched to blend seamlessly with the surrounding concrete, enhancing the overall visual appeal of the structure.

Different types of sealants are available for various concrete applications, including joints in pavements, bridges, buildings, and other structures. These sealants can be based on various materials, such as silicone, polyurethane, acrylic, or asphalt, each offering specific properties and benefits depending on the intended use and environmental conditions.

Overall, sealants are essential in protecting and preserving the integrity of concrete structures, ensuring their long-term performance and minimizing the need for costly repairs and maintenance.

MINERAL ADMIXTURES

Mineral admixtures are materials that are added to concrete during its production to enhance its properties or provide specific characteristics. These admixtures are usually finely divided materials that are either added to the concrete mix or used as a partial replacement for cement.

Mineral admixtures can offer several advantages to concrete, such as improved workability, increased strength, enhanced durability, reduced permeability, and reduced heat of hydration. They can also help mitigate certain issues associated with concrete, such as shrinkage, alkali-silica reaction, and sulfate attack.

3.8 FLY ASH

Fly ash is a widely used mineral admixture in concrete production. It is a finely divided residue that is generated during the combustion of pulverized coal in thermal power

Fig. 3.9: Thermal power plant

plants (Fig. 3.9). Fly ash consists of spherical particles, predominantly composed of silicon dioxide (SiO_2), aluminum oxide (Al_2O_3), iron oxide (Fe_2O_3), and calcium oxide (CaO) (Fig. 3.10). The composition and properties of fly ash can vary depending on the source of coal, combustion conditions, and collection methods. Fly ash typically contains an active SiO_2 content ranging from 30% to 50%. Moreover, its blain surface area measures approximately 4000–4500 cm^2/g, which is 30% to 50% higher than the blain of normal Portland cement. The activation level of fly ash falls between that of silica fume and other supplementary cementitious materials, with higher activation than the latter.

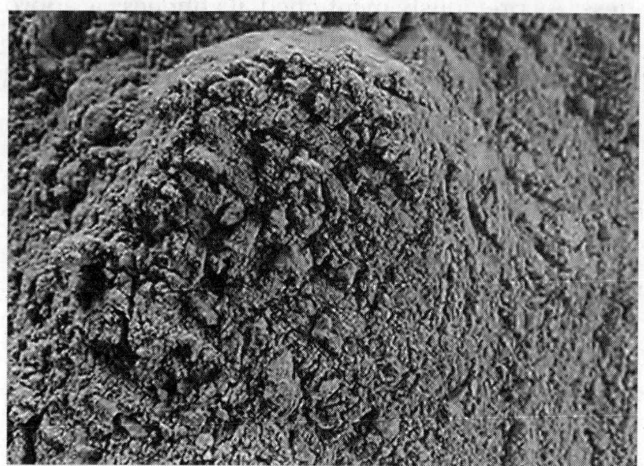

Fig. 3.10: Fly ash

There are two types of fly ash, distinguished by the type of coal burned in the power plant:

1. **Fly ash type F:** This variety of fly ash has low calcium content.
2. **Fly ash type C:** This type of fly ash exhibits a moderate to high calcium content.

Table 3.1 displays the chemical analysis of fly ash type F, while Table 3.2 presents the chemical analysis of fly ash type C. As evident from the tables, there is a disparity in the amount of active SiO_2 between fly ash types F and C. Due to the higher SiO_2 content in type F, it exhibits excellent pozzolanic properties, making it a highly effective pozzolan.

Table 3.1: Chemical analysis of fly ash type F

Material	SiO_2	Al_2O_3	Fe_2O_3	CaO	SO_3	Na_2O	K_2O
Percent	54	24	11.5	5	1.5	1.5	2.5

Table 3.2: Chemical analysis of fly ash type C

Material	SiO_2	Al_2O_3	Fe_2O_3	CaO	SO_3	Na_2O	K_2O
Percent	37	20	7	24	4.5	6	1.5

On the other hand, type C fly ash demonstrates some cementing activity due to its significant CaO content. It can react with water on its own, but the cementing activity is relatively limited. As a result, this type of fly ash is primarily utilized in concrete production for its pozzolanic activity.

3.8.1 Characteristics of Fly Ash

- It appears as a powder ranging from gray to light yellow. The fineness of this powder slightly surpasses that of Portland cement.
- **Specific gravity:** It exhibits a lighter specific gravity than cement, falling within the range of 1.9 to 2.6.
- **Blaine's fineness:** As previously mentioned, its fineness is approximately 30% to 50% greater than that of normal Portland cement. The Blaine's fineness value varies among different producers worldwide but typically ranges from 4000 to 4500 cm^2/g.
- **Concrete usage:** Recommendations for the percentage of using this material in concrete differ. It is advisable to incorporate it between 10% and 35% by weight of the total binder (comprising both Portland cement and supplementary cementitious material).

The incorporation of fly ash in concrete offers several advantages and has become increasingly popular in the construction industry. Some of the key benefits of using fly ash as a mineral admixture include:

1. **Improved workability:** Fly ash acts as a filler material, providing better workability to the concrete mix. It enhances the cohesiveness of the mixture, allowing for easier handling, placing, and compaction of concrete.
2. **Increased strength:** Fly ash is a pozzolanic material, meaning it reacts chemically with calcium hydroxide (a by-product of cement hydration) in the presence of water to form additional cementitious compounds. This pozzolanic reaction results in the development of more refined and denser concrete microstructure, leading to increased compressive strength over time.
3. **Enhanced durability:** The use of fly ash in concrete improves its durability properties. The pozzolanic reaction between fly ash and calcium hydroxide reduces the porosity of the concrete, making it more resistant to penetration by harmful substances, such as chloride ions and sulfate ions. This enhanced

resistance to chemical attack helps in preventing corrosion of reinforcing steel and extends the service life of concrete structures.

4. **Reduced permeability:** The incorporation of fly ash reduces the permeability of concrete, making it less susceptible to water penetration. The finer particles of fly ash fill the voids between cement particles, resulting in a denser concrete matrix. This reduced permeability helps in mitigating issues related to moisture ingress, freeze-thaw cycles, and alkali-aggregate reactions.
5. **Reduced heat of hydration:** Fly ash has a lower heat of hydration compared to cement, which helps in controlling the temperature rise during concrete curing. This is particularly beneficial in large concrete pours and mass concrete applications, as it minimizes the risk of thermal cracking.
6. **Environmental benefits:** The utilization of fly ash in concrete contributes to sustainable construction practices. By incorporating this industrial byproduct into concrete, it reduces the need for raw materials and decreases the amount of fly ash that would otherwise be disposed of in landfills. This helps in conserving natural resources and reducing greenhouse gas emissions associated with cement production.

3.9 SILICA FUME

Silica fume, also known as microsilica, is a highly reactive mineral admixture that is widely used in the production of high-performance concrete. It is obtained as a by-product of silicon and ferrosilicon alloy production through the reduction of quartz or silica in electric arc furnaces. Silica fume consists of very fine, amorphous particles, typically ranging in size from 1 to 100 nanometers. Silica fume is composed of over 90% active SiO_2 and possesses an extremely fine powder texture, exceeding the fineness of Portland cement by more than 50 times. The Blaine's fineness measurement for silica fume ranges from 150,000 to 300,000 cm^2/g. Its pozzolan structure is spherical in nature. Due to its remarkably high activation compared to other supplementary cementitious materials, silica fume is often referred to as a super-pozzolan. For detailed chemical analysis of silica fume, please refer to Table 3.3.

Table 3.3: Chemical analysis of silica fume

Material	SiO_2	C	Fe_2O_3	Al_2O_3	CaO	MgO	Na_2O	K_2O	P_2O_5	SO_3	Cl
Percent	94.43	0.3	0.87	1.32	0.49	0.97	0.31	1.01	0.16	0.1	0.04

3.9.1 Characteristics of Silica Fume

- The powder's appearance is light gray and exceptionally fine, exhibiting a lighter hue than Portland cement (Fig. 3.11).
- **Specific gravity:** It boasts a lower specific gravity than cement, measuring around 2.2.
- **Blaine's fineness:** As previously mentioned, this is an extremely fine powder, and its blain value may vary among different producers worldwide. However, it typically falls within the range of 150,000 to 300,000 cm^2/g.
- **Concrete usage:** For incorporating this material into concrete, there are various recommendations regarding the percentage of use. It is advisable to utilize more

Fig. 3.11: Silica fume

than 5% by weight of the total binder (comprising both Portland cement and supplementary cementitious material) but keep it below 12%.

The incorporation of silica fume in concrete offers several beneficial effects, making it a valuable addition in various construction applications. Here are the key characteristics and advantages of using silica fume as a mineral admixture:

1. **Pozzolanic reactivity:** Silica fume exhibits excellent pozzolanic properties due to its high content of amorphous silicon dioxide (SiO_2). When mixed with calcium hydroxide (a by-product of cement hydration) and water, silica fume undergoes a chemical reaction known as pozzolanic reaction. This reaction results in the formation of additional cementitious compounds, such as calcium silicate hydrate (C-S-H) gel, which enhances the strength and durability of concrete.
2. **Increased strength and dense microstructure:** The pozzolanic reaction of silica fume leads to the formation of a more refined and densely packed concrete microstructure. The small particles of silica fume fill the gaps between cement particles, resulting in a reduced porosity and increased density of the concrete. This densification enhances the compressive strength, flexural strength, and abrasion resistance of the concrete.
3. **Improved durability:** Silica fume significantly enhances the durability of concrete by reducing its permeability. The densified microstructure created by the pozzolanic reaction restricts the movement of water and harmful substances, such as chlorides and sulfates, into the concrete. This improved resistance to penetration helps in preventing corrosion of reinforcing steel, mitigating alkali-silica reaction, and increasing the longevity of concrete structures.
4. **Reduced shrinkage and cracking:** The addition of silica fume to concrete reduces drying shrinkage and the risk of early-age cracking. The fine particles of silica fume fill the voids, reducing the capillary tension within the concrete. This mitigates shrinkage and minimizes the formation of cracks during the early stages of concrete curing.

5. **High temperature resistance:** Silica fume enhances the resistance of concrete to high temperatures. Due to its high surface area and low thermal conductivity, silica fume acts as a barrier that inhibits heat transfer within the concrete. This makes it suitable for applications, such as high-temperature industrial environments, fire-resistant structures, and nuclear power plant constructions.
6. **Improved chemical resistance:** Silica fume improves the resistance of concrete to chemical attack. The densified microstructure and reduced permeability hinder the ingress of aggressive substances, protecting the concrete from chemical deterioration caused by acids, sulfates, and alkalis.

3.10 GROUND GRANULATED BLAST FURNACE SLAG

Ground granulated blast furnace slag (GGBFS), commonly referred to as slag, is a widely used mineral admixture in the production of concrete. It is a by-product generated during the iron manufacturing process in blast furnaces. GGBFS is obtained by quenching molten blast furnace slag in water or steam, followed by drying and grinding into a fine powder. It comprises the residue of melted steel that rapidly cools down after exiting the furnace. The cooling process significantly influences the activity of SiO_2, making it a crucial step in the GGBFS production for concrete.

The GGBFS production process involves two stages:

Stage 1: Occurs in the steel factory during the production process of steel and the subsequent cooling of slag.

Stage 2: Takes place in a cement factory and involves the grinding process, which needs to be separate from cement grinding due to the varying hardness of cement clinker and slag.

GGBFS comprises approximately 30% of active SiO_2. By grinding the slag during GGBFS production, we have the flexibility to adjust the fineness of the final product. Given that GGBFS's activity is considerably lower than that of Portland cement, it requires more extensive grinding compared to cement clinker. Typically, achieving a desirable blain of about 4000 cm^2/g is common for GGBFS. While its activity is inferior to silica fume and fly ash, GGBFS remains an excellent material for producing durable concrete.

Moreover, considering the significant global production of slag from steel manufacturing, utilizing GGBFS in concrete production becomes an environmentally sound practice. Table 3.4 provides the chemical analysis of GGBFS, revealing a SiO_2 content of 35%. With an effective cooling process, we can activate approximately 99% of this SiO_2. However, it is not an ideal slag for use in concrete production.

Table 3.4: Chemical analysis of GGBFS

Material	SiO_2	Al_2O_3	Fe_2O_3	CaO	SO_3	Na_2O	K_2O
Percent	35	13	1	41	9	0.5	0.5

3.10.1 Characteristics of GGBFS

- It presents as a gray to light yellow powder, and its fineness can be adjusted beyond that of Portland cement to regulate its activity. Figure 3.12 displays an image of the slag before grinding.

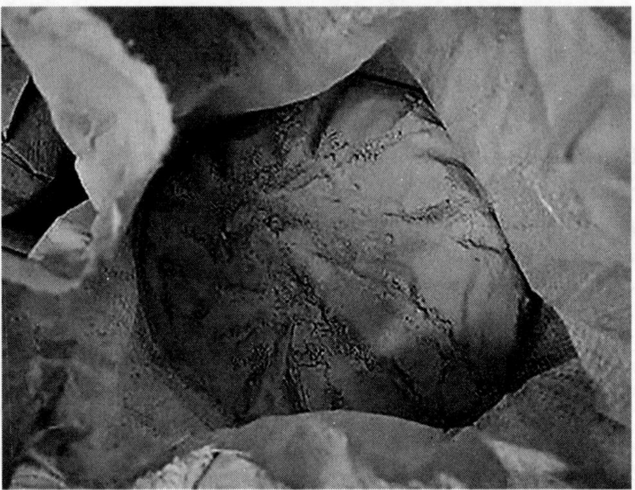

Fig. 3.12: Image of slag

- **Specific gravity:** Generally, it tends to be lighter than cement, with a specific gravity of approximately 2.9.
- **Blaine's fineness:** As previously mentioned, the blain can be tailored during the cement factory process. Typically, the GGBFS blaine's fineness measures around 4000 cm^2/g, being softer than Portland cement due to its lower activity.
- **Concrete usage:** There are various suggestions for the percentage of using this material in concrete. For instance, in Europe, it can be utilized up to 95% of the total binder. However, our recommendation here is to use it between 20% and 50% by weight of the total binder, comprising both Portland cement and supplementary cementitious material.

Here are the key characteristics and advantages of using ground granulated blast furnace slag as a mineral admixture:

1. **Pozzolanic reactivity:** GGBFS exhibits pozzolanic properties due to its chemical composition. It contains amorphous silica (SiO_2), alumina (Al_2O_3), and calcium oxide (CaO), which react with calcium hydroxide (a by-product of cement hydration) in the presence of water, forming additional cementitious compounds. This pozzolanic reaction contributes to the strength and durability of concrete.
2. **Increased strength:** The addition of ground granulated blast furnace slag enhances the compressive and flexural strengths of concrete. The pozzolanic reaction of GGBFS leads to the formation of additional calcium silicate hydrate (C-S-H) gel, which improves the interparticle bonding and overall strength of the concrete. GGBFS can contribute to both early-age and long-term strength development.
3. **Improved durability:** Slag improves the durability of concrete by reducing permeability and enhancing resistance to chemical attack. The finer particles of GGBFS fill the gaps between cement grains, resulting in a denser concrete microstructure. This densification reduces the ingress of water, chlorides, and other harmful substances, thereby enhancing the durability and minimizing the risk of reinforcement corrosion.

4. **Reduced heat of hydration:** Ground granulated blast furnace slag has a lower heat of hydration compared to cement. The addition of GGBFS helps control the heat generated during the hydration process, reducing the risk of thermal cracking in large concrete placements. This is particularly beneficial in massive concrete structures and in hot weather conditions.
5. **Improved workability:** Slag contributes to the workability of concrete by providing better cohesiveness and ease of handling. The finer particles of GGBFS act as a filler, improving the flow and workability of the concrete mix. This can lead to improved placement and compaction characteristics, making it easier to achieve desired concrete finishes.
6. **Sustainable material:** The utilization of ground granulated blast furnace slag promotes sustainable practices in the construction industry. GGBFS is a recycled material that reduces the demand for natural resources. By using slag as a mineral admixture, the environmental impact associated with the production of cement can be reduced. Moreover, the utilization of blast furnace slag helps in minimizing the accumulation of waste materials in landfills.

Chapter 4

Properties of Fresh Concrete

Fresh concrete is described as fully mixed and in a rheological state that maintains its plasticity. This stage encompasses the initial cement hydration phases I and II. The plasticity of fresh concrete allows for activities, such as transportation, placement, compaction, and surface finishing within a specific timeframe. The characteristics of fresh concrete significantly impact construction speed and decision-making processes.

After discussing the components of concrete, let's delve into the properties of freshly mixed concrete. These properties influence how concrete is handled, consolidated, and the sequence of construction activities. Moreover, they can impact the properties of the hardened concrete. These properties are primarily short-term requirements and must meet the following criteria:

1. Easy mixing and transportability.
2. Uniformity within and between batches.
3. Maintenance of fluidity during transportation.
4. Flow properties that ensure complete form filling.
5. Ability to compact fully without segregation.
6. Reasonable setting time.
7. Capability for proper finishing, either against forms or through troweling and other surface treatments.

Compaction plays a critical role in ensuring the long-term properties of hardened concrete. Proper compaction is essential for air removal and achieving a dense concrete structure. Consequently, the compressive strength of concrete can improve with increased density. Traditionally, compaction is achieved using vibrators. However, modern self-compacting concrete can attain dense structures solely through its self-weight, without requiring vibration.

4.1 WORKABILITY OF FRESH CONCRETE

Workability is a crucial property of fresh concrete that denotes its ease of handling, placing, and compacting during construction. A concrete mix with good workability flows easily into formwork, facilitating proper placement and consolidation without excessive effort. Achieving the ideal level of workability is essential for ensuring uniform distribution of aggregates, proper bonding between particles, and ultimately, the structural integrity of the hardened concrete. Various factors influence the workability of fresh concrete, including water content, cementitious materials, aggregate properties, admixtures, and environmental conditions. Balancing these factors is crucial to optimize workability while maintaining the desired strength and durability of the resulting concrete structure. Different methods are employed to assess and measure workability, such as the slump test, flow table test, and compacting factor test, providing valuable insights for concrete mix design and construction practices. Understanding and controlling workability are fundamental aspects of concrete technology, essential for achieving successful outcomes in construction projects.

4.1.1 Factors Affecting Workability

Several key factors influence the workability of fresh concrete, determining its ease of handling, placing, and compaction during construction activities. The water-to-cement ratio plays a significant role, as it affects the hydration process and the lubrication of particles within the concrete mixture. A higher water-to-cement ratio generally results in improved workability but may compromise the strength and durability of the hardened concrete. Additionally, the grading, shape, and surface texture of aggregates influence workability, with well-graded, rounded particles typically enhancing flowability and reducing the risk of segregation. The type and dosage of admixtures, such as plasticizers, superplasticizers, and air-entraining agents, can also significantly impact workability by altering the rheological properties of the concrete mix. Furthermore, environmental factors, such as temperature, humidity, and wind speed can affect workability by influencing the setting time and hydration rate of cementitious materials. Understanding and appropriately managing these factors are essential for optimizing workability while maintaining the desired properties and performance of fresh concrete in construction applications.

4.1.2 Methods to Measure Workability

Slump Test (Fig. 4.1)

- **Preparation:** The test begins with the preparation of a slump cone according to the specifications outlined in IS: 7320-1974. The cone should have a base diameter of 20 cm, a top diameter of 10 cm, and a height of 30 cm. The cone is placed on a smooth, flat surface, such as a steel plate, and dampened to prevent absorption of water from the concrete.
- **Filling the cone:** A representative sample of fresh concrete is obtained from the batch being tested. The concrete is filled into the slump cone in three layers, each approximately one-third of the cone's height. Each layer is compacted with 25 strokes of a tamping rod, uniformly distributed over the cross-section of the cone.
- **Slumping:** After filling, the cone is carefully lifted vertically upward, allowing the concrete to spread freely. The amount of subsidence or slump of the concrete mass is measured immediately using a steel rule perpendicular to the horizontal plane. The difference in height between the original height of the cone and the displaced height of the concrete is recorded as the slump value.
- **Interpretation:** The slump value is interpreted based on the requirements of the specific project or concrete mix design. As per IS: 456, different slump ranges are

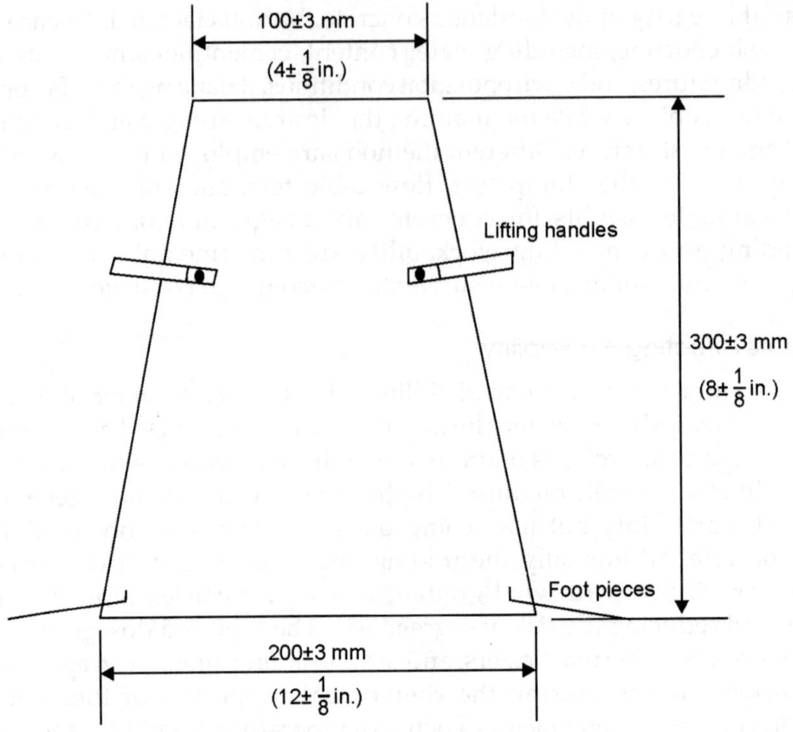

Fig. 4.1: Slump test equipment

recommended for different types of construction, with higher values typically indicating greater workability.

Flow Table Test (Fig. 4.2)

- **Preparation:** The flow table apparatus consists of a rigid metal table measuring approximately 70 cm in diameter, supported on a sturdy base. The table surface is made smooth and free from irregularities. The concrete sample is prepared as per standard procedures.
- **Placing the concrete:** A representative sample of fresh concrete is placed in a cylindrical mold positioned at the center of the flow table. The mold is removed, allowing the concrete to spread and flow freely on the table surface.
- **Interpretation:** The flow value provides an indication of the flowability and consistency of the concrete mix. Higher flow values suggest better workability, while lower values indicate a stiffer or less workable mix.

Compacting Factor Test (Fig. 4.3)

The compacting factor test, as per the Indian Standard IS:1199-1959, outlines a procedure to determine the workability of fresh concrete by measuring the compacting factor.

Preparation of Apparatus

- Ensure that the compacting factor apparatus is clean and free from any debris or previous concrete residue.

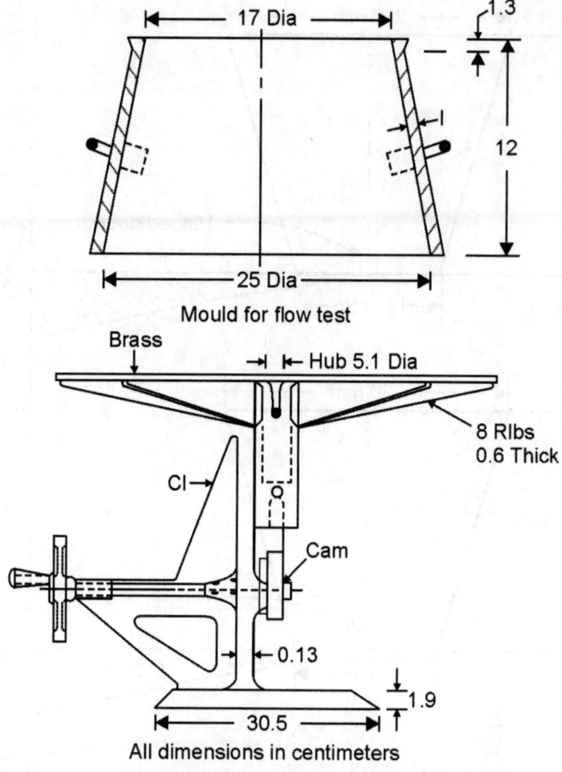

Fig. 4.2: Flow table test

- The apparatus consists of two hoppers, a cylindrical mold, and a tamping rod.

Preparation of Concrete Sample

- Prepare a representative sample of fresh concrete from the batch under consideration.
- The concrete should be thoroughly mixed to achieve uniform distribution of ingredients.
- Ensure that the sample is free from any segregation or bleeding.

Filling the Mold

- Place the clean and dry cylindrical mold on a level, smooth surface.
- Fill the mold with the fresh concrete in three equal layers, compacting each layer thoroughly with a standard tamping rod.
- The tamping rod should be inserted vertically and uniformly distributed over the entire cross-sectional area of the mold. Each layer should be compacted with 25 strokes of the tamping rod.

Compaction Process

- After filling and compacting the mold, lift the mold vertically and remove it from the concrete.

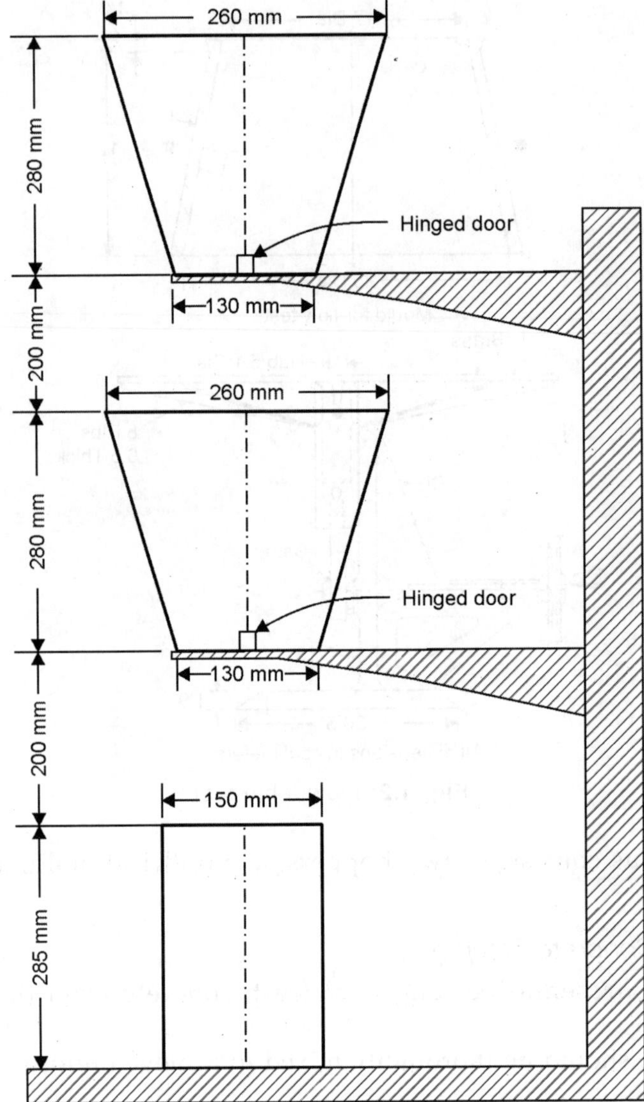

Fig. 4.3: Compacting factor test equipment

- Allow the concrete to spread and flow freely on the smooth surface. Avoid any external compaction or manipulation of the concrete after it is released from the mold.

Weighing the Compacted Concrete

- Weigh the mold filled with compacted concrete using a calibrated weighing scale. Record the mass of the mold and compacted concrete together.
- Ensure accurate measurements to obtain reliable results.

Interpretation

- The compacting factor value obtained from the calculation indicates the workability of the fresh concrete.

- Higher compacting factor values suggest better workability, indicating that the concrete is more easily compacted and has a higher degree of fluidity.
- Lower compacting factor values indicate a stiffer or less workable mix, requiring more effort for compaction.

Vee-Bee Test

- **Preparation:** The Vee-Bee test apparatus consists of a vibrating table, a vibrating plunger, and a calibrated stopwatch. A representative sample of fresh concrete is placed in a cylindrical mold positioned on the vibrating table (Fig. 4.4).
- **Compaction:** The vibrating plunger is inserted into the concrete sample to a depth of 5 cm and subjected to vibration at a frequency of 9,000 ± 500 vibrations per minute. The time taken for the concrete to achieve a specified degree of compaction, typically 60 seconds, is measured using the stopwatch.
- **Interpretation:** The Vee-Bee time provides an indication of the concrete's resistance to segregation and ability to flow under vibration. Shorter Vee-Bee times suggest better workability, while longer times indicate a stiffer or less workable mix.

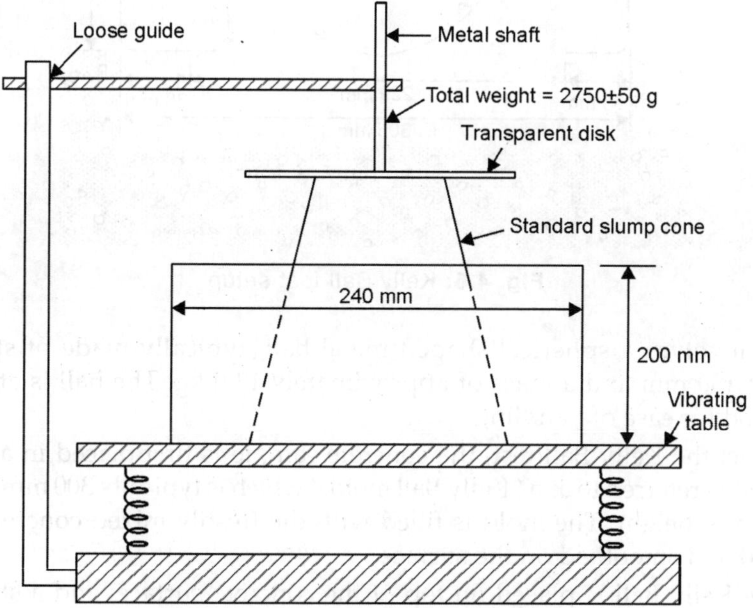

Fig. 4.4: Vee-Bee consistometer

Kelly Ball Test

The Kelly Ball test, also known as the Kelly Ball penetration test or simply the Kelly Ball test, is a method used to determine the workability of freshly mixed concrete (Fig. 4.5). Workability refers to the ease with which concrete can be mixed, placed, and compacted without segregation or excessive bleeding. The Kelly Ball test provides a quick and simple way to assess the consistency of concrete on-site, particularly in situations where other workability tests may not be feasible.

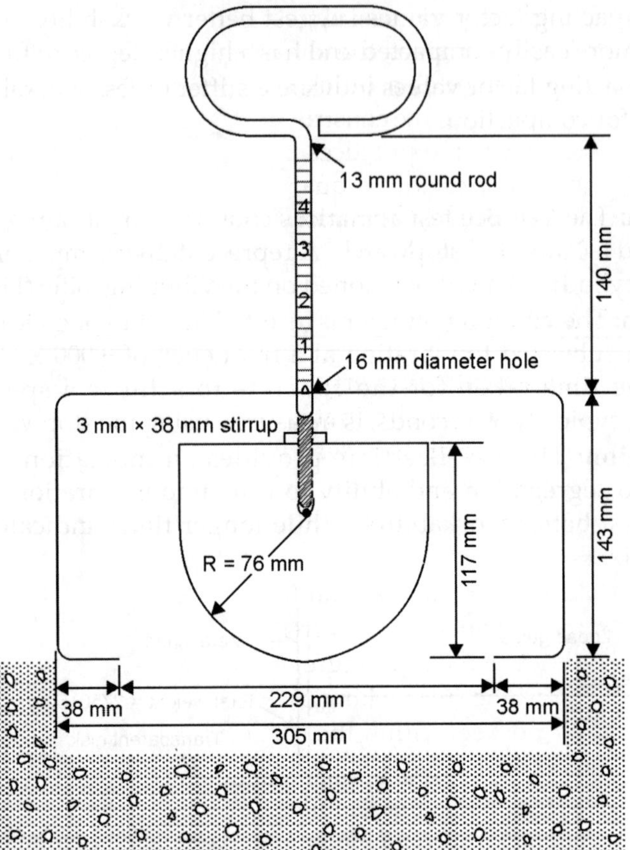

Fig. 4.5: Kelly Ball test setup

The test involves a spherical-shaped metal ball, typically made of steel, with a diameter of 150 mm and a mass of approximately 13.6 kg. The ball is attached to a handle or rod for ease of handling.

To conduct the Kelly Ball test, the concrete sample is first placed in a cylindrical container, often referred to as a "Kelly Ball mold," which is typically 300 mm in diameter and 500 mm in height. The mold is filled with the freshly mixed concrete, which is then leveled and smoothed on the surface.

Next, the Kelly Ball is placed on top of the concrete surface, and a standardized procedure is followed to release the ball onto the concrete. The ball is allowed to penetrate the concrete under its own weight for a specified period, typically around 15 seconds. During this time, the depth of penetration of the Kelly Ball into the concrete is measured.

The depth of penetration is directly related to the workability of the concrete. A greater penetration depth indicates higher workability, while a shallower penetration suggests lower workability. The results of the Kelly Ball test can be compared to established standards or specifications to determine whether the concrete meets the desired workability requirements for the intended application.

The Kelly Ball test is particularly useful for assessing the workability of concrete in situations where other tests, such as the slump test or the Vee-Bee test, may not be suitable or practical. It provides a quick and portable means of evaluating the consistency of concrete directly at the construction site, allowing for timely adjustments to the mix design or construction practices if necessary. However, it is important to note that the Kelly Ball test provides a qualitative measure of workability and may not provide as precise or detailed information as other, more sophisticated workability tests.

4.2 COMPACTABILITY

Compactability is a fundamental property of fresh concrete that denotes its capacity to be densely packed and voids eliminated during the process of placement and compaction. It is essentially about how well the concrete mix can be consolidated to remove air voids and achieve a uniform, dense structure. This property is crucial because it directly impacts the strength, durability, and overall performance of the hardened concrete.

Achieving proper compactability is vital for ensuring the structural integrity and longevity of the concrete element. When fresh concrete is compacted effectively, it promotes better bonding between the aggregate particles, leading to improved load-bearing capacity and resistance to cracking. Additionally, proper compaction helps to eliminate voids and air pockets within the concrete, which can weaken its structure and reduce its durability over time.

Several factors influence the compactability of fresh concrete. Mix design plays a significant role, as the proportion of cement, aggregates, water, and admixtures can affect the concrete's flowability and ease of compaction. The water-cement ratio is particularly important, as it directly impacts the workability and strength of the concrete. Aggregate grading and shape also influence compactability, with well-graded, rounded aggregates typically enhancing flowability and reducing the risk of segregation.

In construction practice, various methods are employed to achieve optimal compactability of fresh concrete. Vibration is one of the most commonly used techniques, where mechanical vibrators are inserted into the concrete mass to agitate and consolidate it. This helps to remove entrapped air and ensure uniform distribution of the concrete within the formwork. Tamping and rolling are alternative methods used for compaction, particularly in cases where access to mechanical vibrators is limited. These techniques involve manually compacting the concrete using handheld or mechanized tools to achieve the desired density.

By optimizing mix design parameters and employing effective compaction techniques, engineers and contractors can enhance the compactability of fresh concrete, thereby improving its strength, durability, and overall performance in service. Proper compaction ensures that the fresh concrete attains the desired density and structural properties required for its intended application, whether it is for structural elements like columns and beams or for pavement and foundation construction.

4.3 MOBILITY

Mobility in concrete refers to its ability to flow freely and fill formwork or molds without segregation or excessive effort during the placement process. It is a crucial property that influences the ease of handling, placing, and compacting fresh concrete in construction applications. Concrete with good mobility exhibits high fluidity and workability, allowing it to spread easily and uniformly within the formwork, even around congested reinforcement, corners, and intricate shapes. This property is essential for ensuring proper consolidation and achieving uniform distribution of aggregates throughout the concrete mass.

Several factors influence the mobility of concrete, including the water-cement ratio, aggregate grading and shape, cementitious materials content, and the use of admixtures, such as plasticizers and superplasticizers. A higher water-cement ratio generally results in improved mobility, as it increases the fluidity of the concrete mixture. Well-graded, rounded aggregates with smooth surfaces also enhance mobility by reducing internal friction and resistance to flow. Admixtures like plasticizers and superplasticizers can significantly improve mobility by reducing the water content required to achieve a given level of workability, thereby enhancing flowability without compromising strength or durability.

Proper control and management of these factors are essential for optimizing the mobility of concrete and ensuring its successful placement and consolidation in construction projects. Engineers and contractors must carefully select and proportion concrete ingredients, considering the specific requirements of the project and the desired properties of the hardened concrete. By achieving the right balance of ingredients and employing appropriate construction techniques, they can ensure that the fresh concrete exhibits optimal mobility, facilitating efficient placement and resulting in high-quality, durable concrete structures.

4.4 STABILITY

Stability in concrete refers to its ability to maintain its shape, integrity, and structural stability during the placement, compaction, and curing processes, as well as throughout its service life. It is a critical property that directly influences the performance and durability of concrete structures. Concrete must possess sufficient stability to resist external forces, such as gravity, lateral loads, and environmental factors, without undergoing excessive deformation, cracking, or failure.

Several factors contribute to the stability of concrete:

1. **Mix design:** The proportioning of concrete ingredients, including cement, aggregates, water, and admixtures, plays a crucial role in determining its stability. A well-balanced mix design ensures that the concrete achieves the desired strength, workability, and durability properties necessary for withstanding various loading conditions.
2. **Water-cement ratio:** The water-cement ratio significantly affects the stability of concrete. Excess water can weaken the concrete matrix, leading to reduced strength and increased susceptibility to cracking and deterioration. Conversely, a

lower water-cement ratio results in a denser, more stable concrete with enhanced durability and resistance to external factors.

3. **Aggregate properties:** The type, size, shape, and grading of aggregates influence the stability of concrete. Well-graded, clean aggregates with smooth surfaces promote good interlocking and bonding within the concrete matrix, enhancing its stability and resistance to deformation and segregation.
4. **Admixtures:** Various chemical admixtures, such as plasticizers, superplasticizers, and air-entraining agents, can influence the stability of concrete. Plasticizers and superplasticizers improve workability and reduce water demand, contributing to better compaction and stability. Air-entraining agents introduce microscopic air bubbles into the concrete, enhancing its freeze-thaw resistance and durability.
5. **Placement and compaction:** Proper placement and compaction techniques are essential for achieving and maintaining the stability of concrete structures. Adequate consolidation ensures that the concrete is uniformly compacted, free from voids and entrapped air, and capable of resisting external loads and environmental conditions.
6. **Curing:** Proper curing is crucial for the long-term stability and durability of concrete. Adequate moisture retention and temperature control during the curing process promote hydration and development of concrete strength, minimizing shrinkage, cracking, and other forms of deterioration.

4.5 CONSISTENCY

Consistency in concrete refers to its degree of fluidity or stiffness, which directly affects its workability and ease of handling during construction. It is a crucial property that influences the ability of concrete to be properly placed, compacted, and finished to achieve the desired shape and surface texture. Consistency is determined by the amount of water present in the concrete mixture relative to its other ingredients, primarily cement and aggregates.

There are generally three main categories of concrete consistency:

1. **Slump consistency:** Slump consistency refers to the measure of the degree of flowability or deformability of fresh concrete. It is typically determined using the slump test, where a cone-shaped mold is filled with fresh concrete, compacted, and then removed to measure the vertical subsidence of the concrete mass. A higher slump value indicates a more fluid or workable concrete mix, while a lower slump value suggests a stiffer or less workable mix.
2. **Flow consistency:** Flow consistency measures the ability of fresh concrete to spread and flow freely within formwork without segregation or excessive bleeding. It is often assessed using the flow table test, where a cylindrical sample of fresh concrete is placed on a horizontal surface and subjected to repeated jolting or vibration. The diameter of the concrete spread after a specified number of jolts is measured, providing an indication of its flowability. Higher flow values indicate better flow consistency and workability.
3. **Consistency by Vee-Bee test:** Consistency by Vee-Bee test evaluates the ability of fresh concrete to flow under vibration. In this test, a vibrating plunger is inserted

into a sample of fresh concrete, and the time taken for the concrete to achieve a specified degree of compaction is measured. Shorter Vee-Bee times indicate better consistency and workability, as the concrete flows more readily under vibration.

The consistency of concrete is influenced by various factors, including the water-cement ratio, aggregate grading, admixtures, and environmental conditions, such as temperature and humidity. Balancing these factors is essential to achieve the desired consistency for the specific construction application while ensuring that the concrete maintains its strength, durability, and other performance properties. By controlling the consistency of concrete, engineers and contractors can optimize its workability and ensure successful construction outcomes.

4.6 SEGREGATION

Segregation in concrete refers to the separation of constituent materials, such as coarse aggregates, fine aggregates, cement paste, and water, resulting in non-uniform distribution within the concrete mass. It is a detrimental phenomenon that can occur during mixing, transportation, placement, and compaction of concrete, leading to variations in composition, density, and strength within the structure. Segregation can manifest in various forms, including aggregate segregation, bleeding, and mortar loss, each posing significant challenges to the integrity and durability of concrete structures.

1. **Aggregate segregation:** One of the most common types of segregation occurs when coarse aggregates separate from the mortar matrix due to differences in size, shape, and density. This can lead to a concentration of aggregates in certain areas of the structure, resulting in decreased strength, increased permeability, and poor bond between concrete layers. Aggregate segregation is particularly problematic in high-slump concrete mixes, where larger aggregates settle to the bottom while the mortar rises to the top during placement and compaction.
2. **Bleeding:** Bleeding is the migration of excess water to the surface of freshly placed concrete, resulting in the accumulation of water and fines at the top layer. This phenomenon occurs due to differences in specific gravity and particle size distribution between the constituent materials. Bleeding can lead to surface defects, such as laitance formation, surface crazing, and reduced durability due to the weakening of the concrete surface layer.
3. **Mortar loss:** Mortar loss, also known as mortar washout or washout segregation, occurs when the cement paste separates from the aggregate particles during handling, transportation, or vibration. This can result in the formation of voids, honeycombs, and weak zones within the concrete structure, compromising its structural integrity and long-term performance. Mortar loss is often associated with over-vibration or excessive movement of concrete during placement, leading to displacement of cement paste and fine aggregates.

Preventing segregation requires careful attention to concrete mix design, proportioning, handling, and construction practices. Some strategies to mitigate segregation include:

- Proper grading and proportioning of aggregates to ensure a well-graded mix with uniform distribution of particle sizes.

- Limiting the water-cement ratio to minimize bleeding and maintain cohesiveness within the concrete mix.
- Using appropriate admixtures, such as air-entraining agents and viscosity-modifying agents, to improve cohesion, reduce bleeding, and enhance workability.
- Employing proper placement techniques, including appropriate vibration and compaction methods, to ensure uniform distribution of concrete and minimize the risk of segregation.
- Monitoring and controlling environmental conditions, such as temperature and humidity, to prevent premature drying and excessive bleeding during concrete placement.

By implementing these measures and maintaining strict quality control throughout the construction process, engineers and contractors can minimize the risk of segregation and ensure the integrity, durability, and performance of concrete structures. Segregation management is essential for achieving uniformity, strength, and durability in concrete construction, ultimately enhancing the service life and reliability of built infrastructure.

4.7 BLEEDING

Bleeding in concrete is a phenomenon where water migrates to the surface of freshly placed concrete, resulting in the accumulation of water and fine particles at the top layer. It is a form of segregation that occurs due to differences in specific gravity and particle size distribution between the constituent materials of concrete, primarily cement paste, aggregates, and water. Bleeding typically occurs during the early stages of concrete placement and consolidation but can persist for several hours or even days, depending on various factors, such as mix design, ambient conditions, and construction practices.

Several factors contribute to bleeding in concrete:

1. **Water-cement ratio:** Excessive water in the concrete mix, often resulting from a high water-cement ratio, increases the likelihood of bleeding. When there is an excess of water, it tends to migrate upwards due to buoyancy, carrying fine particles of cement and fines with it. Lowering the water-cement ratio helps to minimize bleeding and improve the cohesion and strength of the concrete.
2. **Aggregate grading:** The grading and particle size distribution of aggregates can influence bleeding in concrete. Well-graded aggregates with a balanced distribution of particle sizes provide better interlocking and reduce the tendency for water to migrate upwards. On the other hand, poorly graded or gap-graded aggregates may lead to increased bleeding due to uneven distribution of particle sizes.
3. **Admixtures:** The use of certain chemical admixtures, such as air-entraining agents and high-range water reducers (superplasticizers), can affect bleeding behavior. Air-entraining agents introduce microscopic air bubbles into the concrete mix, which can help to reduce bleeding by improving the stability and cohesiveness of the mix. Superplasticizers, when used appropriately, can reduce the water content

of the mix while maintaining workability, thereby minimizing bleeding tendencies.

4. **Mix proportions:** The proportioning of cement, aggregates, water, and admixtures in the concrete mix significantly influences bleeding behavior. Properly proportioned mixes with adequate aggregate content and optimized water-cement ratios tend to exhibit less bleeding compared to poorly proportioned mixes. Careful attention to mix design is essential for achieving the desired performance and minimizing potential issues such as bleeding.
5. **Construction practices:** Construction practices during concrete placement and consolidation can also affect bleeding. Over-vibration or excessive movement of concrete during placement can exacerbate bleeding by causing the separation of water and fines from the rest of the mix. Properly controlling vibration and compaction techniques can help to minimize bleeding and ensure uniform distribution of concrete within the formwork.

The consequences of bleeding in concrete include surface defects, such as laitance formation, surface crazing, and weak surface layers. These defects can compromise the durability, aesthetics, and long-term performance of concrete structures. Therefore, it is essential to manage bleeding effectively by optimizing mix designs, controlling construction practices, and monitoring environmental conditions during concrete placement and curing. By minimizing bleeding, engineers and contractors can ensure the integrity, durability, and quality of concrete structures, ultimately enhancing their service life and reliability in service.

4.7.1 Test for Bleeding

The test for bleeding in concrete is a standardized procedure used to assess the propensity of fresh concrete to segregate and bleed. Bleeding is the migration of excess water to the surface of freshly placed concrete, resulting in the accumulation of water and fine particles at the top layer. This test helps to evaluate the stability and cohesiveness of the concrete mix and provides valuable insights into its workability and performance characteristics.

The test for bleeding typically involves the following steps:

1. **Preparation of concrete samples:** Prepare a representative sample of fresh concrete according to the desired mix design and construction specifications. Ensure that the concrete mix is thoroughly mixed and free from any defects or inconsistencies.
2. **Filling of test apparatus:** Fill a standardized container or cylindrical mold with the freshly mixed concrete sample. Compact the concrete within the mold using appropriate methods to ensure uniform density and distribution of aggregates.
3. **Covering and resting period:** Cover the filled mold with a non-absorbent material, such as plastic sheeting, to prevent evaporation of moisture from the concrete surface. Allow the concrete to rest undisturbed for a specified period, typically 24 hours, to simulate the initial stages of concrete placement and consolidation.
4. **Observation and measurement:** After the resting period, carefully remove the cover from the mold and visually inspect the surface of the concrete for any signs

of bleeding. Look for the presence of water accumulation, surface discoloration, or formation of a thin layer of water and fines at the top layer of the concrete.

5. **Quantitative assessment:** If necessary, quantitative measurements can be performed to assess the extent of bleeding. This may involve measuring the depth of water accumulation on the surface of the concrete or collecting and weighing any water that has separated from the concrete sample.
6. **Interpretation of results:** Based on the observations and measurements obtained from the test, evaluate the bleeding behavior of the concrete sample. Higher levels of bleeding indicate poor stability and cohesion of the concrete mix, while minimal or no bleeding suggests good workability and homogeneity.
7. **Documentation:** Record the test results, including any observations, measurements, and interpretations, in a standardized format. Document the test conditions, including the mix proportions, resting period, and environmental factors, to ensure repeatability and consistency of the test procedure.

By performing the test for bleeding, engineers and technicians can assess the quality and performance characteristics of fresh concrete, identify potential issues related to segregation and workability, and make informed decisions regarding mix adjustments and construction practices to optimize concrete performance in construction projects.

4.8 FACTORS AFFECTING WORKABILITY

The workability of concrete is determined by two key aspects: consistency and cohesiveness. Factors influencing workability can have varying effects on these aspects. Typically, water content, cement content, aggregate characteristics, and admixtures play significant roles in shaping concrete mixtures.

a. **Water content:** Water content is paramount in determining concrete workability. Upon addition to the mix, water is absorbed by cement and aggregate particles, filling voids and creating a lubricating film. Lower water content reduces fluidity, potentially leading to a dry mix, while excessive water can decrease cohesiveness, causing segregation, bleeding, and reduced strength. The water content is often indicated by the water-to-cement (w/c) ratio.
b. **Cement content:** Cement content influences workability in two primary ways. Firstly, higher cement content, at a constant w/c ratio, increases total water content, enhancing consistency. Secondly, cement paste acts as a coating, filler, and lubricant for aggregates. Insufficient cement content results in a harsh mix with poor consistency and finishability, while higher content provides better lubrication. Finer cement particles reduce fluidity but improve cohesiveness, resulting in stickier mixes.
c. **Aggregate characteristics:** Aggregate properties affect workability through surface coating needs, friction, and mobility during mixing, placing, and compaction. Maximum aggregate size, aggregate-to-cement ratio, and fine-to-coarse aggregate ratio influence workability. Larger aggregates require less paste for lubrication, improving consistency, while angular aggregates increase friction, reducing workability. Changes in aggregate proportions affect paste requirement, impacting consistency and cohesiveness.

d. **Admixtures:** Chemical and mineral admixtures alter workability by various means. Air-entraining agents increase paste volume, enhancing consistency and cohesiveness, particularly in low-cement mixtures. Water-reducing admixtures improve fluidity by dispersing cement particles. Mineral admixtures like fly ash and silica fume affect workability differently; fly ash enhances consistency, while silica fume reduces water demand due to its large surface area.

e. **Temperature and time:** Concrete stiffens over time due to factors like water evaporation and hydration. Higher temperatures accelerate hydration and water loss, reducing workability. Ambient conditions and mix composition influence slump loss, necessitating on-site testing for optimal workability determination.

4.9 RHEOLOGY

Rheology is the scientific study concerned with the deformation and flow behavior of materials, particularly in liquid states, but also in the context of "soft solids" exhibiting plastic flow. Originating from experimental observations, rheology is widely considered one of the most suitable methods for examining the fresh properties of cement-based materials. Fluids are generally categorized into two main groups: Newtonian and non-Newtonian. Cement-based materials, due to their composition of various materials with diverse particle size distributions, typically exhibit characteristics of non-Newtonian fluids. When mineral admixtures or superplasticizers are introduced into the cementitious system, observable changes such as thickening or thinning occur during the shearing process of the tested paste. These phenomena of thickening or thinning are closely related to the flowability, viscosity, and other fresh properties of concrete. It is worth noting that viscosity and rheology, although often conflated in literature due to their shared involvement with fluid flow, are distinct concepts. Viscosity quantifies a fluid's resistance to deformation at a given rate, whereas rheology encompasses the broader study of matter flow and its behaviors.

4.10 FACTORS AFFECTING RHEOLOGY

Concrete is a composite material composed of aggregates, cement, water, and mineral and chemical admixtures, with its rheological properties primarily governed by the quality of its constituents and their interactions.

a. **Paste:** The paste is crucial in concrete as it coats aggregates, fills voids between them, and contributes to workability. The volume of paste is a key factor influencing rheological behavior. Generally, high paste volumes exhibit hydrodynamic processes, while low volumes rely on direct frictional contacts between aggregates. Reinhardt et al. (2006) introduced the concept of excess paste thickness, calculated based on various factors, which affects yield stress and plastic viscosity. Additionally, the composition of cementitious materials, such as cement and fly ash, directly impacts rheological behavior by altering paste characteristics.

b. **Aggregate:** Aggregates constitute a significant portion of concrete volume and greatly influence plastic viscosity and yield stress. Aggregate properties, including shape, roughness, and volume fraction, affect workability by influencing packing density and surface morphology. Smooth, rounded aggregates reduce inter-particle friction, while angular aggregates increase it. Changes in coarse and fine aggregate fractions also impact rheological behavior, with increased coarse aggregate volume enhancing consistency and cohesiveness. Gradation and maximum particle size play significant roles, with larger particles requiring less paste and resulting in lower rheological parameter values.

c. **Chemical admixtures:** Superplasticizers, commonly used in concrete, significantly alter yield stress and viscosity by reducing electrostatic and steric hindrance effects. Air-entraining agents influence rheological properties through the formation of air bubbles, which can enhance bonding between particles and act as lubricants. Viscosity modifying agents (VMA) increase plastic viscosity and yield stress, reducing the risk of concrete separation, particularly beneficial for underwater repair and deep foundation walls.

4.11 ANALYSIS OF FRESH CONCRETE

Analyzing fresh concrete involves a comprehensive evaluation of its properties and characteristics to ensure it meets the desired quality standards and performance requirements for a specific construction application. This analysis is typically conducted on freshly mixed concrete before it undergoes setting and hardening. The analysis of fresh concrete encompasses various tests and measurements aimed at assessing its workability, consistency, air content, temperature, and other relevant parameters. These tests provide valuable insights into the behavior and performance of concrete during placement, compaction, and curing processes.

1. **Workability analysis:** Workability refers to the ease with which fresh concrete can be mixed, placed, and compacted without segregation or bleeding. Workability analysis involves tests such as the slump test or the flow table test to measure the consistency and deformability of fresh concrete. These tests help determine whether the concrete mix has the required flow characteristics to fill formwork and achieve proper compaction.
2. **Air content analysis:** The air content of fresh concrete is an essential parameter that influences its durability, freeze-thaw resistance, and resistance to segregation. Air content analysis is typically conducted using methods such as the pressure method or the volumetric method. These tests help ensure that the concrete contains the appropriate amount of entrained air to improve its durability and performance in harsh environmental conditions.
3. **Temperature analysis:** The temperature of fresh concrete plays a crucial role in its setting time, hydration process, and early-age strength development. Temperature analysis involves measuring the temperature of freshly mixed concrete using thermocouples or infrared thermometers. Monitoring the temperature helps prevent issues such as thermal cracking, excessive heat generation, and delayed setting, which can compromise the integrity and durability of the concrete structure.
4. **Consistency analysis:** Consistency refers to the degree of fluidity or stiffness exhibited by fresh concrete, which affects its ability to be properly placed, compacted, and finished. Consistency analysis includes tests such as the Vee-Bee

test or the compaction factor test to assess the flowability and compactability of concrete mixes. These tests help determine whether the concrete has the desired consistency for the intended construction application.

5. **Segregation analysis:** Segregation occurs when the components of fresh concrete, such as aggregates and cement paste, separate and form non-uniform distribution within the concrete mass. Segregation analysis involves visual inspection and quantitative assessments to identify any signs of segregation, such as bleeding, mortar loss, or aggregate settlement. These analyzes help ensure that the concrete mix remains homogeneous and cohesive during placement and compaction.
6. **Mix proportion analysis:** Analyzing the proportions of cement, aggregates, water, and admixtures in the concrete mix is essential for achieving the desired performance and durability of the concrete structure. Mix proportion analysis involves verifying that the concrete mix meets the specified design requirements and adjusting the proportions if necessary to optimize performance and consistency.

To summarize, the analysis of fresh concrete plays a crucial role in ensuring the quality, performance, and durability of concrete structures. By conducting comprehensive tests and measurements, engineers and technicians can identify potential issues, optimize mix designs, and implement appropriate construction practices to achieve superior concrete performance in various construction applications.

Chapter 5

Stages in Concrete Manufacturing

The process of concrete manufacture involves several distinct stages, each crucial in determining the quality and properties of the final product. From the selection and preparation of raw materials such as aggregates, cement, and water to the precise mixing proportions and methods, followed by the placement, compaction, curing, and eventual finishing, every step plays a pivotal role in ensuring the structural integrity, durability, and desired characteristics of the concrete. These stages not only require technical expertise but also demand meticulous attention to detail and adherence to established standards and best practices to achieve optimal results in various construction applications.

5.1 BATCHING OF CONCRETE

Batching of concrete is a fundamental stage in the concrete production process, wherein the various components that constitute concrete are precisely measured and combined in specific proportions to form a homogeneous mixture. The primary ingredients typically include cement, aggregates (such as sand, gravel, or crushed stone), water, and occasionally admixtures.

The process begins with the selection and preparation of raw materials. Aggregates are usually sourced locally and undergo screening and washing to remove impurities that could adversely affect the properties of the concrete. Cement, the binder that holds the mixture together, is carefully stored in silos or other containers to maintain its quality (Fig. 5.1).

Once the raw materials are prepared, the batching process can commence. Batching can be done by weight or volume, depending on the requirements and available equipment. In weight batching, each ingredient is measured by weight using scales or load cells, ensuring precise control over the proportions. Volume batching, on the other hand, involves measuring the materials by volume using containers such as buckets or drums.

Batching equipment, such as batch plants or mixers, is used to facilitate the process. Batch plants are facilities equipped with bins for storing aggregates, cement silos, and weighing equipment. They automatically dispense the required amounts of each ingredient according to predetermined mix designs. Mixers, whether stationary or mobile, are used to combine the ingredients thoroughly to produce a uniform mixture.

Fig. 5.1: Storage of cement and other binders

Accuracy and precision are critical in batching to achieve the desired properties of the concrete. Even slight variations in the proportions of the ingredients can significantly impact the strength, workability, and durability of the concrete. Therefore, proper calibration and maintenance of batching equipment are essential to ensure consistency and reliability in concrete production (Figs 5.2 to 5.7).

Furthermore, adherence to specified mix designs is crucial to meet the requirements of the intended application and achieve the desired performance characteristics of the concrete. Mix designs consider factors such as the desired strength, workability, durability, and environmental conditions to tailor the concrete mixture accordingly.

5.1.1 Volume Batching Method

Volume batching is one of the traditional methods used for batching concrete ingredients. In this method, the proportions of the ingredients are measured by volume

Fig. 5.2: Transition systems for aggregates

Fig. 5.3: Transition system for cement and other powder materials

Fig. 5.4: Weighing system for aggregates utilizing various pneumatic valves

rather than weight. Typically, containers such as buckets, drums, or wheelbarrows are used to measure the volume of each ingredient. The volume of each material is determined based on its density and the space it occupies.

1. **Selection of containers:** Containers of known volumes are selected for measuring each ingredient. These containers should be standardized to ensure consistency in batching.
2. **Volume measurement:** The volume of each ingredient is measured using the selected containers. For example, a specific volume of cement, sand, and aggregate is measured using separate containers.

Fig. 5.5: Weighing system and bucket for cement and alternative binders

Fig. 5.6: Transferring aggregates to the mixer via conveyor belt

Fig. 5.7: Discharge system for cement using pneumatic valve

3. **Mixing:** Once the required volumes of each ingredient are measured, they are combined in a mixing platform or mixer. The materials are then mixed thoroughly until a homogeneous mixture is obtained.
4. **Adjustments:** Volume batching may not be as precise as weigh batching since the density of materials can vary. Therefore, adjustments may be needed based on factors such as moisture content and compaction of aggregates to maintain the desired concrete consistency.

While volume batching is straightforward and does not require sophisticated equipment, it has some limitations. Variations in the moisture content and particle size of aggregates can affect the accuracy of volume measurements, leading to inconsistencies in the concrete mix. Additionally, volume batching may not be suitable for large-scale projects where precise control over the mix proportions is crucial.

5.1.2 Weigh Batching Method

Weigh batching is a more accurate and widely used method for batching concrete ingredients. In this method, the proportions of the ingredients are measured by weight using scales or load cells. Each ingredient is weighed individually to ensure precise control over the mix proportions.

1. **Selection of weighing equipment:** Weigh batching requires accurate weighing equipment such as scales or load cells. These devices are calibrated regularly to maintain accuracy.
2. **Weighing of ingredients:** Each ingredient, including cement, aggregates, water, and admixtures, is weighed separately using the weighing equipment. The weights are measured in kilograms or pounds, depending on the system used.
3. **Mixing:** Once the ingredients are weighed, they are combined in a mixer according to the predetermined mix proportions. The materials are mixed thoroughly to ensure uniform distribution and consistency of the concrete mixture.
4. **Adjustments:** Weigh batching allows for precise adjustments to be made based on factors such as moisture content and other material properties. This ensures that the desired concrete consistency and properties are achieved consistently.

Weigh batching offers several advantages over volume batching, including greater accuracy, better control over mix proportions, and the ability to accommodate variations in material properties. It is particularly suitable for large-scale projects where quality control and consistency are essential.

5.2 MIXING CONCRETE

Mixing concrete is the process of combining various ingredients such as cement, aggregates, water, and admixtures to create a homogeneous mixture suitable for construction purposes. The quality of concrete largely depends on the thoroughness of the mixing process, as it directly influences properties such as strength, durability, workability, and consistency. Proper mixing ensures that the cement particles are evenly distributed throughout the mixture, bonding with the aggregates to form a solid mass. There are different methods of mixing concrete, each with its own advantages and suitability depending on factors such as project scale, equipment availability, and desired properties of the concrete (Figs 5.8 to 5.11).

5.2.1 Methods of Mixing

1. **Hand mixing:** Hand mixing involves the manual blending of concrete ingredients using shovels, hoes, or other hand tools. While it is suitable for small-scale projects or locations where access to machinery is limited, hand mixing may be labor-intensive and less precise compared to machine mixing.
2. **Machine mixing:** Machine mixing employs equipment such as drum mixers, pan mixers, or truck-mounted mixers to achieve efficient and uniform blending of concrete ingredients. Machine mixing is commonly used for larger projects due to its ability to handle large volumes of concrete and ensure consistent quality. Various types of mixers are available, each offering different mixing capabilities and output capacities to suit specific project requirements.

Fig. 5.8: Pan mixer system

Fig. 5.9: Twin shaft mixer system

Fig. 5.10: Discharging system for concrete

Fig. 5.11: Semi-automatic batching control system

5.2.2 Mixing Time

Mixing time refers to the duration for which the concrete ingredients are blended together in the mixer to achieve a homogeneous mixture. The mixing time depends on factors such as the type of mixer, the properties of the materials, and the desired characteristics of the concrete. Generally, mixing times range from 1 to 5 minutes, although this can vary depending on factors such as the type of mixer, batch size, and mix design. Proper mixing time is essential to ensure thorough distribution of cement particles throughout the mixture, which is critical for achieving the desired strength and durability of the concrete.

5.2.3 Performance Attributes of Mixed Concrete

The performance attributes of mixed concrete refer to the properties and characteristics exhibited by the concrete as a result of the mixing process. These attributes include:

1. **Strength:** Proper mixing ensures that the cement particles are evenly distributed throughout the mixture, leading to uniform hydration and optimal strength development.
2. **Durability:** Thorough mixing helps to achieve a dense and compact concrete mixture, which enhances resistance to factors such as moisture penetration, chemical attack, and freeze-thaw cycles, thereby improving durability.
3. **Workability:** Effective mixing ensures that the concrete has the desired workability, or ease of handling and placement, which is essential for proper consolidation and finishing during construction.
4. **Consistency:** Homogeneous mixing results in a consistent mixture with uniform properties, ensuring consistent performance and appearance of the finished concrete structure.

5.2.4 Re-tempering of Concrete

Re-tempering is the process of adding additional water to concrete that has already begun to set in order to restore workability. It is typically done when the concrete has become stiff or difficult to handle due to factors such as prolonged mixing or exposure to hot weather conditions. However, re-tempering should be done judiciously, as excessive water addition can negatively impact the strength, durability, and overall quality of the concrete. It is important to follow established guidelines and recommendations for re-tempering concrete to minimize adverse effects on its performance.

5.3 TRANSPORTING CONCRETE

Transporting concrete involves the process of moving freshly mixed concrete from the production site (such as a batching plant) to the construction site where it will be placed. This stage is crucial in ensuring that the concrete maintains its desired properties and workability until it reaches its final destination. Several methods are commonly used for transporting concrete:

1. **Ready-mix trucks:** Also known as transit mixers, these specialized vehicles have rotating drums where the concrete is continuously mixed during transit. Ready-mix trucks are the most common method of transporting concrete to construction sites due to their ability to deliver large volumes of concrete while maintaining consistency and quality (Fig. 5.12).
2. **Dump trucks:** In situations where ready-mix trucks are unavailable or unsuitable, dump trucks may be used to transport concrete. The concrete is loaded into the dump truck at the batching plant and then transported to the construction site. While dump trucks are less efficient than ready-mix trucks in maintaining concrete quality during transit, they are still used for short-distance transportation or in areas with limited access.
3. **Conveyors and pumps:** For construction sites with difficult access or where concrete needs to be transported vertically or horizontally over long distances, conveyors or concrete pumps may be used. Conveyors can move concrete horizontally or at slight inclines over short distances, while concrete pumps use hydraulic pressure to transport concrete through pipelines to the desired location, making them suitable for high-rise construction or remote sites (Fig. 5.13).

Factors influencing the choice of transportation method include the distance to the construction site, traffic conditions, weather, and handling and placement requirements. Proper planning and coordination are essential to ensure that concrete is transported efficiently and maintains its desired properties upon arrival at the construction site. Additionally, quality control measures, such as monitoring concrete temperature, slump, and air content during transit, are implemented to verify compliance with specifications and ensure the quality of the concrete upon delivery.

5.4 PLACING CONCRETE

Placing concrete encompasses several sequential operations: (1) preparing the site to receive the concrete, (2) conveying and depositing the concrete into forms,

Fig. 5.12: Ready-mix concrete trucks

Fig. 5.13: Concrete transportation through conveyor belt

(3) compacting the concrete, and (4) post-compaction care. Concrete should ideally be deposited close to its final position to minimize segregation and should not be transported over excessive distances. Once placed, concrete must be compacted to eliminate trapped air, which can be achieved through manual rodding or tamping, or by employing mechanical vibrators. This section focuses on the preparation, conveying, placement, and compaction stages.

5.4.1 Site Preparation

Before concrete is ordered and delivered from commercial plants, meticulous site preparation is essential. This involves tasks such as processing steel reinforcement, erecting formwork, and arranging concrete handling equipment. Different structures necessitate distinct preparations.

1. **Foundations:** Preparing foundations for concrete requires meticulous attention due to the extensive excavation and large areas involved. Excavation should reach

into stable, undisturbed soil or rock, and any large voids encountered during excavation must be backfilled with material of similar stiffness to prevent uneven settling. Rock surfaces must be clean and sound, and any free water should be removed to prevent potential issues. In certain situations, the provision of a sump outside the form area may be necessary to facilitate water drainage. Foundations must be free of frost and ice during concrete placement in winter, and the soil should be sufficiently moist but not overly muddy in dry seasons.

2. **Construction joints:** Structural members with significant areas or volumes may necessitate construction joints to accommodate the limitations of concrete supply, construction processes, and time constraints. These joints, whether horizontal or vertical, must be strategically planned to account for factors such as structural member size, concrete supply capabilities, thermal expansion coefficients, construction schedules, and concrete shrinkage properties. Construction joints must not compromise the structure's strength and should be made in a manner that ensures minimal impact on its integrity. Adequate surface preparation and reinforcement continuity across joints are essential.
3. **Formwork:** Before pouring concrete, formwork construction is imperative. Formwork serves as a temporary mold into which concrete is poured, supporting the weight of fresh concrete until it gains sufficient strength to support itself. Formwork can be constructed using steel plates or timber boards and should be sturdy enough to withstand the pressure exerted by wet concrete. Proper coating with oil or parting compound aids in demolding, and moisture must be applied to wood forms to prevent them from absorbing water from the concrete (Fig. 5.14).
4. **Reinforcing steel:** Following formwork erection, reinforcing steel cages are positioned within the formwork before concrete pouring. Main reinforcing bars should be properly secured in position with steel stirrups, and all reinforcing steel must be free of contaminants such as dirt, paint, or grease. Rust should be

Fig. 5.14: Formwork for the transfer block of a tall building

Fig. 5.15: Framework of reinforcing steel

removed, and during concrete placement, steel should be accurately positioned and supported by chairs, ties, or hangers (Fig. 5.15).

5. **Embedded items:** Many concrete structures incorporate embedded fixtures such as manholes, anchor bolts, or pipes, which must be firmly fixed in place before concrete placement. Adjustments to accommodate these items should only be made if they do not compromise the load-bearing capacity of the structure.

5.4.2 Conveying Concrete

Conveying concrete involves several preparatory steps before the actual placement of the material. Once formwork, steelwork, and embedded items are in place, a thorough inspection should confirm the readiness of all equipment and materials. This includes ensuring the appropriate amount of concrete has been ordered, and that the ready-mix supplier is prepared to deliver at the required rate. Transporting equipment such as pumps, cranes, batch trucks, conveyors, and helicopters must be capable of handling the concrete efficiently, with curing materials readily available.

The method of placing fresh concrete can vary depending on factors such as the size of the project, available space, and equipment accessibility. Options include direct discharge from a mixer into forms, crane and bucket placement, pumping, conveyors, buggies, wheelbarrows, pneumatic placers, small railcars, or a combination thereof. In remote or challenging locations, helicopters have been employed to transport equipment and concrete buckets.

Direct discharge involves pouring concrete from a transport truck directly into forms or onto the subgrade, with the option of extending chutes to reach further distances. Chutes must be smooth and of appropriate slope to prevent concrete friction and sticking, minimizing segregation (Fig. 5.16). Buckets are effective for conveying concrete, ranging in capacity from under 1 m^3 for structural use to 10 m^3 for mass concrete. Crane handling is common in building construction, but care must be taken to avoid shaking or jarring the concrete, which can cause segregation.

Other methods of concrete conveyance include belt conveyors, wheelbarrows, and buggies (Fig. 5.17). Belt conveyors can transport concrete over long distances

Fig. 5.16: Concrete conveyed through chutes to a large foundation

Fig. 5.17: Wheelbarrow on construction site

horizontally and vertically to some extent. Wheelbarrows are suitable for short distances, with a maximum haul of about 60 m, while hand-operated carts and power-driven carts can carry varying capacities over moderate distances. Pumping concrete under pressure through pipes or hoses has become increasingly popular, particularly with the development of self-compacting concrete. Special high-pressure pumps now enable concrete to be pumped horizontally up to 1400 m or vertically as high as 420 m, making it a versatile and efficient method for a range of construction projects (Figs 5.18 and 5.19).

Fig. 5.18: Concrete pumping

Fig. 5.19: Machine with a stationary pump

5.5 COMPACTING CONCRETE

After pouring concrete into formworks, immediate compaction is essential. Compaction serves to eliminate trapped air, ensuring thorough consolidation of plastic concrete within all formwork spaces, including corners and around reinforcing steel. This process increases concrete density and stiffness, leading to enhanced compressive

Fig. 5.20: Concrete pump with a boom

strength and reduced permeability, essential for high-quality concrete. Traditionally, laborers used various tools like spades and tampers for consolidation, but nowadays, high-frequency vibrators are predominantly employed (Fig. 5.20).

On construction sites, both internal and external vibrators are commonly utilized. An internal vibrator comprises a poker housing an eccentric shaft, driven by a flexible motor (Fig. 5.21). When immersed in concrete, the poker vibrates harmonically, applying pressure to the surrounding concrete. Pokers come in various sizes, ranging from 20 to 150 mm in diameter, with head lengths from 250 to 750 mm. They generate vibrations with frequencies between 70 to 200 Hz and accelerations from 0.7 to 4 m/s^2, operating at speeds of 5500 to 15,000 vibrations per minute (vpm). However, this process generates noise levels of up to 90 dB, posing potential health risks to workers.

Alternatively, self-compacting concrete eliminates the need for vibration entirely, making it an environmentally friendly option. Figure 5.21 illustrates the vibration process of an internal vibrator.

The external vibrator typically features a flat metal base resembling a plate, incorporating the surface, and pan or screed vibrators (Fig. 5.22). The mortar layer atop the plate induces vibrations on the surface, making it suitable for compacting fresh concrete, particularly for slabs and floor elements. Slabs up to 200 mm thick can be adequately consolidated with this method, while thicker slabs may require supplementary internal vibration. Additionally, apart from consolidating the concrete within the slab, this unit levels the surface and prepares it for final finishing.

Another variant of the external vibrator is the form vibrator, affixed to the exterior of molds or forms. They are utilized in situations where internal vibrators are impractical, such as tunnel linings or densely congested forms. Form vibrators are also employed in the production of pipes, masonry units, and various types of precast concrete. Pneumatically driven units generate vibrations through the rotation of an eccentric weight, allowing for speed adjustment by varying air volume. Vibration

Fig. 5.21: Internal vibrator

Fig. 5.22 Concrete vibrator

should cease when the concrete surface appears flattened and glossy, indicating the cessation of air bubble rise and proper integration of coarse aggregate into the surface.

Occasionally, over-vibration may lead to the sinking of coarse aggregate below the surface, resulting in a frothy appearance. In such instances, the slump should be reduced initially, followed by adjustments to the vibration intensity.

Basic finishing of fresh concrete is typically performed using a trowel just before initial setting. This process aims to create a smooth surface on the concrete element, ensuring a denser, compact, and properly graded surface layer to minimize water evaporation and enhance wear resistance. Adequate finishing of high-quality concrete can significantly reduce the maintenance costs associated with structural elements.

5.6 CURING OF CONCRETE

Curing involves maintaining an appropriate environment for fresh concrete to undergo hydration reactions. The key focus in concrete curing is to ensure adequate moisture is retained, preventing hydration from halting. Insufficient curing can result in the loss of mixed water, initiating harmful processes that compromise concrete quality and reduce the structure's service life in both the short and long term. Curing significantly influences the properties of concrete in its fresh and hardened states.

The curing process should commence within 3 to 18 hours after concrete placement. The duration and methods of curing vary depending on the concrete type and construction conditions. For Portland cement concrete, a minimum of 7 days of moist curing is typically recommended.

While curing may seem straightforward, it is often overlooked despite being the most crucial step in producing robust, long-lasting, and waterproof concrete.

5.6.1 Methods of Curing Concrete

Below are the various methods of concrete curing:

a. **Standard curing:** This involves curing concrete in a humid environment or water at a temperature of 20 ± 2°C and a relative humidity of at least 95%. The standard curing duration is 28 days.

b. **Natural curing:** Natural curing methods include covering, watering, wetting, wind shielding, and heat preservation under ambient temperature conditions (above 5°C). It can be categorized into two types: covering watering curing and plastic film curing. Covering watering curing involves covering concrete with grass curtains, mats, or blankets within 3–12 hours after pouring, followed by periodic watering to maintain moisture. Plastic film curing utilizes plastic film coverings to prevent moisture evaporation, allowing hydration and hardening to occur.

c. **Heat curing:** Heat curing accelerates concrete hydration by applying heat. Common methods include warm shed, steam curing, pressurized steam curing, and dry and radiant heat curing. Steam curing involves exposing concrete to saturated steam or a steam-air mixture at high temperature and humidity. This method increases concrete strength by 10–40% and speeds up construction regardless of external temperature. Pressurized steam curing involves increasing atmospheric pressure (>8 standard atmospheres) and temperature (>174.5°C) to achieve higher concrete strength. Warm shed curing employs thermal insulation materials and heating equipment to maintain a positive temperature environment. Radiant heat curing utilizes heat radiation to increase concrete internal temperature, promoting hydration and achieving high compressive strength in a short time.

d. **Cold curing:** Cooling the interior of large concrete structures is crucial to prevent strength reduction and thermal cracking due to non-uniform heating/cooling. Methods include circulating water in embedded pipes and using liquid nitrogen spray on site.

e. **Curing compound method:** This method involves applying a curing compound to the surface of fresh concrete to prevent moisture loss, forming a moisture-tight membrane. Curing compounds include waxes, natural and synthetic resins, and high-volatility solvents. Incorporating white or gray pigments enhances heat reflectance and provides a clear area for application, making it particularly useful for vertical surfaces like walls and columns.

5.6.2 Importance of Concrete Curing

Neglecting proper concrete curing in structures can lead to various issues:

- Reduction in compressive strength and other mechanical properties compared to laboratory results.
- Formation of significant cracks, diminishing structural performance and load-bearing capacity.
- Development of microcracks, allowing aggressive ions to penetrate concrete elements, thus reducing overall durability.

Concrete curing is crucial for structural integrity. However, in many projects, inadequate attention is given to curing due to payment structures, which often only account for concrete pouring. Consequently, insufficient inspection is conducted, except for highly sensitive projects (Fig. 5.23).

Key considerations for concrete curing in all ambient conditions include:

- **Preventing moisture loss within concrete:** Techniques such as water jets, steam curing, or curing compound admixtures are employed. Hot weather poses challenges due to increased evaporation rates, exacerbated by wind. Special efforts are required to counteract these effects.
- **Temperature control:** Adaptations depend on weather conditions. Cold water may be used in hot weather to regulate concrete temperature, while special blankets or heat sources are utilized in cold conditions. Measures are taken to prevent the formation of ice and snow on structures.
- **Sufficient curing duration:** Duration is critical, especially for crack prevention. Ideal curing times vary based on structure type, weather, and concrete

Fig. 5.23: Curing of concrete using curing compound

Fig. 5.24: Curing through water jet

characteristics. Although a week is recommended for optimal results, practical constraints often limit curing to a minimum of 48 hours, provided stringent control measures are in place (Fig. 5.24).

5.7 FINISHING THE CONCRETE SURFACE

Achieving a high-quality surface finish for concrete elements is crucial for preventing cracking and ensuring durability, particularly in structures like flooring where specialized loading conditions apply. Smoothing the concrete surface is a fundamental step in this process.

For most structures, hand trowels are commonly used for smoothing. It is vital to protect the surface from foot traffic until the concrete sets completely, and proper curing is essential to prevent cracking.

However, for flooring applications such as parking or industrial floors, achieving a superior finish often requires the use of electric trowels, as depicted in Fig. 5.25. These

Fig. 5.25: Electrical trowel

specialized tools are designed to effectively smooth concrete surfaces. To optimize surface quality, applying silicate hardener powders before electric trowel usage is recommended.

Electric trowels should only be employed once the concrete has set, as their weight can damage freshly poured concrete. In some cases, electric trowels can also help prevent plastic shrinkage cracking. If such cracks occur, a second pass with the electric trowel can be utilized to eliminate them before proceeding with concrete curing to further safeguard against cracking.

5.8 AUTOGENOUS HEALING OF CONCRETE

Autogenous healing of concrete refers to the natural process through which cracks in concrete can partially or completely self-heal over time without the need for external intervention. This phenomenon occurs due to the rehydration of certain materials within the concrete matrix, typically calcium silicates, which can precipitate and fill small cracks.

The autogenous healing process is primarily driven by the presence of moisture and the continued hydration of unreacted cement particles within the concrete. When cracks form, water from the surrounding environment can penetrate the concrete, allowing hydration to occur in the crack planes. As a result, calcium silicate hydrate (C-S-H) gel can form within the crack, effectively sealing it and restoring some of the concrete's structural integrity.

While autogenous healing can be effective for repairing very small cracks, its effectiveness diminishes with the size and width of the cracks. Additionally, environmental factors such as temperature, humidity, and the presence of aggressive chemicals can influence the rate and extent of healing.

Research into autogenous healing aims to better understand the mechanisms involved and explore ways to enhance the process, potentially through the use of supplementary cementitious materials or specialized additives that can promote healing. However, it is important to note that autogenous healing is generally limited in its ability to repair significant cracks, and it is not a substitute for proper maintenance and repair practices in concrete structures.

Rheology of Concrete

6.1 INTRODUCTION

Rheology can be defined as the study of how materials deform and flow, focusing on the relationships between stress, strain, rate of strain, and time. It specifically pertains to materials with flow properties more complex than simple fluids like liquids or gases. In the context of concrete, rheological principles and techniques encompass the deformation of hardened concrete, the handling and placement of freshly mixed concrete, and the behavior of its constituent components, such as cement slurries and pastes. However, this chapter solely addresses the rheological properties of fresh concrete. These properties, including workability, encompass stability, mobility, and compactability, which are crucial for evaluating the suitability of any concrete mix, as depicted in Fig. 6.1. In discussing the rheological properties of fresh concrete, these parameters are redefined in terms of the forces involved in transmitting mechanical stresses onto the concrete. During its handling and placement, fresh concrete experiences both normal and shearing forces.

Stability refers to the condition where aggregate particles remain uniformly dispersed within the matrix, maintaining consistent particle size distribution during transportation, placement, and compaction. It is assessed based on concrete's segregation and bleeding tendencies. Segregation occurs when weak matrix cannot adequately hold aggregate particles in homogeneous dispersion, and its resistance depends on the cohesion within the mix. Both wet and dry concrete mixes can experience segregation. Wet segregation arises from excessive water content, causing

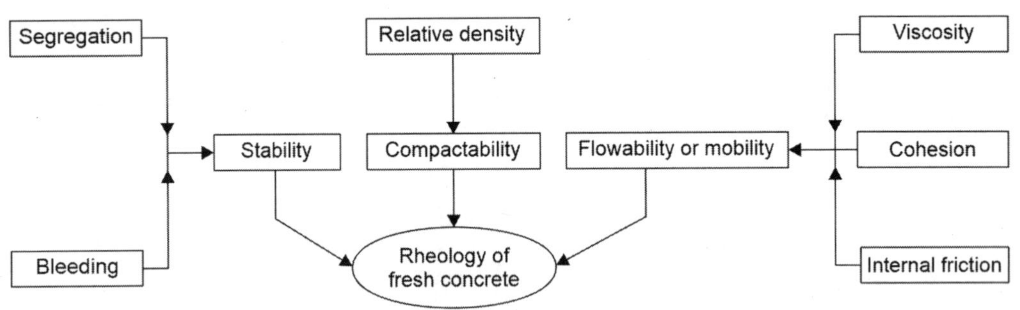

Fig. 6.1: Parameters defining the rheology of fresh concrete

the paste to lose its ability to retain aggregate particles during handling. Dry segregation occurs with low water-cement ratios, resulting in a crumbly mix. However, vibration during compaction can improve cohesion and shear resistance in crumbly mixes by momentarily liquefying the matrix. Bleeding, on the other hand, occurs when unstable mortar releases excess water, which should be minimized.

Mobility in fresh concrete refers to its ability to flow under mechanical stresses, constrained by cohesive, viscous, and frictional forces. Cohesive forces arise from matrix-aggregate adhesion, providing tensile strength and resisting segregation. Matrix viscosity influences the ease of aggregate movement, with low-stress conditions causing the mix to behave as a highly viscous solid, transitioning to liquid-like behavior as stresses increase. Internal friction occurs as aggregates translate and rotate within the mix, with resistance influenced by factors like aggregate shape and texture, mix richness, water-cement ratio, and cement type. The angle of internal friction significantly impacts concrete mobility, evaluated through laboratory triaxial compression tests or field tests like the Vee-Bee test in conjunction with the basic compacting factor test.

Compactability refers to the ease with which fresh concrete can be compacted, involving the expulsion of entrapped air and repositioning of aggregate particles to form a dense mass without inducing segregation. The compactability of concrete is typically assessed using the compacting factor test. However, this test has its limitations, such as cohesive mixtures sticking in test apparatus hoppers and producing inconsistent results with low or very low workabilities. To address these limitations, the compacting factor test can be augmented with two additional measurements. Firstly, the density of uncompacted concrete is determined by placing it loosely into the base container without compaction. Secondly, the density of mechanically vibrated concrete is measured by compacting it in three layers using an internal vibrator. These additional measurements, combined with the standard compacting factor test results, offer insights into the relative ease of transitioning from a loose to a compacted state. The difference between the actual compacted state and the theoretical maximum compaction provides a relative measure of concrete void content, offering indications of durability, permeability, and relative strength of hardened concrete. Understanding the rheological properties of concrete aids in selecting concrete mixtures that can be efficiently compacted in forms. Current workability tests, such as slump, compacting factor, Vee-Bee, and other remolding tests, have limited scope as they assess only one parameter, earning them the designation of single-point tests.

6.2 REPRESENTATION OF RHEOLOGICAL BEHAVIOR

Newtonian liquids, which adhere to Newton's law of viscous flow where shear stress is directly proportional to the rate of shear strain, are known as ideal liquids. The constant of proportionality serves as a physical characteristic of these materials. However, fresh concrete exhibits non-Newtonian flow behavior. The ratio of shear stress to shear rate is not constant but varies with the shear rate of measurement and may also be influenced by the shear history of the concrete sample being analyzed. Nevertheless, at low shear rates pertinent to practical applications, the behavior can

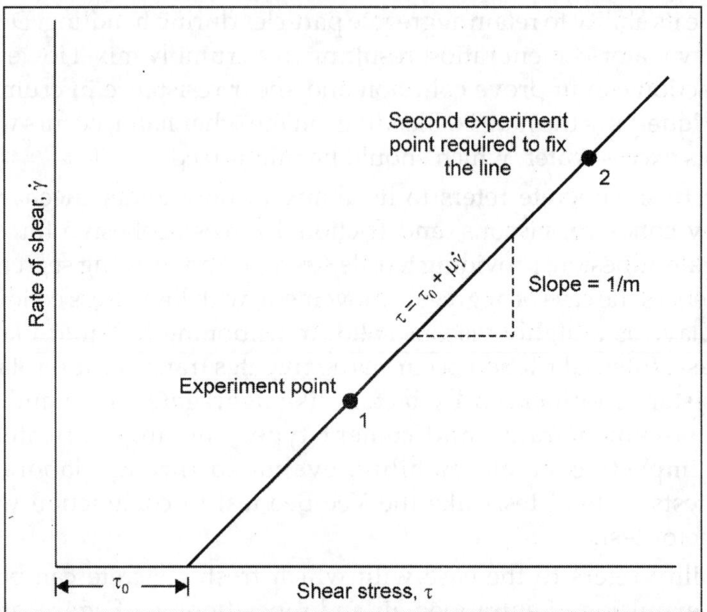

Fig. 6.2: Bingham's model

be approximated by a linear relationship that intersects the stress axis at a non-zero value, indicating the presence of a minimum stress required for flow initiation. This minimum stress is referred to as the yield stress and denoted by the symbol τ_0. Thus, the basic flow equation for concrete, as depicted in Fig. 6.2, can be expressed as:

$$\tau = \tau_0 + \mu\gamma$$

In the Bingham model, τ_0 represents the yield stress, indicating the material's cohesion, while m is a constant with dimensions of viscosity, known as plastic viscosity. This mathematical relationship characterizes the flow properties of the material, relating its shear stress, cohesion, plastic viscosity, and the rate of shear loading. To establish a straight line in the Bingham model, a minimum of two points are required. Consequently, workability assessment of concrete cannot be adequately defined by single-point tests, which provide only one parameter. Therefore, they must be complemented by other tests to achieve a comprehensive understanding of concrete rheology. For instance, the Vee-Bee test can be combined with the compacting factor test to assess mobility and compactability. Tattersall proposed a method for measuring mobility characteristics using a single test that yields multiple points (shear conditions). This method involves determining the power required to mix concrete at various speeds and calculating torque by dividing the power by the speed. The torque is then related to the mixing speed through the following relation:

$$T = g + hN$$

In the equation, T represents the measured torque at N revolutions per second (rps), while g and h are constants that are proportional to the cohesion and plastic viscosity of the mixture, respectively.

It has been observed that mixtures with identical values of g and h will exhibit the same consistency, compacting factor, and Vee-Bee time. Conversely, mixtures with different g and h values may demonstrate similarity in one of the three standard tests, but will behave differently in the others.

Concrete behavior diverges significantly from the Bingham model in at least one of the following aspects:

1. The definition of yield stress is ambiguous.
2. The flow curve is not linear except within a very limited range of shear rates.

If the flow curve exhibits concave upward behavior, where the slope increases with shear rate, it indicates that the applied shearing forces are disrupting the structure present in the material when it is unstressed. This disruption progresses further with higher shear rates. For example, in the curve depicted as ABC in Fig. 6.3, as the shear rate is gradually increased up to point C, the resulting curve is obtained. However, if the shear rate is then steadily decreased to zero, the downward curve may not align perfectly with the upward curve.

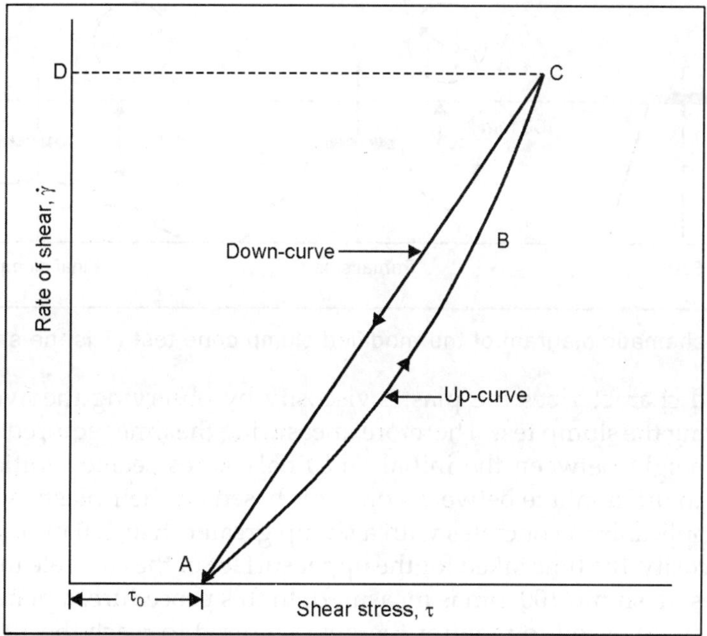

Fig. 6.3: Deformation curve for fresh concrete

If point C represents the breakdown in the material's structure due to shear, and this breakdown process is immediately reversed, then decreasing the shear rate from point D will lead to a gradual rebuilding of the structure to the same state as it was on the upward curve. However, since time is required for the structure to rebuild, the shear stress at any particular shear rate on the downward curve will be less than that on the upward curve at the same shear rate. As a result, the two curves will not coincide, and a hysteresis loop will form.

Despite these complexities, the Bingham model can still be applied to fresh concrete under practical conditions, provided its limitations are recognized and acknowledged.

6.3 MEASUREMENT OF RHEOLOGY BY THE MODIFIED SLUMP TEST

A straightforward, resilient, and cost-effective field test method has been proposed by Ferraris, CF *et al.* 1998. This method simplifies the rheological behavior of concrete to two key physical properties or parameters: yield stress and plastic viscosity. Currently, the most commonly used field test, the slump test, only assesses the yield stress (Fig. 6.4). However, the plastic viscosity of concrete is becoming increasingly important in modern concrete applications. For high-performance concretes, it often becomes the crucial parameter that governs pumpability and ease of finishing. This section outlines the modified standard slump test apparatus, test procedure, and calculations that enable the evaluation of the two Bingham rheological parameters—yield stress and plastic viscosity—in the field.

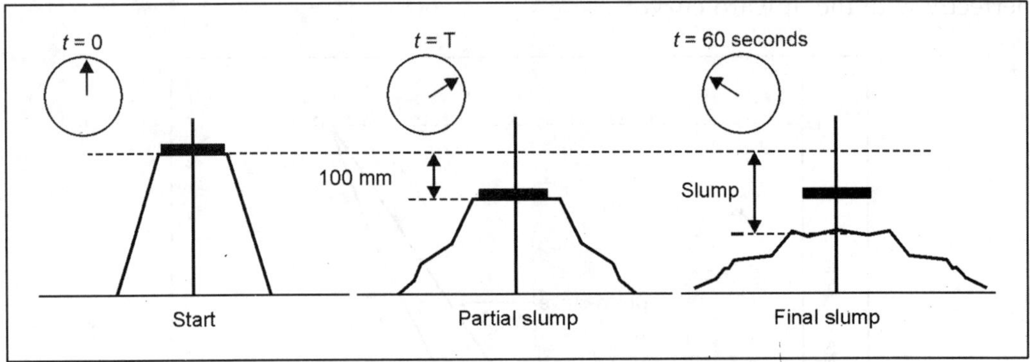

Fig. 6.4: Schematic diagram of the modified slump cone test (T is the slump time)

The method characterizes the plastic viscosity by observing the average rate of slumping during the slump test. Therefore, measuring the time required to achieve an intermediate height between the initial and final values seemed initially to be an effective way to differentiate between concretes based on their plastic viscosity. This approach is applicable to concretes with a slump greater than 100 mm. To determine the plastic viscosity, the time taken for the upper surface of the concrete in the standard slump cone test to slump 100 mm is measured. In this procedure, a plate slides along a centrally positioned rod to monitor the time required to reach the 100 mm slump. The partial slump time is recorded using a stopwatch operated by the observer, based on a visual criterion (similar to the Vee-Bee test). The stopwatch is started when the cone is lifted, and it is stopped when the sliding plate on the fresh concrete reaches the stop on the rod.

6.3.1 Procedure for Measuring the Slump Time

The dimensions of the apparatus and the test setup are depicted in Fig. 6.5. The concrete is placed following the same procedure as in the standard slump test. The steps involved in the procedure are as follows:

1. The rod connected to the horizontal base of the standard slump test apparatus is thoroughly cleaned and lubricated up to the stop.

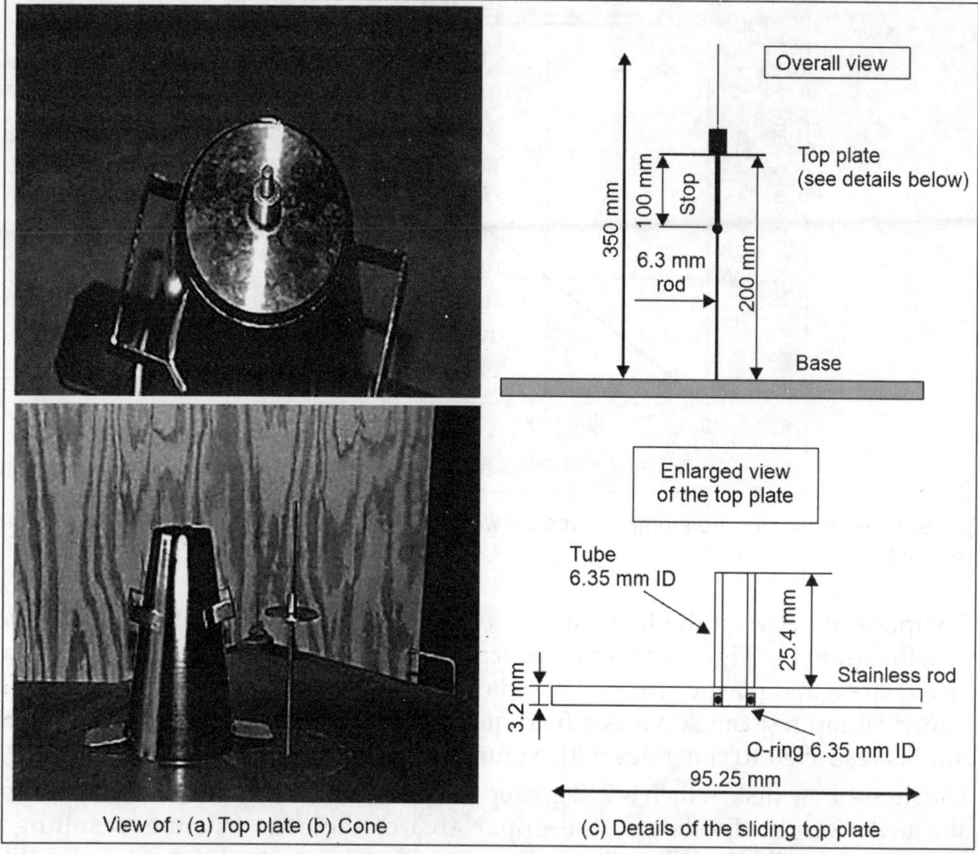

View of : (a) Top plate (b) Cone

(c) Details of the sliding top plate

Fig. 6.5: The details of the modified slump test apparatus

2. The base and the inner wall of the slump cone are moistened using a damp sponge.
3. The slump cone is positioned on the base, ensuring that the rod is centered with respect to the opening at the top of the cone. The cone is secured onto the base using the attachments provided for this purpose.
4. The cone is filled in three layers of equal volume, and each layer is compacted by tapping it 25 times with the standard tamping rod.
5. The surface of the concrete is leveled off with the top of the cone.
6. Any protruding part of the rod above the concrete specimen is wiped clean with a cloth.
7. The upper plate disk is lowered along the rod until it makes contact with the surface of the concrete. The disk is equipped with a rubber O-ring seal to prevent fine materials from interfering with its descent.
8. The mould is raised vertically while simultaneously starting the stopwatch, which has a minimum time interval of 0.01 seconds.
9. While the concrete is slumping, the disk is continuously monitored through the top of the cone, and the stopwatch is halted as soon as the disk comes to a stop.
10. Once the slump has stabilized, or no later than one minute after the test begins, the disk is removed, and the slump is measured using a ruler.

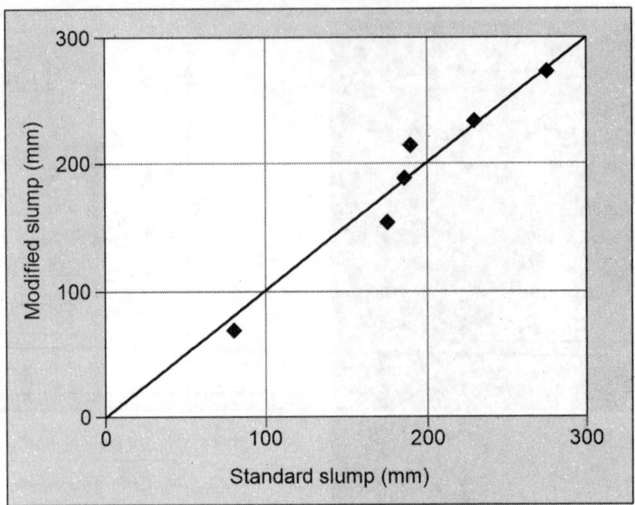

Fig. 6.6: Comparison of the slump values between the standard slump test and the modified slump test

Comparison between the final slumps obtained from the standard and modified tests is illustrated in Fig. 6.6. Semi-empirical models have been proposed to estimate the yield stress and plastic viscosity based on the final slump and slumping time. The modified slump test can serve as a field quality control measure, although its applicability is restricted to concretes with a slump ranging from 120 to 260 mm.

The mass of the disk, which is 212 g, exerts a maximum vertical stress on the sample equal to its weight divided by the upper area of the cone frustum, resulting in approximately 0.27 kPa. When the disk reaches the stop, with the concrete height h being 200 mm, the vertical compression stress at the base of the sample is determined by ρgh (where ρ is approximately 2400 kg/m^3, representing the density of the fresh concrete, and g is the acceleration due to gravity), yielding approximately 4.8 kPa. Consequently, it can be observed that the vertical stress due to the disk is at most about 6% of the stress induced by the concrete. Additionally, the frictional resistance of the concrete along the rod tends to decrease the final slump.

The essential rheological parameters derived from the modified slump test can be calculated using the following relation:

$$\tau_0 = \rho(300 - s)/270$$

In the equation, where ρ represents the density in kg/m^3, τ_0 denotes the yield stress in Pa, and S is measured in mm, a reasonable estimate of the Bingham yield stress is obtained. However, it tends to consistently underestimate the yield stress, especially in the low slump range characteristic of self-leveling concretes. On average, the error for the yield stress in the range of 100 to 2000 Pa amounts to 195 Pa. For highly fluid mixtures, an empirically enhanced equation can be employed:

$$\tau_0 = \rho(300 - s)/347 + 212$$

Thus, this test will be more useful in determining the plastic viscosities of concretes with HRWRAs.

6.3.2 A Semi-empirical Model for Evaluation of the Plastic Viscosity

The assessment of plastic viscosity through modified slump test results relies on the premise that when concretes exhibit identical final slumps and densities, variations in slump time can be ascribed to differences in plastic viscosity. Dimensional analysis reveals that the factor $\mu/(\rho gT)$ (where m represents plastic viscosity and T signifies slump time) is dependent on the final slump. For concrete mixes with slumps below 260 mm, the most accurate representation of the data is provided by the following equations:

$$\mu = 1.08(S - 175)\rho T \times 10^{-3} \quad \text{for } 200 < S < 260 \text{ mm}$$
$$= 25\rho T \times 10^{-3} \quad \text{for } S < 200 \text{ mm}$$

where ρ = density in kg/m^3 (in the present case ρ = 2400 kg/m^3), T = slumping time in seconds, S = final slump in mm, m = viscosity in Pa·s. The model exhibits an average error of 66 Pa·s across all concretes with slumps ranging from 120 to 260 mm. Nomographs are provided to estimate the yield stress (in Pa) and plastic viscosity of concrete (in Pa·s) based on the results of the modified slump test, assuming a concrete density of 2400 kg/m^3 (Fig. 6.7). The first graph determines the yield stress from slump measurements, while the second graph allows for the estimation of plastic viscosity by interpolating between values corresponding to the nearest curve based on the coordinates of slump and time (T). The modified slump test serves as a practical quality control procedure in the field, while the rheometer functions as a developmental tool for determining the optimal mix design for specific applications.

It has been noted that the three-parameter Herschel–Bulkley model offers a more accurate description of the nonlinear behavior observed in fresh concrete compared to the two-parameter Bingham linear model. The primary rationale for adopting the Herschel–Bulkley model stems from its ability to adequately handle self-leveling concretes. When using the Bingham model, there's often an issue of calculating negative yield stress values, particularly in self-leveling concretes, rendering the results meaningless. In contrast, the Herschel–Bulkley model consistently provides positive yield stress values that exhibit reasonable correlation with the outcomes of the slump test (either slump or slump flow, depending on the concrete mixture). However, in practical scenarios, the Bingham model can still be useful with modifications to the method of determining yield stress and plastic viscosity parameters. By making simple adjustments to the Bingham equations, better fits to the data can be achieved.

The addition of HRWRA, a water reducer, has been observed to significantly decrease the yield stress compared to the plastic viscosity in concrete. This discrepancy suggests that the ideal granular proportions for achieving desired rheological properties differ between ordinary concrete (without HRWRAs) and self-leveling concretes (with HRWRAs).

Furthermore, when HRWRA is present, the contribution of cement to the yield stress is notably diminished. This phenomenon clarifies why, in concrete mixes with very low yield stress and normal or high plastic viscosity, such as self-leveling concretes, an optimal composition typically includes a higher proportion of fine materials.

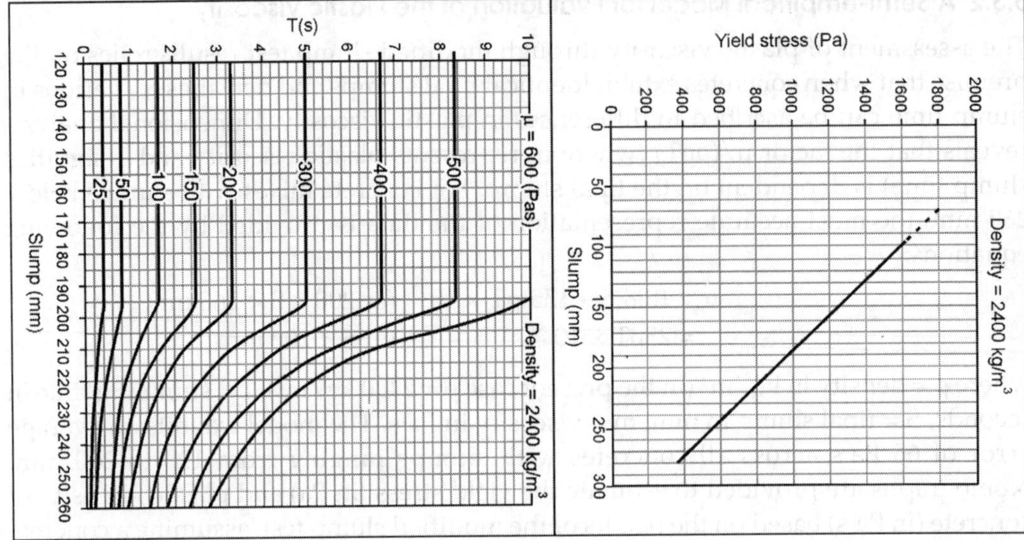

Fig. 6.7: Nomographs for estimating the yield stress and plastic viscosity of concrete

6.4 FACTORS AFFECTING RHEOLOGICAL PROPERTIES

Similar to workability, the rheological characteristics of fresh concrete are influenced by various factors, including the proportions of its constituents, properties of the ingredients, presence of admixtures, duration of mixing, and time elapsed after mixing. While these factors have previously been detailed, this section delves into their specific impacts on the flow properties of concrete.

6.4.1 Mix Proportions

In the process of proportioning concrete, the aim is to achieve the necessary workability during construction while ensuring that the hardened concrete meets the required performance standards.

A concrete mix with an excessive amount of coarse aggregate will lack sufficient mortar to fill the voids, resulting in decreased cohesion and mobility. Such a mix is commonly referred to as 'harsh' and demands more effort for placement and compaction. Harshness may also arise from a low air content, which can be mitigated by increasing entrained air to reduce the excessive use of fine aggregate. Conversely, an overabundance of fine aggregate or entrained air in the mixture significantly enhances cohesion, making the concrete difficult to manipulate. High fine aggregate content increases particle surface area, necessitating more paste to coat these surfaces to maintain adequate mobility. Consequently, this can lead to heightened drying shrinkage and an increased likelihood of cracking.

In practical scenarios, concrete is typically proportioned with an excess of fine aggregate and a higher cement content compared to what would be required for a mixture with an optimal fine aggregate content. A higher cement content imparts stickiness and sluggishness to the concrete, especially within the normal slump range for cast-in-situ concrete. Moreover, a lower water-cement ratio and increased cement content reduce the workability of rich mixes compared to their immediate post-mixing measurements.

6.4.2 Consistency

The consistency of concrete, as assessed by the slump test, serves as an indicator of the relative water content in the concrete mixture. An elevation in the water content or slump beyond what is necessary for achieving workability leads to increased fluidity and reduced internal friction. This decrease in mixture cohesion heightens the risk of segregation and excessive bleeding. Therefore, an excess water content does not enhance the rheological properties of concrete. Conversely, insufficient slump or water content diminishes mobility and compactability, posing challenges during placement and consolidation. Regarding the rheological properties of concrete, a one percent increase in air entrainment is equivalent to either a one percent increase in fine aggregate or a three percent increase in water content. Additionally, an overly dry mix may result in decreased cohesion and an uptick in dry segregation.

6.4.3 Hardening and Stiffening

Increased temperature, utilization of rapid-hardening cement, insufficient gypsum in cement, and the application of accelerating admixtures accelerate the hardening rate of concrete, thereby diminishing its mobility. Additionally, dry and porous aggregates can swiftly decrease workability by either absorbing water from the mixture or expanding the surface area requiring wetting.

6.4.4 Aggregate Shape and Texture

The rheology of concrete is significantly influenced by the shape and texture of aggregate particles. Rough and highly angular aggregate particles tend to fill a higher percentage of voids with mortar, necessitating greater amounts of fine aggregate and correspondingly higher water content. Likewise, angular fine aggregate increases internal friction within the concrete mixture, requiring a higher water content compared to well-rounded natural sand.

6.4.5 Aggregate Grading

A well-graded aggregate contributes to good workability in concrete. The absence of a specific size of aggregate (gap-graded) or alterations in size distribution can significantly impact the void system and workability. These effects are more pronounced in fine aggregate compared to coarse aggregate. As fine aggregate becomes finer, the water requirement increases, making the concrete mixture stickier. Conversely, as fine aggregate becomes coarser, cohesion decreases, resulting in a harsher mixture and an increased likelihood of bleeding. Adjustments to the grading of fine aggregate are necessary to preserve workability amidst these changes.

6.4.6 Maximum Aggregate Size

Increasing the maximum size of aggregate will decrease the amount of fine aggregate needed to achieve a specific level of workability. Consequently, this reduction in fine aggregate content will decrease the surface area requiring wetting and subsequently reduce the amount of cement necessary to maintain a constant water-cement ratio.

6.4.7 Admixtures

Among the plethora of admixtures utilized in concrete to enhance performance, those significantly affecting concrete rheology include plasticizers, superplasticizers, air-entraining agents, accelerators, and retarders. These admixtures serve three main purposes:

1. Enhancing workability while maintaining long-term strength and durability.
2. Achieving equivalent workability with reduced water content, leading to higher strength.
3. Achieving identical workability and strength with less cement content, provided the reduced cement content is sufficient for durability considerations.

Commercially available plasticizers, typically based on lignosulfonate salt (0.15 percent), can reduce water content by up to 10 percent without adverse effects. Superplasticizers enable the creation of flowing or self-leveling concrete, requiring minimal compaction effort to fill corners and congested reinforcement areas. A maximum yield value of 350 Pa is generally recommended for self-leveling concrete. This level of workability can be achieved through the addition of ultrapure lignosulfate or synthetic napthalene or melamine resins. However, concrete with very high workability attainable with superplasticizers is prone to segregation.

As previously discussed, in a normal water-cement system, particles are suspended in a high electrolyte concentration, causing them to come close enough to adhere, a process known as flocculation. Admixtures alter this condition in the cement-water suspension to prevent the formation of flocculated structures by transforming interparticle attraction into repulsion.

Plasticizers or superplasticizers interact with cement particles by forming a membrane of charged molecules around each particle. This membrane prevents particles from approaching closely enough to adhere, thus preventing flocculation. The membrane acts as a steric barrier, inhibiting close contact between particles. By increasing the thickness of the absorbed membrane, the attraction between particles can be reduced to zero, thereby reducing the yield value through deflocculation or dispersion of cement particles.

Additionally, the absorption of ionized compounds generates repulsive electrical forces between particles, increasing plastic viscosity through the secondary electroviscous effect. Admixtures in this group prevent close contact between cement particles through a combination of electrostatic and steric repulsions, weakening the structure that can form at rest and reducing the yield value. However, beyond an optimal percentage, increasing the concentration of the plasticizer does not significantly decrease the yield rate. The reduction in yield value increases with increasing cement content in the mix.

Changes in plastic viscosity vary depending on the sand content of the concrete. Concrete with low sand content (coarse overall grading) experiences an increase in plastic viscosity when the cement is deflocculated, as separated coarse particles come closer together, increasing resistance to flow. Conversely, concrete with high sand content relies less on cement because there is sufficient sand to fill voids in the coarse aggregate, preventing closer aggregation of particles and maintaining lower plastic viscosity.

Air-entraining agents introduce spherical air bubbles ranging from 10 to 250 μm in diameter by altering the surface tension of the aqueous phase in the concrete mix. This process is achieved through compounds featuring a negatively charged head group (such as –COO, SO_3^{2-}, SO_4^{2-}) that is hydrophilic (attracting water) and a non-polar tail that is hydrophobic (repelling water). Commonly used materials include abietic and pemeric acid salts, sodium olerate, sodium caprate, alkyl sulfates, among others. These compounds generate air bubbles with an apparent negative charge, forming bridges between cement particles and increasing the yield value. These bubbles act like ball bearings, allowing larger particles to flow past each other more easily, thus reducing the plastic viscosity.

Air-entrainment significantly alters the rheological properties of concrete by enhancing cohesion and reducing the tendency for bleeding. For instance, incorporating four to six percent air-entrainment by volume increases the mix's cohesion, enabling a reduction in sand content by approximately five percent.

Accelerators or retarders modify the workability time of a given concrete mixture, either reducing or extending it. The duration of improved workability retention is crucial for applications where concrete needs to be transported or manipulated before placement. The decrease in workability is akin to the stiffening of concrete caused by slow chemical reactions during the induction period.

As these admixtures alter the nature of the membrane around cement particles and the composition of the aqueous solution, they influence the rate of stiffening, particularly noticeable with superplasticizers. A retarder plasticizer diminishes workability loss and prolongs retention time by slowing down the setting process. Superplasticizers provide substantial improvements in workability without the need for retarders, which would be necessary with conventional plasticizers at such high dosages.

Moreover, it has been observed that the original flowing consistency can be maintained by administering a second dose of superplasticizer up to 60 minutes for melamine resin and up to 150 minutes for naphthalene resin. Occasionally, superplasticizers and retarders are combined to achieve slower stiffening than when used individually.

6.5 MIXTURE ADJUSTMENTS

Adequate consideration of the rheological properties of a mixture can lead to significant reductions in construction and material expenses. Alterations in the rheological characteristics of concrete are frequently identifiable through visual observation. It is imperative to make necessary adjustments as the properties of materials and field conditions evolve.

6.6 RHEOLOGY MODELS OF CONCRETE

There are currently four established rheological models for cement-based materials, outlined as follows:

a. **Bingham model:** Several studies have regarded cement-based materials as plastic fluids, which can be effectively characterized by the Bingham model, represented by:

$$\tau = \tau_0 + \mu\gamma$$

where τ is shear stress (Pa), γ is share rate (s – 1), τ_0 is yield stress for the tested paste, and μ means the plastic viscosity (Pa·s). In this model, the tested paste can flow when the share stress exceeds a critical value τ_0.

b. **Modified Bingham model:** In practical observations, it has been recognized that the stress-strain relationship of tested paste at low shear rates isn't strictly linear. To account for this, a quadratic term ($c\gamma^2$) is incorporated into the Bingham model to offer further refinement, as depicted.

$$\tau = \tau_0 + \mu\gamma + c\gamma^2$$

where c is correction index.

c. **Casson model:** The Casson fluid model operates on two main principles: (1) it assumes the presence of interaction forces among solid particles suspended within a Newtonian fluid system, and (2) when the shear stress is relatively small, the particles can agglomerate together and generate a rigid rod, and the length of the rigid rod could inversely proportionally decrease with an increase in the shear stress. This Casson model can be represented as follows:

$$\tau = \tau_0 + \mu_\infty\gamma + 2\sqrt{\mu_\infty\tau_0})\sqrt{\gamma}$$

where μ_∞ is ultimate viscosity (Pa·s).

d. **Herschel-Bulkley model:** In the Herschel-Bulkley model, the paste can flow only when the shear stress exceeds a critical shear stress, and the shear rate will increase based on a power-law when the shear stress is increasing. The Herschel-Bulkley model can be presented as:

$$\tau = \tau_0 + m\gamma^n$$

where m is consistency coefficient (Pa·s), n means rheological behavior index. It is clear that the n can reflect the difference between the Newtonian fluid and non-Newtonian fluid. When n = 1, this model is similar to that shown in the Bingham model; when $n < 1$, the thinning of the tested paste can be observed during the shearing process; when $n > 1$, the thickening of the tested paste can be observed during the shearing process. In the Herschel-Bulkley model, the fluid viscosity can be expressed by:

$$\mu = \frac{3m}{n+2}\gamma_{max}^{n-1}$$

where γ_{max} is the maximum shear rate during the rheological testing process.

Properties of Hardened Concrete

Hardened concrete refers to concrete that has undergone the curing process and has achieved its full strength and durability. Several properties characterize hardened concrete, including:

1. **Compressive strength:** This is the most commonly measured property of hardened concrete. It indicates the maximum load-carrying capacity of concrete under compression. Compressive strength is typically determined by testing cylindrical or cubical specimens in a laboratory following standardized procedures.
2. **Tensile strength:** While concrete is strong in compression, its tensile strength is relatively low. Cracking may occur under tensile stress. Techniques such as adding reinforcement (rebar or fibers) or prestressing can enhance concrete's tensile strength.
3. **Flexural strength:** Also known as bending strength, flexural strength measures the ability of concrete to withstand bending stresses. It is crucial for structural elements like beams and slabs. Flexural strength depends on factors such as concrete's compressive strength, tensile strength, and the presence of reinforcement.
4. **Durability:** Durability encompasses several aspects, including resistance to environmental factors (such as freeze-thaw cycles, chemical exposure, and abrasion), resistance to deterioration over time, and ability to maintain structural integrity. Proper mix design, curing, and construction practices are essential for achieving durable concrete.
5. **Permeability:** Permeability refers to the ability of concrete to allow fluids (such as water or chemicals) to pass through. Low permeability is desirable for structures like bridges and marine structures to prevent corrosion of reinforcement and other forms of degradation.
6. **Density:** Concrete density influences various properties, including strength, durability, and thermal conductivity. Higher density concrete typically exhibits better strength and durability characteristics but may be more challenging to place and handle during construction.
7. **Shrinkage:** Concrete undergoes shrinkage as it cures due to moisture loss. Shrinkage can lead to cracking and other forms of distress in concrete structures. Proper mix design, curing practices, and the use of shrinkage-compensating admixtures can help mitigate shrinkage-related issues.

8. **Modulus of elasticity:** Modulus of elasticity (also known as Young's modulus) represents the stiffness of concrete. It defines how much deformation a concrete member will experience under applied loads. Modulus of elasticity depends on factors, such as concrete's composition, curing conditions, and age.
9. **Creep:** Creep refers to the gradual deformation of concrete under sustained loads over time. It is an important consideration in the design of long-span structures and prestressed concrete elements.

Understanding and controlling these properties of hardened concrete are essential for designing durable and safe structures in various construction applications. Proper mix design, quality control during construction, and adherence to best practices in curing and protection can help achieve desired concrete properties.

7.1 UNIAXIAL AND MULTIAXIAL STRENGTH OF CONCRETE

Concrete, a fundamental building material in civil engineering, exhibits distinct mechanical properties when subjected to different loading conditions. Two essential aspects in understanding concrete's behavior are its uniaxial and multiaxial strength. Uniaxial strength refers to concrete's ability to withstand stress in a single principal direction, primarily characterized by its compressive strength. On the other hand, multiaxial strength encompasses concrete's response to stress in multiple principal directions simultaneously, incorporating considerations of tensile, compressive, and shear strengths. While uniaxial strength is pivotal in designing elements experiencing predominantly axial loads, such as columns and footings, multiaxial strength becomes critical for structures subjected to complex loading conditions like beams, slabs, and bridges. This essay elaborates on the definitions, parameters, influencing factors, and applications of uniaxial and multiaxial strength of concrete, delineating their significance in structural engineering practices.

7.1.1 Uniaxial Strength of Concrete

Definition: Uniaxial strength refers to the strength of concrete when it is subjected to stress in only one principal direction.

Main parameter: The primary parameter considered under uniaxial loading is the compressive strength of concrete.

Compressive strength: This is the maximum stress that concrete can withstand under direct compression. It is typically measured by testing cylindrical or cubical specimens of concrete in a laboratory environment. The compressive strength is crucial for designing structural elements, such as columns, footings, and walls.

Factors influencing compressive strength: Several factors influence the compressive strength of concrete, including the water-cement ratio, aggregate quality, curing conditions, and concrete mix design.

Applications: Uniaxial strength is predominantly relevant in structures where loads act predominantly in one direction, such as gravity loads in columns and foundations.

7.1.2 Multiaxial Strength of Concrete

Definition: Multiaxial strength refers to the strength of concrete when it is subjected to stress in multiple principal directions simultaneously.

Types of stresses: In real-world scenarios, concrete elements experience a combination of axial loads, bending moments, and shear forces, leading to multiaxial stress states. This includes combinations of compression, tension, and shear stresses.

Tensile and shear strength: Unlike compressive strength, concrete's tensile and shear strengths are considerably lower. Special attention is given to reinforcing concrete elements to enhance their tensile and shear capacities. Steel reinforcement bars (rebar) or fibers are often used to strengthen concrete against tensile and shear stresses.

Interaction effects: In multiaxial loading conditions, the interaction between different stress components must be considered. This interaction can affect the overall behavior and strength of concrete elements. Proper analysis techniques, such as finite element analysis, are employed to assess these interactions accurately.

Applications: Multiaxial strength considerations are crucial for designing structural elements subjected to complex loading conditions, such as beams, slabs, and bridges. These structures experience combinations of axial loads, bending moments, and shear forces, requiring careful consideration of concrete's multiaxial strength properties.

Key Differences

1. **Loading conditions:** Uniaxial strength is concerned with stress in only one principal direction, while multiaxial strength accounts for stress in multiple principal directions simultaneously.
2. **Main parameter:** Compressive strength is the primary parameter for uniaxial strength, while multiaxial strength encompasses a combination of tensile, compressive, and shear strengths.
3. **Reinforcement:** Multiaxial strength often necessitates the use of reinforcement to enhance tensile and shear capacities, whereas uniaxial strength is primarily determined by the intrinsic properties of concrete under compression.

7.2 COMPRESSIVE STRENGTH

In the realm of materials such as concrete, which feature void spaces of varying sizes and shapes within the matrix, along with microcracks between the matrix and aggregates, understanding the failure mechanisms under loading conditions is essential. Although the failure modes can be complex and contingent upon the type of stress applied, a brief overview proves invaluable in grasping and managing the factors influencing concrete strength.

In compression, the failure mode tends to be less brittle, as significantly more energy is required to initiate and propagate cracks within the matrix. It is widely acknowledged that in uniaxial compression tests conducted on medium- or low-strength concrete, no cracks are typically initiated within the matrix until approximately 40–50% of the failure stress is reached. However, even at this juncture, a stable network of cracks, known as shear-bond cracks, already exists in the vicinity of the coarse aggregate. As stress levels escalate, cracks begin to initiate in a stochastic manner. Certain cracks within the matrix and near the coarse aggregate (referred to as shear-bond cracks) eventually coalesce in a confined region when the loading reaches roughly 80% of the ultimate value, while others remain closed. Subsequently, significant cracks develop within these localized zones, aligned closely with the direction of the applied load, signifying the failure of the compression specimen.

Concrete failure during compressive loading can also be depicted as illustrated in Fig. 7.1. The initiation and propagation of vertical cracks lead to the expansion of concrete. Ultimately, the final failure predominantly occurs through splitting, as depicted in Fig. 7.2, although occasionally failure may occur due to the formation of a shear band.

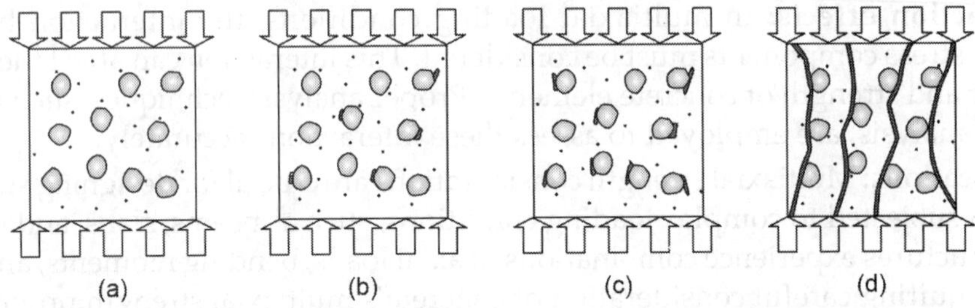

Fig. 7.1: Failure process of concrete under compression: (a) Shear-bond crack formation (load below 40% of ultimate value); (b) Initiation of load-induced cracks (load between 40% to 80% of ultimate value); (c) Concentration of cracks (load greater than 80% of ultimate value); (d) Formation of major cracks (indicative of failure)

7.2.1 Specimens for Compression Testing

There are two primary types of specimens utilized for uniaxial compression testing: the cube specimen and the cylinder specimen. The cube specimen method is commonly employed in India, Europe and China, whereas the cylinder specimen method is predominant in North America and also accepted in Europe.

Fig. 7.2: Common failure mode of concrete under compression

a. **Cube specimen:** The standard size for cube specimens is typically 150 × 150 × 150 mm, although the nominal size should be chosen to be at least 3.5 times the maximum aggregate size. Preparation involves pouring concrete into a cubic mold in at least two layers, with no layer thicker than 100 mm. Each layer should be compacted using a hemispherical-tipped steel rod (16 mm diameter) or a steel compacting bar, ensuring at least 25 strokes per layer. Compacted specimens are left in the mold for a minimum of 16 hours (but no longer than 3 days) under protected conditions to prevent dehydration at 20 ± 5°C. Post-demolding, specimens should be cured at 20 ± 1°C in water or a chamber with a relative humidity of at least 95%. Cube specimens typically exhibit a height-to-width ratio of 1, with at least five surfaces exposed during molding, facilitating testing without further surface preparation (Fig. 7.3).

b. **Cylinder specimen:** Cylindrical specimens of various sizes, with a length-to-diameter ratio of 2 and a diameter at least 3 times the nominal maximum aggregate

Fig. 7.3: Cube specimens (left) and cylindrical specimens (right)

size is considered. The widely adopted standard size for compression testing is 150 × 300 mm (Fig 7.4). Preparation consists pouring concrete into the cylindrical mold in three approximately equal layers; each compacted with 25 strokes using a hemispherical-tipped steel rod (16 ± 2 mm). After 16–24 hours from casting, specimens should be demolded and cured at 23.0 ± 2.0°C in a water tank or moist conditions. Cylinder specimens possess a length-to-diameter ratio of 2, and their upper surface is typically not smooth, necessitating grinding or capping to achieve a level and smooth compression surface before testing.

Fig. 7.4: Concrete compression testing equipment

Variations in compressive strength are observed among specimens of the same concrete mix. For instance, cylindrical and prismatic specimens with a height or length to lateral dimension ratio of 2 may yield compressive strengths ranging from 75 to 85 percent of the cube strength for normal-strength concrete. The impact of specimen height/lateral dimension ratio on compressive strength is illustrated in Fig. 7.5.

7.3 FLEXURAL STRENGTH

Determining the flexural tensile strength is crucial for estimating the load at which concrete members may crack. Due to the difficulty of directly measuring concrete's tensile strength, flexural testing is employed to compute it. The flexural tensile strength, or modulus of rupture, is determined from such tests and is particularly relevant in designing pavement slabs and airfield runways where flexural tension is a critical factor. This modulus is typically obtained by testing standard specimens under

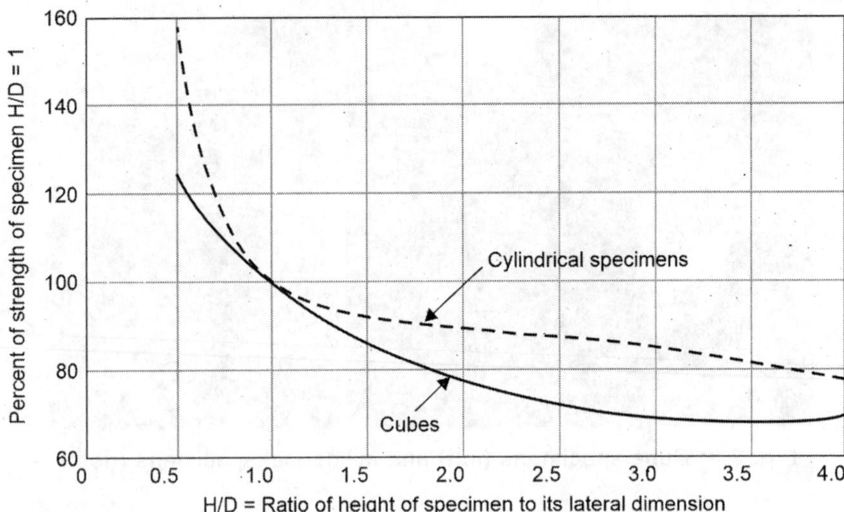

Fig. 7.5: The influence of the ratio between specimen height and lateral dimension on compressive strength

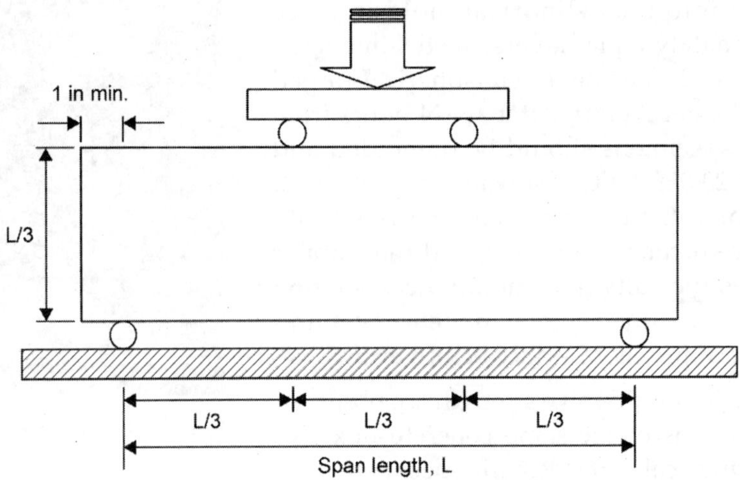

Fig. 7.6: Flexural strength test setup

symmetrical two-point loading (Fig. 7.6). However, the computation assumes linear material behavior up to failure, providing only a rough estimation. Various factors such as specimen size, casting, curing, loading manner, and rate of loading affect the results. Despite its limitations, flexure testing machines adhere to prescribed standards for accurate determination of strength. Notably, the flexure test tends to yield higher strength estimates compared to direct tension tests due to the assumption of linear material behavior. Conversely, direct tension tests often yield lower apparent tensile strength, partly due to potential eccentricities. Additionally, direct tension tests may be more prone to weak elements occurring within the specimen due to uniform stress distribution.

7.4 TENSILE STRENGTH

In addition to the flexure test, methods for determining the tensile strength of concrete can be broadly categorized as direct and indirect approaches. Direct methods encounter challenges in securely holding the specimen in the testing machine to avoid stress concentration and in applying a uniaxial tensile load without introducing eccentricity. Even slight eccentricities in load application can lead to bending and axial force conditions, causing concrete to fail at an apparent tensile stress rather than its true tensile strength. Given the complexities of conducting direct tension tests, several indirect methods have been developed. These methods typically involve applying a compressive force to a concrete specimen in a manner that induces tensile stresses leading to failure. The resulting stress at failure represents the concrete's tensile strength.

The splitting test, also known as the splitting tensile strength test, is a widely used indirect method for determining the tensile strength of concrete. In this test, compressive line loads are applied along the opposite generators of a horizontally placed concrete cylinder between two platens, as illustrated in Fig. 7.7. The line loading induces a relatively uniform tensile stress over nearly two-thirds of the loaded diameter, calculated through elastic analysis. This tensile stress, acting perpendicular to the applied compression, is given by $2P/\pi DL = 0.637P/DL$, where P is the applied load, and D and L are the diameter and length of the cylinder, respectively. Eventually, the specimen fails by splitting along the loaded diameter, allowing for the determination of tensile strength based on the failure load P. The test can also be conducted on cubes, either by splitting along the middle parallel to the edges using opposite compressive forces applied through 15 mm square bars, or along one of the diagonal planes by

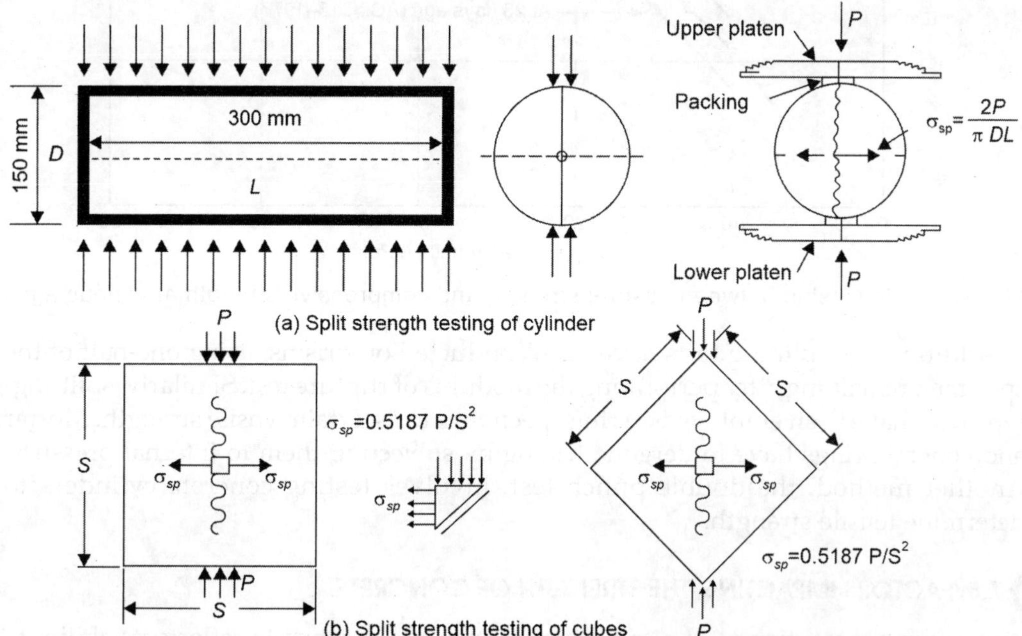

Fig. 7.7: Loading arrangement for split strength determination

applying compressive forces along opposite edges. In cube side-splitting, the tensile strength is determined using $0.642P/S^2$, and in diagonal splitting, it is calculated using $0.5187P/S^2$, where P is the load at failure and S is the side length of the cube.

The relationships between compressive strength and split tensile strength, as well as flexural strength and split tensile strength, are illustrated in Figs 7.8 and 7.9, respectively. The advantages of the splitting test for determining tensile strength are outlined below:

1. The test is straightforward to conduct and yields more consistent results compared to other tension tests.
2. The strength obtained is closer to the actual tensile strength of the concrete compared to results from the modulus of rupture test.
3. The same molds can be utilized for casting specimens for both compression and tension tests.

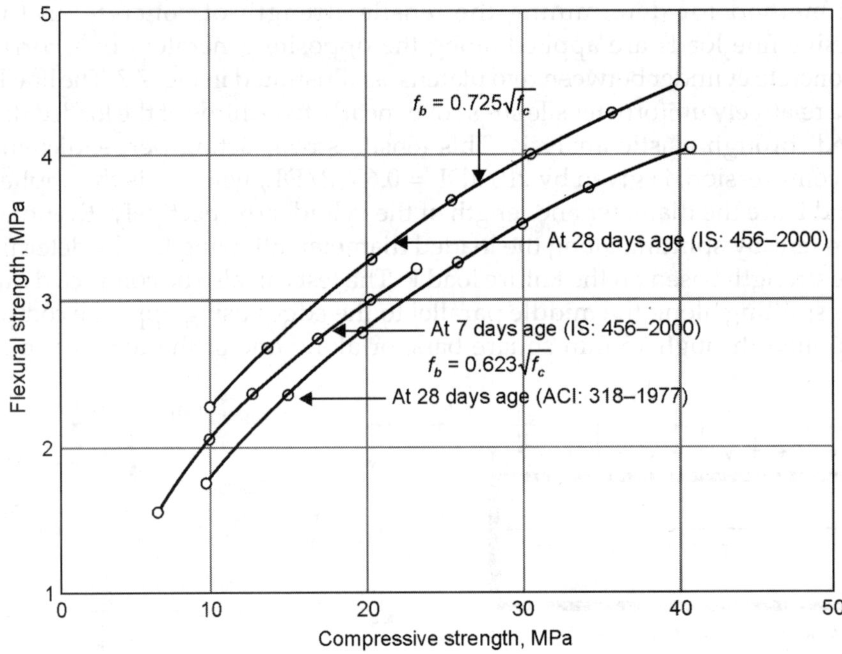

Fig. 7.8: Relationship between flexural strength and compressive strength at various ages

Additionally, splitting tests have been conducted on prisms, using one-half of the specimen remaining after performing the modulus of rupture test. Similarly, splitting-type tests have been employed on ring specimens to ascertain tensile strength. Mortar and concrete rings have undergone testing by subjecting them to internal pressure. Another method, the double punch test, involves testing concrete cylinders to determine tensile strength.

7.5 FACTORS IMPACTING THE STRENGTH OF CONCRETE

As previously mentioned, the compressive strength of concrete reflects its ability to withstand compressive stress and is inherently linked to the breakdown of the concrete

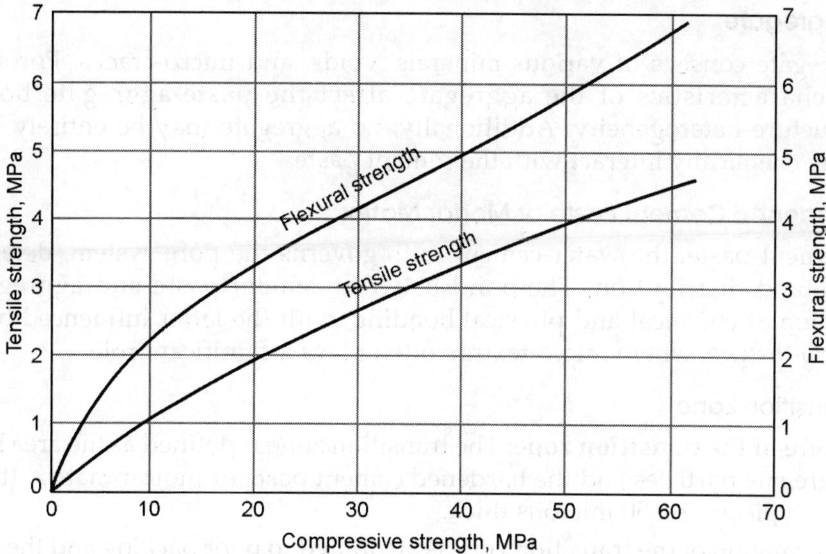

Fig. 7.9: Relationship between compressive strength, tensile strength and flexural strength

matrix. Consequently, strength tests are inherently destructive, leading to failure. Typically, the three-phase theory is employed to analyze the strength characteristics of concrete. According to this theory, concrete is conceptualized as comprising three main phases: aggregate (both coarse and fine), hardened cement paste or mortar matrix, and a transition zone. Each phase can be further subdivided into multiple components. Strain incompatibilities exist among these phases, leading to gradual micro-cracking. These strain incompatibilities are depicted in Fig. 7.10. The strength of concrete is influenced by the properties of these phases and their interactions with one another.

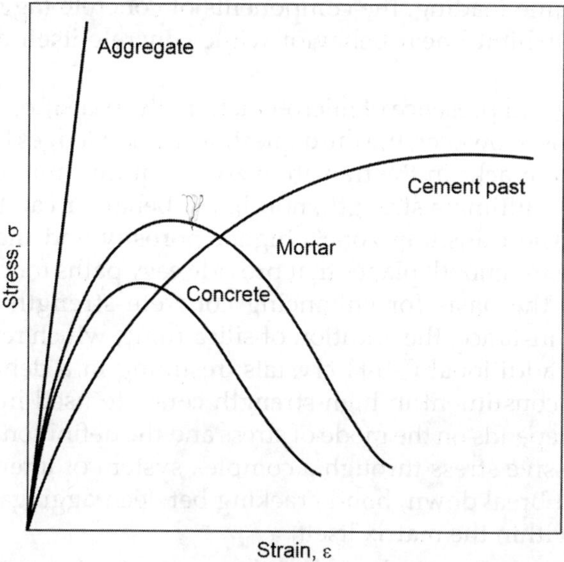

Fig. 7.10: Strain inconsistencies among different phases of concrete

7.5.1 Aggregate

The aggregate consists of various minerals, voids, and micro-cracks. Porosity and surface characteristics of the aggregate affect the paste-aggregate bond and microstructure heterogeneity. Additionally, no aggregate may be entirely inert, as some may chemically interact with the cement paste.

7.5.2 Hardened Cement Paste or Mortar Matrix

In the cement paste, the water-cement ratio governs the pore system, determining pore size and distribution. The bond between cement paste and aggregate is a combination of chemical and physical bonding, with the latter influenced by micro and macro-texture, where micro-texture often plays a significant role.

7.5.3 Transition Zone

Structure of the transition zone: The transition zone is defined as the area between large aggregate particles and the hardened cement paste or mortar matrix. It forms a thin shell, typically 10–50 microns thick.

i. The formation of the transition zone is attributed to poor packing and the creation of water films around large particles during mixing. Due to a higher water-cement ratio, the transition zone is more porous than the bulk cement paste or mortar matrix. Additionally, micro-cracks often develop within the transition zone even before external loading is applied.
ii. Influence of the transition zone on concrete properties: Generally weaker than both the aggregate and the hardened cement paste, the transition zone, despite occupying less volume, has a significant impact on concrete properties. Its presence helps explain why:
    a. cement paste or mortar matrix is typically stronger than concrete when tested under the same water-cement ratio and age.
    b. the permeability of concrete is higher than that of cement paste.
    c. under the same loading, the components of concrete (aggregate and cement paste) may exhibit linear behavior while concrete itself displays non-linear behavior.

The high porosity and presence of micro-cracks in the transition zone easily explain the first two questions. However, the third question acknowledges that the propagation of pre-existing micro-cracks in the transition zone requires minimal energy. Even at 40% of the concrete's ultimate strength, non-linear behavior can be observed due to this phenomenon. The transition zone's higher porosity and the presence of large $Ca(OH)_2$ crystals create smooth planes that provide easy paths for cracks to propagate. This insight forms the basis for enhancing concrete strength by improving the microstructure. For instance, the addition of silica fume, which reacts with $Ca(OH)_2$, removes it to form additional C-S-H crystals, resulting in a denser interface. Silica fume is a common constituent in high-strength concrete used in practice. Concrete strength primarily depends on the mode of stress and the definition of failure. Concrete fails under compressive stress through a complex system of internal micro-cracking and microstructural breakdown, bond cracking between aggregate and matrix, and cleavage cracking within the matrix itself.

A sketch showing factors influencing the strength of concrete is depicted in Fig. 7.11.

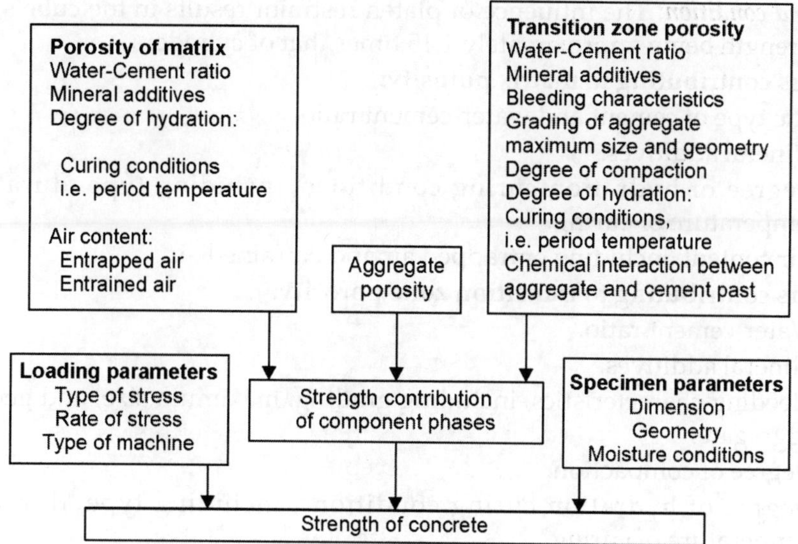

Fig. 7.11: Factors influencing the strength of concrete

The cracking primarily occurs in tensile or shear/tensile nature, with cleavage cracking becoming predominant as ultimate failure approaches, leading to final rupture. Factors influencing the strength of concrete can be categorized into four groups:

a. **Factors associated with the testing method:**

i. *Specimen parameters*:

- Dimensions, including the size of the test specimen: Larger defects such as voids and cracks are more likely with larger specimens, resulting in smaller apparent strength. Therefore, smaller specimens tend to yield higher apparent strength.
- Size of the specimen relative to the size of the aggregate.
- Geometry of the test specimen, such as cube or cylinder.
- Moisture conditions of the specimen.
- Support conditions of the specimen.

ii. *Loading parameters*:

- Type of loading or stress applied (axial, bending, or shear).
- Rate of loading applied to the specimen: A faster load rate typically results in a higher ultimate load. It's crucial to adhere to standard loading rates, which are 0.15–0.34 MPa/s for ASTM and 0.2–0.4 MPa/s for BS. Concrete strength tends to decrease with decreasing loading rates, as slower rates allow more time for crack propagation, requiring lower stress for crack failure to occur.
- Nature of loading to which the specimen is subjected, such as static, sustained, dynamic, etc.
- Type of testing machine.
- Assumptions made in the stress-to-failure load analysis, including the type of stress situation that may exist, such as uniaxial, biaxial, and triaxial.

End condition: The influence of platen restraint results in the cube's apparent strength being approximately 1.15 times that of cylinders.

b. **Factors contributing to matrix porosity:**
   i. The type of cement and water-cement ratio.
   ii. Mineral additives.
   iii. Degree of hydration curing conditions, including type, duration, and temperature of curing.
   iv. Air content, including entrapped air and entrained air.

c. **Factors contributing to transition zone porosity:**
   i. Water-cement ratio.
   ii. Mineral additives.
   iii. Bleeding characteristics, including grading, maximum size, and geometry of aggregate.
   iv. Degree of compaction.
   v. Degree of hydration curing conditions, including type, duration, and temperature of curing.
   vi. Chemical interaction between aggregate and cement paste.

The level of compaction significantly influences the porosity of the transition zone. The impact of compaction on the compressive strength of concrete is demonstrated in Fig. 7.12.

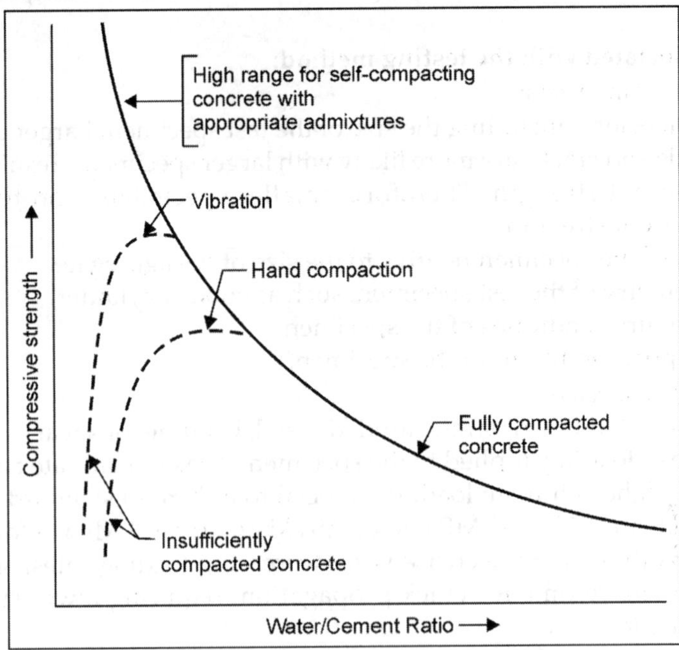

Fig. 7.12: The effect of degree of compaction on the compressive strength of concrete

d. **Aggregate porosity:** For mixes with the same water-cement ratio, those containing larger aggregates tend to exhibit lower strength. This phenomenon arises from the existence of a weak zone at the interface between the aggregate and paste, where initial cracking occurs. Larger aggregates facilitate the formation of larger cracks at the interface, enabling easier interaction with paste cracks and other interfacial cracks.

7.6 STRESS-STRAIN RELATIONSHIP

Obtaining a complete stress-strain curve of concrete requires a proper loading control mechanism, particularly considering the post-peak response. In uniaxial compression tests, the load cell measures load, while sensors like strain gauges, extensometers, or LVDTs measure deformation. For normal-strength concrete tested on a very stiff machine, stroke control suffices to capture the post-peak response. However, with high-strength concrete, stroke control may not provide adequate downward movement as a feedback signal, leading to specimen failure around the peak load. In such cases, alternative control methods are necessary. One approach is circumferential control, using a roller chain tied transversely on the specimen to ensure stable and reliable control throughout the post-peak response, as depicted in Fig. 7.13. In uniaxial tension tests, obtaining a complete stress-deformation curve is more challenging. Traditionally, two methods are employed to stabilize the response in the post-peak region. One method, called loading-sharing, Fig. 7.14, utilizes an elastic load-sharing system parallel to the specimen to avoid unstable failure near the peak load caused by sudden energy release. However, this method is prone to inaccuracies, especially in the post-peak region, due to errors in strain gauge measurements leading to significant load calculation errors.

Recognizing the limitations of the parallel load-sharing method, endeavors were undertaken to conduct tensile tests on specimens with two edge notches using closed-loop control, as depicted in Fig. 7.15. Tensile failure in concrete typically involves the

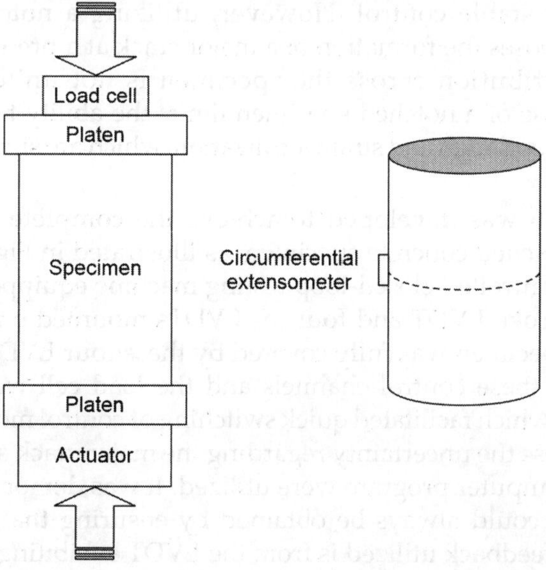

Fig. 7.13: Circumferentially controlled test setup

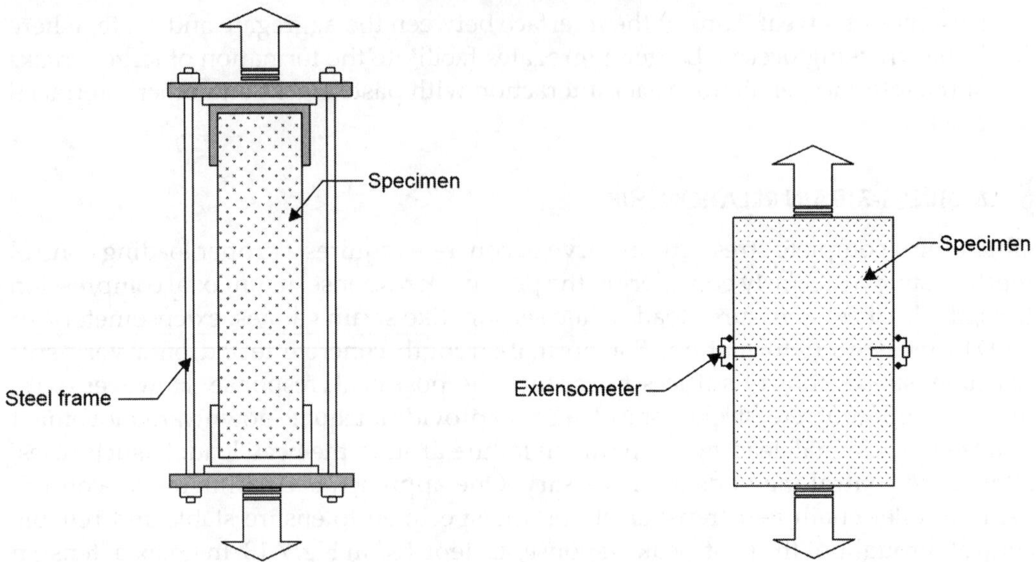

Fig. 7.14: Concrete tension test conducted with loading sharing system

Fig. 7.15: Notched specimen used for uniaxial tension test

opening of a single 'major' crack. By controlling the crack opening in a closed-loop manner, gradual failure can be achieved, thereby avoiding instability near the peak load.

Introducing two edge notches in the specimen significantly weakens its cross-section, promoting the formation of a major crack at this location. Typically, a pair of displacement sensors is employed, with one on each side of the specimen covering the notch, and their average output serves as a feedback control signal. Because the location of the major crack is predetermined by the notch, its opening consistently increases, enabling stable control. However, utilizing a notched specimen has drawbacks, as it imposes the formation of a major crack at a predetermined position, and the stress distribution across the specimen is not uniformly distributed. Consequently, the use of a notched specimen limits the ability to study phenomena such as damage accumulation and strain localization, which are significant in the failure process.

A novel approach was developed to achieve the complete stress-deformation response of an unnotched concrete specimen, as illustrated in Fig. 7.16. This method utilizes a digitally controlled closed-loop testing machine equipped with five control channels: one for stroke LVDT and four for LVDTs mounted on the specimen. The test section of the specimen was fully covered by these four LVDTs. Throughout the test, the outputs of these control channels and the load cell were monitored by a computer program, which facilitated quick switching of control modes from one LVDT to another. To address the uncertainty regarding the major crack's location, the LVDT arrangement and computer program were utilized. It was demonstrated that a stable post-peak response could always be obtained by ensuring that, at any given time during the test, the feedback utilized is from the LVDT exhibiting the largest slope of the response-time curve. Additionally, an acoustic emission (AE) measurement system comprising six channels was employed in the experiments. Monitoring signals from the AE transducers provided valuable insights, aiding in decisions regarding control switching.

For the plain concrete specimen under test, a dependable result was obtained, and the stress-deformation curve is depicted in Fig. 7.17. In Fig. 7.17, 'deformation' refers to displacement measured by the LVDT, which controlled the post-peak region. The curve can be segmented into three sections: the linear elastic part, the nonlinear pre-peak part, and the post-peak part. In the initial segment, the concrete exhibits elastic behavior, characterized by uniform deformation and a "global" material response. In the subsequent segment, as damage occurs (evidenced by AE events), the material modulus begins to decrease, leading to nonlinear behavior in the stress-deformation curves. Since damage doesn't occur uniformly across the specimen, the material's behavior ceases to be "global." Following the peak load, a major crack forms in the specimen. The behavior in this region can be elucidated using

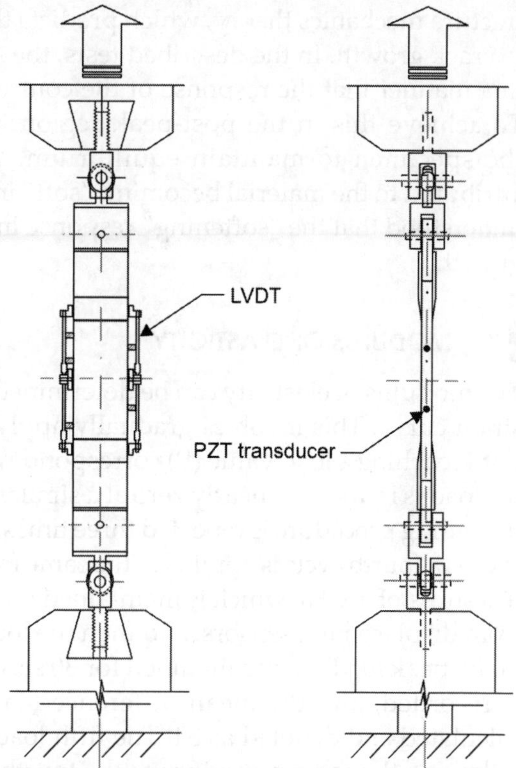

Fig. 7.16: Uniaxial tension test setup for unnotched concrete specimen

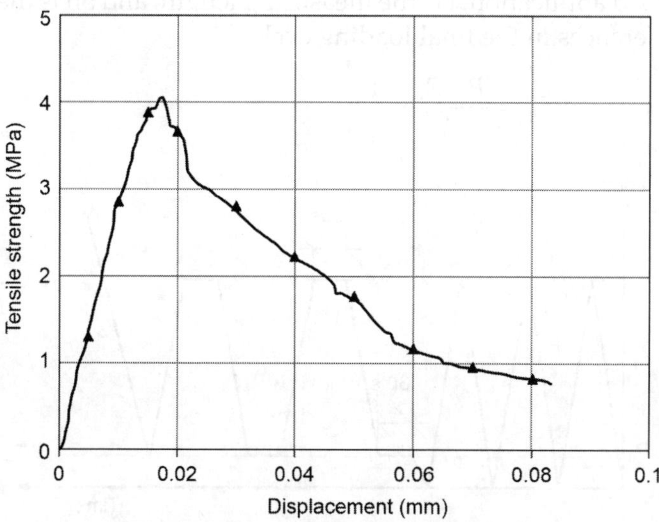

Fig. 7.17: The stress-deformation curve of an unnotched concrete specimen

fracture mechanics theory, which predicts that the specimen's stiffness decreases due to crack growth. In the described tests, the test machine was instructed to apply load in a manner that the response of the controlling LVDT increased linearly with time. To achieve this in the post-peak region, the machine had to reduce the load on the specimen to maintain equilibrium. This reduction in load was previously attributed to the material becoming "soft" in the post-peak region. However, it is now understood that the "softening" response in tension is actually a result of single crack growth.

7.7 MODULUS OF ELASTICITY

The modulus of elasticity can be determined directly from a specially designed stress-strain curve. This involves gradually applying load at a rate of 2–3 MPa per second until reaching a load value (P) corresponding to 40% of the peak load (Fig. 7.18). Then, the load is reduced to nearly zero at a similar rate as it was increased, and this loading/unloading procedure is repeated three times. Following the completion of three loading cycles, a fourth cycle is applied at the same rate to a value (P_0) approximately equivalent to a stress of 5 MPa, which is maintained for 30 seconds. Deformation (δb) is measured from displacement sensors, and then the load is increased to P (corresponding to 40% of the peak load) and maintained for 30 seconds. The corresponding deformation (δa) is recorded, and the mean difference (δa – δb) between the two deformations is calculated and denoted as 54. The fifth loading cycle begins with the base load of P_0, following the same procedure as the fourth cycle. The mean deformation change (δ5) recorded by the gauges is calculated, and if the difference between δ4 and δ5 is not greater than 0.003 mm, the gauges are removed. Subsequently, the load is increased until failure of the specimen, from which the modulus of elasticity of concrete in compression (E^s) can be determined. In the equations, P represents the load corresponding to a stress level of 5 MPa, P represents the load corresponding to 0.4 fc, A is the area of load application, l is the measuring length, and 5n is the mean value of deformation differences in the final loading cycle.

$$E_h^s = \frac{P - P_0}{A} \times \frac{1}{\delta_n}$$

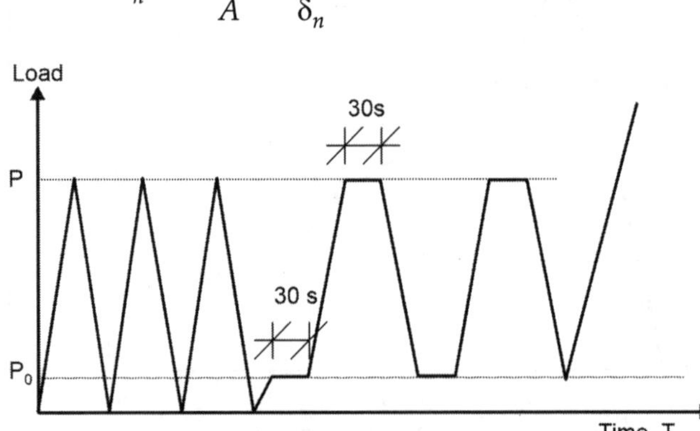

Fig. 7.18: A loading time diagram is utilized to assess the modulus of elasticity of concrete

7.8 DIMENSIONAL STABILITY— SHRINKAGE AND CREEP

Dimensional stability in construction materials pertains to their ability to maintain their dimensions over an extended period without causing structural issues. For concrete, factors such as drying shrinkage and creep contribute to potential dimensional changes, distinct from those caused by external loads.

Creep refers to the gradual deformation of concrete under sustained loads, while shrinkage involves its contraction even without applied loads. These phenomena, alongside elastic strains, typically exhibit similar magnitudes. The collective term "volume change" encompasses alterations due to shrinkage, creep, temperature variations, and potential chemical degradation.

Shrinkage and creep are often discussed together as they stem from the deformation of hydrated cement paste within concrete, while the aggregate serves to mitigate these effects by restraining deformation. Shrinkage strains encompass plastic and drying shrinkage variations, with the latter being particularly notable.

7.8.1 Plastic Shrinkage

Plastic shrinkage occurs on the surface of freshly cast concrete, typically within a few hours, while the concrete underneath remains in its plastic state. Without proper curing methods, such as adequate hydration or protection from environmental factors like temperature, sunlight, wind speed, and humidity, the surface undergoes evaporation, resulting in water loss. This loss is usually compensated by water migrating from within the concrete. However, when the rate of surface water loss surpasses the rate of internal water movement, local reductions in volume occur, known as plastic shrinkage. Studies have shown plastic shrinkage to exceed 6,000 microstrain for paste and 2,000 microstrain for concrete, potentially reaching up to 10,000 microstrain in extreme cases. Despite the plastic state of concrete at this stage, significant stress isn't typically induced, allowing for further work to mitigate potential cracks.

During plastic shrinkage, solid and heavier components in the surface layer may move downward. However, this movement can be hindered by large coarse aggregates or top-layer reinforcement. In such cases, the concrete above the aggregates or bars may bend over them, resulting in cracks known as plastic shrinkage cracks. These cracks are typically shallow, ranging from 38 to 50 mm in depth and 300 to 450 mm in length. They commonly form perpendicular to the wind direction and run parallel to each other (Fig. 7.19). Plastic shrinkage cracks serve as pathways for water and chemicals, such as chloride ions, to penetrate the concrete and reach the steel reinforcement, which can significantly impact the durability of concrete structures by promoting corrosion of the reinforcement.

Preventing plastic shrinkage is most effectively achieved by shielding the concrete surface from wind and sunlight during construction and promptly covering it after

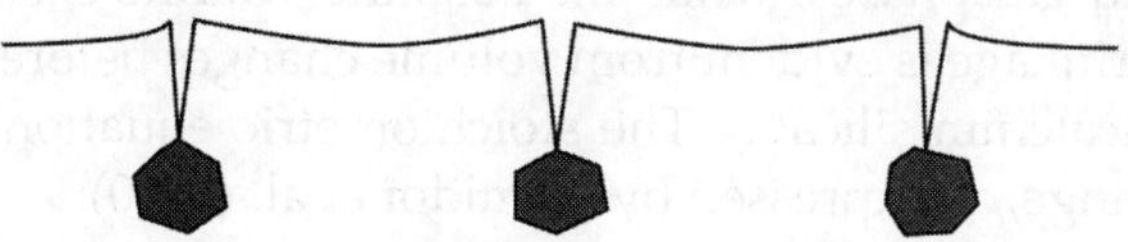

Fig. 7.19: Formation of plastic shrinkage crack

finishing to reduce evaporation rates. BS 8110-1:1997 outlines minimum curing and protection periods (Table 7.1) to mitigate plastic shrinkage and ensure proper property development in fresh concrete. Similarly, ACI 308R (Guide to External Curing of Concrete) provides regulations for maintaining concrete temperatures above 10°C. Modifying concrete mix designs, particularly through the use of air entrainment, can also help reduce plastic shrinkage. In cases where cracks have already formed, remedial measures typically involve sealing them against water ingress by applying cement or low-viscosity polymers.

Table 7.1: Minimum periods of curing and protection

Types of cement	*Ambient conditions after casting*	*Minimum period of curing and protection*	
		Average concrete surface temperature	
		5–10°C	*t°C (10–25°C)*
Portland cement, SRPC	Average	4 days	$60/(t + 10)$ days
	Poor	6 days	$80/(t + 10)$ days
All except Portland cement and	Average	6 days	$80/(t + 10)$ days
SRPC, and all with GGBS or PFA	Poor	10 days	$140/(t + 10)$ days
All	Good	No special requirements	

Note: SRPC, sulfate-resisting Portland cement; GGBS, ground granulated blase-furnace slag; PFA, pulverized fuel ash

7.8.2 Autogenous Shrinkage

Autogenous shrinkage refers to the macroscopic volume reduction of concrete within the first day after casting, occurring independently of moisture transfer to the surrounding environment. This shrinkage stems from self-desiccation due to cement hydration, leading to chemical shrinkage, where the total volume of hydration products is smaller than the sum of water and cement minerals. Initially described in the 1930s by Lyman (1934) as a factor contributing to overall shrinkage, autogenous shrinkage was observed only at very low water-to-cement (w/c) ratios, well below practical ranges, and received limited attention. However, with advancements like superplasticizers allowing for lower w/c ratios, approaching or even below 0.42, autogenous shrinkage has become a significant concern in modern concrete practice, particularly with the incorporation of materials like silica fume.

To grasp autogenous shrinkage, it is essential to first explore chemical shrinkage. When cement encounters water, ions dissolve and react to produce hydrates, leading to a reduction in the total absolute volume of the cement system—a phenomenon known as chemical shrinkage. Initially discovered by Le Chatelier (1900), chemical shrinkage distinguishes between apparent and absolute volume of cement paste. The apparent volume represents the external volume of a sample, including spaces occupied by solid, liquid, and gas phases, while the absolute volume excludes the gas phase space. Chemical shrinkage is evident from volume changes before and after complete reaction of C_3S (tricalcium silicate). The stoichiometric equation for fully hydrated C_3S reflects this change, as expressed by Damidot et al. (1990):

$$C_3S + 5.2H \rightarrow C_{1.75}SH_{3.9} + 1.3CH$$

Upon substituting the molecular weights and densities of all products into equation, it becomes evident that the hydration of C_3S leads to a decrease in the absolute volume of the system (Nawa and Horita, 2004):

$$C_3S + 5.2H \rightarrow C_{1.75}SH_{3.9} + 1.3CH$$

$$72.8\ cm^3 + 93.6\ cm^3 \rightarrow 95.9\ cm^3 + 42.9\ cm^3$$

$$166.4\ cm^3 \rightarrow 138.8\ cm^3$$

It is evident that there's approximately a 16.5% volume reduction after hydration if the reactants adhere to their stoichiometric proportions. It is important to note that autogenous shrinkage and chemical shrinkage exhibit some disparities. Figure 7.20 schematically illustrates the relationship between autogenous shrinkage and chemical shrinkage. During the plastic stage of cement paste, the apparent volume change or autogenous shrinkage aligns closely with the reduction in absolute volume or chemical shrinkage. However, as hydration products form a structural skeleton, autogenous shrinkage can be constrained by the skeleton, deviating from theoretical chemical shrinkage.

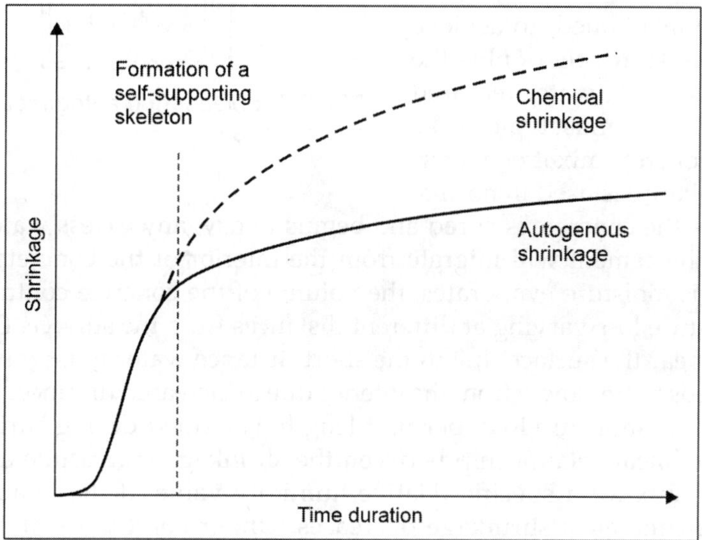

Fig. 7.20: Relationship between autogenous shrinkage and chemical shrinkage

Numerous techniques have been developed to measure autogenous shrinkage, typically categorized into two approaches: measuring volume change or monitoring changes in linear length. Volume change of cement paste can be assessed by immersing the specimen in a tightly sealed rubber balloon and measuring the water displaced by the specimen. Alternatively, linear length change can be measured using a strain gauge embedded in the specimen. During hydration, the cement paste undergoes deformation, generating internal strain indicative of autogenous shrinkage. It is crucial to measure autogenous shrinkage without moisture transfer, necessitating tight sealing of the specimen with materials like Teflon sheets or rubber membranes, as depicted in Fig. 7.21.

To achieve high-fidelity measurement or monitoring of internal strains in concrete, embedded fiber-optic sensors have been widely adopted in the past decade. These sensors include point sensors, such as those based on fiber Bragg gratings, or distributed sensors, like those based on Rayleigh scattering-based optical frequency domain reflectometry systems. Recent advancements in embedded optical fiber and coaxial cable strain sensors have attained resolutions as fine as 0.1 micro-strain (Du et al., 2017; Huang et al., 2012).

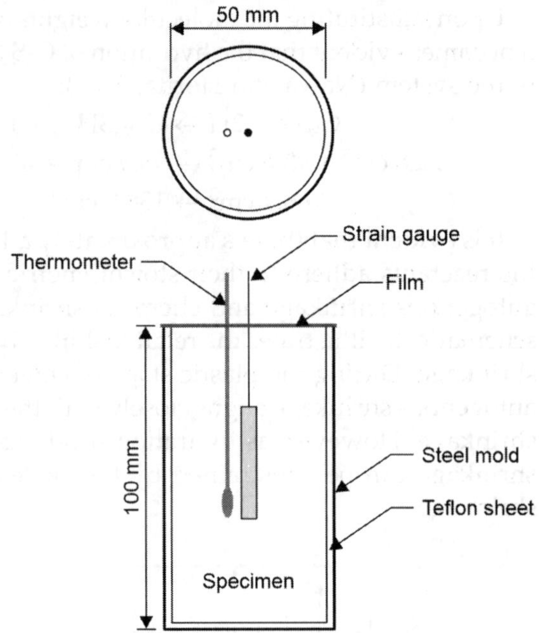

Fig. 7.21: Measuring autogenous shrinkage in cement paste

7.8.3 Drying Shrinkage

As previously mentioned, to achieve workable concrete, nearly double the theoretical amount of water required for cement hydration must typically be added to the concrete mix if no water-reducing admixture is used in normal concrete. Once the concrete is cured and begins to dry, any excess water that hasn't reacted with the cement will migrate from the interior of the concrete mass to the surface. As this moisture evaporates, the volume of the concrete contracts, with the extent of moisture loss varying at different distances from the surface. Drying occurs most rapidly near the surface due to the short distance water must travel to escape, while it proceeds more slowly from the interior due to increased distance. The reduction in volume due to moisture loss, per unit length, is termed drying shrinkage. There exists a nearly linear relationship between the shrinkage magnitude and the water content of the mix for a specific relative humidity value. If the relative humidity increases, the concrete's shrinkage decreases. Under conditions of 100% relative humidity or when submerged in water, concrete may actually experience a slight increase in volume as gel formation continues due to ideal hydration conditions.

The drying shrinkage of Portland cement concrete is primarily governed by three fundamental mechanisms. One of these mechanisms is disjointing pressure, which is influenced by water absorbed on the surface of C-S-H (calcium-silicate-hydrate) phases. Water is absorbed within the layers of C-S-H across all relative humidities, with the thickness of the water layer increasing as humidity rises. At relative humidities exceeding 10%, a water film can form on the surfaces bounded by narrow spaces, as illustrated in Fig. 7.22. When the distance between two layers is restricted due to van der Waals forces of attraction, the absorbed water molecules between the C-S-H surfaces may generate a pressure known as disjointing pressure, resulting in expansion. However, as the relative humidity decreases, the disjointing pressure diminishes accordingly, causing the separated surfaces to come closer again due to van der Waals forces and leading to volume reduction or shrinkage. Disjointing pressure significantly influences shrinkage when relative humidity surpasses 75% but has no impact when the relative humidity is below 45%.

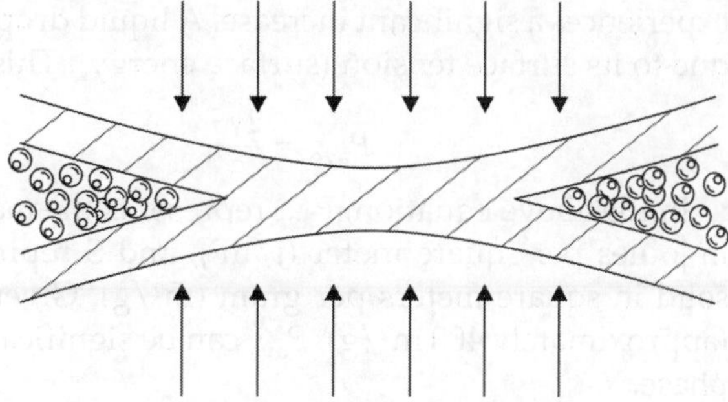

Fig. 7.22: Absorbed water film

The second mechanism contributing to drying shrinkage is the capillary surface tension effect. As hydration progresses, the air volume expands, either due to chemical shrinkage or the self-desiccation effect. Consequently, the interface between air and water in capillary pores also increases. The formation of an interface, known as a meniscus, generates stress referred to as capillary stress. Capillary tension effects arise from the formation of menisci within capillary pores, leading to uniform hydrostatic compression within the solid phase. This compression draws the voids within the C-S-H matrix closer together. The capillary surface tension effect can be understood through the examination of the Kelvin and Laplace equations. The Kelvin equation is expressed as:

$$\ln(\text{RH}) = -\frac{2\sigma}{r}\frac{M}{\nu RT}\cos\theta$$

or

$$\frac{2\sigma}{r}\cos\theta = \frac{\nu RT}{M}\ln(\text{RH})$$

In the provided equations, *RH* represents the relative humidity, σ denotes the surface tension of water in contact with air, *M* represents the molar mass of water, θ stands for the contact angle between water and solid, *r* signifies the radius of the pore, *v* represents the density of water, *R* denotes the ideal gas constant, and *T* indicates the temperature on the Kelvin scale. The Laplace equation can be expressed as:

$$p_c - p_\nu = \frac{2\sigma}{r}\cos\theta$$

or

$$\Delta p = \frac{2\sigma}{r}\cos\theta$$

where, p_c represents the capillary pressure of water within a pore, p_v denotes the vapor pressure, and Δp signifies the suction pressure. Upon substituting the Kelvin equation into the Laplace equation, we obtain:

$$\Delta p = -\frac{\nu RT}{M}\ln(\text{RH}) = -\frac{\ln(\text{RH})}{K}$$

From the above equation, it is evident that suction pressure increases as internal humidity decreases. Put differently, decreasing internal relative humidity generates greater pressure, resulting in concrete shrinkage. Below approximately 45% relative humidity, neither disjointing pressure nor capillary stress exists, and shrinkage must be attributed to a change in surface energy. As the most strongly adsorbed water (equivalent to one or two molecular layers) is removed, the solid's surface free energy experiences a significant increase. A liquid droplet is subjected to hydrostatic pressure due to its surface tension (surface energy). This pressure can be described as:

$$P_{ave} = \frac{2\gamma S}{3}$$

In the above equation, P_{ave} represents the mean pressure, γ denotes surface energy in joules per square meter (J/m²), and S represents the specific surface area of the solid in square meters per gram (m²/g). Given that S is large in the case of C–S–H (approximately 400 m²/g), P_{ave} can be significant, leading to compression in the solid phase.

Drying shrinkage induces stress within concrete. Consider a concrete cylinder as an example. Because the concrete near the cylinder surface dries faster than the interior, initial shrinkage strains are greater near the surface than in the interior. This differential shrinkage results in a set of internal self-balancing forces—compression in the interior and tension on the outside. These stresses induced can be explained by imagining the separation of the cylindrical core from its outer shell, allowing them to shrink independently based on the effective quantities of water lost. As deformations must be compatible at the core-shell junction, shear stresses are generated between them. For the upper half of the cylinder, vertical equilibrium necessitates shear stresses inducing compression in the core and tension in the shell, as depicted in Fig. 7.23.

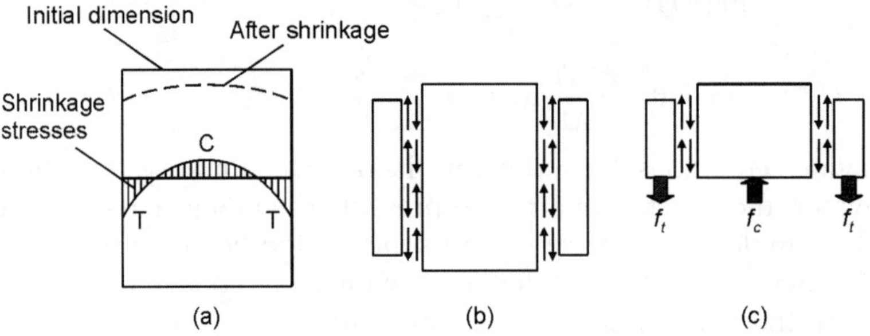

Fig. 7.23: Self-balanced stresses arising from drying shrinkage

These self-balancing shrinkage stresses may influence flexural strength and splitting strength measurements. In flexural strength tests, the presence of self-balancing stress can underestimate a concrete's apparent flexural strength obtained from beam bending. Conversely, in split tensile strength tests, the self-balancing stress may require a higher peak load to fracture a cylinder, leading to an overestimation of concrete's splitting tensile strength.

Moreover, besides the self-balancing stresses resulting from differential shrinkage, overall shrinkage creates stresses when members are restrained in the direction of shrinkage. Tensile cracking due to shrinkage occurs in any structural element restrained by its boundaries, such as a beam-column joint illustrated in Fig. 7.24.

It is imperative to control shrinkage since it allows water passage, mars appearance, reduces shear strength, and exposes reinforcement to atmospheric conditions.

The extent of ultimate shrinkage primarily depends on the initial water content of concrete and the relative humidity of the surrounding environment. Shrinkage strain,

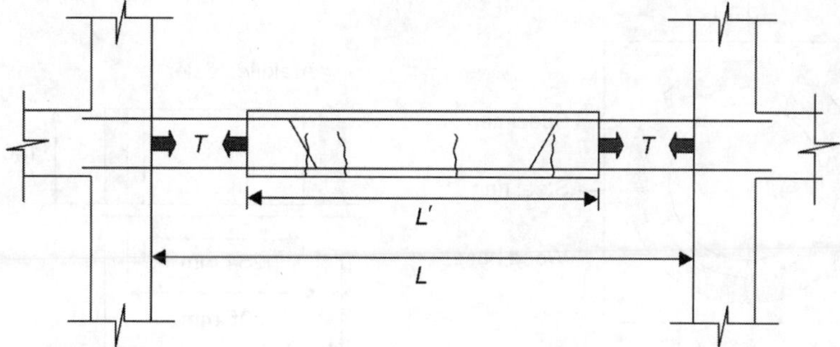

Fig. 7.24: Crack formation due to restraint from shrinkage

represented by ε_{sh}, varies over time, with approximately 90% of ultimate shrinkage occurring within the first year. Both the rate and magnitude of total shrinkage increase with higher surface-to-volume ratios. This is because greater surface areas facilitate quicker moisture evaporation. For plain concrete members, the shrinkage strain typically ranges from 0.0004 to 0.0007 under standard conditions, whereas for reinforced concrete members, it falls between 0.0002 and 0.0003. This indicates that reinforcement aids in mitigating shrinkage.

Fig. 7.25: Measurement of free-drying shrinkage using a Demec gauge on a cylinder specimen

Free-drying shrinkage can be assessed using a Demec gauge on cylindrical, prismatic, or ring-shaped specimens (Fig. 7.25). These specimens are moved to a shrinkage test room after curing to a specified age. The room is maintained at a temperature of 23 ± 2°C and a relative humidity of 50 ± 4%, adhering to ASTM standards (C157/157M and C596). Shrinkage is typically measured at various ages using a Demec gauge, such as the CT 171M, with a maximum displacement measurement of 5 mm.

In addition to conducting free shrinkage tests, it's often necessary to perform restrained shrinkage tests to assess concrete's susceptibility to cracking. Restraint shrinkage investigations typically involve three types of specimens: bars, plates, and rings. The bar-type test allows for the development of uniaxial stress in specimens with large-sized aggregates. However, ensuring a constant restraint and end conditions can be challenging, making this test type complicated. Plate-type testing evaluates both biaxial and plastic shrinkage, offering a biaxial restraint influenced by geometry and boundary conditions. Ring-type specimens are convenient to cast, and their closed-loop shape eliminates end effects. Ring tests are commonly utilized for investigating restrained shrinkage cracking. In these tests, ring-shaped specimens are cast around a rigid inner steel core (as depicted in Fig. 7.26) to provide restraint when the specimen tends to shrink. The degree of cracking depends on the restraint conditions and the drying environment. The restraint induces tensile stresses in the concrete ring, peaking at the inner surface of the specimen. If the developed tensile stress exceeds the tensile strength of concrete, cracking initiates. This method has been standardized as ASTM

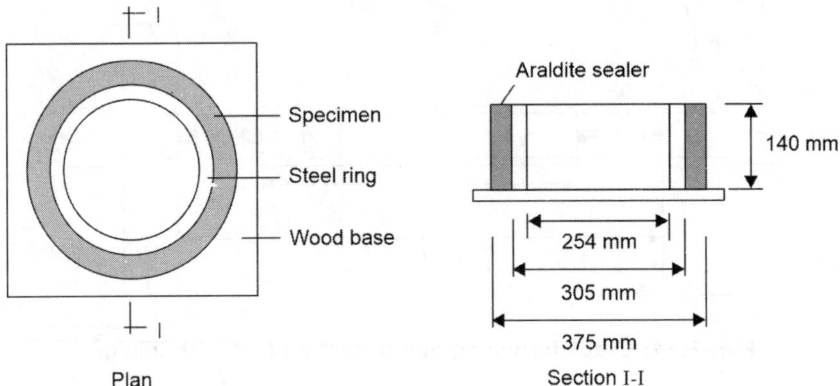

Fig. 7.26: Ring-shaped specimen for restrained shrinkage testing

C1581/1581M to determine the age at cracking and induced tensile stresses in mortar/concrete specimens under restrained shrinkage conditions.

Conventional circular ring testing presents several drawbacks. Firstly, it is challenging to anticipate the location of initial cracking due to equal potential for cracking around the circumference of the ring. Secondly, in cases where a steel ring lacks sufficient stiffness, concrete with higher toughness may not produce visible cracks but rather more subtle fine cracks, potentially compromising concrete durability. The low cracking sensitivity (whether in mortar or concrete) is influenced by geometry and non-stress intensity effects. In circular ring tests, the sample geometry may not induce enough stress to produce visible cracks at specific locations.

The deterioration process in concrete is multifaceted, often accelerated by early-age cracking. Therefore, assessing the cracking sensitivity of a material is crucial in evaluating concrete durability. To enhance the crack propagation rate of mortar or concrete and differentiate materials' cracking sensitivity within shorter timeframes, a novel ellipse-type ring for restrained shrinkage testing was developed. In this setup, the development of shrinkage diffusive stress is faster along the long principal axis compared to the short principal axis, resulting in more predictable crack occurrence. This testing apparatus not only allows for the detection of mortar or concrete extension in a shorter duration but also facilitates early detection of shrinkage cracks. Furthermore, the new method incorporates an electrical conduction line along the circumference of the elliptical ring-shaped specimen. Continuous monitoring of the line's resistance enables precise detection of the timing of crack occurrence (Fig. 7.27).

7.8.4 Shrinkage Control

Because shrinkage cracking can accelerate the deterioration of concrete structures, shortening their useful lifespan, numerous efforts have been made to mitigate or control shrinkage. One effective approach is the use of expansive concrete, also known as shrinkage-compensating concrete. Another method involves the utilization of reinforcement to reduce shrinkage. Since reinforcement does not shrink, it can counteract the shrinkage of concrete through mutual bonding. This process generates compression stress in the reinforcement steel and tension stress in the concrete, which

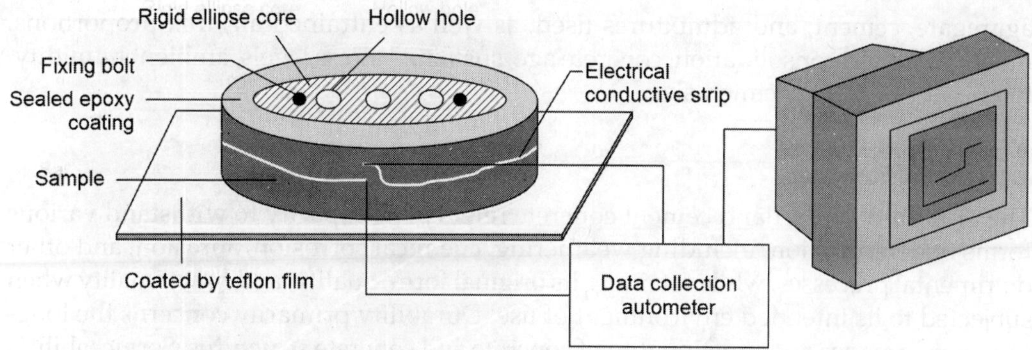

Fig. 7.27: Elliptical ring test for constrained shrinkage

are self-balanced. When employing reinforcement steel to mitigate shrinkage, it is essential to carefully manage the magnitude of the tensile stress induced in the concrete to ensure it remains within the tensile strength limits. Consequently, finer steel bars are preferred over thick steel bars if the area of the reinforcement steel is fixed.

Utilizing fibers to control shrinkage is another widely adopted method. By incorporating fibers into the concrete mix, shrinkage can be reduced owing to the restraining effect of the fibers. Additionally, the bonding between the concrete and fibers, known as the bridging effect of the fibers, allows for the control of shrinkage crack width. For early-age shrinkage crack control, polymeric fibers, such as polyvinyl alcohol, are commonly employed. In recent years, the use of shrinkage reducers, a type of chemical admixture comprising a blend of propylene glycol derivatives, has garnered increased attention for shrinkage control. Shrinkage-reducing admixtures (SRAs) were first invented in 1982 and later patented in 1985. Subsequent studies have demonstrated that SRAs can delay the onset of cracking by reducing free shrinkage and improve long-term drying shrinkage performance by up to 50%. Even in concrete with proper curing, where drying shrinkage is minimized, the effect of SRA still results in a substantial reduction in shrinkage. SRAs are also considered crucial in advanced cement-based materials like ultra-high-performance concrete (UHPC), where shrinkage is a critical issue hindering practical applications.

7.8.5 Creep of Concrete

Creep in concrete refers to the gradual increase in strain over time under sustained stress. Shrinkage and creep are considered simultaneous, with their effects assumed to be additive for simplicity. Upon removal of the sustained load, the strain immediately decreases by an amount equal to the elastic strain at that age. This instant recovery is followed by a gradual decrease in strain, known as creep recovery, which contributes to the total creep strain experienced by the concrete. Viewing a loaded concrete specimen as under constant strain, creep progressively reduces stress over time, a phenomenon termed relaxation.

The rate of creep diminishes over time, with creep strains typically reaching terminal values after five years. While around 80 to 85 percent of shrinkage strains occur within six months, only about 75 percent of creep strains develop within 12 months. Various factors influence both shrinkage and creep similarly. These include the types of aggregate, cement, and admixtures used, as well as entrained air, mix proportions, mixing time and consolidation, concrete age, sustained stress levels, ambient humidity, temperature, and specimen size.

7.9 DURABILITY

The durability of Portland cement concrete refers to its capacity to withstand various forms of deterioration, including weathering, chemical corrosion, abrasion, and other detrimental processes, while retaining its original form, quality, and functionality when subjected to its intended environment of use. Durability primarily concerns the long-term performance and functionality of concrete and concrete structures. Serviceability, in this context, denotes the ability of the structure to fulfill its designated functions even after being exposed to particular environmental conditions.

7.9.1 Factors Influencing Durability

Concrete deterioration can be classified into three main categories: physical, chemical, and mechanical causes. These factors often interact, either independently or in combination.

Physical causes encompass various forms of surface wear, such as abrasion, erosion, and cavitation, as well as the impact of high temperatures and disparities in thermal expansion between aggregates and hardened cement paste. Examples include the detrimental effects of freezing-thawing cycles and deicing salts, as well as cracking induced by volume changes, temperature differentials, salt crystallization in pores, structural loading, restrained shrinkage, and exposure to fire.

Chemical degradation typically arises from internal or external chemical attacks on the cement matrix. Portland cement, being alkaline, is susceptible to reaction with acids in the presence of moisture, leading to weakening of the matrix and leaching of its constituents. Common chemical causes of concrete durability issues include hydrolysis of cement paste, carbonation, cation-exchange reactions, and expansion reactions such as sulfate expansion, alkali-aggregate expansion, and steel corrosion.

Mechanical causes involve impact and excessive loading. Concrete deterioration usually results from a combination of environmental factors and structural loading. Common durability problems include corrosion of reinforcing steel, freeze/thaw damage often associated with salt scaling, alkali-aggregate reactions, and sulfate attack. These attacks typically initiate due to mass transfer and can lead to cracking and spalling of concrete structures.

7.9.2 Role of Water-Cement Ratio

The alteration in volume within concrete leads to the formation of cracks, which subsequently cause its disintegration. It is important to note that permeability plays a significant role in this volume change, with a higher water-cement ratio being the primary factor contributing to increased permeability. Thus, the use of a higher water-cement ratio initiates a cyclic process in concrete: higher water-cement ratio → increased permeability → volume change → formation of cracks → disintegration → concrete failure. Therefore, achieving durable concrete necessitates employing the lowest feasible water-cement ratio to produce a dense and impermeable concrete structure.

It is widely acknowledged that concrete with a low water-cement ratio exhibits a superior quality of hydration products (gel) and, consequently, a finer microstructure compared to concrete with a high water-cement ratio. In low water-cement ratio concretes, the interconnected network of capillaries is so fine that water cannot flow through them effectively, resulting in significantly reduced permeability, making these concretes almost impervious to water. Furthermore, the diffusion of chloride ions in low water-cement ratio concretes is notably slower, approximately 10 to 15 times slower than in high water-cement ratio concretes. Additionally, low water-cement ratio concretes exhibit lower sensitivity to carbonation, external chemical attacks, and other detrimental factors that compromise concrete durability. Employing a low water-cement ratio and ensuring adequate concrete cover provides the best protection against reinforcing steel corrosion.

The introduction and utilization of superplasticizers have transformed the production of durable concrete by substantially reducing the water-cement ratio. Currently, flowing or self-leveling concretes are being manufactured with water-cement ratios as low as 0.25 or even 0.20. This technological advancement, combined with the use of cementing mineral additives, has facilitated the production of highly durable high-performance concrete.

However, in low water-cement ratio concretes, there may not be sufficient water available to fully hydrate all cement particles, resulting in only surface hydration of cement particles and leaving a considerable amount of unhydrated cement grain cores. These unhydrated cores serve as reserve strength. If cracks develop due to structural or environmental factors, moisture or water penetrating through micro or macro-cracks causes the hydration of the unhydrated core. The hydration products formed seal the cracks and restore the concrete's integrity, ensuring long-term durability.

7.9.3 Permeability

The capillary pores within concrete act as conduits or a transport system for deteriorating agents. However, it is worth noting that in the initial stages, micro-cracks are so fine that they may not significantly increase permeability. Nevertheless, as time progresses, the propagation of these micro-cracks due to drying shrinkage, thermal shrinkage, and externally applied loads will enhance the permeability of the system.

The cement paste is comprised of C–S–H gel, $Ca(OH)_2$, and both water-filled and empty capillary voids. The gel possesses a porosity of approximately 28%, with a permeability around 7.5×10^{-16}, which is roughly one-thousandth of that of the cement paste. Consequently, the contribution of gel pores to the permeability of the cement paste is minimal. The size and quantity of capillary voids or pores are influenced by the water-cement ratio. Lower water-cement ratios result in fewer and finer capillary voids, which are rapidly filled within a few days by hydration products of cement. However, excessively large voids resulting from high water-cement ratios, around 0.7, may remain unfilled by hydration products and contribute to the permeability of the paste. Despite both cement paste and good-quality normal aggregates having very low coefficients of permeability, rendering them nearly impermeable, mortar and concrete still exhibit significant permeability. This increased permeability in mortar or concrete within actual structures is attributed to the formation of micro-cracks in the transition zone (due to shrinkage and thermal stresses), macro-cracks (due to volume changes and higher structural stresses), and the presence of entrapped air (due to insufficient compaction).

The incorporation of aggregates, especially larger sizes, significantly enhances permeability. As discussed earlier, this increase in permeability arises from the formation of micro-cracks in the vulnerable transition zone during the early stages. Reports indicate that the size of these cracks in the transition zone is notably larger than that of the capillary voids within the cement paste.

The permeability of pozzolanic cement pastes, initially higher compared to Ordinary Portland Cement (OPC), tends to decrease as curing progresses. During the first 7 to 15 days of cement hydration, only the clinker fraction is involved. Pozzolanic materials or fly ash gradually convert soluble and leachable $Ca(OH)_2$ into cementitious products at a slower rate, within an already established rigid pore structure. The resulting precipitation of cementitious product within the pores formed by clinker hydration may not completely fill the larger voids but effectively blocks smaller capillaries connecting these larger pores or reduces their openings significantly. Consequently, the porosity of pozzolanic cement pastes remains equal to or slightly higher than OPC, but their permeability decreases. Concrete containing cements with 35% fly ash has been observed to be two to five times less permeable than concrete made with OPC or blast-furnace-slag cements. Furthermore, concretes using pozzolanic cements exhibit a better flexural/compressive strength ratio and a reduced tendency to crack compared to those using OPC.

7.9.4 Factors Contributing to Durability Issues

Durability factors can be classified as either external or internal causes. External factors encompass physical, chemical, and mechanical influences and are further categorized as follows:

1. Environmental factors, including extreme temperature variations, abrasion, and electrostatic actions.
2. Chemical attacks from natural or industrial liquids and gases.

   Internal causes consist of:

   a. Alkali-aggregate reactions.
   b. Volume changes resulting from disparities in the thermal properties of the aggregate and cement paste.

Common types of chemical deterioration include:

i. Cement leaching
ii. Carbonation
iii. Chloride ion infiltration
iv. Sulfate erosion
v. Exposure to marine environments
vi. Natural slightly acidic water.

The resistance to these deterioration agents varies according to cement type, ranking as follows: Ordinary Portland Cement (OPC) and Rapid Hardening Cement (RHC) exhibit lower resistance, followed by Portland Blast Furnace Cement or Low Heat

Cement, and then Sulfate-Resistant Portland Cement, Pozzolanic Cement, and Super Sulfated Cement, in increasing order of resistance.

Chloride Ion Penetration

The presence of chloride ions in concrete can have detrimental effects on both the concrete itself and the reinforcement within it. Firstly, chloride ion penetration causes concrete to swell approximately 2 to 2.5 times more than observed with water penetration, resulting in a slight reduction in concrete strength. Secondly, when chloride ions are near the reinforcement steel, they make it susceptible to corrosion. If the ratio of hydroxide to chloride near the reinforcement steel falls below 0.3, passivation is disrupted, leading to inevitable corrosion. Thus, it is imperative to prevent chlorides from entering the concrete.

According to IS:456-2000 standards, the allowable chloride content in concrete, concerning reinforcement corrosion, is limited to acid-soluble chloride contents of 0.4 and 0.6 kg/m^3 of concrete in prestressed and reinforced concretes, respectively, at the time of concrete placement. Some of the chlorides present in the concrete materials can be chemically fixed through reactions with C_3A compound of Portland cement, forming calcium chloro-aluminate hydrate. This not only elucidates the favorable performance of Portland cement with high calcium aluminate content but also suggests such cements as a solution to the problem. It is not advisable to use sulfate-resisting cements in environments with excessive chlorides, as they have lower C_3A content and thus less capability to form calcium chloro-aluminate hydrate. Reducing the water-cement ratio, which decreases permeability and subsequently reduces chloride ion penetration into concrete, significantly prevents steel corrosion.

Using blended cements containing pozzolanic materials or slag is recommended, as the diffusion of chlorides through the pastes of these cements occurs at a significantly slower rate compared to Ordinary Portland Cement (OPC) and sulfate-resisting cements. Among these options, a cement with 65% slag content is considered most suitable, while sulfate-resisting cement is least suitable in chloride-rich environments. When pozzolanic materials are present, a content of 33% is deemed highly effective in reducing chloride diffusion into concrete. However, the replacement percentage of cement by pozzolana is limited to 25% according to IS: 1489-1991, and slag is restricted to 65% according to IS: 455-1989. Nevertheless, by incorporating pozzolana or slag as mineral additives, concrete with desirable performance can be achieved. Therefore, in extremely aggressive environments with high chloride concentrations, a higher percentage of such materials can be utilized.

Carbonation

Concrete is inherently alkaline, providing effective protection to embedded reinforcement. The alkaline environment facilitates the formation of a protective oxide film, passivating the steel and shielding it from corrosion. Initially, concrete exhibits a pH value ranging from approximately 12 to 13. However, due to factors such as leaching, carbonation, and subpar construction practices, the pH value decreases rapidly over time. Once the pH value of the concrete cover drops below 10, corrosion of steel reinforcement becomes inevitable, jeopardizing the durability of the concrete. This outcome is influenced by the concrete's quality and porosity, particularly in the cover area. Dense, high-quality concrete offers superior protection to embedded steel. Therefore, it is crucial to produce concrete with a low water- cement ratio to minimize unblocked capillary pores. Higher-strength concretes, which typically have lower water-cement ratios, are preferred.

Regarding the carbonation process, atmospheric carbon dioxide reacts with water on the concrete surface, resulting in carbonation, or the conversion of concrete to an acidic state. This chemical reaction commences at the surface and gradually progresses into the interior of the concrete mass, typically quantified as the depth of carbonation. Due to the lower stability of hydrated calcium silicates and aluminates compared to calcium carbonate, concrete carbonation is unavoidable. In cracked portions, carbonation penetrates deeper along the cracks, as illustrated in Fig. 7.28(a).

Carbonation of concrete yields various benefits to ordinary concrete properties but can also significantly impact the durability of reinforced concrete structures. When the concrete is dense and properly compacted, carbonation decreases total porosity, specific surface area of cement pastes, and water permeability. Consequently, this enhances resistance to sulfate and aggressive chloride ion penetration. However, in reinforced concrete, these positive effects are counterbalanced by a significant decrease in alkalinity or a drop in pH value.

Upon carbonation, the concrete's pH value decreases from approximately 13.5 to 8.3. As a result, the steel reinforcement loses its passivation by the alkaline concrete surrounding it. In the presence of moisture and oxygen, oxidation of the reinforcement steel occurs, leading to corrosion (rusting). This corrosion causes the volume of the steel to increase, ultimately resulting in cracking and spalling of the concrete.

Sulfate Attack

Sulfates are commonly present in groundwater, subsoil, and seawater, either naturally occurring or as a result of industrial waste disposal. They can pose a significant threat to concrete durability. Calcium, sodium, magnesium, and ammonium sulfates, in increasing order of hazard, can cause an increase in concrete volume and subsequent cracking. Calcium sulfate reacts with calcium aluminate in cement hydrates, forming expansive ettringite. Sodium sulfate reacts with calcium hydroxide to produce expansive gypsum in the presence of aluminates, potentially leading to ettringite formation. Magnesium sulfate reacts with cement compounds, decomposing the cement itself and generating gypsum and ettringite as byproducts.

Acid Attack

Concrete structures are frequently utilized for storing liquids, including those that can be detrimental to concrete integrity. In industrial settings, concrete floors often encounter liquids that cause damage, as depicted in Fig. 7.28(b). Additionally, in moist environments, exposure to sulfur dioxide (SO_2), carbon monoxide (CO), and other acidic fumes in the atmosphere can adversely affect concrete by dissolving and removing portions of the set cement. It's noteworthy that no type of Portland cement is resistant to acid. Furthermore, concrete is susceptible to degradation when exposed

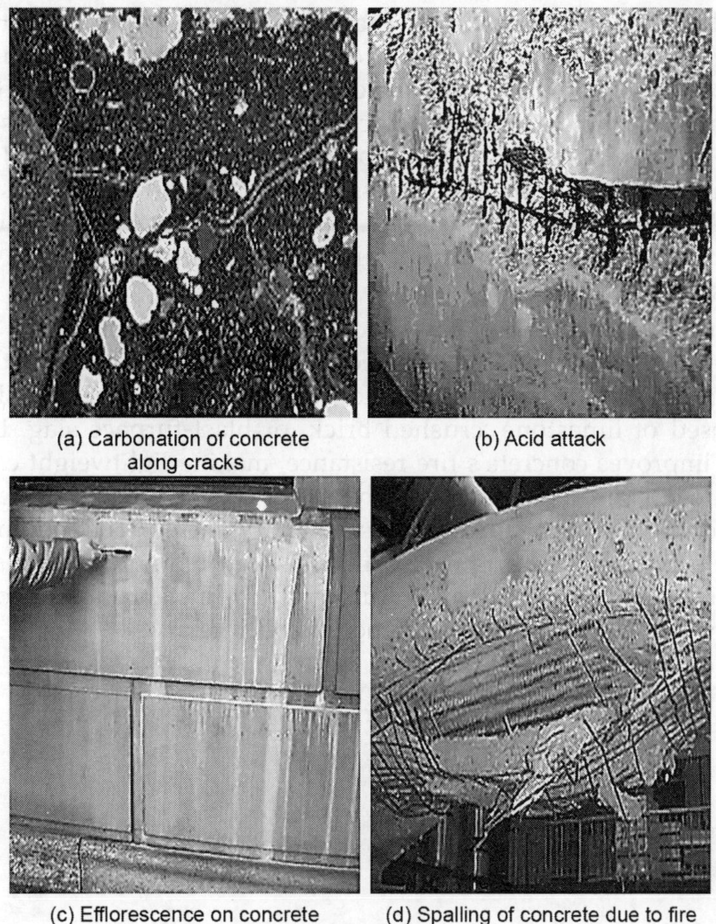

(a) Carbonation of concrete along cracks (b) Acid attack

(c) Efflorescence on concrete (d) Spalling of concrete due to fire

Fig. 7.28: Concrete deterioration

to water containing free CO_2, and even sewage water can gradually lead to concrete deterioration.

Efflorescence

Water seeping through cracks, faulty joints, or areas of poorly compacted porous concrete dissolves some of the readily soluble calcium hydroxide and other solids. Upon evaporation, this water leaves behind calcium carbonate deposits on the concrete surface, as depicted in Fig. 7.28(c). These deposits, resulting from the leaching of calcium hydroxide followed by carbonation and evaporation, are referred to as efflorescence. Efflorescence can also be caused by unwashed seashore aggregate, gypsum, and alkaline aggregate. Various types of salts have been identified in samples of efflorescence.

Fire Resistance

In general, concrete exhibits favorable properties in terms of fire resistance, characterized by a relatively high period of satisfactory performance under fire exposure without emitting toxic fumes. The duration during which structural concrete maintains its structural integrity under fire conditions is referred to as its fire rating. Prolonged exposure to temperatures exceeding 35°C, combined with significant moisture loss from concrete, results in decreased strength and modulus of elasticity. The decrease in strength at elevated temperatures is more pronounced in saturated concrete compared to dry concrete. Excessive moisture during a fire is the primary cause of spalling, as illustrated in Fig. 7.28(d). Generally, the moisture content of concrete is the most crucial factor influencing its structural behavior at high temperatures.

Leaner concrete mixes tend to experience relatively less strength loss compared to richer mixes. Flexural strength is more affected than compressive strength. The loss of strength is notably lower in concrete made with aggregates lacking silica, such as those composed of limestone, crushed brick, or blast-furnace slag. Low thermal conductivity improves concrete's fire resistance, making lightweight concrete more resistant to fire than ordinary concrete. The use of calcined material aggregates with low density contributes to enhanced fire resistance in concrete. The endothermic nature of carbonate aggregates during calcination at high temperatures results in heat absorption and delays further temperature rise. For instance, the incorporation of dolomite gravel enhances the fire resistance of concrete.

Concrete Mix Design

8.1 MIX DESIGN

The process of concrete mix design involves determining the selection and proportions of raw materials necessary to meet specific requirements, such as strength, durability, and workability. The desired characteristics of hardened concrete are typically set by the structural designer, while the properties of fresh concrete are influenced by construction methods, including placement and transportation techniques. These factors, alongside on-site construction expertise, guide the composition of the mix. Mix design entails selecting suitable ingredients and determining their relative quantities to produce an economical concrete with essential properties, including workability, strength, and durability. It is important to note that mix design often involves a trial-and-error approach, making it more of an art than a precise science. The variability of materials used and their inherent properties means that achieving an optimal mix is based on informed estimations rather than exact measurements. Consequently, to ensure an effective mix, trial batches are typically prepared and adjustments made as necessary until a satisfactory mix is achieved.

8.2 PRINCIPAL REQUIREMENTS FOR CONCRETE

The primary objective of mix design is to achieve a concrete product that meets predetermined requirements, encompassing various properties:

a. **Quality (strength and durability):** The strength and permeability of hydrated cement paste are interlinked, primarily controlled by the water-to-cement (w/c) ratio and hydration level. Durability, crucially affected by permeability, correlates with strength. Therefore, typical mix designs prioritize strength and workability. However, in scenarios where concrete faces specific environmental conditions, factors ensuring durability, such as w/c ratio limits, minimum cement content, and adequate reinforcement cover, are also considered.

b. **Workability:** Workability in fresh concrete is multifaceted, involving properties like consistency and cohesiveness. While no single test fully captures workability, the slump test, assessing the concrete's flow during placement, is commonly used due to its simplicity and quantifiability. Occasionally, the Vee-Bee test may be utilized as well.

c. **Economy:** Admixtures carry the highest unit cost among concrete constituents, followed by cement, with aggregates being considerably more cost-effective. Admixtures are often employed in minimal quantities for specific properties. To minimize costs, efforts focus on reducing cement content without compromising desired properties like strength and durability.

Furthermore, potential cost savings can be achieved by substituting a portion of Portland cement with more economical alternatives such as fly ash or ground blast-furnace slag.

Under normal conditions, considering workability and strength suffices for concrete design. However, for specialized situations, additional factors like dimensional stability and enhanced durability must be factored into the design process.

8.3 WEIGHT METHOD AND ABSOLUTE VOLUME METHOD

Concrete mix design can be approached through two methods: the weight method and the absolute volume method. In the weight method, the unit weight of fresh concrete is typically derived from past experience with commonly used raw materials. This known unit weight is then utilized to calculate the weight of the final unknown component of concrete, often the sand. If the unit weight of fresh concrete (wet concrete) is established, the calculation proceeds as follows:

$$W_{\text{wet concrete}} = W_{\text{cement}} + W_{\text{water}} + W_{\text{aggregate}} + W_{\text{sand}} + W_{\text{admixture}}$$

Once the weights of cement, water, coarse aggregate, and admixtures are established, the weight of sand can be calculated using the provided equation. Typically, the unit weight of wet concrete falls within the range of 2300 to 2400 kg/m^3.

In the absolute volume method, the total volume (1 m^3) equals the sum of the volume of each ingredient, including water, air, cement, and coarse aggregate. Hence, the equation is formulated as follows:

$$\frac{W_{\text{cement}}}{\rho_{\text{cement}}} + \frac{W_{\text{water}}}{\rho_{\text{water}}} + \frac{W_{\text{aggregate}}}{\rho_{\text{aggregate}}} + \frac{W_{\text{sand}}}{\rho_{\text{sand}}} + \frac{W_{\text{admixture}}}{\rho_{\text{admixture}}} + \text{Volume\% (air)} = 1$$

Once the weights of cement, water, coarse aggregate, and admixture are established, their respective volumes can be computed, given their known densities. Utilizing the determined air volume during concrete mix design, the volume of sand—typically the final unknown component—can be calculated using the provided equation. Since measuring the weight of each ingredient is typically more straightforward than measuring volume, concrete design proportions are commonly expressed as weight ratios. Therefore, proportions derived from the volume method must be converted to weight units by multiplying the volume by the material's density.

8.4 FACTORS TO BE CONSIDERED IN CONCRETE MIX DESIGN

In preceding sections, a thorough examination of the diverse factors impacting concrete properties has been provided. This section delves into the technical and economic considerations crucial in concrete mix design. Primarily, the anticipated concrete strength must be prioritized, typically stipulated by the structural designer.

While the strength at 28 days commonly serves as the design benchmark for structural applications, other factors such as formwork demolding time may necessitate considering strength at different ages. Employing quality-control measures aids in minimizing strength variability, ensuring attainment of the projected strength.

Presently, a significant portion of concrete is procured from commercial concrete suppliers. In these pre-designed mixes, adherence to specifications encompassing various properties is imperative. These specifications often include parameters, such as maximum water/cement ratio, minimum cement content, anticipated strength, desired workability, maximum aggregate size, and air content.

8.4.1 Water/Cement Ratio

While the water/cement (w/c) ratio can be estimated using Abram's law based on the projected concrete strength, in concrete design, the w/c ratio necessary to achieve a specified mean compressive strength is typically determined from established relationships derived from similar ingredient mixes or through trial mixes with actual ingredients, including admixtures. These relationships are often synthesized into tables or graphs for easy reference, such as Tables 8.1 and 8.2 provided as examples. These tables can serve as initial estimates for the w/c ratio for the listed cements.

Table 8.1: Relation between w/c and average compressive strength of concrete according to ACI 211.1-91

Average compressive strength at 28 days (MPa)	*Effective water/cement ratio (by mass)*	
	Non-air-entrained concrete	*Air-entrained concrete*
45	0.38	–
40	0.42	–
35	0.47	0.39
30	0.54	0.45
25	0.61	0.52
20	0.69	0.60
15	0.79	0.70

Table 8.2: Relation between w/c and specified compressive strength of concrete according to ACI 318-83

Specific compressive strength at 28 days (MPa)	*Absolute water/cement ratio (by mass)*	
	Non-air-entrained concrete	*Air-entrained concrete*
30	0.40	–
25	0.50	0.39
20	0.60	0.49
17	0.66	0.54

It is essential to ensure that the w/c ratio chosen based on strength considerations also meets durability requirements. Additionally, establishing this w/c ratio for durability should precede structural design commencement to leverage the advantages of higher concrete strength in design calculations if necessary.

When supplementary cementitious materials are utilized in concrete, the water/binder ratio by mass becomes significant. The water/binder ratio is equated to the w/c ratio of a Portland cement mix. In the mass method, the water/binder ratio equals the w/c ratio of the Portland cement-only mix. Conversely, in the absolute volume method, because supplementary cementitious materials typically have a lower specific gravity than Portland cement, the volume replaced by these materials exceeds that of Portland cement. Consequently, in the volume method, the mass of the cementitious material is smaller than that of the cement in the Portland cement-only mix, resulting in a higher water/cementitious material ratio than in the Portland cement-only mix. Regardless of the approach used, partial cement replacement by pozzolans generally reduces early-age strength.

8.4.2 Durability

Stringent control of the water/cement (w/c) ratio is imperative in severe exposure conditions, as it significantly influences the permeability and diffusivity of cement paste and, consequently, the resulting concrete. Moreover, adequate cover for embedded reinforcing steel is essential. However, the w/c ratio can be indirectly assessed through factors, such as mix workability, cement content, and strength. If the w/c ratio is determined based on durability requirements, cement content can be reduced by using larger-size aggregates.

The requirements for the water/binder ratio and minimum cover thickness for reinforced concrete by ACI 318-83 are provided in Tables 8.3 and 8.4. It is important to note that air entrainment is essential in conditions involving freezing and thawing or exposure to deicing salts, as shown in Table 8.5. However, entrained air does not protect concrete containing coarse aggregates that undergo disruptive volume changes when frozen in a saturated condition.

Table 8.3: Requirements of ACI 318-83 for water/cement ratio and strength for special exposure conditions

Exposure condition	*Maximum water/ cement ratio, normal-density aggregate concrete*	*Minimum design strength in MPa, low-density aggregate concrete*
Concrete intended to be watertight		
Exposure to fresh water	0.50	25
Exposed to brackish or seawater	0.45	30
Concrete exposed to freezing and thawing in a moist condition		
Curbs, gutters, guardrails, or thin sections	0.45	30
Other elements	0.50	25
In presence of deicing chemicals	0.45	30
For corrosion protection of reinforced concrete exposed to deicing salts, brackish water, seawater, or spray from these sources	0.40[a]	33[a]

[a] If minimum cover required in Table 8.4 is increased by 10 mm, water/cement ratio may be increased to 0.45 for normal density concrete or design strength reduced to 30MPa for low-density concrete.

Table 8.4: Requirements of ACI 318-83 for minimum cover for protection of reinforcement

Exposure condition	*Minimum cover in mm*		
	Reinforced concrete cast in suit	*Precast concrete*	*Prestressed concrete*
Concrete cast against, or permeability exposed to earth	70	–	70
Concrete exposed to earth or weather			
Wall panels	40–50	20–40	30
Slabs and joists	40–50	–	30
Other members	40–50	30–50	40
Concrete not exposed to weather or in contact with earth			
Slabs, walls, joists	20–40	15–30	20
Beams, columns	40	10–40	20–40
Shells, folded plate members	15–20	10–15	10
Nonprestressed reinforcement	–	–	20
Concrete exposed to deicing slats, brackish water, seawater, or spray from these sources			
Walls and slabs	50	40	–
Other members	60	50	–

Table 8.5: Recommended air content of concretes containing aggregates of different maximum size, according to ACI 201.2R-77

Maximum size of aggregate (mm)	*Recommended total air content of concrete (%) for level of exposure*	
	Moderate	*Severe*
10	6.0	7.5
12.5	5.5	7.0
20	5.0	6.0
25	4.5	6.0
40	4.5	5.5
50	4.0	5.0
70	3.5	4.5
150	3.0	4.0

8.4.3 Workability

As previously discussed, concrete workability encompasses two key aspects: flowability and cohesiveness. Determining workability involves considering two main factors: the geometry of the member to be cast, including cross-sectional size and reinforcement spacing, and the compaction method, including the type of compaction equipment and duration of consolidation.

When dealing with narrow or intricate cross-sections for casting, concrete must exhibit high fluidity to ensure complete compaction. Similarly, when facing complex shapes, achieving full compaction becomes more challenging. Therefore, selecting appropriate compaction equipment, such as plate-type or poker-type vibrators, and determining the duration of compaction are vital to ensure thorough consolidation throughout construction. Guidance on workability for various construction types is provided in Tables 8.6 and 8.7.

Table 8.6: Workability, slump, and compacting factor of concretes with 19 or 38 mm maximum size of aggregate

Degree of workability	*Slump*		*Compacting factor*	*Use for which concrete is suitable*
	mm	*inch*		
Very low	0–25	0–1	0.78	Roads vibrated by power-operated machines. At the more workable end of this group, concrete may be compacted in certain cases with hand-operated machines
Low	25–50	1–2	0.85	Roads vibrated by hand-operated machines. At the more workable end of this group, concrete may be manually compacted in roads using aggregate of rounded or irregular shape. Mass concrete foundations without vibrated or lightly reinforced sections with vibration
Medium	25–100	2–4	0.92	At the less workable end of this group, manually compacted flat slabs using crushed aggregate. Normal reinforced concrete manually compacted and heavily reinforced sections with vibration
High	100–175	4–7	0.95	For sections with congested reinforcement. Not normally suitable for vibration

Table 8.7: Recommended values of slump for various types of construction as given by ACI 211.1-91

Types of construction	*Range of slump**	
	(mm)	*(inch)*
Reinforced foundation walls and footings	25–75	1–3
Plain footings, caissons and substructure walls	25–75	1–3
Beams and reinforced walls	25–100	1–4
Building columns	25–100	1–4
Pavements and slabs	25–75	1–3
Mass concrete	25–75	1–2

* The upper limit of slump may be increased by 20 mm for compaction by hand

Once the desired workability is determined, estimating the water content of the mix (mass of water per unit volume of concrete) becomes possible by considering the workability requirement. Water content values for different maximum aggregate sizes and slump values (indicating workability), with and without air entrainment (Table 8.8). These values are applicable for well-shaped coarse aggregates, and although water requirement can be influenced by aggregate texture and shape, the provided values offer sufficiently accurate initial estimates.

8.4.4 Cement Type and Content

The selection of cement types is contingent upon several factors, including the required hydration rate and strength development, susceptibility to chemical attack, and thermal considerations. While these factors have been previously discussed, it is worth emphasizing the necessity of choosing a cement with a high rate of heat of hydration for cold-weather concreting, and conversely, a low rate of heat of hydration for mass concreting. Additionally, in hot weather conditions, employing a lower water/cement ratio may be essential to achieve satisfactory early-age strength. Given that cement is typically more costly than aggregate, it is preferable to minimize the cement content as much as possible, provided it can satisfy the strength, durability, and workability requirements.

Furthermore, maintaining a low to moderate cement content provides the technical advantage of reducing hydration heat and minimizing the potential for cracking. This is particularly important in mass concrete, where controlling hydration heat is crucial, and in structural concrete, where minimizing shrinkage cracks is essential. Technically, the cement content is derived from the water/binder ratio and the mixing water requirement determined by the desired workability. However, the cement content must also meet the minimum requirement specified for durability considerations.

Table 8.8: Approximate requirement for mixing water and air content for different workabilities and nominal maximum sizes of aggregates, according to ACI 211.1-91

Workability or air content	*Water content (kg/m^3) of concrete for indicated maximum aggregate size in mm*							
	9.5	*12.5*	*19*	*25*	*37.5*	*50*	*75*	*150*
	Non-air entrained concrete							
Slump								
25–50 mm	207	199	190	179	166	154	130	113
75–100 mm	228	216	205	193	181	169	145	124
150–175 mm	243	228	216	202	190	178	160	–
Approximate entrapped air content (%)	3	2.5	2	1.5	1	0.5	0.3	0.2
	Air-entrained concrete							
Slump								
25–50 mm	181	175	168	160	150	142	122	107
75–100 mm	202	193	184	175	165	157	133	119
150–175 mm	216	205	197	184	174	166	154	–
Recommended average total air content (%)								
Mild exposure	4.5	4.0	3.5	3.0	2.5	2.0	1.5[a]	1.0[a]
Moderate exposure	6.0	5.5	5.0	4.5	4.5	4.0	3.5[a]	3.0[a]
Extreme exposure[b]	7.5	7.0	6.0	6.0	5.5	5.0	4.5[a]	4.0[a]

[a] For concrete containing large aggregate which will be wet-screened over 40 mm sieve prior to testing of air content, the percentage of air expected in the material smaller than 40 mm should be as tabulated in the 40 mm column. However, initial proportioning calculations should be based on the air content as a percentage of the whole mix

[b] These values are based on the criterion that a 9% air content is needed in the mortar of concrete

Notes: Slump values for concrete containing aggregate larger than 40 mm are based on slump test made after removal of particles larger than 40 mm by wet-screening.

Water contents for nominal maximum size of aggregate of 75 mm and 150 mm are average values for reasonable well-shaped coarse aggregates, well graded from coarse to fine.

8.4.5 Major Aggregate Properties and Aggregate Content

In the design of concrete, the determination of aggregate size takes precedence as it significantly influences concrete properties. In reinforced concrete structures, the maximum aggregate size is dictated by the member geometry and reinforcement spacing. Typically, the maximum aggregate size should be smaller than 1/4 to 1/5 of the smallest dimension of the member and 3/4 of the net spacing distance of reinforcement. While it is generally desirable to use as large a maximum aggregate size as possible, the benefits in concrete properties plateau beyond approximately 40 mm. For high-strength concrete, the maximum aggregate size is often limited to 20 mm. However, in mass concrete applications such as dam construction, larger maximum aggregate sizes, extending to a few hundred millimeters, may be suitable. Factors influencing the choice of maximum aggregate size may also include material availability and cost considerations. For example, when various sizes are screened from a pit, it is generally preferable not to reject the largest size, provided it meets acceptable technical criteria.

Another crucial aspect of aggregate is its grading. In all scenarios, dense-graded or well-graded aggregate is preferred, with a focus on achieving uniformity. When dealing with coarse aggregate, uniformity can be relatively easier to achieve by utilizing separate stockpiles for each size fraction. For mass concrete projects with a maximum aggregate size larger than 40 mm, combining coarse aggregate fractions to maximize density and minimize voids. However, when it comes to fine aggregate, maintaining uniform grading is essential. Fine aggregate, often sourced directly from riverbeds, can vary significantly from one location to another. This becomes particularly crucial when the water content of the mix is controlled by the mixer operator based on consistent workability. A sudden shift towards finer grading necessitates additional water to preserve workability, resulting in lower strength of the batch. Moreover, an excess of fine aggregate may hinder full compaction, leading to a decrease in strength.

Table 8.9 provides the idealized combined grading for nominal maximum aggregate sizes of 150 mm and 75 mm. To illustrate the proportioning of crushed coarse aggregate fractions to achieve the ideal combined grading as shown in the first column of Table 8.9, consider four size fractions: 150 to 75 mm, 75 to 37.5 mm, 37.5 to 19 mm, and 19 to 4.76 mm. The gradings of these fractions are detailed in Table 8.10. In concrete mix design, determining the aggregate content is a critical process. Since aggregate typically occupies 65% to 75% of the total volume of concrete, it significantly influences concrete properties and costs.

Table 8.9: 'Ideal' combined grading for coarse aggregate of nominal maximum size of 150 and 75 mm

Sieve size (mm)	*Cumulative percentage passing for nominal size of aggregate in mm*			
	150 mm		*75 mm*	
	Crushed	*Rounded*	*Crushed*	*Rounded*
150	100	100	–	–
125	85	89	–	–
100	70	78	–	–
75	55	64	100	100
50	38	49	69	75
37.5	28	39	52	61
25	19	28	34	44
19	13	21	25	33
9.5	5	9	9	14

Table 8.10: Example of grading of individual coarse aggregate fractions to be combined into an "ideal" grading for mass concrete

Sieve size (mm)	*Cumulative percentage passing for fraction (%)*			
	150–75 mm	*75–37.5 mm*	*37.5–19 mm*	*19–4.76 mm*
175	100	–	–	–
150	98	–	–	–
100	30	100	–	–
75	10	92	–	–
50	2	30	100	–
37.5	0	6	94	–
25	0	4	36	100
19	0	0	4	92
9.5	0	0	2	30
4.76	0	0	0	2

Decisions regarding aggregate content in a concrete mix design involve determining the total aggregate-to-binder ratio and the fine aggregate-to-coarse aggregate ratio. Table 8.11 offers the dry bulk volume of coarse aggregate per unit volume of concrete, which is dependent on both the fineness modulus of the fine aggregate and the maximum size of the aggregate. Subsequently, the mass of the coarse aggregate can be computed by multiplying the dry bulk volume by the density (or unit weight) of the dry coarse aggregate.

Table 8.11: Dry bulk volume of coarse aggregate per unit volume of concrete as given by ACI 211.1-91

Maximum size of aggregate (mm)	*Dry bulk volume of rodded coarse aggregate per unit volume of concrete for different fineness modulus of sand*			
	2.40	2.60	2.80	3.00
9.5	0.50	0.48	0.46	0.44
12.5	0.59	0.57	0.55	0.53
19	0.66	0.64	0.62	0.60
25	0.71	0.69	0.67	0.65
37.5	0.75	0.73	0.71	0.69
50	0.78	0.76	0.74	0.72
75	0.82	0.80	0.78	0.76
150	0.87	0.85	0.83	0.81

The estimation of fine aggregate content per unit volume of concrete can be achieved through either the mass method or the volume method. In the mass method, the mass of cement, coarse aggregate, and water is subtracted from the mass of a unit volume of concrete, often determined from previous experience with the materials used. Alternatively, in the absence of such data, Table 8.12 can serve as an initial estimate, with adjustments made based on trial mixes.

A more precise estimate can obtained from the following equation:

$$\rho = 10\gamma_a(100 - A) + C\left(1 - \frac{\gamma_a}{\gamma}\right) - W(\gamma_a - 1)\ (\text{kg/m}^3)$$

Table 8.12: First estimate of density (unit weight) of fresh concrete as given by ACI 211.1-81

Maximum size of aggregate (mm)	*First estimate of density (unit weight) of fresh concrete (kg/m³)*	
	Non-air entrained	*Air entrained*
9.5	2280	2200
12.5	2310	2230
19	2345	2275
25	2380	2290
37.5	2410	2350
50	2445	2345
75	2490	2405
150	2530	2435

where

ρ = density (unit weight) of fresh concrete, kg/m^3

γ_a= weighted average bulk specific gravity (SSD) of combined fine and coarse aggregate; clearly, this needs to be determined from tests

A = air content, %

C = cement content, kg/m^3

γ = specific gravity of cement

W = mixing water requirement, kg/m^3

The volume method is an exact procedure for calculating the required amount of fine aggregate. Here, the mass of fine aggregate, A_f, is given by:

$$A_f = \gamma_f \left[1000 - \left(W + \frac{C}{\lambda} + \frac{A_c}{\gamma_c} + 10A\right)\right] (\text{kg/m}^3)$$

where

A_c = coarse aggregate content, kg/m^3

γ_f = SSD of fine aggregate

γ_c = SSD of coarse aggregate

8.5 APPROACHES FOR CONCRETE MIX DESIGN

Numerous approaches to concrete design have been proposed, broadly classified into three main categories: prescriptive method, statistical method, and close-packing-based method.

8.5.1 Prescriptive Method

The process of traditional concrete mixture design involves determining mixture proportions through either prescriptive or performance-based design methods. Here, the method proposed by American Concrete Institute (ACI 211.1-91) is introduced. Prior to commencing concrete mix design, it is essential to gather fundamental information regarding raw materials and background data, which includes:

a. Results of sieve analysis and fineness modulus of fine and coarse aggregate
b. Dry-rodded density (unit weight) of coarse aggregate
c. Bulk specific gravity of each raw material
d. Absorption capacity or moisture content of the aggregates
e. Variations in the approximate mixing water requirement concerning slump, air content, and grading of available aggregates
f. Correlations between strength and water/cement ratio for different combinations of cement and aggregate
g. Job specifications, if applicable, such as maximum water/cement ratio, minimum air content, minimum slump, maximum aggregate size, and desired strength at early ages (typically, 28-day compressive strength is specified).

Regardless of whether concrete characteristics are specified or left to the discretion of the mix designer, batch weights in kilograms per cubic meter of concrete can be calculated through the following steps:

Step 1: *Selection of slump.* If not specified, an appropriate slump value for the particular work can be chosen from Table 8.7 based on the type of structure.

Step 2: *Determination of maximum aggregate size.* For a given volume of coarse aggregate, using a larger maximum size of well-graded aggregate results in less void space, reducing the mortar requirement in a unit volume of concrete. The largest economically available size should be selected, ensuring it meets general requirements regarding form dimensions, slab depth, and spacing between reinforcing bars.

Step 3: *Estimation of mixing water and air content.* The amount of water per unit volume of concrete required for a given slump value depends on aggregate characteristics and air content. In the absence of specific data, an estimate of mixing water, with or without air entrainment, can be obtained from Table 8.8 for trial batches.

Step 4: *Selection of water/cement ratio.* The relationship between strength and water/cement ratio for the materials to be used should ideally be established. In the absence of such data, conservative values can be selected from Table 8.1. The chosen ratio should meet both strength and durability criteria.

Step 5: *Calculation of cement content.* The required cement content is determined by dividing the mixing water content obtained in step 3 by the water/cement ratio determined in step 4.

Step 6: *Estimation of coarse aggregate content.* To minimize concrete costs, aggregates should be maximized. For properly graded materials, statistics show that finer sand and larger coarse aggregate particles allow for a higher volume of coarse aggregate in a concrete mixture with satisfactory workability. Table 8.11 illustrates that the volume of coarse aggregate in a unit volume of concrete depends on its maximum size and the fineness modulus of the fine aggregate. Differences in mortar requirements due to particle shape and grading are compensated for automatically by variations in dry-rodded void content.

Step 7: *Determination of fine aggregate content.* After completing step 6, all concrete ingredients have been estimated except for the fine aggregate. The quantity of fine aggregate can be calculated using either the weight method or the volume method.

In accordance with the weight method, if the unit weight of wet fresh concrete is available based on past experiences, the necessary weight of fine aggregate can be calculated as the variance between the unit weight of concrete and the combined weight of water, cement, and coarse aggregate. In instances where a reliable estimate of the unit weight of concrete is unavailable, Table 8.12 serves as a reference to select the unit weight of fresh concrete. It has been observed that even a rough approximation of the unit weight suffices for generating trial concrete.

$$U_m = 10G_a(100 - \overline{A}) + C_m\left(1 - \frac{G_a}{G_c}\right) - W_m(G_a - 1)\,\text{kg/m}^3$$

where

U_m = weight of fresh concrete, kg/m^3

G_a = weighted average SSD of combined fine aggregate and coarse aggregate, assuming reasonable weight proportions

G_c = specific gravity of cement

A = air content, %

W_m = mixing water content, kg/m^3

C_m = cement content, kg/m^3

In the absolute volume method, the volume occupied by the known ingredients (water, air, cement, and coarse aggregate) is deducted from the unit volume of concrete to determine the necessary volume of fine aggregate. Subsequently, this volume is converted into weight units by multiplying it by the density of fine aggregates.

Step 8: *Adjustment of free water content.* The mix proportions determined through steps 1 to 7 presume that aggregates are in a saturated surface dry (SSD) condition. However, stock aggregates typically aren't in a balanced state and may be either air-dry or wet, affecting their ability to absorb or release water during the mixing process. Additionally, the use of liquid admixtures introduces extra water into the mix. Failure to consider water from these sources when adjusting mixing water can lead to inaccuracies in the actual water/cement ratio of the trial mix. Therefore, it is crucial to accurately calculate the moisture content of aggregates and the additional water from liquid admixtures, and subsequently adjust the amount of mixing water accordingly. Detailed procedures for this adjustment will be illustrated in the sample computations.

Step 9: *Trial mixes.* Laboratory trials are essential due to the numerous assumptions made in the preceding theoretical calculations. These trials involve conducting small batches (e.g. 0.02 m^3 or 50 kg of concrete) to check and adjust the mix proportions for actual concrete. Fresh concrete should undergo testing for slump, cohesiveness, finishing properties, air content, and unit weight. Hardened concrete specimens, cured under standard conditions, should be tested for strength at specified ages. If any property fails to meet the design requirements, adjustments to the mix proportions are necessary. For instance:

a. Inadequate slump can be rectified by adjusting the estimated water content, increasing or decreasing it by 6 kg/m^3 for every 25 mm increase or decrease in slump.

b. If the desired air content is not achieved, the dosage of air-entraining admixture should be adjusted accordingly. The water content is then adjusted by 3 kg/m³ for each 1% decrease or increase in air content.

c. If the estimated density of fresh concrete by the mass method is not achieved and is significant, mix proportions should be adjusted, considering any changes in air content.

d. If projected strength cannot be met, the water-to-binder ratio should be reduced by 0.05 for every 5 MPa shortfall.

Step 10: *Adjustment of mix proportions:* Following multiple trial runs, upon achieving a mixture that meets the desired standards for workability and strength, the mix proportions determined from the laboratory-scale trial batch can be finalized and scaled up for the production of larger quantities in field batches.

Example I: Concrete Mix Design

Concrete is needed for a column expected to be moderately exposed to freezing and thawing. The column has a cross-section measuring 300 × 300 mm, with the smallest spacing between reinforcing steel set at 30 mm. The specified compressive strength of the concrete at 28 days is 40 MPa, with a desired slump range of 80 to 100 mm. The material properties are outlined as follows:

a. The cement utilized is Portland cement, possessing a specific gravity of 3.15.

b. Available coarse aggregate features a maximum size of 20 mm, a dry-rodded unit weight of 1600 kg/m^3, a SSD of 2.68, an absorption capacity of 0.5%, and a moisture content (OD) of 0.25%.

c. Fine aggregate boasts a SSD of 2.65, an absorption capacity of 1.3%, a moisture content (SSD) of 3%, and a fineness modulus of 2.60. The aggregates conform to the ASTM C33-84 requirements for grading.

With the provided data, the concrete mix design process will be meticulously executed following the prescribed steps.

Step 1: *Slump selection*: The specified slump aligns with Table 8.7, ensuring consistency.

Step 2: *Determination of maximum aggregate size*: The maximum aggregate size of 20 mm conforms to the prescribed limitations of 1/5 of the minimum dimension between forms and 3/4 of the minimum clear space.

Step 3: *Estimation of mixing water and air content*: As the concrete will face freezing and thawing conditions, air entrainment is essential. Following Table 8.8, the recommended mixing water quantity is 180 kg/m^3, with a suggested air content of 5.0% for moderate exposure.

Step 4: *Water/cement ratio (w/c)*: Referring to both Table 3.1 and Table 8.3, the estimated w/c ratio necessary to achieve a 28-day compressive strength of 40 MPa is 0.35.

Step 5: *Determination of cement content*: Based on steps 3 and 4, the required cement content amounts to 180/0.35 = 514 kg/m^3.

Step 6: *Assessment of coarse aggregate content*: Referring to Table 8.11 for a fine aggregate fineness modulus of 2.60, the volume of dry-rodded coarse aggregate per unit volume of concrete is determined to be 0.64. Consequently, 0.64m^3 of coarse aggregate will be present per unit volume of concrete. Therefore, the oven-dry weight of the coarse aggregate equals 0.64 × 1600 = 1.024 kg. Subsequently, the weight at saturated-surface-dry (SSD) condition is calculated as 1024 × 1.005 = 1029 kg.

Step 7: *Assessment of fine aggregate content*: The fine aggregate content can be estimated using either the weight method or the volume method.

a. **Weight method:** Referring to Table 8.12, the estimated concrete weight is 2280 kg/m^3.

$$U_m = (10)(2.67)(100-5) + 514(1-2.67/3.15) - 180(2.67-1)$$
$$= 2314 \text{ kg/m}^3$$

Using the previously calculated weights of water, cement, and coarse aggregate, the SSD weight of the fine aggregate can be determined as follows:

$$2314 - 180 - 514 - 1{,}029 = 591 \text{ kg}$$

b. **Volume method:** Utilizing the known weights and specific gravities of water, cement, and coarse aggregate, along with the air volume, the volumes occupied by each constituent per cubic meter can be obtained as follows:

$$\text{Water} = \frac{180}{1000} = 0.180 \text{ m}^3$$

$$\text{Cement} = \frac{514}{1000 \times 3.15} = 0.163 \text{ m}^3$$

$$\text{Coarse aggregate (SSD)} = \frac{1029}{1000 \times 2.68} = 0.384 \text{ m}^3$$

$$\text{Air} = 0.05 \text{ m}^3$$

Therefore, the fine aggregate must occupy a volume of 1 – (0.180 + 0.163 + 0.384 + 0.05) = 0.223 m^3. The required SSD weight of the fine aggregate is 0.223 × 2.65 × 1000 = 591 kg.

Step 8: *Adjustment for aggregate moisture*: Given that the aggregates will not be in either SSD or OD condition in the field, it is crucial to adjust the aggregate weights to account for the water content present in the aggregates. Since absorbed water does not contribute to the mix water, only surface water needs to be taken into account. With the provided moisture contents, the aggregate weights become:

Coarse aggregate (stock): From

$$W\text{ (stock)} = W\text{ (OD)} [1 + MC(OD)]$$

Get: $W\text{ (stock)} = 1024 \times 1.0025 = 1026 \text{ kg}$

The extra water needed for coarse aggregate absorption is:

$$W\text{ (SSD)} - W\text{ (stock)} = 1029 - 1026 = 3 \text{ kg}$$

Fine aggregate (stock): 591 × 1.03 = 609 kg/m^3

Extra water provided by fine aggregate: 609 – 591 = 18 kg

The mixing water is then: 180 + 3 – 18 = 165 kg

Thus, the estimated batch weights per m^3 are as follows: water, 165 kg; cement, 514 kg; coarse aggregate, 1026 kg; fine aggregate, 609 kg; total, 2314 kg.

Step 9: *Trial mixing*: It is essential to conduct trial mixes using the calculated proportions. The concrete properties in the trial mix should be compared against the desired properties, and adjustments to the mix design must be made accordingly, as outlined.

Example II: Raw Material Calculation for a Given Concrete Mix Ratio

A concrete mix has a proportion of 1:0.4:1.8:2.5 (P:W:S:A). In the powder content, 90% is Portland cement and 10% is solid silica fume (SF). The concrete also uses 0.25% retarder and 1.5% superplasticizer. The absorption for sand is 1.2% and for aggregate is 0.9%. The MC (OD) is 2.5% for sand and 0.4% for coarse aggregate. The solid content is 35% in retarder and 40% in superplasticizer. The SF used is a slurry with 50% of water. To cast 5 beams (100 × 100 × 500 mm) and 18 cylinders (100 × 200 mm), how much of each individual ingredient should be used (consider 5% extra amount)?

Solution

1. The total volume of concrete specimen is

$$5 \times 0.1 \times 0.1 \times 0.5 + 18 \times 3.14159 \times (0.1/2)^2 \times 0.2 = 0.053274 \text{ m}^3$$

2. The total weight is (assuming the unit weight of concrete is 2400 kg/m³)

$$2400 \times 0.053274 \times (1 + 0.05) = 134.2492 \text{ kg}$$

(Note that P:W:S:A refers to the SSD states)

3. The weight of cement and SF is:

$$W_{C+SF} = 134.2492/(1 + 0.4 + 1.8 + 2.5 + 0.0025 + 0.015)$$
$$= 23.480 \text{ kg}$$
$$W_C = 23.48 \times 0.9 = 21.132 \text{ kg}$$

4. For sand $W_{SSD} = 1.8 \times 23.480 = 42.265$ kg

Absorption capability (AB) $= (W_{SSD} - W_{OD})/W_{OD}$

MC (OD) $= (W_{stock} - W_{OD})/W_{OD}$

So $W_{stock}/W_{SSD} = [1 + \text{MC (OD)}]/(1 + \text{AB})$

Thus $W_{stock} = (1 + 0.025)/(1 + 0.012) \times 42.265 = 42.808$ kg

Water provided by sand $= 42.808 - 42.265 = 0.543$ kg

5. For aggregate $W_{SSD} = 2.5 \times 23.48 = 58.701$ kg

$W_{stock} = (1 + 0.004)/(1 + 0.009) \times 58.701 = 58.410$ kg

Water required by aggregate $= 58.410 - 58.701 = -0.291$ kg

6. For tetarder $W_{solid} = 0.0025 \times 23.48 = 0.059$ kg

$W_{solution} = 0.059/0.035 = 0.168$ kg

Water provided by retarder solution

$= 0.168 - 0.059 = 0.109$ kg

7. For superplasticizer $W_{solid} = 0.015 \times 23.48 = 0.352$ kg

$W_{solution} = 0.352/0.4 = 0.881$ kg

Water provided by superplasticizer solution $= 0.881 - 0.352 = 0.528$ kg

8. For SF $W_{solid} = 0.1 \times 23.48 = 2.348$ kg

$W_{solution} = 2.348/0.5 = 4.696$

Water provided by superplasticizer solution $= 4.696 - 2.348 = 2.348$ kg

9. For water $\text{Water} = 0.4 \times 23.48 - (0.543 - 0.291 + 0.109 + 0.528 + 2.348)$
$= 6.155 \text{ kg}$

This example provides the method that can be used to make adjustments to the mixing water in practice.

8.5.2 Statistical Method

Efforts have been made to enhance forecasting accuracy, efficiency, and resource savings. Consequently, statistical methods and approaches play a vital role in understanding, optimizing, and predicting the behavior of objects through data analysis, offering objectivity and comprehensiveness.

Introducing the Response Surface Methodology

Response surface methodology (RSM): The section starts by clarifying fundamental terms to provide valuable insights for designers irrespective of their statistical background.

- **Data:** Values acquired from observation, experiment, or calculation, utilized in scientific research, technical design, verification, decision-making, etc.
- **Variables:** Independent factors in optimization problems typically controlled by decision-makers.
- **Response:** Decision factors determining the desired outcome for the problem, guiding the search for optimal results.
- **Input:** Specific mixed decision variables.
- **Output:** Objectives of the desired outcome.
- **Run:** An experimental trial.

RSM is a widely used statistical design method for modeling and analyzing problems where multiple variables influence a desired response. Its advantages include evaluating factor interactions within the experimental region, identifying optimal responses based on various priorities, and establishing nonlinear relationships. As depicted in Fig. 8.1, the RSM process involves five main steps: formulating the problem, selecting the design approach, conducting experimental runs, statistically analyzing the data, and determining optimized solutions.

Step 1: *Formulating the problem* involves transforming the intricate concrete design challenge into a functional relationship solution. Designers must select variables, define their ranges of variation, identify responses, and determine evaluation methods. For example, variables such as water-to-binder ratio, composition and properties of cementitious materials, binder-to- aggregate ratio, dosage of superplasticizer and fiber, mixing process, and curing schedule are considered. Correspondingly, responses including environmental impact, cost, mechanical properties, and workability are chosen. Additionally, the range of constituents must be specified.

$$i = 1, 2, \ldots, q \quad 0 \leq L_i \leq x_i \leq U_i \leq 1$$

where L_i and U_i refer to the lower and the upper constraints, respectively.

Step 2: *Selecting the design approach* follows the transformation of the concrete design problem into a functional relationship solution. For addressing the relationship between water-to-binder ratio and slump flow, the choice of an appropriate design approach is

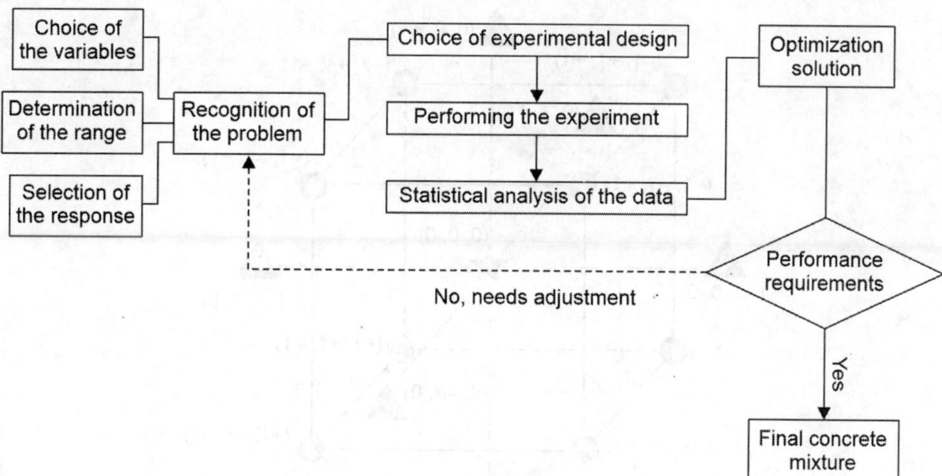

Fig. 8.1: The flow sheet of the statistical method

crucial. Utilizing a second-order model-based strategy proves effective in tackling the complexities of concrete design challenges. The following equation illustrates the use of an optimal predictor quadratic model to identify the optimal conditions for the responses.

$$Y = \beta_0 + \sum \beta_i x_i + \sum \beta_{ii} x_i^2 + \sum \beta_{ij} x_i x_j$$

Y represents the response, x_i denotes the design factors, β signifies the unknown parameters to be estimated from the experimental data, β_{ii} stands for the quadratic coefficients, β_{ij} corresponds to the coefficients of interaction, and ε represents the random error term encompassing experimental uncertainties.

Following the selection of design approaches, specific runs are determined to construct the model. For instance, in utilizing a Central Composite Design (CCD) as part of the RSM, runs involve factorial points positioned at the corners of the cube, axial points at the center of each face, and center points within the cube's center (Fig. 8.2).

Step 3: *Performing runs*. Involves the actual execution of experiments.

Step 4: *Statistical analysis of the data*. Once the model has been established, including confirmation tests such as analysis of variance (ANOVA).

Step 5: *Determining optimized solutions*. Following the establishment of the regression model linking mix design variables and responses, all independent variables are concurrently and independently adjusted to optimize the objective functions. A global desirability function, as developed by Derringer et al. (Derringer and Suich, 1980), is:

$$D = \left(d_1^{r_1} \times d_2^{r_2} \times d_3^{r_3} \times \ldots \times d_n^{r_n}\right)^{1/\sum r_i} = \left[\prod_{i=1}^{n} d_i^{r_i}\right]^{1/\sum r_i}$$

where n is the number of responses included in the optimization, and r_i is the relative importance of each individual functions d_i. Importance (r_i) varies from 1 to 5, from least to most important, respectively. Individual desirability functions (d_i) range

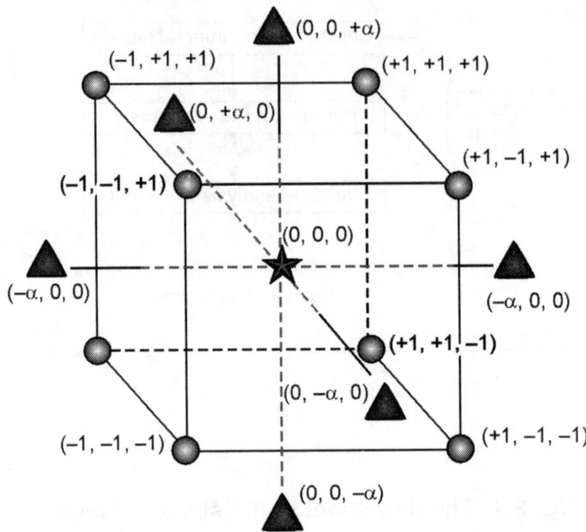

Fig. 8.2: Center, axis and factorial points in CCD

between 0 (completely undesired response) and 1 (fully desired response). For a value of D close to 1, the response values are near the target values. For each variable and response, four different goals could be assigned, namely maximize, minimize, target, and in range. Besides, a weight factor is defined, ranging between 0.1 and 10, which represents the shape of the desirability for each goal. The values higher than 1 give more emphasis to the goal and those lower than 1 have the opposite effect.

After that, solutions of concrete could be calculated, and the theoretical solutions are also confirmed by comparing the predicted value to the ensured value.

Artificial neural network (ANN): ANN is a machine learning algorithm designed to mimic the learning capabilities of the human brain, making it adept at processing complex and nonlinear problems. Recently, ANN has found applications in predicting and optimizing concrete properties. One advantage of ANN is its ability to model relationships between numerous decision variables and objectives while mitigating the risk of over-fitting. However, despite its potential, ANN is not widely used in concrete design, possibly due to its opaque nature. Unlike traditional methods, the internal structure of an ANN resembles a black box, providing little insight into the causal relationships between inputs and outputs (Fig. 8.3).

In reality, an ANN comprises a multi-layer feed-forward perceptron network consisting of five fundamental elements: inputs, weights, sum function, activation function, and outputs, akin to biological neurons. By adjusting the weights and thresholds between layers, designers can facilitate information flow from input to output layers. The weighted sum of input components is computed as follows:

$$\text{net}_j = \sum w_{ij} x_i + b_j$$

where net_j is the weighted sum of the j_{th} neuron received from the lower layer with n neurons, w_{ij} is the weight between the i_{th} neuron and the j_{th} neuron in the preceding

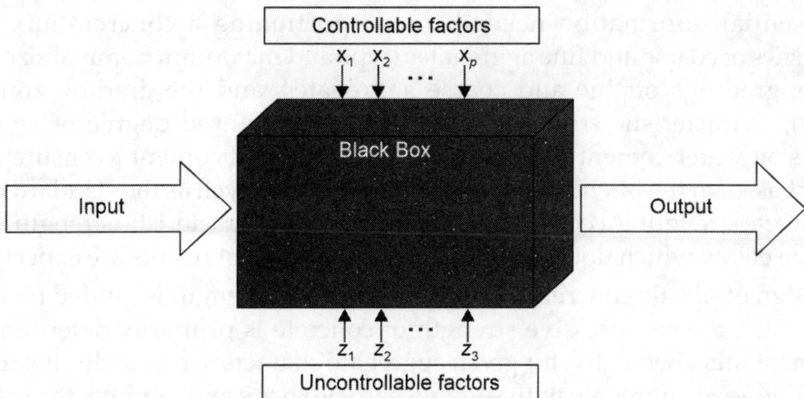

Fig. 8.3: The black box of the complex relationship between the composition of raw materials and the performances

layer, x_i is the output of the i_{th} neuron, and b_j is a fix value as internal addition. Typical ANN goes through three steps.

Step 1: *Data collection.* Designers gather data either through personal experimentation or by sourcing it from existing literature. This data comprises variables (such as OPC, SF, and alternative content) and responses (such as slump flow, strength, and energy consumption), similar to that used in RSM.

Step 2: *Determination of ANN structure.* The fundamental structure of an ANN consists of the input layer, hidden layer, and output layer. The number of nodes in the input and output layers is decided based on the parameters of the research problem or determined through trial and error. Additionally, the activation function for the hidden and output layers needs to be defined. Through a series of trials, the number of layers and other parameters of the ANN models are determined by minimizing the mean square error (MSE) of the training data, aiming to achieve high accuracy in the ANN model.

Step 3: *Data processing.* The collected data used to develop ANN models must be normalized within specific limits to remove nonsingular data, enhance result accuracy, expedite convergence, and reduce calculation time. Most normalization techniques involve linear or logarithmic functions.

8.6 CONCRETE MIX PROPORTIONING—IS GUIDELINES

The concrete mix proportioning process according to IS guidelines aims to achieve specific properties, including the workability of fresh concrete, as well as the strength and durability requirements of hardened concrete at specified ages, all while maximizing overall cost-effectiveness. These guidelines are applicable to ordinary and standard concrete grades with a maximum 28-day cube compressive strength up to 55 MPa and a workability (slump) range of 25 to 125 mm. These concrete mixes are commonly used in various structural elements such as reinforced concrete beams, columns, walls, foundations, footings, caissons, substructure walls, and pavements.

The essential information needed for proportioning a concrete mix includes characteristics of coarse and fine aggregates (type and maximum nominal size of coarse aggregate, gradings of fine and coarse aggregates, and the grading zone of fine aggregate), characteristic strength at 28 days (f_{ck}), required degree of workability, limitations on water-cement ratio, and minimum cement content to ensure adequate durability based on the intended exposure conditions, as well as the standard deviation (S) for concrete strength. According to IS:456-2000, the characteristic strength is defined as the value below which not more than five percent of test results are expected to fall.

The design of plastic concrete mixes with medium strength is guided by two main criteria. Firstly, the compressive strength of concrete is primarily determined by its water-cement ratio. Secondly, for given aggregate characteristics, including maximum size of well-graded aggregate with suitable particle shape and grading, the workability of the concrete mix depends on factors such as water content, entrained air content, and the addition of specific chemical admixtures. However, workability is largely independent of mix proportions, especially the amount of cementitious material.

8.6.1 Mix Design Procedure

The initial revision of IS:10262, which addresses Concrete Mix Proportioning Guidelines, adopted a format reminiscent of the ACI mix proportioning method. Unlike European nations, which lack a unified concrete mix design method due to considering mix design as part of concrete production, they instead regulate through EN 206-1. The specific method used for concrete mix proportioning, whether it's the British DoE method, DIN, or any other, is inconsequential as long as it meets the specified requirements and standards.

The process for mix proportioning, as outlined in IS:10262, is illustrated in the form of a schematic flowchart depicted in Fig. 8.4. Below are the outlined steps for this procedure:

1. **Establishing the fundamental attributes of accessible fine and coarse aggregates involves determining the following properties:**
   a. Maximum nominal size of coarse aggregate
   b. Gradings of both fine and coarse aggregates
   c. Gradings zone of the fine aggregate
   d. Unit weight, specific gravities, and absorption capacities of both coarse and fine aggregates. If needed, multiple coarse aggregate fractions of different sizes may be amalgamated to ensure that the overall grading of coarse aggregate aligns with the specifications outlined in Table 2 of IS 383 for the specific nominal maximum aggregate size.
2. **Determining the free water-cement ratio:**
   a. The mean target strength, f_t, is calculated based on the specified characteristic compressive strength at 28 days, f_{ck}, and the quality control level using:

$$f_t = f_{ck} + kS = f_{ck} + 1.65\ S$$

   where S represents the standard deviation and k denotes the statistical coefficient dependent on the accepted proportion of low results. For the characteristic compressive strength defined in IS 456-2000, k equals 1.65.

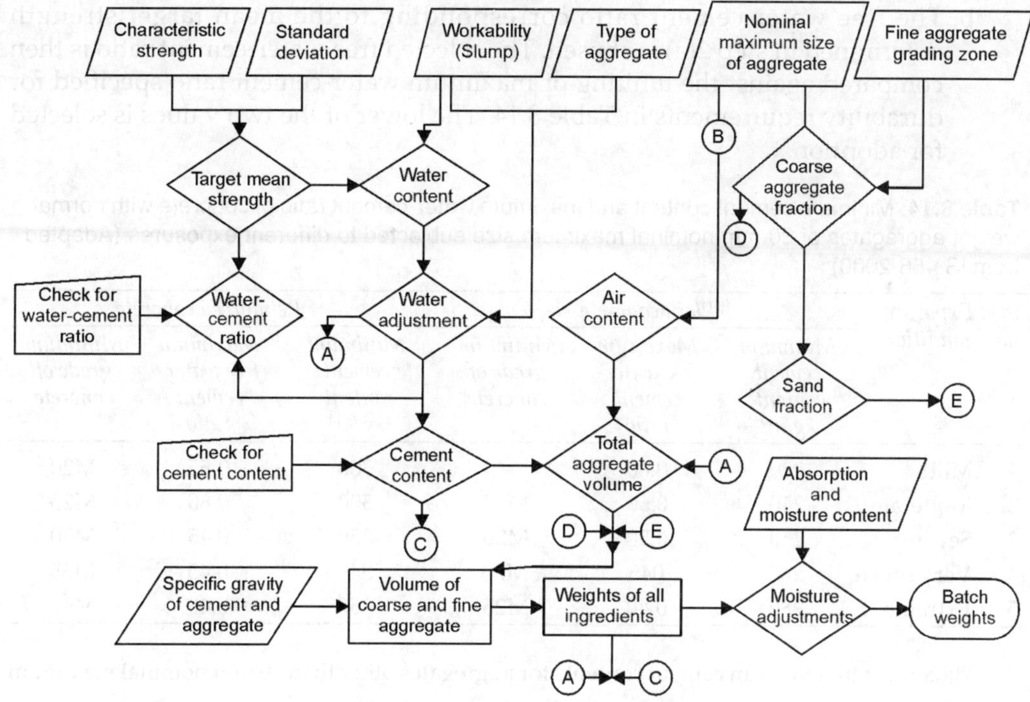

Fig. 8.4: Schematic flowchart for concrete mix proportioning—IS guidelines

The standard deviation, which reflects the level of control, can be statistically estimated from variations in test results obtained from trial mixes conducted either in the field or laboratory. It must be based on a minimum of 30 strength samples. Calculating the standard deviation should occur as early as possible when the mix is initially employed and should be updated after any alteration in mix design. In cases where adequate test results for a specific grade of concrete are unavailable, the standard deviation value provided in Table 8.13 may be adopted. However, as soon as sufficient results become available, the mix should be redesigned utilizing the actual calculated standard deviation. Alternatively, if there are ample past records for a similar grade, the existing standard deviation value may be utilized.

Table 8.13: Assumed standard deviation

Group no.	*Grade of concrete*	*Assumed standard deviation, MPa*	*Quality control*
1.	M10, M15	3.5	The values correspond to the site control having proper storage of cement; weigh batching of all materials; controlled addition of water; regular checking of all materials, aggregate grading and moisture content; and periodical checking of workability and strength. Where there is deviation from the above, values given in the above table shall be increased by 1.0 MPa.
2.	M20, M24	4.0	
3.	M30, M35, M40, M45, M50, M55	5.0	

b. The free water-cement ratio corresponding to the mean target strength determined in step 2(a) is chosen. The selected free water-cement ratio is then compared against the limiting or maximum water-cement ratio specified for durability requirements in Table 8.14. The lower of the two values is selected for adoption.

Table 8.14: Minimum cement content and maximum water-cement ratio of concrete with normal-weight aggregates of 20 mm nominal maximum size subjected to different exposures (Adapted from IS 456-2000)

Sl. no.	*Exposure condition*	*Plain concrete*			*Reinforced concrete*		
		Minimum cement content, kg/m³	*Maximum free water-cement ratio*	*Minimum grade of concrete*	*Minimum cement content, kg/m³*	*Maximum free water-cement ratio*	*Minimum grade of concrete*
1.	Mild	220	0.60	–	300	0.55	M20
2.	Moderate	240	0.60	M15	300	0.60	M25
3.	Severe	250	0.50	M20	320	0.45	M30
4.	Very severe	260	045	M20	340	0.45	M35
5.	Extreme	280	0.40	M25	360	0.40	M40

Adjustment to minimum cement contents for aggregates other than 20 mm nominal maximum size.

	Nominal maximum size, mm	*Adjustment to minimum cement content, kg/m³*
1.	10	+40
2.	20	0
3.	40	–30

3. **Determination of free water content:** The water content per unit volume of concrete, based on aggregates in a saturated surface dry condition, is chosen from Table 8.15, considering the standard reference conditions regarding the type of aggregate and desired workability. This initial water content is then modified according to Table 8.15 to account for any variations in the type of coarse aggregate and workability from the standard reference values.
4. **Determination of cement content:**
   a. Calculate the minimum cement and supplementary cementitious material content per unit volume of concrete by dividing the final free water content, adjusted in step (3), by the free water-cement ratio obtained in step 2(b).
   b. Compare the cementitious material content derived in the previous step with the minimum value dictated by durability requirements, and select the greater of the two values for adoption.
5. **Determination of coarse aggregate volume proportion:** The volume proportion (p) of coarse aggregate with a specified nominal maximum size is estimated from Table 8.16, considering a reference water-cement ratio of 0.5 and the grading zone of the fine aggregate used. This estimate is then adjusted accordingly for the chosen water-cement ratios.

Table 8.15: Maximum water content for nominal maximum size of aggregate

Sl. no.	*Nominal maximum size of aggregate, mm*	*Maximum water content, kg*	*Validity or reference conditions*
1.	10	208	Applicable to angular crushed coarse aggregate
2.	20	186	Water content corresponds to saturated surface dry aggregate
3.	40	165	Applicable to slump range of 25 to 50 mm

Adjustments in the water content for the change in type of aggregate and workability

Change in condition stipulated above	*Adjustment required in water content*
A. Shape of aggregate	
1. Sub-angular aggregates	–10 kg
2. Gravel with some crushed particles	–20 kg
3. Rounded gravel	–25 kg
B. Workability	
1. For each additional 25 mm slump	+ 3%
2. Required water content may be established by trial	
3. Use of chemical admixtures conforming to IS:9103	Water reducing admixtures and superplasticizers usually decrease water content by 5 to 10% and 20% and above, respectively, at appropriate dosages

For concrete requiring increased workability, such as pumpable mixes or those placed around densely packed reinforcing steel, the estimated coarse aggregate content may be reduced by up to 10%, provided that the slump, water-cement ratio, and concrete strength properties align with the requirements outlined in IS 456 and project specifications.

Table 8.16: Proportion of coarse aggregate to total aggregate for different zones of fine aggregate

Sl. no.	*Nominal maximum size of aggregate, mm*	*Volume fraction of coarse aggregate to total aggregate p for different zones of fine aggregate*			
		Zone IV	*Zone III*	*Zone II*	*Zone I*
1.	10	0.50	0.48	0.46	0.44
2.	20	0.66	0.64	0.62	0.60
3.	40	0.75	0.73	0.71	0.69

6. **Calculation of total absolute volume of aggregates:** The total absolute volume of coarse and fine aggregates in a saturated surface dry condition is computed by subtracting the sum of absolute volumes of cementitious material, water (determined in steps 2 and 3), chemical admixture, and entrained air (if applicable) from the unit volume of concrete. Hence, the total absolute volume of aggregates, denoted as V_a (m^3), is determined by the following formula:

$$V_a = 1.0 - \left[v + \frac{C}{S_c \times 1000} + \frac{W}{1000} \right]$$

where W, C, v and S_c are the mass of water (kg), mass of cement (kg), air content (m^3) per cubic meter of concrete and the specific gravity of cement, respectively.

7. **Determination of absolute volumes of fine and coarse aggregates:** The volume of total aggregate obtained in step 6 is divided into coarse and fine aggregate fractions by volume in accordance with coarse aggregate proportion p already determined in step 5. The absolute volumes of coarse aggregate (V_{ca}) and fine aggregate (V_{fa}) per unit volume of concrete are determined as:

$$V_{ca} = pV_a \text{ and } V_{fa} = (1-p)\,V_a$$

where p represents the ratio of coarse aggregate in the total absolute volume of aggregates. Therefore, contents of fine and coarse aggregates by mass are:

$$C_{fa} = (S_{fa} \times 1000)V_{fa} \text{ and } C_{ca} = (S_{ca} \times 1000)V_{ca}$$

where S_{fa} and S_{ca} are the specific gravities of saturated surface dry fine and coarse aggregates, respectively, in kg/liter. Thus, the concrete mix proportions for the first trial mix by mass (kg) are:

$$\begin{array}{ccccccc} \text{Cement} & : & \text{Water} & : & \text{Fine aggregate} & : & \text{Coarse aggregate} \\ C & : & W & : & V_{fa}S_{fa}(1000) & : & V_{ca}S_{ca}(1000) \end{array}$$

The above concrete mix proportions can be expressed by volume (m^3) as where are the bulk densities (kg/m^3) of cement, fine and coarse aggregates, respectively.

$$\begin{array}{ccccccc} \text{Cement} & : & \text{Water} & : & \text{Fine aggregate} & : & \text{Coarse aggregate} \\ \dfrac{C}{\gamma_c} & : & \dfrac{W}{1000} & : & \dfrac{V_{fa}S_{fa}(1000)}{\gamma_{fa}} & : & \dfrac{V_{ca}S_{ca}(1000)}{\gamma_{ca}} \end{array}$$

where γ_c, γ_{fa} and γ_{ca} are the bulk densities (kg/m^3) of cement, fine and coarse aggregates, respectively.

8. **Adjustments for aggregate moisture and final proportions:** As aggregates are batched based on actual weight, adjustments are made to the amount of mixing water added to account for absorption and the existing moisture content. This adjustment aims to achieve an equivalent of saturated surface dry condition for the aggregates before determining the final proportions.

9. **Trial batch preparation and testing:**
   a. Determine the concrete mix proportions for the initial trial mix (trial mix no. 1) and assess its workability based on slump measurement. Observe the mix for segregation, bleeding, and finishing properties. If the slump of the first trial mix differs from the specified value, adjust the water and/or admixture content to achieve the correct slump.
   b. Recalculate the mix proportions while maintaining the pre-selected free water-cement ratio for trial mix No. 2. Additionally, formulate two more trial mixes, No. 3 and No. 4, with the same water content as trial mix No. 2, but varying the free water-cement ratio by ±10 percent of the preselected value.
   c. Test the fresh concrete from each trial batch for unit weight, yield, and air content. Cast three 150 mm cubes from each batch. After 28 days of moist curing, test the wet cubes for strength.

10. **Determination of final mix proportions:** Analyze trial mixes No. 2 to 4 to extract pertinent data, particularly regarding the correlation between compressive strength and water-cement ratio. Compute the water-cement ratio needed to

achieve the mean target strength using this correlation. Recalculate the mix proportions to accommodate the adjusted water-cement ratio while maintaining the water content at the same level as determined in trial mix No. 2.

For field trials, manufacture the concrete using the actual concrete production method intended for field use.

Example III

Designing a pumpable concrete mix of M35 grade, with a slump ranging between 100 and 125 mm, utilizing G-43 OPC in accordance with IS:8112. The mix is intended for a reinforced concrete structure exposed to very severe environmental conditions during its service life. Preliminary mix proportions will be estimated using IS:10262 guidelines for concrete mix proportioning, with the understanding that final mix proportions will be contingent upon actual site conditions, which may vary depending on location and other factors.

The coarse aggregates present at the site consist of crushed angular particles with nominal maximum sizes of 10 mm and 20 mm, possessing a specific gravity of 2.67, a moisture content of 1.0%, and an absorption of 0.5%. The available fine aggregate has a fineness modulus of 2.80 (grading zone-I), a specific gravity of 2.62, a moisture content of 4.0%, and an absorption of 1.0%. The G-43 Portland cement available has a specific gravity of 3.15. The bulk densities of cement, fine aggregates, and coarse aggregates are 1450, 1700, and 1800 kg/m^3, respectively. Other requirements include:

- Standard deviation (from past records): 2.0 MPa
- Air content: 4.0–5.0%
- Maximum allowable free water-cement ratio: 0.45
- Minimum cement content: 340 kg/m^3
- Maximum cement content (IS 1343-1980): 450 kg/m^3
- Chemical admixture type: Superplasticizer conforming to IS 9103
- Density of water: 1000 kg/m^3

Solution

Mix Proportions

Considering the coarsest grading curve No. 1 of Fig. 8.5 for the combined aggregate, it is determined that to achieve this grading, the coarse aggregates of 20 mm and 10 mm sizes need to be mixed in a ratio of 55:45. The maximum nominal size for the combined aggregate is 20 mm.

The target mean strength, f_t, is calculated as $f_{ck} + kS$, resulting in 38.3 MPa. The corresponding free water-cement ratio from Fig. 8.6 is 0.39. However, based on experience, a water-cement ratio of 0.40 is adopted, which falls within the acceptable range.

a. **Selection of water content:** Referring to Table 8.15, the maximum water content for a slump range of 25 to 50 mm for 20 mm nominal size aggregate under saturated surface dry conditions is 186 liters.

   Adjustments: Given the required workability range of 100–125 mm slump, which differs from the reference value, adjustments in the water content are necessary to accommodate this variation. The estimated water content for a 125 mm slump is determined accordingly.

$$= 186 \times \left[1 + \frac{3}{100} \times \frac{125 - 50}{25}\right] = 203 \text{ liters}$$

Since superplasticizer is utilized, the water content can be decreased by more than 20%. The desired reduction in water content is determined through trials with superplasticizer. For instance, let us consider a superplasticizer with a manufacturer-recommended dosage of 2.0% by mass of cementitious material as a water-reducing admixture, resulting in a reduction in water content of approximately 30%. Hence, the adjusted water content would be calculated as follows: Water content = 203 × 0.70 = 142 liters or kg/m^3.

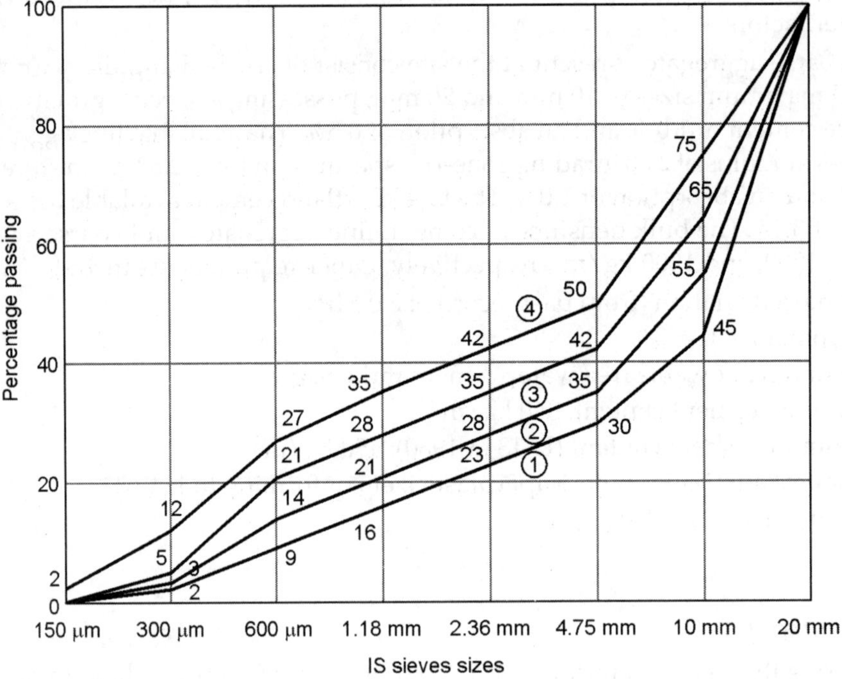

Fig. 8.5: Recommended grading curves for 20 mm nominal maximum size aggregate

b. **Determination of cement content:**

Water-cement ratio = 0.40

Hence, cement content = 142/0.40 = 355 kg/m^3.

The calculated cement content is more than the minimum cement content of 340 kg/m^3 recommended in Table 8.14 and less than the maximum 450 kg/m^3 prescribed in Clause 8.1.1 of IS 1343-1980.

c. **Volume fractions of coarse and fine aggregates:** The volume proportion of coarse aggregate (20 mm nominal maximum size) to total aggregate, with fine aggregate belonging to Zone I and a water-cement ratio of 0.50 as obtained from Table 8.16, is 0.60.

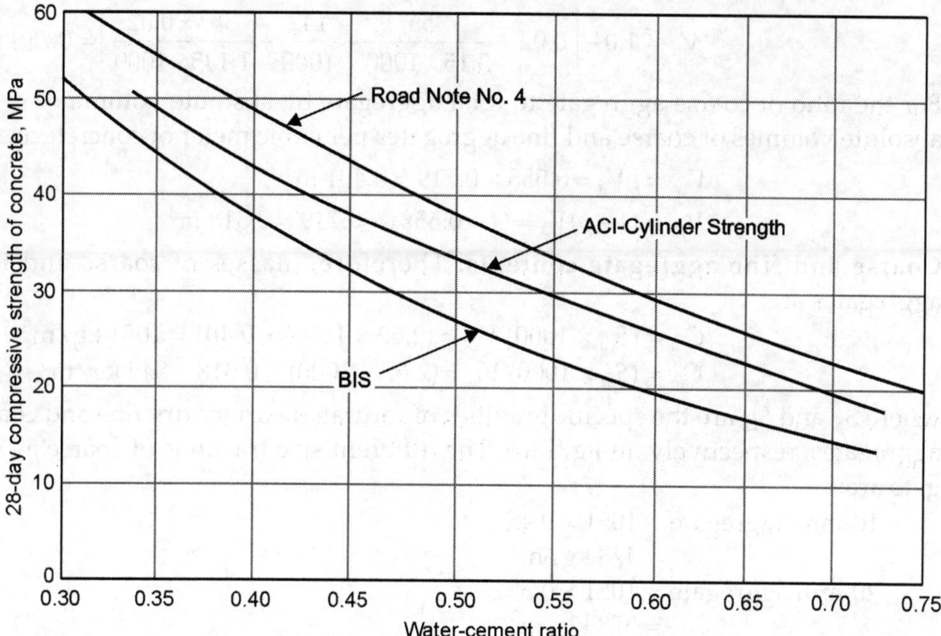

Fig. 8.6: Generalized relationship between water-cement ratio and compressive strength of concrete

Adjustments: Since the selected water-cement ratio of 0.40 differs from the reference value of 0.50, adjustments are necessary for this change. Consequently, the volume of coarse aggregate needs to be increased to decrease the fine aggregate content.

Considering the selected water-cement ratio is lower by 0.10 from the reference value, the proportion of the volume of coarse aggregate is increased by 0.02 (at a rate of ± 0.01 for every ± 0.05 change in water-cement ratio). Thus, the corrected volume fraction of coarse aggregate for the water-cement ratio of 0.40 is $p = 0.62$.

If the coarse aggregate is not crushed (angular), the volume of coarse aggregate needs to be suitably increased based on experience.

For pumpable concrete, the volume fraction of coarse aggregate should be reduced by 10 percent.

Therefore, volume fraction of coarse aggregate for pumpable concrete,

$$p = 0.62 \times 0.9 = 0.558$$

Volume fraction of fine aggregate,

$$1 - p = 1 - 0.558 = 0.442$$

Total absolute volume of aggregates V_a (m^3) is given by eq.

$$V_a = 1.0 - \left[v + \frac{C}{S_c \times 1000} + \frac{W}{1000} + \frac{S}{S_s \times 1000} \right]$$

where S and S_s are the mass and specific gravity of chemical admixture (superplasticizer), respectively. Air content, V, for 20 mm maximum nominal size aggregate is 2%, i.e. 0.02.

$$V_a = 1.0 - \left[0.02 + \frac{355}{3.15 \times 1000} + \frac{142}{1000} + \frac{355 \times 0.02}{1.145 \times 1000}\right] = 0.719 \text{ m}^3$$

For the ratio of coarse aggregate to total aggregate by absolute volume of p, the absolute volumes of coarse and fine aggregates per cubic meter of concrete are:

$$V_{ca} = pV_a = 0.558 \times 0.719 = 0.401 \text{ m}^3$$
$$V_{fa} = (1 - p)V_a = (1 - 0.558) \times 0.719 = 0.318 \text{ m}^3$$

d. **Coarse and fine aggregate contents:** Therefore, masses of coarse and fine aggregates are:

$$C_{ca} = (S_{ca} \times 1000)\, V_{ca} = (2.62 \times 1000) \times 0.401 = 1051 \text{ kg/m}^3$$
$$C_{fa} = (S_{fa} \times 1000)\, V_{fa} = (2.67 \times 1000) \times 0.318 = 849 \text{ kg/m}^3$$

where S_{fa} and S_{ca} are the specific gravities of saturated surface dry fine and coarse aggregates, respectively, in kg/liter. The different size fractions of coarse aggregate are:

10-mm aggregate = 1051 × 0.45
= 473 kg/m³

20-mm aggregate = 1051 × 0.55
= 578 kg/m³

Mix proportions:

i. **Mix proportions by mass:**

Cement		Water		Fine aggregate		Coarse aggregate 10 mm		Coarse aggregate 20 mm		Admixture
355	:	142	:	849	:	473	:	578	:	7.1 (kg/m³)
1.0	:	0.40	:	2.39	:	1.33	:	1.63	:	0.2

ii. **Mix proportions by volume:**

Cement		Water		Fine aggregate		Coarse aggregate 10 mm		Coarse aggregate 20 mm		Admixture
$\frac{355}{1450}$	:	$\frac{142}{1000}$	:	$\frac{849}{1700}$	:	$\frac{473}{1800}$	:	$\frac{578}{1800}$	:	– (m³)
1.0	:	0.40	:	2.04	:	1.07	:	1.31	:	0.2

e. **Adjustments for aggregate moisture:** Since there is moisture in both the coarse and fine aggregates their trial batch masses must be adjusted as:

Weight of fine aggregate = 849 × 1.04 = 883 kg

Weight of coarse aggregate = 1051 × 1.01 = 1062 kg

The amount of mixing water also needs adjustment because both the coarse and fine aggregates are wet and will contribute to free water available for cement paste. Free water present in the aggregate:

Fine aggregate = 849 × (0.04 – 0.01) = + 25.47 kg

Coarse aggregate = 1051 × (0.01 – 0.005) = + 5.26 kg

Free-water in aggregate = + 30.73 kg

Therefore, the amount of water to be added at the batching plant is = 142 – 30.73 = 111.27 kg. The final trial batch quantities per cubic meter of concrete are:

Nominal water-cement ratio	*Water (kg/m³) effective w/c ratio*	*Cement (kg/m³)*	*Fine aggregate (kg/m³)*	*Coarse aggregate (kg/m³)*		*Admixture (kg/m³)*
				10 nm	*20 nm*	
0.40	111.27	355	883	478	584	7.1
–	0.31	1.0	2.49	1.35	1.65	0.02

Example IV

Utilizing IS10262 guidelines for concrete mix proportioning, formulate a M25 concrete mix suitable for a reinforced concrete structure expected to encounter mild exposure conditions throughout its service life. The mix should fulfill the following specifications:

a. **Design stipulations:**
   Degree of workability: Medium (75–100 mm slump)
   Degree of quality control: Weigh batching, occasional supervision, no past experience with this grade, S = 5.5 MPa.

b. **Characteristics of materials:**
   Cement
   Type and grade: Ordinary Portland cement, G-43
   Specific gravity: 3.15
   Bulk desity: 1450 kg/m³

Aggregates	*Fine aggregate*	*Coarse aggregate*
Type	River sand (zone II)	Crushed granite
Maximum nominal size	–	20 mm
Specific gravity	2.60	2.65
Bulk density (kg/m³)	1700	1800
Fineness modulus	2.3	6.0
Free surface moisture (%)	2.0	1.0

Mix Proportions

Target mean strength, f_t, is calculated as $f_{ck} + kS$, resulting in 34.1 MPa.

a. **Free water-cement ratio:** Considering compressive strength considerations, a value of 0.43 is obtained. Alternatively, from durability considerations, a value of 0.55 is derived. Hence, a water-cement ratio of 0.43 may be adopted. However, based on experience, the water-cement ratio is selected as 0.45 (< 0.55).

b. **Determination of water content:** The maximum water content for a slump range of 25 to 50 mm for 20 mm nominal size aggregate under saturated surface dry condition is 186 liters.
   Adjustments: Since the workability (slump) range of 75–100 mm differs from the reference value, adjustments in the water content are required for this variation.
   Estimated water content for 75–100 mm slump:

$$= 186 \times \left[1 + \frac{3}{100} \times \frac{100 - 50}{25}\right] = 197.2 \text{ liters}$$

c. **Determination of cement content:** Given water-cement ratio = 0.45, thus cement content = 197.2/0.45 = 438 kg/m³.

The calculated cement content falls within the recommended range of minimum 300 kg/m^3 and maximum 450 kg/m^3 and Clause 8.1.1 of IS 1343-1980.

d. **Volume fractions of coarse and fine aggregates:** The volume proportion of coarse aggregate (20 mm nominal maximum size) to total aggregate, with fine aggregate belonging to grading Zone II, for a water-cement ratio of 0.50 as obtained as 0.62.

Adjustments: Since the selected water-cement ratio of 0.45 is lower than the reference value of 0.50 by 0.05, the volume fraction of coarse aggregate is increased at a rate of ± 0.01 for every ± 0.05 change in water-cement ratio, the volume fraction of coarse aggregate is adjusted by 0.01 to reduce the fine aggregate content. Consequently, the corrected volume fraction of coarse aggregate for the water-cement ratio of 0.45 is determined as $p = 0.63$. The volume fraction of fine aggregate content, calculated as $1 - p$, results in $1 - 0.63 = 0.37$.

e. **Volumes of fine and coarse aggregates:**

$$V_a = 1 - \left(0.02 + \frac{438}{3.15 \times 1000} + \frac{197.2}{1000}\right) = 0.644\ \text{m}^3$$

Therefore, the absolute volumes of fine and coarse aggregates per unit volume of concrete are:

$$V_{fa} = 0.37 \times 0.644 = 0.238\ \text{m}^3$$
$$V_{ca} = 0.63 \times 0.644 = 0.406\ \text{m}^3$$

f. **Mix proportions:** The quantities of saturated surface dry fine and coarse aggregates are:

$$C_{fa} = (2.60 \times 1000) \times 0.238 = 619\ \text{kg/m}^3$$
$$C_{ca} = (2.65 \times 1000) \times 0.238 = 630\ \text{kg/m}^3$$

i. Mix proportions by (saturated surface dry) mass

Cement		Water		Fine aggregate		Coarse aggregate	
438	:	197.2	:	619	:	1076	(kg/m^3)
1.0	:	0.45	:	1.41	:	2.46	

ii. Mix proportions by volume

Cement		Water		Fine aggregate		Coarse aggregate	
$\left(\frac{438}{1450}\right)$	:	$\left(\frac{197.2}{1000}\right)$	:	$\left(\frac{619}{1700}\right)$	:	$\left(\frac{1076}{1800}\right)$	(kg/m^3)
1.0	:	0.45	:	1.21	:	1.98	

g. **Adjustments for aggregate moisture:** Since there is moisture in both the coarse and fine aggregate their trial batch masses must be adjusted as:

Weight of fine aggregate = 619 × 1.02 = 631 kg

Weight of coarse aggregate = 1076 × 1.01 = 1087 kg

Free-water present in the fine and coarse aggregates,

$$= 619 \times 0.02 + 1087 \times 0.01 = 23.2\ \text{kg}$$

Therefore, the amount of water to be added at the batching plant is

$$= 197.2 - 23.2 = 174\ \text{kg}$$

The final trial batch quantities per cubic meter of concrete are:

Nominal water-cement ratio	*Water (kg/m^3) effective w/c ratio*	*Cement (kg/m^3)*	*Fine aggregate (kg/m^3)*	*Coarse aggregate (kg/m^3)*
0.45	174	438	631	1087
–	0.40	1.0	1.44	2.48

Chapter 9

Durability of Concrete

The durability of Portland cement concrete denotes its capacity to withstand various forms of deterioration, including weathering, chemical corrosion, and abrasion, while retaining its original quality and functionality in its intended service environment. It primarily concerns the long-term performance of concrete and concrete structures, ensuring they maintain their functionality even when subjected to specific environmental conditions. Serviceability, in this context, pertains to a structure's ability to fulfill its designated functions following exposure to its environment.

9.1 WHY DURABILITY?

Concrete has traditionally been specified based on its compressive strength after 28 days of casting. Conversely, reinforced concrete (RC) structures are typically designed with a substantial safety margin, resulting in strength levels well above the allowable stress. Consequently, intrinsic strength deficiencies seldom cause concrete structure failures. Instead, premature failures often stem from gradual deterioration due to durability issues, leading to structures failing before their intended service life. This durability challenge has grown significantly, evolving from a "multimillion-dollar opportunity" in the 1980s to a trillion-dollar market in recent years. For instance, in the United States, over 2.5 million concrete bridge decks required repair within two decades of operation. Reports from the American Society of Civil Engineers (ASCE) highlight the substantial investment required to restore infrastructure to normal operation conditions, with estimates reaching $1.6 trillion over five years in 2005. Efforts such as the Fixing America's Surface Transportation (FAST) Act, initiated in 2015 under President Obama, and subsequent infrastructure investment drives under President Trump and President Biden's proposed $3.5 trillion plan in 2021 have aimed to address these challenges. While these efforts have improved America's infrastructure to a cumulative GPA of C- as per ASCE's 2021 report card, the investment gap remains significant, with the total shortfall increasing from $2.1 trillion to nearly $2.59 trillion over a decade. In the United Kingdom, for example, the initial construction cost of eight high bridges in Southern England's circular expressway was £28 million. However, by 2004, the repair costs for these bridges had soared to £120 million, nearly six times the initial construction expenditure.

Numerous researchers have extensively investigated durability issues, exploring individual deterioration mechanisms as well as the combined impact of environmental factors and mechanical loading. These studies have led to the development of durability-oriented design principles by various countries.

9.2 FACTORS INFLUENCING DURABILITY

Concrete deterioration stems from three main categories: physical, chemical, and mechanical causes, which often interact in a combined manner.

Physical causes encompass surface wear due to abrasion, erosion, and cavitation, as well as effects from high temperatures and disparities in thermal expansion between aggregates and hardened cement paste. Examples include the impact of freeze-thaw cycles and deicing salts, as well as cracking induced by volume changes, temperature gradients, salt crystallization, structural loading, restrained shrinkage, and exposure to fire.

Chemical degradation typically arises from internal or external chemical attacks on the cement matrix. Portland cement's alkalinity makes it prone to reactions with acids in the presence of moisture, leading to matrix weakening and leaching of constituents. Common chemical causes of concrete durability issues include hydrolysis of cement paste, carbonation, cation-exchange reactions, and expansion-inducing reactions like sulfate attack, alkali-aggregate reactions, and steel corrosion.

Mechanical causes involve impacts and overloading.

Concrete deterioration usually results from environmental factors affecting exposed structures or the mechanical loading they endure. Often, a structure's degradation is a consequence of the combined effects of environmental factors and loading. Common durability issues in concrete structures include reinforcing steel corrosion, freeze/thaw damage (often associated with salt scaling), alkali-aggregate reactions, sulfate attack, among others. These attacks commonly initiate due to mass transfer and lead to concrete cracking and spalling.

9.3 TRANSPORT PROPERTIES

The durability of concrete is significantly influenced by its transport properties, such as permeability and diffusivity. Permeability refers to the rate at which a fluid can flow into a porous material under pressure. Measuring the permeability of concrete involves assessing the rate of water flow through a concrete sample. The porosity of concrete, which includes pores within the bulk cement paste, interfacial transition zones between aggregate and cement paste, and microcracks, greatly impacts its permeability. Water flow through concrete follows Darcy's law, with the flow rate during steady-state conditions described by this law as follows:

$$\frac{dq}{dt} = K\frac{\Delta HA}{L}$$

In the equation, where dq/dt represents the flow rate, K denotes the permeability coefficient, ΔH signifies the pressure gradient, A represents the surface area of the specimen, and L stands for the thickness of the specimen. As previously mentioned, concrete permeability is influenced by the presence of pores within the material, encompassing two key aspects: the overall porosity percentage and the distribution of pore sizes or their connectivity. Concrete consists of aggregates, hardened cement paste, and the interface between aggregates and paste. Table 9.1 illustrates the permeability coefficient for hardened cement paste (HCP), aggregates, and concrete. For fully matured hardened cement paste, despite its notable porosity, the permeability coefficient remains remarkably low. This coefficient for matured hardened cement paste is comparable to that observed in low-porosity aggregates composed of rocks. The minimal permeability coefficient is indicative of water encountering difficulty in traversing very fine gel pores, with permeability predominantly governed by an interconnected network of capillary pores. Typically, pores smaller than 0.1 μm are considered detrimental. As hydration progresses, the capillary network becomes increasingly convoluted as interconnected pores are obstructed by the formation of C–S–H. Despite both hardened cement paste and aggregates exhibiting low permeability coefficients, concrete possesses a permeability coefficient one to two orders of magnitude higher than those of hardened cement paste and aggregates. This disparity can be ascribed to the interface between hardened cement paste and aggregates, characterized by significantly higher porosity, enabling pervasive permeation throughout the material at standard aggregate volume fractions.

Table 9.1: Typical values of permeability coefficients of concrete materials

Type	*Porosity (%)*	*Average pore size*	*Permeability coefficient*
HCP	20	100 nm	6×10^{-12} cm/sec
Aggregate	3–10	10 μm	$1–10 \times 10^{-12}$ cm/sec
Concrete	6–20	100 nm–500 mm	$100–300 \times 10^{-12}$ cm/sec

Diffusivity in concrete refers to the velocity at which ions or moisture migrate under the influence of a concentration gradient, as illustrated in Fig. 9.1. Unlike permeability, which is driven by pressure disparities, diffusivity is propelled by concentration differences. Permeability characterizes water flow within water-filled pores of concrete, while diffusivity delineates the movement of ions or water vapor under both saturated and unsaturated conditions. These parameters are interconnected, and knowledge of one allows for the indirect determination of the other. This relationship can be established through empirical or analytical equations, such as the Katz-Thompson

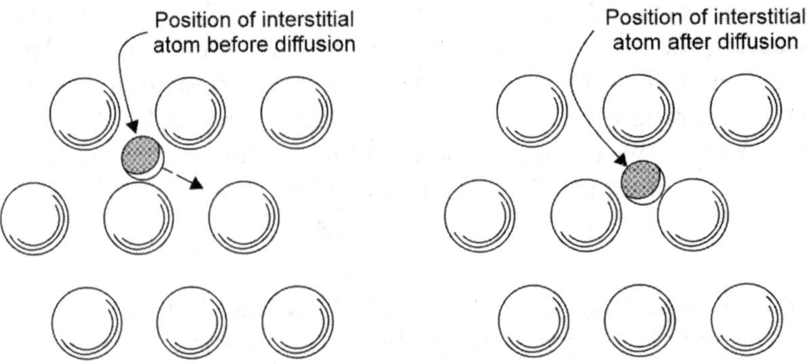

Fig. 9.1: Diffusion phenomenon

equation. Fick's law is often employed to describe diffusivity, comprising two laws: Fick's first law, which describes steady-state diffusion and is linear in form.

$$J = -D\frac{\partial C}{\partial x}$$

In the equation, J represents the diffusion flux or the rate of mass transport (kg/m^2-sec), D denotes the diffusion coefficient (m^2/sec), C signifies the concentration of a specific ion or gas (kg/m^3), and x denotes the position (m) along the axis indicating the direction from high to low concentrations. Fick's second law, on the other hand, can elucidate non-steady state diffusion and is expressed as:

$$\frac{\partial C}{\partial t} = -D\frac{\partial^2 C}{\partial x^2}$$

The solution of Fick's second law for a semi-infinite plane has the form:

$$C(x, t) = C_0\left[1 - erf\left(\frac{x}{2\sqrt{Dt}}\right)\right]$$

In the equation, $C(x, t)$ represents the concentration of ions or gas at a specific distance x and time t, C_0 denotes the concentration at the higher surface, and erf symbolizes the error function.

Permeability coefficient and diffusivity coefficient serve distinct roles in concrete dynamics. Permeability governs the flow of water within concrete or between its sections under a hydraulic gradient. On the other hand, the diffusion coefficient regulates the movement of ions, moisture, or gases, such as oxygen, through concrete, whether it is dry or wet, or the migration of ions like chloride within the pore solution. It is important to note that the diffusion coefficient varies depending on the substance diffusing. Generally, as both permeability and diffusivity are linked to concrete's pore structure, concrete with low permeability typically exhibits low diffusivity. Methods aimed at reducing permeability and diffusivity, such as minimizing the water-to-cement ratio to decrease capillary porosity, ensuring sufficient cement content for proper compaction, and implementing appropriate curing methods to prevent surface cracks, are beneficial for enhancing concrete durability.

9.4 MEASUREMENT OF TRANSPORT PROPERTIES

The aim of a permeability test is to assess how quickly a liquid can flow through a test specimen when subjected to a specific pressure. Concrete, being porous, allows water to pass through it slowly under pressure. Two common approaches are employed to evaluate concrete permeability using water: the steady-flow method and the penetration-depth method. In the steady-flow method, a pressure head is applied to one end of a saturated specimen, as depicted in Fig. 9.2. Once a steady-flow state is achieved, the outflow is measured to determine the permeability coefficient, employing Darcy's law:

$$k_1 = \frac{(dq/dt)L}{\Delta HA}$$

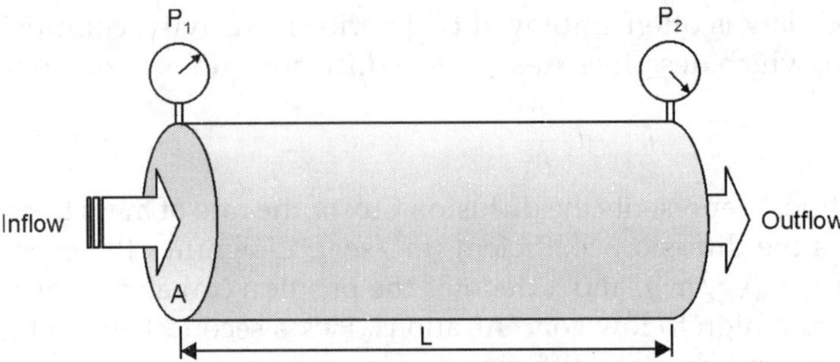

Fig. 9.2: Steady-flow permeability test

In the equation, k_1 represents the permeability coefficient (m/sec), dq/dt denotes the steady-flow rate (m^3/sec), L indicates the thickness or length of the specimen (m), ΔH signifies the drop in hydraulic head across the sample (m), and A stands for the cross-sectional area of the sample (m^2).

To attain a steady-flow state, water must permeate all pores within the sample, ensuring that pore surfaces offer minimal friction or capillary resistance to water passage. Negative pressures arising from self-desiccation during cement hydration and the presence of entrapped air can both influence the permeation test. For instance, studies have shown that the presence of 1% air voids in the pore water can increase the duration required to achieve steady-state water flow by one order of magnitude. Achieving steady-state flow conditions can be time-consuming, particularly in high-performance modern concrete characterized by dense, low-porosity structures. In some cases, it may be impractical to achieve such conditions within a year. Consequently, the significant time investment required for concrete testing and the challenges in achieving steady-state outflow can be considered drawbacks of the steady-flow method.

For assessing the permeability of high-performance concrete, the penetration-depth method is often employed. This method typically utilizes a permeability cell, as illustrated in Fig. 9.3. The cell comprises plastic tubes at the top and bottom, with the concrete specimen positioned in between. To ensure a unidirectional flow condition, the circumferential surface of the concrete specimen is sealed with epoxy. In operation, the top tube is filled with water while the bottom one contains air, with the air pressure in the bottom tube adjustable via a vacuum process.

Fig. 9.3: Permeability cell

To subject the unsaturated concrete specimen to pressure, the specimens are placed in an autoclave, as depicted in Fig. 9.4, and pressure is applied. This creates a pressure head at the top end of the concrete specimen through the water in the tube, while the opposite end remains under normal atmospheric conditions. Water penetration can be evaluated either by measuring the volume of water entering the sample or by splitting the cylinder after the test and measuring the average depth of discoloration resulting from wetting, which represents the penetration depth.

Fig. 9.4: Penetration depth test with an autoclave

Assuming uniaxial water flow, the penetration depth can be utilized to determine the permeability coefficient, which corresponds to that used in Darcy's law, derived as:

$$k_1 = \frac{x^2 v}{2\Delta HT}$$

In the equation, x stands for the depth of concrete penetration (m), v represents the fraction of concrete volume occupied by pores, and T denotes the duration of pressure application (sec). The value of v accounts for discrete pores, like air voids, which are typically unfilled with water unless subjected to pressure. This value can be determined by measuring the increase in concrete mass during the penetration test. It is important to note that only voids within the portion of the specimen penetrated by water are taken into consideration, leading to the expression:

$$v = \frac{\Delta W}{DAx}$$

In this equation, ΔW represents the increase in specimen weight during the penetration test, D stands for the density of concrete, and A denotes the cross-sectional area. Through the penetration-depth method, the depth of water penetration can serve as a qualitative indicator of concrete permeability. In summary, the steady-flow method is suitable for concretes exhibiting relatively higher permeability, whereas the penetration-depth method is more suitable for concretes with very low permeability. It is worth noting that there can be significant variability in permeability test results for similar concrete under identical conditions, including age and equipment usage.

In concrete technology, chloride is commonly chosen as the diffusion testing medium for several reasons. Firstly, chloride ions are known to induce corrosion in reinforcing steel, making them relevant for assessing concrete durability. Secondly, the small size (radius) of chloride ions, at 181×10^{-12} m, makes them suitable for diffusion testing purposes. Traditionally, two methods are used to evaluate chloride diffusion in concrete: rapid permeability test and diffusion cell test method.

In the rapid permeability test, a standard specimen with a nominal diameter of 100 mm and a thickness of 50 mm is prepared from a cylindrical sample, either cored from field concrete or cast in the laboratory. Before mounting the specimen into the test facility, its side surface is sealed with a rapid-setting coating, and the specimen is vacuum desiccated for 3 hours and vacuum-soaked for 18 ± 2 hours. The test facility consists of positive and negative terminals made of plexiglass plates, with an empty cell and a circular opening matching the specimen's diameter on one surface. The specimen is mounted with two surfaces connected to the terminal openings using sealing material. Subsequently, a 3% NaCl solution is added to fill the cell on the negative terminal, and 0.3 N NaOH is added to fill the cell on the positive terminal. Figure 9.5 shows the experimental setup of the rapid chloride test. A constant voltage of 60 V is then applied for 6 hours. The total charge passing through the concrete specimen during testing serves as an index of concrete diffusivity. Table 9.2 outlines the classifications of concrete quality based on this index.

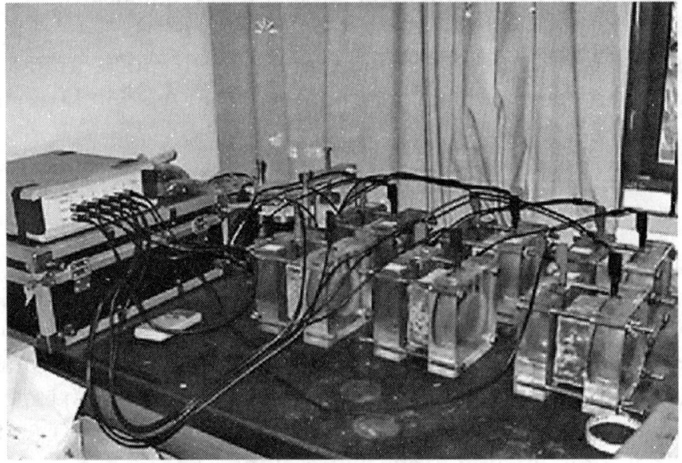

Fig. 9.5: Rapid chloride permeability test setup

Table 9.2: Classification of concrete quality using chloride ion penetrability

Charge passed (Coulombs)	*Chloride ion penetrability*
>4000	High
2000–4000	Moderate
1000–2000	Low
100–1000	Very low
<100	Negligible

The latter method is regarded as a practical test approach for assessing the chloride diffusivity of concrete. In this method, specimens measuring ϕ100 × 20 mm (ϕ3.94 × 0.79 inches) are sandwiched between two chambers, and the edges are sealed with epoxy resin (Fig. 9.6). Once the epoxy resin has cured, saturated calcium hydroxide solution is introduced into the chambers, and the specimens are submerged in the solution for a duration of 5 days. This step aims to prevent any anomalous effects arising from sorption rather than the diffusion of chloride ions. Subsequently, a NaCl solution with a concentration of 5 M is introduced into chamber A to initiate the chloride diffusion test. The chambers are maintained at a temperature of 23 ± 2°C, and the concentration of chloride diffused through the specimens in chamber B is periodically monitored.

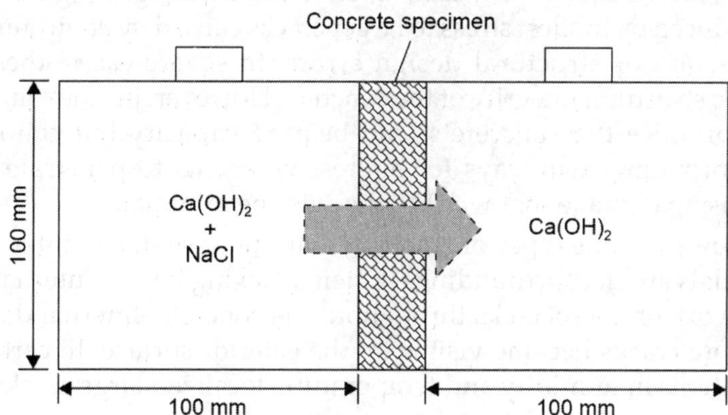

Fig. 9.6: Measurement of diffusion coefficient

In typical experimental results, the curve depicting chloride concentration in chamber B exhibits significant nonlinearity between chloride concentration and time at the outset. However, after approximately 30 weeks of testing, the curve transitions to a more linear pattern. This suggests that chloride diffusion has reached a steady state. The linear correlation between chloride ion concentration and time can be represented as:

$$C = kt - A$$

In this equation, C represents the cumulative concentration of chloride ion penetration at time t in chamber B, k denotes the slope of the chloride concentration-time curve at steady-state, and A is a constant. During steady-state, the flux of chloride ions through the specimens can be characterized by Fick's first law of diffusion. Specifically, for the steady-state scenario, this law can be expressed as:

$$C = \frac{DC_A}{l^2}t - A$$

In the equation, D represents the diffusion coefficient in the steady-state, C_A stands for the concentration of chloride ions in chamber A, and l denotes the thickness of the slice specimen. By comparing the two equations mentioned above, the diffusion coefficient can be formulated as follows:

$$D = \frac{kl^2}{C_A}$$

It is evident that with knowledge of the slope of the chloride concentration-time curve (flux) during steady state, the diffusion coefficient can be determined. In essence, the latter method closely resembles the actual scenario of chloride penetration in concrete and offers a means to ascertain the diffusion coefficient. Nonetheless, it entails significant time and labor investment.

9.5 CRACKING IN CONCRETE

Cracking in concrete is a significant factor impacting its durability. When concrete develops cracks, its permeability and diffusivity increase significantly, accelerating deterioration. Various factors can lead to concrete cracking, ranging from internal microcracks induced by modest stress to larger cracks caused by environmental factors, construction issues, or structural design errors. In severe cases, these cracks can compromise the structural integrity of the concrete. However, in many instances, cracks may not compromise the concrete's load-bearing capacity but can still affect its durability by providing pathways for aggressive agents to penetrate the material, potentially causing damage that would otherwise be minimal.

Table 9.3 shows various types of cracking that can arise due to interactions within concrete materials and its surroundings. Often, cracking begins internally, gradually forming a network of microcracks throughout the concrete. Internal damage may be significant before cracks become visible on the exterior surface. In certain scenarios, such as fluctuations in humidity and temperature, localized large cracks may emerge

Table 9.3: Causes of cracking in concrete due to interaction with surroundings

Component	*Type*	*Cause of distress*	*Environmental factor(s)*	*Variable to control*
Cement	Unsoundness	Volume expansion	Moisture	Free lime and magnesia
	Temperature cracking	Thermal stress	Temperature	Heat of hydration, rate of cooling
Aggregate	Alkali-silica reaction	Volume expansion	Supply of moisture	Alkali in cement, composition of aggregate
	D-cracking	Hydraulic pressure	Freezing and thawing	Absorption and maximum size of aggregate
Cement paste	Plastic shrinkage	Moisture loss	Wind, temperature, relative humidity	Temperature of concrete, protection of surface
	Drying shrinkage	Moisture loss	Relative humidity	Mix design, rate of drying
	Sulfate attack	Volume expansion	Sulfate ions	Mix design, cement type, admixtures
	Thermal expansion	Volume expansion	Temperature change	Temperature rise, rate of change
Concrete	Settlement	Consolidation of concrete around reinforcement	–	Concrete slump, cover, bar diameter
Reinforcement	Electro-chemical corrosion	Volume expansion	Oxygen, moisture	Cover, permeability of concrete

in the structure, even appearing on the surface. Cracking patterns can serve as indicators of concrete deterioration, aiding in determining the underlying causes Table 9.4. Concrete that exhibits resistance to cracking under normal environmental conditions may not remain unscathed under extreme circumstances like fire hazards and earthquakes.

Table 9.4: Type of cracking in concrete structures

Nature of crack	*Cause of cracking*	*Remarks*
Large, irregular, frequently with height differential	Inadequate support, overloading	Slabs on ground, structural concrete
Large, regularly spaced	Shrinkage cracking, thermal cracking	Slabs on ground, structural concrete, mass concrete
Coarse, irregular "map cracking"	Alkali-silica reaction	Extrusion of gel
Fine, irregular "map cracking" (crazing)	Excessive bleeding, plastic shrinkage	Finishing too early, excessive troweling
Fine cracks roughly parallel to each other on surface of slabs	Plastic shrinkage	Perpendicular to direction of wind
Cracks parallel to sides of slabs adjacent to joints (D-cracking)	Excessive moisture content, porous aggregate	Deterioration of concrete slab due to destruction of aggregates by frost
Cracks above and parallel to reinforcing bars	Settlement cracking	Structural slabs due to consolidation of plastic concrete around reinforcing bars near upper surface
Cracking along reinforcing bar placements, frequently with rust staining	Corrosion of reinforcement	Aggravated by the presence of chlorides

The most effective approach to controlling cracking is during the design and construction stages. By carefully selecting materials and anticipating potential issues through a thorough assessment of the expected service environment, cracking can often be prevented.

Chemical attacks on concrete entail the infiltration of moisture, serving either as a carrier for aggressive agents or as a participant in damaging reactions. Therefore, precautions taken in mix design and construction practices to hinder water ingress into concrete can enhance its durability. Ensuring low permeability in concrete involves employing appropriate amounts (neither excessive nor insufficient) of cementitious materials and maintaining low water-to-cement ratios. Additionally, proper placement, consolidation, and finishing techniques, along with adequate moist curing, contribute to achieving concrete with low permeability and enhanced durability.

Cracks arising from drying shrinkage and thermal expansion stem from tensile stresses resulting from differential strains during uneven drying, temperature fluctuations, or uneven restraint. Therefore, shrinkage and thermal cracking resemble flexural cracking and can be managed by strategically placing reinforcements and/or incorporating fibers for distributed micro-reinforcement. This approach reduces the occurrence of cracking and promotes the formation of multiple fine cracks rather than a single large crack. Finer cracks are less likely to contribute to durability issues. For cases of severe exposure, crack widths less than 0.10 mm are preferred over wider cracks.

9.6 MAJOR DURABILITY PROBLEMS

9.6.1 Corrosion of Reinforcing Steel

The corrosion of reinforcing steel stands as one of the most critical durability challenges globally. Ideally, in a well-designed, properly constructed, and maintained structure, corrosion of steel within concrete should be minimal during its intended service life. This is because concrete creates a highly alkaline environment, with pH levels typically ranging from 12.5 to 13.5, which effectively passivates the steel. However, this favorable condition isn't always sustained over time due to concrete deterioration, leading to corrosion of the reinforcement. Beyond the typical corrosion caused by exposure to oxygen and water in areas like cracks and spalling concrete, two main mechanisms exacerbate rebar corrosion: carbonation-induced corrosion and chloride-induced/ catalyzed corrosion. Carbonation- induced corrosion arises from a general breakdown of passivity due to concrete neutralization, while chloride-induced corrosion stems from a localized breakdown of the passive film on the steel.

Carbonation-induced Corrosion

Carbonation-induced corrosion occurs when carbon dioxide from the atmosphere infiltrates concrete. The chemical process involves carbon dioxide molecules entering the concrete and interacting with calcium hydroxide, a hydration byproduct in the cement paste. This reaction leads to the carbonation of calcium hydroxide into calcium carbonate, represented as $Ca(OH)_2$ reacting to form $CaCO_3$:

$$CO_2 + Ca(OH)_2 \rightarrow CaCO_3 + H_2O$$

The primary focus lies on the reaction of carbonation, particularly concerning concrete composed of Portland cement. While the carbonation of C–S–H is feasible when calcium hydroxide becomes depleted, the main interest lies in the carbonation of calcium hydroxide. Other compounds in hydrated cement paste, such as ettringite, may also undergo decomposition, potentially altering the mineralogy. Generally, carbonation can induce shrinkage in concrete. In Portland cement concrete, carbonation might even lead to increased strength. Although carbonation itself isn't necessarily problematic, its effects on reinforced concrete can be severe. The chemical processes during carbonation lead to a significant decrease in concrete alkalinity, dropping from an average pH of 12–14 to 8–9, due to the consumption of calcium hydroxide. This reduction in alkalinity disrupts the passive environment, rendering the reinforcement susceptible to corrosion. Consequently, when carbonation reaches the rebar cover and encounters oxygen and moisture, corrosion ensues. The depth of carbonation within reinforced concrete plays a crucial role in reinforcement protection; deeper carbonation increases the risk of steel corrosion. Another consequence of carbonation is the potential liberation of chlorides, including those bound within calcium chloroaluminate hydrates like Friedel's salt and those bound to hydrated phases, which can further exacerbate the aggressiveness of the pore solution.

The speed at which carbonation progresses, measured by how quickly the carbonation front advances into the concrete, escalates with higher concentrations of carbon dioxide, particularly evident in concretes with elevated water-to-cement ratios. Additionally, the pace of carbonation is influenced by various environmental factors such as relative humidity and temperature, along with concrete quality attributes, primarily its alkalinity and permeability. Concrete quality stands out as the foremost parameter dictating the carbonation rate. This quality is determined by factors like binder composition (whether Portland cement or blended cement was utilized), water-to-cement or water-to-binder ratios, and curing conditions. The permeability of concrete significantly impacts carbon dioxide diffusion and, consequently, the rate of carbonation. Lowering the water-to-cement or water-to-binder ratio reduces capillary porosity and thus permeability, potentially slowing down carbonation penetration. The type of cement also plays a role; blended cements, due to hydration of pozzolanic materials or ground granulated blast furnace slag, may exhibit a higher carbonation rate owing to reduced calcium hydroxide content. Consequently, blended cements may undergo deeper carbonation compared to Portland cement concrete under similar water-to-binder ratios. Curing conditions are crucial, as proper curing can densify concrete, hindering permeation or diffusion. Effective curing can offset the lower alkalinity of cements with fly ash or GGBS additives through reduced permeability of their cement pastes. Carbonation rates rise with temperature and vary according to concrete humidity levels. In extremely dry or saturated environments, carbonation is inhibited since CO_2 diffusion is restricted. The carbonation rate may correlate with environmental humidity levels, with the 60–70% relative humidity range being particularly conducive to promoting carbonation.

The rate of carbonation-induced corrosion on steel is commonly quantified by the penetration rate of the corrosion front into the steel bar, typically measured in micrometers per year. Corrosion rates are categorized as negligible if below 2 μm/year, low between 2 and 5 μm/year, moderate between 5 and 10 μm/year, intermediate between 10 and 50 μm/year, high between 50 and 100 μm/year, and very high for values exceeding 100 μm/year. In high-quality concrete, carbonation-induced corrosion is considered negligible when relative humidity (RH) is below 80%, implying that corrosion progresses primarily when concrete is wet (i.e. RH > 80%). Over time, corrosion rates tend to decrease, and the presence of corrosion products can further reduce the corrosion rate. Page (1992) has demonstrated the correlation between corrosion rates in carbonated concrete and environmental relative humidity. The highest corrosion rates, ranging from 100 to 200 μm per year, are typically observed in extremely wet environments with relative humidity nearing 100%. Under typical atmospheric exposure conditions with RH between 70–80%, maximum corrosion rates range between 5 and 50 μm per year.

Chloride-induced Corrosion

Chloride-induced corrosion in structural concrete primarily occurs when there are sufficient free chloride ions present in the cement matrix surrounding the steel rebar. These chloride ions can enter concrete during mixing through admixture components like chloride accelerators, chloride-contaminated aggregates, or mix water from sources such as seawater or salt spray. Alternatively, they can penetrate the hardened concrete later on from external sources like seawater or deicing salt applied to concrete pavements. If chlorides are present during mixing, corrosion may initiate at an early service stage. In cases where chlorides penetrate the concrete in the service environment, rebar corrosion begins once a certain level of chloride accumulation occurs at the rebar surface. Chloride ions diffuse through the concrete cover to the rebar surface, where they accumulate until reaching a critical level, typically between 0.6 and 0.9 kilograms per cubic meter of concrete. At this point, the protective oxidized passivation film on the steel dissolves, leading to localized breakdown and the formation of a galvanic cell. Anodic areas experience oxidation of iron, while cathodic areas undergo reduction. This separation of anodes and cathodes significantly influences the corrosion pattern. In the vicinity of anodic areas, positive iron ion concentration rises, lowering pH and allowing soluble iron-chloride complexes to form and diffuse away from the rebar, perpetuating corrosion. As these complexes break down at a distance from the electrode, iron hydroxides precipitate, chloride migrates back to the anode, and the autocatalytic process deepens corrosion pits rather than spreading corrosion along the rebar. Corrosion product expansion, particularly if FeO forms, can cause cracking and spalling of the concrete cover, ultimately compromising structural integrity. Chloride-induced corrosion is localized, with corrosion accumulating in specific areas surrounded by non-corroded regions. The threshold chloride ion concentration, determining the initiation of corrosion, is a function of pH, specifically the ratio of free chloride to hydroxyl ions ($[Cl^-]/[OH^-]$). Most specifications and guidelines define the permissible chloride content in concrete as a percentage by weight of the original cement used, typically less than 0.2%. ACI 318 specifies maximum water-soluble chloride contents by weight of cement at 0.15–0.4% for reinforced concrete and 0.06% for prestressed concrete, depending on exposure class. Sometimes, the critical chloride level is specified in terms of weight of chloride per unit volume of concrete, often in the range of 0.6–1.2 kg/m^3, particularly for assessing chlorides in existing structures.

Under typical atmospheric conditions, the rate of chloride-induced corrosion can range from tens of micrometers per year to localized values of 1 mm per year for steel, as relative humidity increases from 70 to 95% and chloride content escalates from 1% by mass of cement to higher levels. Structures with high chloride content, such as bridge decks, retaining walls, and seawater-exposed pillars, often experience elevated corrosion rates. Corrosion rates tend to rise with increasing temperatures. Once corrosion initiates in chloride-contaminated structures, significant reduction in reinforcement cross-section can occur relatively quickly, even under normal atmospheric exposure conditions. The lower threshold of relative humidity required for negligible chloride-induced corrosion rates is considerably lower than that for carbonation-induced corrosion. Temperature and humidity influence corrosion rates by affecting electrochemical reactions at the steel/concrete interface and ion transport between anodes and cathodes. Concrete resistivity has long been associated with corrosion rates, particularly at moderate or low temperatures. Under similar humidity and temperature conditions, blended cements with higher resistivity may exhibit lower corrosion rates compared to Portland cement.

The onset of corrosion in reinforcing steel is often indicated by rust stains and minute cracks on the concrete surface. This is typically due to the expansion associated with corrosion product formation and the leaching of rust. Without prompt repairs, corrosion damage can escalate, leading to severe consequences such as longitudinal cracks parallel to the reinforcement, delamination, spalling of the concrete cover, and exposure of the steel, ultimately reducing its cross-section and potentially resulting in catastrophic collapse. The financial impact of reinforcing steel corrosion damage can be substantial. For instance, a survey conducted by the China Academy of Engineering in 2002 estimated the annual cost of reinforcing steel corrosion in China to be around CNY 100 billion. Therefore, it is crucial to understand the mechanisms of steel corrosion and explore effective methods for repairing the resulting damage.

9.6.2 Corrosion Mechanisms

The corrosion of reinforcing steel in concrete is an electrochemical process involving oxidation and reduction reactions, leading to the formation of iron oxides and hydroxides as corrosion products. This process is characterized by the presence of both anodic and cathodic areas, each with distinct potential differences arising from various factors such as differences in the composition and structure of the concrete cover, exposure conditions, and contact with dissimilar materials. Corrosion cells are typically formed due to contact between dissimilar materials, variations in surface characteristics, and differences in the concentrations of alkalis, chloride, and oxygen.

Four components are necessary for corrosion to occur in a macro cell: the anode, cathode, electrolyte, and metallic path. The anode is where oxidation (corrosion) takes place, involving the loss of electrons and the formation of metal ions. The cathode is where reduction occurs, involving the gain of electrons. The electrolyte is usually a liquid containing ions that migrate in an electric field, while the metallic path allows for electron movement between the anode and cathode. In the context of steel corrosion in concrete, the anode, cathode, and metallic path are typically represented by the same steel rebar, while the moistened concrete serves as the electrolyte. Corrosion ceases if any of these components is removed, providing the foundation for corrosion control.

The process of corrosion is depicted in Fig. 9.7 with relevant chemical reactions annotated. At the anode site, iron dissociates to form ferrous ions and electrons:

$$Fe \rightarrow Fe^{2+} + 2e^- \quad \text{anodic reaction}$$

Electrons travel through the metal towards the cathodic site, while ferrous ions dissolve into the pore solution. At the cathodic site, electrons react with oxygen and water to produce hydroxyl ions:

$$4e^- + O_2 + 2H_2O \rightarrow 4(OH)^- \quad \text{cathode reaction}$$

Hydroxyl ions migrate to the anode via the pore solution and react to generate corrosion products at the anode:

$$Fe^{2+} + 2(OH)^- \rightarrow Fe(OH)_2 \quad \text{ferrous hydroxide}$$

$$4Fe(OH)_2 + 2H_2O + O_2 \rightarrow 4Fe(OH)_3 \quad \text{ferric hydroxide}$$

The equations above demonstrate that oxygen and water are essential for initiating and sustaining corrosion. In a completely dry atmosphere, likely below a relative humidity of 40%, corrosion typically does not occur. It has been proposed that the optimal relative humidity for corrosion is between 70–80%. Under higher relative humidity conditions (above 80%) or in immersion scenarios, oxygen diffusion is significantly reduced, resulting in more uniform environmental conditions along the steel and consequently less corrosion. Corrosion requires ions to travel through the

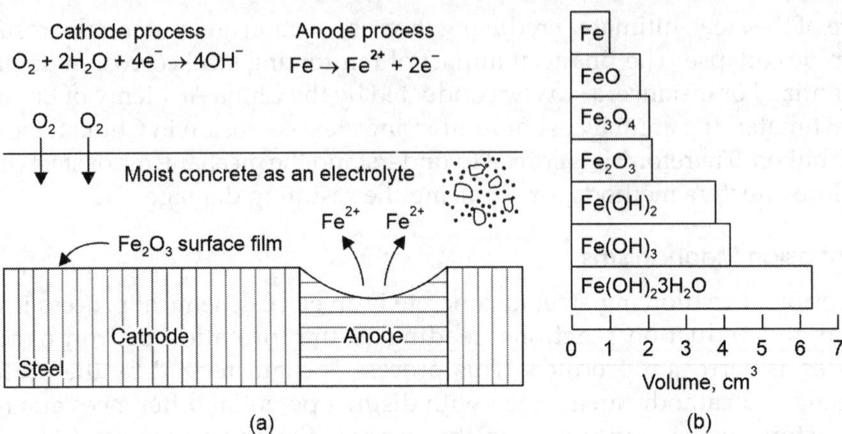

Fig. 9.7: Reinforcing steel corrosion and expansion of corrosion products: (a) corrosion process; (b) volume expansion of corrosion products

pores in the surrounding concrete, as well as oxygen diffusion through the concrete cover. Thus, the corrosion rate is influenced by factors, such as electrical resistance, diffusivity, and thickness of the concrete cover.

The degree of steel corrosion in concrete hinges on factors including the electrolyte conductivity, potential difference between anodic and cathodic areas, and the rate at which oxygen reaches the cathode, thereby regulating the velocity of the anodic reaction. In concrete, the strong polarization of anodic zones under aqueous and highly alkaline conditions elevates the steel's potential near that of the cathode, leading to passivation of the steel surface by the formation of an oxide layer containing Fe_3O_4, Fe_2O_3, and/or γ- FeOOH. This passivation film inhibits further reactions, preserving the steel over extended periods. Additionally, concrete's increased electrical resistivity following hydration can impede the flow of electrical currents within the material, especially in high-density concrete. However, when carbonation reaches the vicinity of the steel bar, reduced alkalinity dissolves the passivation film, initiating or resuming corrosion reactions. Similarly, if chloride ions breach the reinforcement and exceed the threshold concentration, they can also disrupt the passivation film, though the specific mechanisms remain a topic of debate. Generally, the breakdown of the passivation film can be described as:

$$Fe^{2+} + 2Cl^- \rightarrow FeCl_2$$

The reaction described is more rapid than the typical anodic reaction, and the dissolved ferrous ions can interact with hydroxyl ions, water, and oxygen to produce corrosion products. Notably, chloride ions are not depleted in this process; rather, they act as a catalyst, expediting and intensifying the corrosion of steel. Thus, chloride is a particularly detrimental contaminant in reinforced concrete.

Because severe corrosion poses a significant risk to structural integrity, engineers must actively detect or monitor corrosion to inform maintenance decisions. Various methods are employed for detection and monitoring, including visual inspection, electrical and electrochemical techniques (such as half-cell potential measurement, electrical tomography, and four-electrode configuration), as well as radiographic, fiber-optic, ultrasonic, magnetic perturbation or flux, and acoustic emission methods. Detailed methodologies are available in the existing literature. Here, we provide a brief overview of two techniques: half-cell potential measurement and acoustic emission.

9.7 PREVENTION OF STEEL CORROSION

Efforts to mitigate steel corrosion, particularly in rebar, have intensified over recent decades due to the substantial costs involved. Typically, corrosion prevention methods are passive in nature. The primary focus is on minimizing chloride content in concrete, often achieved through meticulous control of raw materials to ensure levels remain below critical thresholds. This preserves the protective layer on the rebar, preventing corrosion initiation.

Another vital aspect is ensuring adequate rebar protection through meticulous design and control of concrete cover. Design codes typically stipulate parameters such as minimum cover thickness, concrete properties (including design strength and water/cement ratio), and allowable crack widths. These measures, when adhered to, significantly delay the penetration of corrosive agents like CO_2 and chloride ions to the rebar. However, increasing cover thickness may diminish rebar effectiveness and elevate the risk of cracking due to various stressors, such as tension, shrinkage, and temperature fluctuations.

Enhancing concrete quality emerges as a primary defense mechanism. This involves reducing water/cement ratios, increasing binder content, and enhancing strength. Such improvements not only control carbonation and chloride ingress rates but also disrupt one of the key components of corrosion cells: the electrolyte. By densifying concrete, moisture and air infiltration are minimized, reducing electrolyte formation and corrosion likelihood.

Cathodic protection methods, such as utilizing zinc as an anode, offer additional safeguards for reinforcing steel. In this process, corrosion predominantly occurs at the sacrificial zinc anode, shielding the steel from deterioration.

Other strategies for protecting against corrosion include the use of coated rebar, cathodic protection, corrosion-resistant rebar, and corrosion inhibitors. Employing epoxy coating on reinforcing steel can significantly improve durability by acting as a barrier, obstructing aggressive substances from reaching the steel surface, and offering electrical insulation. Epoxy coatings can be applied in different forms, either as a liquid or as a powder that is heat-fused onto the surface.

Generally, the performance of epoxy-coated rebars in environments with chloride exposure, such as bridge decks and parking garages subject to chloride deicing salts during winter, has been widely regarded as excellent. However, significant issues related to the corrosion of epoxy-coated bars have been documented in substructures. The primary contributing factor to this poor performance has been identified as the extent of damage to the epoxy coating prior to concrete casting. Hence, proper training is essential for the correct production, handling, application of the coating, and repairing of field damage to epoxy-coated bars. Furthermore, the bond properties between concrete and epoxy-coated rebars are not as robust as those between concrete and conventional rebars, necessitating improvement.

To address the issue of poor interfacial bonding, enamel coatings have been proposed as alternatives to epoxy coatings. However, since enamels require high-temperature formation around 800°C, their cost-effectiveness may not match that of epoxies. Similar to epoxy coatings, enamels only provide physical barriers, meaning damage to the coating during construction may compromise corrosion protection during service. A promising avenue for a new generation of coatings involves providing not only a physical barrier but also a surface passivation mechanism. Some chemically bonded phosphate ceramic coatings are currently under evaluation, expected to offer a dense, ceramic-like barrier and an iron hydrogen phosphate hydrate passivation layer.

Zinc coating, or galvanizing, of steel is another effective method for corrosion resistance, functioning as both a sacrificial and barrier-type coating. However, one drawback is that, like other metal coatings, zinc corrodes over time. The rate of corrosion depends on environmental conditions and determines the coating's effective service life. Zinc's stability is influenced by the pH of the surrounding solution, remaining stable below pH 12.5 but dissolving at an increasing rate above this level. Corrosion products may deposit on the coating surface, sealing it and halting hydrogen gas evolution, thus passivating the zinc coating. However, when galvanized rebars are used alongside ungalvanized bars, the depletion of the galvanized bars accelerates. Therefore, when using galvanized and ungalvanized bars together in a structure, meticulous care must be taken to ensure complete electrical isolation between them.

Beyond its role as a rebar coating, zinc is widely employed for cathodic protection methods to safeguard reinforcing steel. In such applications, zinc serves as an anode, experiencing corrosion before the steel can be affected.

Several studies have investigated the utilization of stainless steel bars, revealing that the chloride threshold for corrosion initiation in non-welded AISI 304 stainless steel rebars is three to five times higher than that of conventional rebars. However, welding the bar decreases the critical chloride level by 50%. Since the 1990s, there has been growing interest in fiber-reinforced polymer (FRP) bars, including carbon, glass, and basalt variants, as an alternative to steel rebars. Nonetheless, the use of stainless steel or FRP rebars remains a costly solution, and FRP bars exhibit more significant sensitivity to high temperatures compared to steel.

Corrosion inhibitors are considered beneficial not only as a preventive measure for new structures but also as a surface-applied admixture for existing structures. Various types of corrosion inhibitors include adsorption inhibitors that target specific partial reactions of corrosion processes, film-forming inhibitors that partially or fully block surfaces, and passivators that promote steel passivation. These inhibitors primarily combat localized or pitting corrosion caused by chloride ions or pH fluctuations. When added to concrete, corrosion inhibitors can delay corrosion initiation and/or reduce corrosion rates after depassivation. Mixed-in inhibitors are generally considered more reliable and easier to implement. Laboratory tests have shown that certain corrosion inhibitors may not significantly affect the chloride ion threshold for corrosion initiation but can lower corrosion rates post-initiation. However, the long-term effectiveness of these products in field conditions remains inconclusive due to limited observation periods.

9.8 DETERIORATION CAUSED BY FREEZE-THAW CYCLING

Concrete, inherently porous, undergoes a transformation as cement and water react to form a solidified paste binding coarse and fine aggregates. This process leaves behind capillary pores within the originally water-filled spaces among cement grains. Capillary pores vary in size from approximately 5 nm to 1 μm, sometimes even larger. Alongside capillary pores, cement paste contains a considerable volume of gel pores. The water content and capillary forces within these pores play a vital role in the durability of hardened concrete, particularly in environments where freeze-thaw cycles are common, leading to the deterioration of surface layers.

The degradation of concrete due to freeze-thaw cycling is attributed to the presence of water within the material, although it cannot be solely explained by water expansion upon freezing. While pure water freezes at 0°C, water within concrete is a solution of various salts, thus lowering its freezing point. Additionally, the freezing temperature of water depends on pore size, which varies widely in concrete. As a result, there is no singular freezing point. For instance, in saturated Portland cement paste, free water within pores larger than 0.1 mm freezes between 0°C and –10°C; water within pores ranging from 0.1 to 0.01 mm freezes between –20°C and –30°C; and water within gel pores (pores less than 10 nm) freezes below –35°C.

Freezing typically initiates in outer layers and larger pores before extending to inner parts and smaller pores if the temperature drops further. Gel pores, too small to accommodate ice formation, largely remain unaffected, with freezing predominantly occurring in capillary pores. Larger voids, resulting from incomplete compaction, are typically air-filled and less susceptible to initial frost action.

When water freezes, it expands by approximately 9%, exerting hydraulic pressure on unfrozen water in capillary pores as freezing occurs gradually inward. If this pressure isn't relieved, it can lead to internal tensile stresses, potentially causing localized concrete failure. Upon thawing, the expansion caused by ice persists, creating space for additional water absorption during subsequent freezing cycles, leading to further expansion. As a result, repeated freeze-thaw cycles can accumulate damage, with concrete in cold regions being particularly susceptible.

There are two processes that could increase hydraulic pressure in capillary pores. Firstly, there is a thermodynamic imbalance between gel water and ice, leading to gel water diffusion into capillaries, expanding the ice body and increasing hydraulic pressure. Secondly, osmotic pressure rises due to local solute concentration increases caused by pure water removal during freezing. Damage from freeze-thaw cycling varies from surface scaling to complete disintegration, with ice layer formation starting at the concrete surface and progressing inward. Concrete members that remain wet for extended periods are especially vulnerable to frost damage, particularly in fully saturated pore systems where pressure release relies on microstructure expansion, often resulting in cracking.

Frost damage in concrete is linked to the degree of saturation (DOS), indicating the ratio of fluid-filled pores to total pore volume. Studies have identified a critical DOS for specific concretes, typically ranging from 86% to 88%, below which frost damage is minimal but accelerates above this threshold. The critical DOS depends on factors like particle size, homogeneity, freezing rate, and air entrainment.

The presence of deicing salts, such as calcium chloride and sodium chloride, exacerbates concrete degradation during freeze-thaw cycles. These salts lower ice formation temperatures but also increase concrete DOS due to their hygroscopic nature. They cause disruptive effects, induce differential stresses, create temperature shocks, and lead to salt crystallization in pore supersaturated solutions. Despite some positive effects, such as lowered freezing temperatures, the negative impacts generally outweigh them, resulting in early appearance of scaling and detachment of cement paste from aggregates (Fig. 9.8).

Fig. 9.8: Scaling deterioration caused by freezing-thawing

Moreover, chloride deicing chemicals, especially magnesium chloride, dissolve cement hydration products, forming calcium oxychloride that continues damaging concrete even during thawing periods. Typically, mass loss or dynamic modulus decrease serves as indicators of freeze-thaw-induced degradation, and concrete resistance to such damage. To prevent or mitigate freeze-thaw damage, air-entraining agents can be utilized. These chemical admixtures deliberately introduce air into cement paste within enclosed spaces, enhancing resistance to freeze-thaw cycles. Common air-entraining agents include animal and vegetable fats and oils, natural wood resins, and wetting agents containing alkali salts of organic compounds.

9.9 DURABILITY IN A MARINE ENVIRONMENT

Numerous infrastructures are constructed in marine environments, including sea bridges, tunnels, oil platforms, and piers. Marine environments can be categorized into three main zones: underwater, tidal, and atmospheric. Additionally, a splash zone is often recognized between the tidal and atmospheric zones. Concrete structures in the tidal zone face particularly severe deterioration due to a combination of chemical and physical factors (Fig. 9.9).

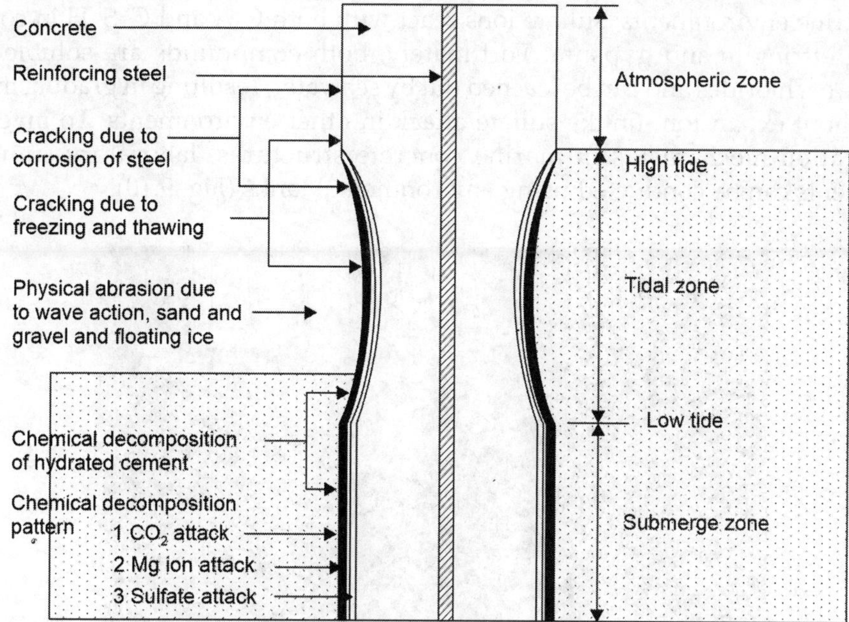

Fig. 9.9: Deterioration mechanisms of concrete structure in marine environment

In the tidal zone, concrete structures are exposed to various types of attacks, including physical erosion, salt crystallization pressure, sulfate attack product leaching, freezing/thawing in cold climates, and chloride penetration. This zone extends between the mean high and mean low water levels, experiencing periodic immersion and drying cycles, typically on a daily basis. Such wet-dry cycling significantly accelerates the ingress of chloride from seawater, leading to steel reinforcement corrosion once the threshold concentration is exceeded. This corrosion, the most common and severe deterioration mechanism, results in the accumulation of corrosion products on the steel surface, leading to expansion and eventual spalling of the concrete surface. When coupled with other physicochemical mechanisms, such as those listed above, this corrosion process hastens the degradation of marine concrete structures, particularly those situated in the tidal zone.

Within the tidal zone, structural elements face abrasion from ice and debris, exacerbated by the alternating motion of waves and tides. High-velocity waves, along with surface irregularities, can induce cavitation in marine concrete structures, where minute bubbles form and collapse rapidly, generating intense impact waves that splatter against the concrete surface, particularly damaging high-strength concrete. Cavitation-induced deterioration can manifest as the tearing out of large concrete pieces.

Cyclic drying and capillary suction occur just above sea level, leading to the transportation of dissolved salts into the concrete. Subsequent evaporation results in salt crystallization within pores, creating stresses that can cause microcracking. Below the low-tide line, where continual immersion occurs, steel and concrete structures typically experience less severe attack compared to those exposed in tidal or splash zones.

In marine environments, sulfate ions react with both C_3A and C–S–H in concrete, forming ettringite and gypsum. Fortunately, both compounds are soluble in the presence of chlorides and can be leached out by seawater, resulting in gradual material loss without expansion, unlike sulfate attack in other environments. To investigate deterioration mechanisms in marine concrete structures, laboratory simulation experiments can be conducted using environmental tanks (Fig. 9.10).

Fig. 9.10: Seawater tank for marine environmental simulation test

9.10 GENERAL METHODS TO ENHANCE THE DURABILITY OF CONCRETE

In practical scenarios, concrete structures face degradation due to the combined influence of various environmental factors. For instance, marine structures are often subjected to erosion, chloride diffusion, and sulfate attack simultaneously, illustrating multifactorial deterioration. Moreover, concrete structures must withstand mechanical loads amid exposure to diverse environments. Thus, studying deterioration mechanisms under the combined effects of mechanical loading and environmental factors is more realistic. While researchers have initiated studies in this direction, further efforts are required to fully comprehend these mechanisms.

Despite the complexity of multifactorial degradation, several general methods are known to enhance concrete durability. Chemical mechanisms of deterioration, such as sulfate attack and steel corrosion, involve substance migrations, both from external surroundings (e.g. chloride, sulfate, oxygen, carbon dioxide, and moisture) and within concrete itself (e.g. alkalis). Therefore, reducing concrete's transport properties is crucial for enhancing durability. This can be achieved through improved compaction, reduced porosity and pore connectivity, and crack mitigation. Compaction can be enhanced by optimizing fresh concrete manipulation, while pore structure refinement can be attained by adjusting water-to-cement or water-to-binder ratios, incorporating supplementary cementitious materials, or modifying pore structures with polymers. Crack mitigation strategies, depending on their origins, may involve fiber reinforcement, enhanced curing, shrinkage-reducing admixtures, expansion agents, internal curing, or specific expansion control methods.

Since many chemical deteriorations involve reactions with specific cement components or hydration products, reducing their availability is a fundamental approach to enhancing durability. For instance, using sulfate-resistant cements instead of general-purpose cement can mitigate sulfate attack. A broader method to improve resistance against multiple deterioration mechanisms, such as carbonation, sulfate attack, alkali-aggregate reaction, and leaching, is to reduce alkalinity, particularly the amount of calcium hydroxide, by incorporating quality supplementary cementitious materials.

Given that water is critical for most deterioration mechanisms, preventing moisture ingress theoretically prevents deterioration. This can be achieved practically by using film-forming admixtures to block pore networks, coating concrete surfaces with waterproof or super-hydrophobic coatings, or enhancing drainage in the surrounding environment.

Chapter 10

Ready-mixed Concrete

10.1 HISTORICAL DEVELOPMENT

The development of ready-mixed concrete (RMC) is a fascinating journey that traces back through centuries of innovation and adaptation.

1. **Early use of concrete:** Concrete has been used in construction for thousands of years. Ancient civilizations like the Egyptians, Greeks, and Romans used various forms of concrete in their structures. However, these early concrete mixes were typically prepared on-site and used immediately.
2. **Industrial revolution:** The industrial revolution marked a significant turning point in construction practices. With the advent of mechanization and mass production, there was a growing need for more efficient construction methods. This led to the exploration of pre-mixed concrete formulations.
3. **Emergence of concrete plants:** In the late 19th century, as urbanization accelerated, the demand for concrete increased. This prompted the establishment of the first concrete plants, where concrete could be batched, mixed, and delivered to construction sites.
4. **Invention of the ready-mixed concrete truck:** One of the key milestones in the development of RMC was the invention of the ready-mixed concrete truck. This innovation, which occurred in the early 20th century, enabled the transportation of freshly mixed concrete to construction sites. It revolutionized the industry by providing a more convenient and consistent supply of concrete.
5. **Standardization and quality control:** As the use of RMC became more widespread, there was a growing emphasis on standardization and quality control. Industry standards were developed to ensure that RMC met specific criteria for strength, durability, and consistency.
6. **Advancements in technology:** Over the years, advancements in technology have further improved the production and delivery of RMC. Innovations such as computerized batching systems, specialized additives, and improved mixing techniques have enhanced the performance and versatility of RMC.
7. **Environmental considerations:** In recent decades, there has been a greater focus on sustainability and environmental responsibility in construction practices. As a result, there has been a shift towards using alternative materials in concrete mixes, as well as implementing more eco-friendly production methods.

8. **Globalization and market growth:** Today, ready-mixed concrete is a multi-billion-dollar industry that operates on a global scale. It plays a vital role in modern construction projects, offering convenience, consistency, and reliability.

10.2 ADVANTAGES OF READY-MIXED CONCRETE

Ready-mixed concrete (RMC) offers several advantages over traditional on-site mixed concrete, making it a preferred choice for many construction projects. Some of the key advantages are:

1. **Consistency and quality control:** RMC is produced in specialized batching plants under controlled conditions, ensuring uniformity and consistency in the mix. This results in higher quality concrete with predictable properties, such as strength, durability, and workability.
2. **Time and labor savings:** Using RMC eliminates the need for on-site batching, mixing, and handling of raw materials, which can be time-consuming and labor-intensive. Construction crews can focus on other tasks, leading to increased productivity and faster project completion.
3. **Reduced wastage:** RMC is delivered in the exact quantity needed for the project, minimizing material wastage and reducing the environmental impact associated with excess concrete disposal.
4. **Improved workability:** Ready-mixed concrete can be customized to meet specific project requirements, such as desired slump or setting time. This allows for better workability and placement, resulting in smoother finishes and reduced labor efforts.
5. **Cost efficiency:** While the initial cost of RMC may be slightly higher than on-site mixed concrete due to transportation and batching plant expenses, the overall cost savings can be significant. Factors such as reduced labor costs, decreased construction time, and minimized wastage contribute to long-term cost efficiency.
6. **Enhanced safety:** RMC eliminates the need for on-site concrete mixing equipment, reducing the risk of accidents and injuries associated with handling heavy machinery and hazardous materials.
7. **Greater control over supply:** Using RMC provides construction managers with greater control over the supply chain, ensuring a steady and reliable source of concrete throughout the project. This minimizes disruptions and delays due to material shortages or inconsistencies.
8. **Versatility and customization:** Ready-mixed concrete can be tailored to meet specific project requirements, including strength, durability, and aesthetic considerations. Additives and admixtures can be incorporated into the mix to enhance performance and achieve desired characteristics.
9. **Support for sustainable practices:** Many RMC producers prioritize sustainability by incorporating recycled materials, optimizing energy usage, and implementing efficient waste management practices. This aligns with the growing demand for environmentally responsible construction solutions.

10.3 PRODUCTION METHODS

In the production of ready-mixed concrete involves various processes, including handling raw materials, batching ingredients, mixing the concrete, and loading delivery vehicles. There is no universally agreed-upon "best approach," as each plant makes choices based on economic factors and market demands specific to its location. Due to the short shelf life of the product, plants are strategically situated near potential markets. Designing a ready-mixed concrete plant requires an accurate understanding of local market size, the types of concrete commonly used, and realistic projections for demand as well as:

i. Types of materials
ii. Storage capacity
iii. Processing sequences
iv. Truck mixer capacity and throughput
v. Planning requirements
vi. Quality control requirements
vii. Duration of operation
viii. Health and safety regulations

10.3.1 Material Types

The variety of cement types required in a region depends on the expected demand for different concrete types, while the availability of aggregates is determined by local sources, including gravel, limestone, granite, sand, and crushed rock fines, whether sourced from land or marine locations. Typically, plants stock 20 mm and 10 mm maximum-size coarse aggregates, and sometimes 40 mm, based on local preferences.

A dual-silo plant equipped to store Portland cement (PC) alongside ground granulated blast furnace slag (GGBFS) or pulverized fuel ash (PFA) can produce standard concrete and certain grades of sulfate-resistant concrete. However, it may not be equipped to produce rapid-hardening concrete without the need to empty and refill a silo with rapid-hardening cement.

10.3.2 Storage Capacity

Efficient handling of incoming materials in bulk is essential for cost-effective production of ready-mixed concrete. The current legal weight limit on vehicles, based on a maximum axle load of 10 tons, significantly impacts the delivery costs of cements and aggregates. Cement tankers typically deliver up to 20 tons of cement, and during periods of increased concrete demand, ready-mixed concrete producers depend on cement suppliers' tanker fleets to replenish silos. However, fluctuations in cement pricing may prompt ready-mixed concrete companies to opt for direct collection from the source. Modern tippers can transport up to 24 tons of aggregates, influencing the design of storage facilities such as cement silos and aggregate bins to accommodate bulk delivery vehicle capacities.

When plants are strategically located near aggregate sources such as quarries, gravel pits, railheads, or wharves, the need for extensive storage facilities at the ready-mixed concrete plants is reduced. Maintaining the moisture content of aggregates, particularly sand, is crucial for determining aggregate storage capacity and layout.

10.3.3 Processing Sequence

Batching, often accompanied by mixing options, is crucial for ready-mixed concrete production. The maximum batch size significantly impacts plant production rates, although most plants are not designed to load a truck mixer with materials in a single batch.

Accurate weighing of solid constituent materials has long been essential for producing quality concrete, with recent years witnessing notable automation advancements in the batching process. Improved reliability of automatic controls and computerization allows for more sophisticated adjustments. While balanced mechanical lever systems remain common for weighing equipment, load cell weighing and some continuous weighing systems are also utilized. Discharge control from storage and weigh hoppers primarily relies on gates operated by compressed air cylinders (Fig. 10.1).

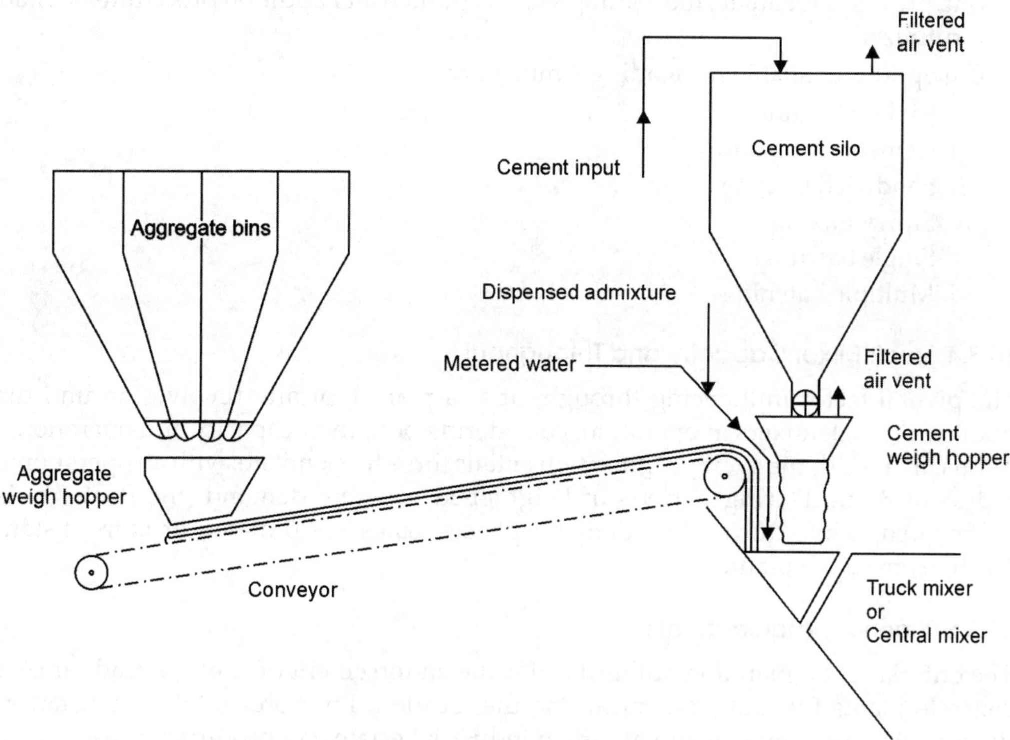

Fig. 10.1: Weigh hopper system

Emphasis on calibration underscores the importance of conducting routine and specialized checks of the weighing process with ease, influencing plant layouts. Flow meters are widely used for water measurements, though some plants still weigh water. Dispensers are almost universally employed for measuring admixtures, with ease of calibration influencing their design and installation.

Modern truck mixers' ability to thoroughly mix various concrete types affects the justification for including a mixer in the processing sequence. Local market demand for lean mix concretes often dictates the inclusion of a mixer in plant design, especially for semi-dry concretes frequently collected in tippers.

Typically, plants where all concrete must pass through the mixer are primarily located in urban areas. A common compromise involves having two production streams: a "dry-leg" directly feeding the truck mixer, and a "wet-leg" passing through a mixer. These "wet-leg" mixers often have limited capacity.

In addition to raising capital costs, including a mixer undoubtedly increases a plant's energy requirements and maintenance costs. Therefore, deciding whether to include or omit a mixer in the production process can significantly impact the commercial viability of the plant.

The predominant method of ready-mixed concrete production involves loading batched materials into a truck mixer and mixing them through drum rotation. Achieving uniformity within batches is primarily influenced by the loading method employed. Practices have adapted to suit local material characteristics, but if concrete mixing proves inadequate, the loading sequence and water addition procedures should be scrutinized.

The options available for loading a mixer are:

i. Ribbon loading
ii. Cement-last loading
iii. Sandwich loading
iv. Slurry mixing
v. Single batching
vi. Multiple batching

10.3.4 Truck Mixer Capacity and Throughput

The pivotal factor influencing throughput at a plant typically revolves around the number of truck mixers in operation, considering both their capacity and operational radius. In the UK, the average utilization entails three truck mixers with an operational radius of 8 km. During periods of heightened concrete demand, the fleet size is augmented, while during low-demand phases, sales are pursued at more distant locations from the plant.

10.3.5 Planning Requirements

The criteria set by planning authorities for the endorsement of sites for ready-mixed concrete plants fluctuate depending on the location. Environmental circumstances diverge between a quarry and an urban industrial estate, yet producers must adhere to the standards outlined by the Environmental Protection Acts.

10.3.6 Quality Control Requirements

With the multitude of methods currently utilized for specifying concrete, it is imperative for a responsible ready-mixed concrete producer aiming to fulfill market demands to implement a highly comprehensive quality system. This entails establishing protocols for sampling, crafting cube specimens, curing, and conducting tests under standardized conditions, necessitating the establishment of a laboratory for collating test data and formulating new mixes. The expense associated with quality control facilities has prompted the consolidation of plants within a company into regional clusters, with quality control operations overseen from a central technical hub. The provision of laboratory facilities, mobile sampling and testing units, as well as staffing requirements to monitor constituent materials and ensure compliance with orders received, constitutes a pivotal aspect of any company's quality system, with the establishment and maintenance of such a laboratory and control system constituting a significant investment.

10.3.7 Duration of Operations

The anticipated duration of plant operation plays a crucial role in determining the type of plant suitable for installation. While truly mobile plants are rare, transportable ones are prevalent, with many ready-mixed concrete producers opting to establish plants on significant construction sites for the project's duration. Regardless of the operational timeframe, substantial investment in foundations, services, assembly and disassembly, access roads, paved areas, wash-down facilities, and effluent disposal is necessary. Regardless of the relatively short operational period, maintaining product quality remains paramount, thus upholding standards of good practice remains unchanged.

10.3.8 Health and Safety

For ready-mixed concrete plants, the Health and Safety Executive has recommended particular attention to the following areas:

i. **Conveyor safety:** Ensuring adequate guarding on conveyors and conveyor drives, positioning the bottom pulley for spillage clearance, and providing safe access for tracking correction and belt adjustment during operation.

ii. **Mixer access:** Implementing interlocking systems for mixer access points to prevent hand and arm injuries.

iii. **Emergency procedures:** Proper placement of belt isolators and establishment of lockout procedures to ensure plant isolation from power when maintenance requires guard removal.

iv. **Traffic management:** Directing incoming cement tankers, aggregate tippers, and outgoing truck mixers to minimize reversing, segregating vehicles and pedestrians, and utilizing audible warning systems.

v. **Inspection points:** Installing grids and pulpits at ground hopper tipping points for inspection purposes.

vi. **Inspection systems:** Establishing a safe system for visually checking fresh concrete during mixing.

vii. **Access safety:** Providing edge protection and safe access for maintenance and operating personnel throughout the plant.

viii. **Silos and tanks:** Ensuring safe entry into silos and tanks, equipping with relevant safety gear including lighting and anchorages.

ix. **Site security:** Implementing site security measures to prevent unauthorized access by the public.

10.4 ORGANIZING PRODUCTION AND DELIVERY

Companies vary in how they organize and control production and delivery operations. Some manage operations at the depot level, while others, especially larger and medium-sized companies, have centralized shipping offices catering to specific markets. While computerization is suitable for meeting these requirements, its economic feasibility is influenced by geography and market conditions. Effective credit control systems are integral to any company's organization due to the short turnaround time between order placement and delivery, coupled with the inability to reclaim delivered products.

Management systems utilizing computer technology have been developed to enhance productivity levels. The degree of computerization varies among companies, ranging from comprehensive automation of all functions to the use of small personal computers for specific tasks, such as printing batching instructions instead of manually preparing batch books. Software and hardware packages are available to cover various aspects, including order processing, delivery execution with batch control, material scheduling at plants, and administrative tasks such as invoicing.

10.5 DELIVERY

10.5.1 Truck Mixers

Ready-mixed concrete is not just a commodity; it is also a service, with approximately 20 million cubic meters delivered annually via truckmixers. The evolution of the truck mixer from a basic mobile site mixer in the late 1940s to a sophisticated vehicle capable of efficiently mixing, delivering, and distributing concrete has been remarkable. Indeed, the economic feasibility of ready-mixed concrete hinges on the effective utilization of this specialized fleet of truckmixers.

10.5.2 Mixing

The adaptable truck mixer serves three primary functions in the production process:

i. **At a ready-mixed concrete plant:** Dry batched materials, along with water, are loaded into the truck mixer, and mixing occurs at the plant. While in transit, the drum can be rotated slowly to maintain agitation. Upon arrival at the site, the drum is spun at mixing speed for a brief period to ensure thorough remixing before discharge.

ii. **On-site mixing:** The truck mixer is loaded with dry batched materials at the plant and transported to the site. Upon arrival, mixing water is added, and mixing is completed before discharge.

iii. **Agitation:** The truck mixer is loaded with pre-mixed concrete from a plant mixer. During transit, the drum can be rotated slowly to keep the mix agitated, and at the site, the drum is spun at mixing speed to ensure complete remixing before discharge.

10.5.3 Delivery

The truck mixer vehicles come in capacities ranging from 2 to 9 cubic meters, but the most commonly used ones typically hold 6 cubic meters of concrete (Fig. 10.2). Ready-mixed concrete, with its limited "shelf life" lasting only a few hours, primarily operates as a "local delivery" service. On average, the distance from the depot to the point of delivery is approximately 8 km, although this distance varies between urban and rural areas. While longer deliveries are feasible, their economic viability requires thorough examination.

Fig. 10.2: A 6 cubic meter truck mixer

10.5.4 Distribution

Upon arrival at the site, the typical truck mixer is capable of:

i. Mixing the concrete and, if necessary, modifying the properties of the plastic concrete by adding measured water.
ii. Discharging the concrete directly using a fitted chute and extensions.
iii. Adjusting the discharge rate to meet the specific placing requirements on site.

10.5.5 Type of Vehicles

The mixer unit, installed on a commercial vehicle chassis, comprises an abrasion-resistant steel drum set at an inclination of approximately 16°. Inside the drum are blades designed to mix and agitate the ingredients as the drum rotates in one direction, while also facilitating the discharge of mixed concrete when the drum is reversed. Power to rotate the drum can be derived from the main truck engine, utilizing a hydraulic power drive to the drum; a separate engine (commonly referred to as a "donkey" engine) with hydraulic drive; or a separate engine with a mechanical coupling to the drum. Replacement of the drum is feasible when it becomes worn, with the rate

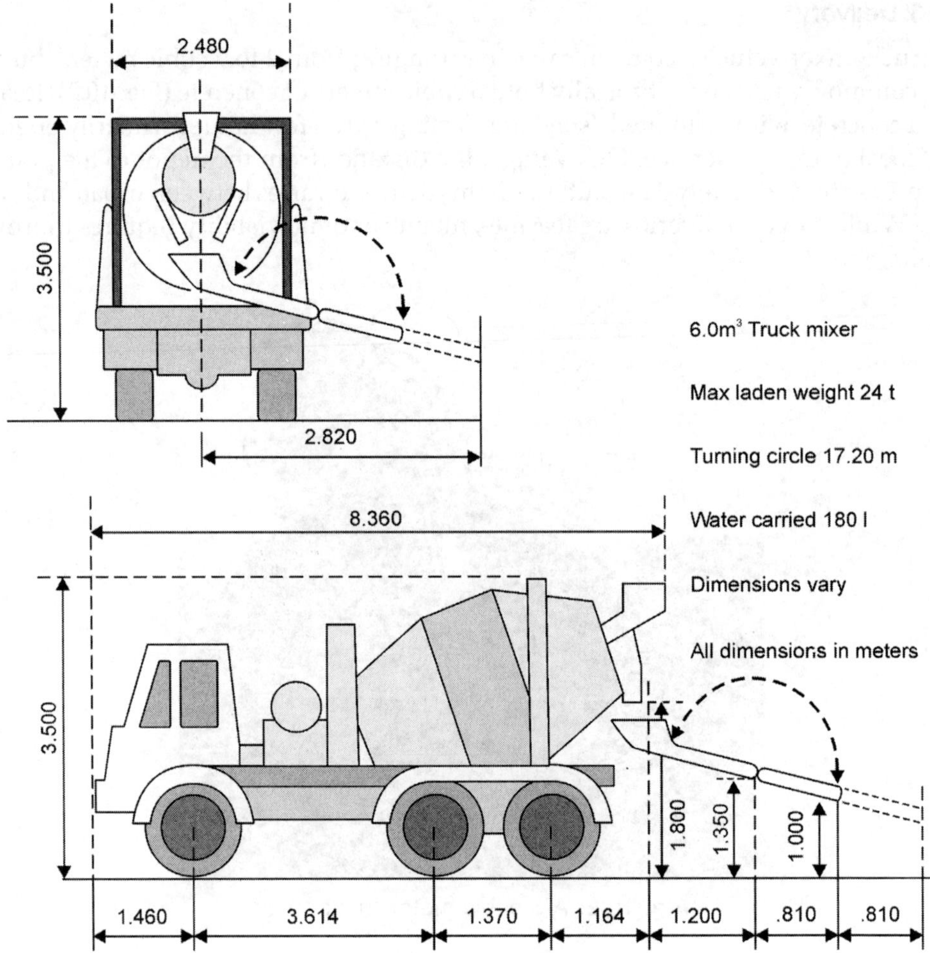

Fig. 10.3: Typical truck mixer dimensions

of wear significantly influenced by the abrasive nature of the aggregates. However, most companies typically anticipate a mixer lifespan exceeding four years (Fig. 10.3).

10.5.6 Tippers

A considerable quantity of concrete is obtained directly from ready-mixed concrete plants using tippers. In plants equipped with a wet-leg system, the mixed concrete is discharged directly into the tipper. In cases where there is no central mixer at the plant, the components are batched into a truck mixer, mixed, and then discharged from the truck mixer into the tipper. If needed, a ramp is used to elevate the discharge chute above the sides of the tipper for efficient transfer.

10.5.7 Conveyers

Some truck mixers are equipped with conveyors attached to them. The utility of a belt conveyor is demonstrated in Fig. 10.4. Another truck mixer can be employed to supply material to the conveyor.

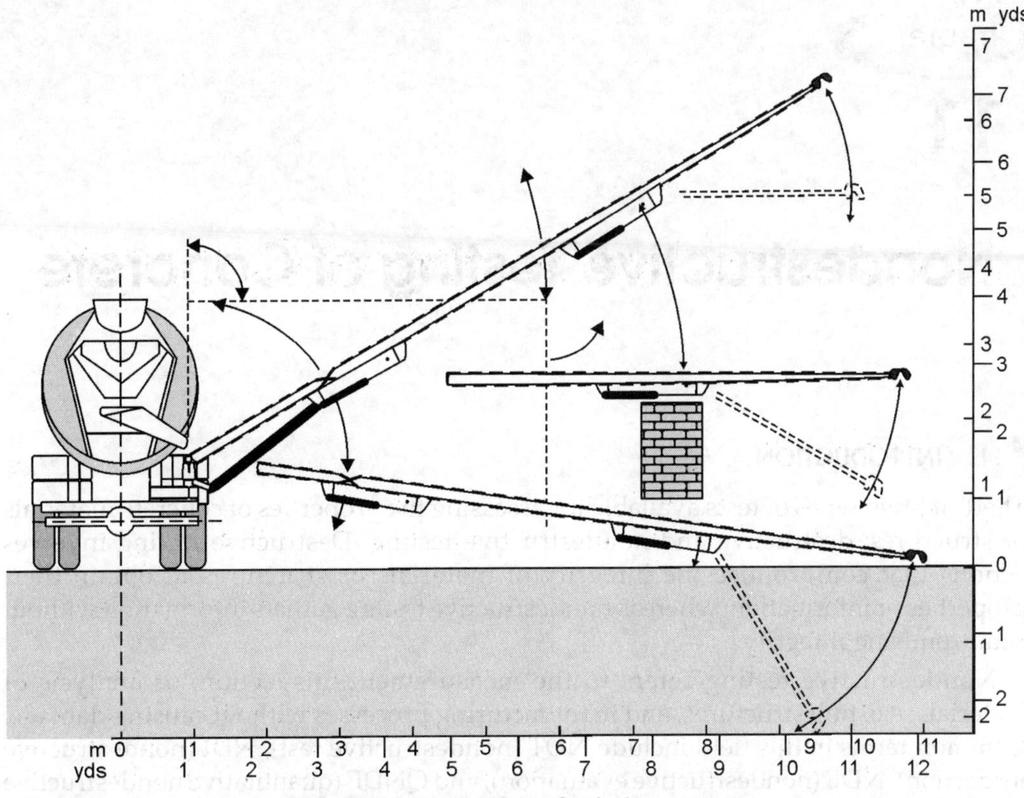

Fig. 10.4: Application of a belt conveyor

10.6 QUALITY ASSURANCE

Ensuring confidence in the qualities of concrete necessitates:

i. Objectively defining the required qualities of fresh and hardened concrete.
ii. Conducting production, delivery, and on-site processes under controlled conditions that enable tracing of the entire process from constituent materials to cured concrete.
iii. Validating all testing performed in control and compliance procedures.

The ready-mixed concrete producer can only deliver what is specified in the order, as the contract to supply exists solely between the purchaser and the supplier. Thus, the concrete producer's role concludes upon producing and delivering the concrete down the discharge chute. They have no authority over how the concrete is placed, compacted, finished, cured, or protected.

Production control testing by the ready-mixed concrete producer must adhere to agreed standards. However, compliance testing by the purchaser holds limited value unless it aligns with the same agreed standards. Quality assurance encompasses the entire process, not solely production, yet ensuring quality in the production process remains a significant component.

Chapter

11

Nondestructive Testing of Concrete

11.1 INTRODUCTION

There are two types of tests available for assessing the properties of concrete materials or structures: destructive and nondestructive testing. Destructive testing involves actions that compromise the integrity of materials or structures to obtain their properties or information, whereas nondestructive testing gathers information without compromising integrity.

Nondestructive testing refers to the measurement, inspection, or analysis of materials, existing structures, and manufacturing processes without causing damage. Common terms in this field include NDT (nondestructive test), NDI (nondestructive inspection), NDE (nondestructive evaluation), and QNDE (quantitative nondestructive evaluation). The first three terms are interchangeable, while QNDE emphasizes quantitative analysis and can be more challenging to implement.

The application fields of nondestructive testing encompass various areas:

a. Quality control of concrete materials and structures, involving monitoring hydration processes, evaluating strength development, monitoring curing processes, assessing welding quality of reinforcing steel, and detecting porosity in matured concrete members.
b. In-service inspections of concrete materials and structures, including assessments of corrosion degree and rate, residual strength, fatigue damage, existing crack length, debonding of interfaces, and impact damage.

Nondestructive testing in concrete engineering (NDT-CE) plays a crucial role in evaluating the quality and maturity of concrete structures during construction, aiding decision-making and expediting construction procedures. It serves as a quality control tool for new constructions, assessing reliability, integrity, and construction conditions comprehensively or selectively.

NDT-CE proves invaluable for evaluating the serviceability and stability of concrete structures, informing maintenance and renovation decisions for aged buildings and infrastructure by estimating material and structural performance. It facilitates the localization and measurement of defects or damage within structures for repair or removal purposes, as well as locating prestressed elements to prevent accidental damage during drilling.

Overall, NDT-CE significantly contributes to evaluating and ensuring building safety and preserving invaluable monuments cost-effectively, quickly, and efficiently. Practical NDT-CE techniques should meet several key requirements:

- Effectiveness in determining relevant quantities
- Accuracy in determining the shape, size, and depth of defects
- Insensitivity to surface conditions and object shape
- Efficiency in terms of labor and equipment, with simplicity and speed of use
- Economic viability, with low equipment and maintenance costs
- Non-intrusive to the surrounding environment
- Safety for operators and equipment
- Convenience for users
- Preferably non-contacting
- Capability to inspect both large and localized areas

While it may be challenging for any specific NDT-CE technique to meet all requirements, it should aim to fulfill as many as possible. The performance of concrete in a building often differs from laboratory conditions, highlighting the importance of *in situ* testing directly on concrete structures.

It is often stated that numerous nondestructive testing (NDT) methods have been attempted on concrete structures, but none have proven entirely satisfactory. This assertion holds partial truth because concrete, being the most commonly used building material, is inherently heterogeneous, porous, and subject to significant variability. The average properties of concrete are influenced by factors, such as the types and proportions of raw materials, variations in water content, curing conditions, microstructure of hardened binders, cement mix composition, as well as the type, shape, orientation, size, and distribution of aggregates, and the condition of concrete reinforcement. Moreover, the sheer scale of building or bridge structures presents challenges for achieving precise results.

Furthermore, limitations are inherent to NDT-CE techniques themselves, despite their potential strengths in certain areas. To effectively utilize NDT-CE techniques, a deep understanding of the specific challenges posed by the concrete structures or materials being tested is essential. Accurate selection of NDT-CE techniques requires a solid grasp of the underlying principles of testing techniques and the devices employed. This typically necessitates interdisciplinary collaboration, thorough familiarity with the specimen, instrument calibration, and skilled operators.

Since the 1980s, advancements in NDT-CE techniques have progressed significantly, driven by developments in digital electronics and computer technology. Automation has become prevalent, with computer-controlled instruments facilitating automated measurements, analysis, and display of test results in user-friendly formats. This process, known as digital signal processing, has substantially improved the efficiency and accuracy of data analysis. Notable advancements were observed in the 1990s, particularly in ultrasonic pulse-echo testing, radar and impact echo techniques, data analysis methods, and the interpretation and simulation of test results.

In NDT-CE, an allowable tolerance approach is commonly adopted. This entails acknowledging the inherent detection limits of NDT methods and permitting flaws or

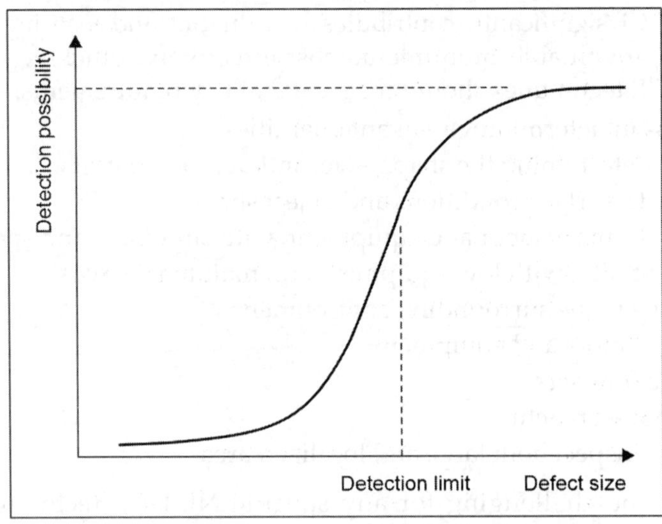

Fig. 11.1: No clear cutoff in detection resolution

cracks to remain if their size falls below a critical threshold. Additionally, inspection intervals for different concrete structures may be adjusted based on their significance and economic considerations. Probability theory is often employed in NDT-CE to account for uncertainties in detection resolution, as illustrated in Fig. 11.1.

11.2 PRINCIPLES AND CLASSIFICATIONS

In general, NDT serves as a means to understand the properties or internal structures of components under inspection, particularly for components that are optically opaque, without causing damage. There exist numerous NDT techniques, including mechanical, elastic wave, electromagnetic, and optical techniques. Four main aspects characterize a specific NDT technique. Firstly, the physical principle upon which the technique is founded, referred to as the principle, serves as the foundation. Secondly, the method employed in realizing the measurement represents the approach taken. Thirdly, the equipment utilized to carry out the function specified is crucial, and lastly, the signal processing scheme adopted plays a vital role.

Of these aspects, the principle holds the utmost significance as it determines how received signals are linked to material properties and interpreted regarding structural conditions and qualities. The efficacy and limitations of an NDT technique are fundamentally governed by the underlying physical principles. The method denotes the manner in which measurements are realized and represents a key aspect of an NDT technique. There are various possible methods following a principle; for instance, wave-related NDT techniques may employ transmission or reflection methods. Equipment serves as the physical medium for conducting NDT measurements and is designed in alignment with the principle and method. The suitability of an NDT technique largely hinges on the capabilities of the equipment employed.

The signal processing scheme is crucial for extracting useful information from gathered signals. While data interpretation is primarily based on the principles of the method, signal processing also plays a significant role. In modern NDT measurements, signal processing, particularly digital signal processing (DSP), has become indispensable due to advancements in computer technology and mathematical analysis tools. It is important to differentiate between the terms "signal" and "information." A signal is the direct measurement obtained by a sensor, whereas information is interpreted from the signal. Signals act as carriers of information, and the goal is to have fewer signals that carry more meaningful information, thus minimizing noise and maximizing interpretability.

NDT techniques can be categorized based on four main aspects: the physical principle they adhere to, the methods they employ, the equipment utilized, and the signal processing scheme applied. Additionally, classification can be based on the intended objectives or goals of the technique. In practice, a wide array of NDT-CE techniques exists. Some examples include mechanical techniques, such as building dynamics, impact echo, ultrasound, and acoustic emission techniques. There are also electromagnetic techniques like eddy current, electrochemical methods, microwaves, nuclear magnetic resonance, magnetic methods, and radiography. Optical methods, including interferometry, infrared thermography, and fiber optic sensors, are also utilized. Imaging techniques like computer tomography are employed as NDT-CE techniques as well. Classification based on the physical working principle generally divides NDT-CE techniques into three categories: direct measurement techniques, load-induced reaction measurement techniques, and measurements conducted through an inquiring agency.

11.2.1 Direct Measurement NDT Techniques

In some cases, the properties or characteristics of a material can be directly measured or inferred through NDT measurements. This type of testing is known as direct NDT-CE technique. Direct-measurement NDT-CE techniques rely on fundamental physical principles. For instance, density measurement involves weighing the object provided its volume is known. This technique can also determine moisture content in a concrete sample by weighing the sample, drying it, and reweighing it to measure the weight difference, which directly correlates with moisture content. Another example is the half-cell potential measurement technique, commonly used for electrochemical NDT-CE assessments of reinforced concrete structures. This technique measures the macrocurrent of corroding steel bars in reinforced concrete, allowing for easy deduction of corrosion condition. The magnetic leakage technique is another direct NDT-CE method, which measures the premagnetized magnetic field of steel-reinforced concrete. Changes in the magnetic field indicate steel rebar fracture.

While direct NDT-CE testing techniques are typically straightforward, they may not always be suitable for *in situ* applications. For instance, the weighing-drying-weighing technique may not be feasible for on-site testing. Nonetheless, such techniques remain valuable in practice, particularly for testing structures in a minimally destructive manner, such as by extracting samples from columns, beams, slabs, or walls through coring.

11.2.2 Load-induced Reaction Measurement NDT Techniques

This technique involves subjecting the object under test to a controlled level of loading to observe its response, ensuring that the load remains within a reasonable range to avoid damaging the test specimen. Signals collected during this process reflect the characteristics of the test object. Building dynamics serves as an example of this approach. In building dynamics, the natural or eigen frequency of a structure (such as a building or a bridge) is excited by a random load and subsequently measured. Additionally, mode shapes can be determined as necessary. These data can then be compared with theoretical predictions from the structure's model to extract information regarding its integrity, stiffness, stability, and any macroscopic defects. Another instance of this technique is the impact echo method, which assesses the dynamic response of a structure to an applied impact load.

11.2.3 Measurement through Inquiring Agent NDT Techniques

These methods utilize an inquiring agent, typically in the form of a wave packet, to probe materials under inspection. They can be categorized into active and passive techniques. In active techniques, a wave packet is generated by the test instrument and transmitted into the materials being inspected. Examples include ultrasonic testing and microwave testing. The wave packet, acting as the probe agency, interacts with the material matrix and any embedded objects, if present. Subsequently, it emits a signal carrying information about the specimen. On the other hand, passive techniques involve the wave packet originating from the tested specimen itself, providing information about the processes occurring within the specimen. An example is the acoustic emission NDT-CE technique.

The most commonly used inquiring agents in NDT-CE include mechanical waves (such as acoustic and ultrasonic waves) and electromagnetic waves [including ultrahigh frequencies (UHF), L-band, and S-band microwaves]. Additionally, infrared light, visible light, X-rays, and gamma-ray radiation are also utilized. From a physical perspective, infrared light, visible light, X-rays, and gamma-ray radiation are fundamentally electromagnetic waves.

11.3 COMPONENTS OF NDT

As previously stated, NDT-CE refers to nondestructive testing in concrete engineering, which represents a relatively recent field within NDT applications. Large-scale experiments in this area began in the 1980s.

NDT-CE activities can be categorized based on two main aspects: the test objects or issues being addressed, and the testing methods employed. However, these categories are interconnected. A single problem may necessitate the use of multiple NDT techniques, or conversely, a single technique may be applicable to various test objects or issues.

11.3.1 Testing Objects

The subjects of NDT-CE testing encompass a variety of structures, including masonry buildings, typically low-rise residential or office buildings constructed from concrete blocks, as well as concrete bridges, high-rise buildings, dams, highways, and airport runways. In contrast to NDT applications in other domains, structures examined in NDT-CE are often larger, possess more intricate shapes, and exhibit complex properties. Consequently, NDT-CE typically necessitates meticulously crafted inspection strategies and the utilization of multiple techniques.

11.3.2 Testing Problems

The challenges in NDT-CE testing can be categorized based on load-carrying capabilities and resistance to environmental factors:

a. **Strength:** Determining the strength of concrete on-site can differ significantly from laboratory measurements, with variations over the service life of the concrete. Assessing the residual strength of fire-damaged concrete and determining steel yield stress after natural disasters are critical maintenance tasks requiring NDT-CE.
b. **Cracks and fractures:** Concrete's tendency to crack under tensile stresses poses durability issues, as cracks can facilitate the ingress of harmful agents. Detecting crack properties, including length, width, position, and propagation rate, is essential for evaluating their severity.
c. **Thickness:** Accurate measurement of pavement, retaining wall, reinforcing steel cover, and slab thickness is crucial for quality assurance in construction and maintenance of concrete structures.
d. **Moisture:** Moisture presence in concrete structures can lead to various durability problems such as corrosion, leaching, alkali-aggregate reaction, and leakage. Detecting moisture location and content is a common NDT-CE concern.
e. **Corrosion:** Corrosion represents a severe durability issue, often causing concrete cover cracking and spalling. Detecting corrosion occurrence, rate, and degree is vital, especially for prestressed concrete structures.
f. **Debonding:** Separation of bonded materials indicates significant damage or deterioration in concrete structures. Debonding issues, frequently caused by corrosion-induced loss of adhesive effect or shear stress damage to interfaces, are common challenges addressed by NDT-CE.

11.3.3 Testing Methods

The classification and overview of commonly used NDT-CE methods were briefly discussed earlier, with detailed descriptions provided in the following sections. Below is a concise introduction to most NDT-CE methods:

a. **Mechanical wave techniques (MWT):** These methods utilize mechanical waves as the working mechanism, governed by principles of wave generation and propagation. Ultrasonic waves, acoustic waves, and subacoustic waves fall under this category. MWT techniques offer advantages, such as accuracy, deep penetration, low cost, ease of operation, and safety. They are commonly used for measurement, detection, and monitoring in civil engineering applications.
   i. *Ultrasonic techniques (UT)*: UT operates within the ultrasonic band, typically between 0.1 and 25 MHz. It involves introducing high-frequency sound waves into materials to detect surface and subsurface flaws. UT offers accuracy,

convenience, and versatility in defect detection. Piezoelectric transducers are commonly used to generate ultrasound, with pulse wave ultrasound being the dominant technique. Signal processing plays a crucial role in UT for data analysis and interpretation.

ii. *Acoustic emission (AE)*: AE is a passive NDT method that detects energy released from microcracks, dislocations, and inclusions in concrete. It provides valuable information about active cracks that pose risks to structures.

iii. *Impact echo (IE)*: IE involves generating an impact on a concrete specimen and analyzing its response to determine properties, such as dynamic modulus and Poisson's ratio. Time-domain and frequency-domain analysis of the received response help interpret material properties and assess structural damage.

b. **The electromagnetic wave technique (EMT)** is a powerful method widely used in NDT for concrete engineering due to its applicability to non-metallic materials. EMT employs electromagnetic waves as the probing agent and is considered an active method capable of both contact and non-contact measurements. It offers numerous advantages over other techniques.

Electromagnetic waves span a broad frequency range, including radio waves, high-frequency waves (RF), very high-frequency waves (VHF), ultra-high-frequency waves, microwaves (L-band, S-band), infrared light (IR), and light, among others. In NDT engineering, these waves are categorized based on their frequency range, with EMT typically utilizing frequencies from RF to the S-band, particularly microwaves ranging from 90 MHz to 1 GHz.

EMT is particularly suitable for testing non-metallic materials, offering deep penetration and high sensitivity in detecting metal objects within non-metal matrices, such as steel bars in concrete. It can detect flat defects that may be challenging to identify using X-ray techniques and is not influenced by aggregate size or type. For instance, radar, a microwave-based technique, can detect small objects like 6-mm-diameter steel bars and 20 by 20 mm voids within concrete with a cover thickness of approximately 200 mm.

The operation of EMT systems is fast and straightforward. However, they may have limitations, such as the inability to penetrate beyond metallic sheets and provide information on structures beyond them. Additionally, EMT equipment tends to be relatively expensive.

EMT relies on physical laws governing microwave generation, propagation, and reception, similar to those encountered in ultrasonic testing. Key parameters measured during EMT include amplitude, phase, frequency, and time of flight, which are used to deduce information about the properties of the test object, including its structure and mechanical properties. These parameters depend on electromagnetic parameters of the material, such as permittivity, permeability, and conductivity, as well as geometrical parameters like thickness and orientation.

The microwave NDT technique is highly versatile, offering applications in building inspections, quality control, and various detection tasks, such as locating steel objects, moisture assessment, water content measurement, and crack detection. It is particularly effective in determining the lateral positions of rebars, identifying metallic ducts, T-girders, and anchors in prefabricated concrete elements, as well as measuring cover thickness and moisture levels in concrete. With microwaves, it is possible to observe artificial birefringence properties in ceramics and cement, enabling visualization of internal structures within specimens.

A prominent instrument within EMT is ground-penetrating radar (GPR), known for its effectiveness in profiling bridge piles during scour investigations. To optimize GPR survey design, it is recommended to select a maximum frequency that ensures clutter reduction, typically with a wavelength at least ten times larger than the characteristic dimension of geological materials. Operating within the frequency range of 90 MHz to 1 GHz and a pulse repetition frequency of 25 Hz, GPR can yield significant results, such as identifying scour depths, sediment layers, and water depths swiftly and accurately across large areas, including extensive airport pavements.

The EMT provides a dependable means of assessing structural integrity and accurately locating tendons and metal ducts, particularly those with a diameter of 85 mm. It offers valuable insights into the geometric dimensions of structures. EMT is adept at identifying defects in concrete components, including voids in tendon ducts and compression faults, as well as honeycombing within concrete ranging from 80 to 160 mm in size. Notably, EMT demonstrates insensitivity to aggregate size variations. For instance, in concrete with aggregate sizes ranging from 8 to 32 mm and cover thickness of 340 ± 10 mm, EMT can pinpoint the lateral position of reinforcement with a precision of ±10 mm. Furthermore, the utilization of a microwave moisture content meter facilitates real-time monitoring of water content in clay substrates.

c. **Optical techniques:** These methodologies employ light waves as the probing mechanism and are categorized as active techniques. They primarily rely on interferometry and energy transportation principles. Notably, interferometric methods leverage the interference of two light sources to assess surface alterations in concrete specimens. Examples of these methods encompass holographic, moiré, and electronic speckle pattern interferometry techniques.

   Infrared thermography operates on the principles of radiation theory. By detecting variations in surface temperature arising from discrepancies in material radiation beneath the surface, infrared thermography can identify instances of debonding and moisture presence within concrete materials or structures.

d. **Electrical and electrochemical methods:** These approaches typically gauge electrical parameters like potential, current, or resistivity, which can be affected by changes in the properties of concrete materials or structures. Consequently, these electrical measurements are employed to infer concrete properties. Examples include noncontact resistivity measurement, half-cell potential measurement, and corrosion current measurement.

   Various other electrical methods for detecting reinforcement corrosion exist. One such technique relies on electrical resistance measurements on a thin section of *in situ* reinforcement. The electrical resistance of the reinforcement bar is inversely correlated with its thickness; hence, as corrosion gradually consumes the thin slice, it becomes thinner, leading to a corresponding increase in resistance. In this method, to facilitate measurements, the probe is typically integrated into a Wheatstone bridge network (Fig. 11.2). One probe arm is shielded from corrosion, while the other arm represents the in-place portion of the reinforcement. The measured resistance ratio serves to monitor the corrosion rate. However, notable drawbacks include the necessity of positioning the exposed probe arm during construction and the associated challenges of sampling techniques required to locate probes in large structures susceptible to localized corrosion.

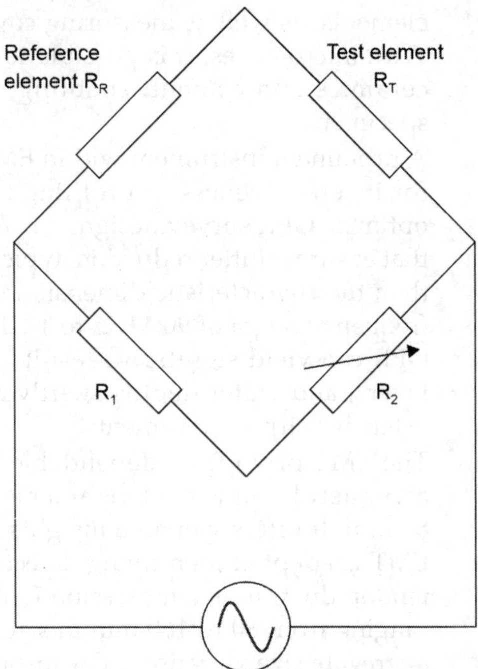

Fig. 11.2: Basic circuit for the electrical resistance probe technique

e. **Magnetic methods:** Magnetic techniques utilize magnetic fields as a fundamental tool for detecting or interpreting material properties. In the context of concrete structures, there are currently three distinct aspects of magnetic field phenomena: (1) alternating current excitation of conducting materials and their magnetic inductance; (2) direct current excitation, resulting in magnetic flux leakage fields around defects in ferromagnetic materials; and (3) nuclear magnetic resonance.

The magnetic induction method is applicable primarily to ferromagnetic materials, where the test equipment circuitry resembles a basic transformer, with the test object acting as a core (Fig. 11.3). By placing a piece of metal close to the transformer coil, the inductance increases, and the change in induced current

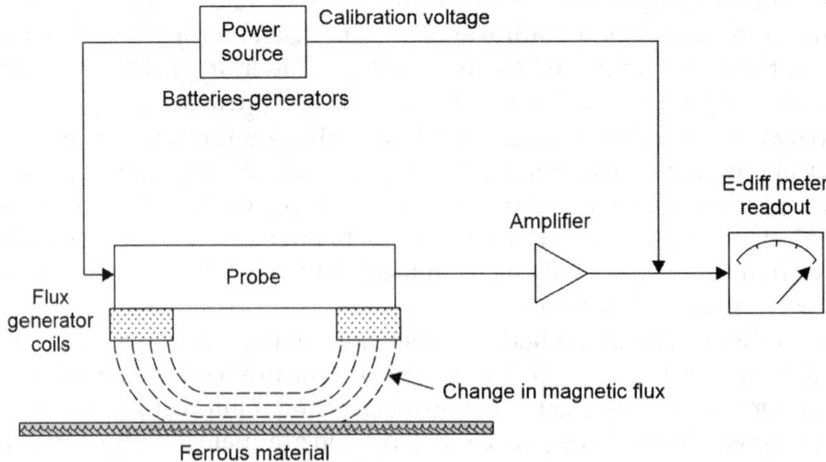

Fig. 11.3: Principle of an induction meter used to locate the reinforcement

depends on the magnetization characteristics, location, and geometry of the metal. This theory has led to the development of equipment for determining the location, sizes, and depth of reinforcement or concrete covers, such as cover meters used to detect embedded steel.

Magnetic flux leakage (MFL) nondestructive testing involves magnetizing a test part, typically a ferromagnetic material, and scanning its surface with a flux-sensitive sensor for the leakage field. When ferromagnetic materials are magnetized, magnetic lines of force pass through the material, increasing in density and strength towards the outer surface. Cracks or defects in materials can perturb the magnetic flux, leading to changes in magnetic permeability and leakage flux. Detection of such discontinuities relies on sensing the leakage flux along with the test member. MFL techniques are suitable for detecting surface or near-surface anomalies in ferromagnetic materials, such as reduction in reinforcement area and tendon breakage in prestressed cables. However, they may not detect internal defects in thick parts where magnetic lines of flux bypass the defect with little leakage. These techniques typically do not require mechanical contact with the testing object and are conducive to automatic signal recognition schemes, facilitating automated, high-speed inspection.

Nuclear magnetic resonance (NMR) relies on the interaction between nuclear magnetic dipole moments and a magnetic field. This phenomenon occurs in electrons, atoms, molecules, and nuclei when subjected to specific radiation frequencies due to space quantization in a magnetic field. In concrete, NMR can determine moisture content by detecting signals from hydrogen nuclei in water molecules. However, this technique requires meticulous surface preparation, ensuring the object is clean and demagnetized. Additionally, high-current electric power is necessary for magnetization, and skilled operators are essential for result interpretation.

Magnetic particle testing is another nondestructive method, primarily used for steel structures. During this process, the object is magnetized and coated with magnetic powder. Surface or near-surface discontinuities in the magnetized material can cause leakage in the magnetic field, altering the orientation of particles above those areas. Alternatively, wet fluorescent particles visible in backlight through a borescope can be utilized. This technique is effective for detecting surface cracks, laps, voids, seams, and other irregularities, with the capability to identify subsurface defects up to approximately 0.635 mm (0.25″) in depth. Magnetic particle testing is fast, straightforward, and cost-effective, but it has limited depth penetration. Despite this limitation, it remains a widely adopted method for nondestructive detection of surface and near-surface discontinuities in ferromagnetic materials, integrated into numerous standards and specifications.

f. **Building dynamics:** Building dynamics involves measuring the vibration of concrete structures under random dynamic loading with minimal amplitude. The measured waveform is analyzed in both time and frequency domains to determine fundamental frequencies and modal modes. This analysis extends to assessing changes in structure stiffness to evaluate the extent of damage.

These techniques are widely utilized in structural engineering. Simple methods are effective for assessing localized integrity, such as delamination, while more complex methods are applied in pile integrity testing, determining member thickness, and examining changes in member stiffness due to cracking or deterioration.

Dynamic response methods for NDT purposes generally fall into three categories: modal analysis, resonant techniques, and damping techniques. Test equipment for building dynamics typically consists of two parts: one for generating mechanical vibrations and the other for sensing these vibrations. The pulse-echo method, involving the measurement of reflected shock waves caused by a surface hammer and subsequent analysis in time and/or frequency domains, is commonly used and straightforward.

For large structures, dynamic response testing may involve hammer impacts or application of vibrating loads, with vibration response recorded by accelerometers. By measuring natural frequencies and/or vibration attenuation rates, information about dynamic properties, defects, damage, and even individual member stiffness can be obtained.

Resonant frequency techniques are also widely used for deriving dynamic properties of building structures. Since every elastic object has multiple resonant frequencies related to stiffness and mass distribution, various physical characteristics can be determined from induced vibration characteristics. Fundamental flexural and extensional modes are typically the easiest to excite and are important for NDT inspection.

When a test object vibrates in one of its natural or resonant modes due to an applied external force, its mode shape reveals its configuration and composition. This method primarily determines dynamic modulus of elasticity, stiffness, and Poisson's ratio. Various factors, such as mix proportions, aggregate properties, specimen size, and curing conditions, can influence resonant frequency method results in concrete structure inspection.

Radiography or radiometry are NDT methods that utilize X-rays or gamma rays to detect internal defects or examine the microstructure of concrete materials or structures. These techniques rely on radioactive sources, including X-rays, gamma rays, or neutrons. Both X-rays and gamma rays have extremely small wavelengths, with X-rays ranging from 3 to 0.03 nm and gamma rays having even smaller wavelengths. As the wavelength decreases, the energy of the radiation increases. Consequently, X-rays and gamma rays, being at the high-energy end of the electromagnetic spectrum, can penetrate matter with some degree of attenuation.

Radiographic and radiometric methods utilize X-rays or gamma rays to detect internal defects or assess the composition of concrete materials or structures. The absorption coefficient, which varies based on material composition, determines the intensity measured by detectors or radiation-sensitive film, providing insights into the material. In radiographic techniques, a radiation source and photographic film are positioned on opposite sides of the test object, resulting in a photographic image of the interior after exposure. These methods are generally efficient and accurate, offering unique insights. However, they require sophisticated technology, significant initial investment, and specialized training and licensing. X-rays can penetrate approximately 1 meter of concrete, revealing details such as aggregate distribution, air void configuration, segregation, and cracks, albeit at a high cost and voltage requirement.

Gamma-ray equipment, not reliant on electricity, has gained popularity but necessitates proper shielding and additional safety precautions due to radioactive materials. Gamma-ray techniques excel in locating reinforcements, concrete voids, or assessing post-tensioned structure grouting quality.

In radiometric approaches, a radiation source and detector are positioned either together or on opposing sides of a concrete member. The number of electric pulses detected correlates with the member's dimensions or physical properties like density or composition. While gamma-rays are commonly used in concrete radiometry, neutron radiometry finds application in asphalt concrete and soil. Geiger-Müller tubes are frequently employed for gamma-ray detection. Gamma-rays passing through concrete are absorbed, transmitted, or scattered, enabling both direct transmission and backscatter modes of examination. Direct transmission mode penetrates 50–300 mm into concrete, while backscatter mode primarily assesses the surface layer within 100 mm. Applications include monitoring density and consolidation degree in fresh concrete using internally embedded probes and noncontact backscatter measurement for thin pavement density monitoring.

h. **Computer tomography:** Computer tomography, a potent post-processing method for X-ray or gamma-ray measurements, enables the slicing of inspected objects into three dimensions with thin segments and subsequent reconstruction into a comprehensive image of the internal microstructure.

Given that mechanical waves (acoustic and ultrasonic) and electromagnetic waves are the primary agents in NDT-CE, comprehending fundamental wave theory becomes crucial for effective NDT-CE management. Therefore, the ensuing sections focus on reviewing wave theories, encompassing aspects such as wave reflection and transmission.

11.4 COMMONLY USED NDT TECHNIQUES

11.4.1 Ultrasonic Technique

As previously discussed, ultrasonic technique (UT) relies on the dynamic movements or vibrations within materials, known as acoustics. All materials consist of atoms, which can undergo vibrational motion around their equilibrium positions. While various atomic vibrational patterns exist, most are irrelevant to acoustics and ultrasonic testing. Acoustics specifically deals with particles containing multiple atoms that move collectively to generate mechanical waves.

When a material isn't stressed beyond its elastic limit, its particles undergo elastic oscillations when displaced from their equilibrium positions, leading to internal restoration forces (electrostatic). These forces, combined with particle inertia, result in the oscillatory motion of the medium. UT encompasses several methods, including pulse velocity, pulse-echo, frequency shift, ultrasonic resonance spectroscopy, 3D imaging, time of flight diffraction (TOFD), and synthetic aperture focusing technique (SAFT). While all UT methods adhere to elastic wave laws, each follows distinct physical principles.

Elastic waves exhibit two types in a homogeneous isotropic solid medium: longitudinal and transverse waves. Consequently, knowing the ultrasonic velocities and material density enables straightforward deduction of elastic modulus, forming the foundation of the pulse velocity method.

Two other significant wave types in solids are surface waves and plate waves. Surface waves, also known as Rayleigh waves, propagate from the surface of a relatively thick solid material, penetrating to a depth of approximately one wavelength. These waves exhibit both longitudinal and transverse motion, resulting in an elliptical orbit motion. The major axis of this elliptical motion is perpendicular to the surface of the solid. As the depth of an individual atom from the surface increases, the width of its elliptical motion decreases. Surface waves are generated when a longitudinal wave intersects a surface near the second critical angle, and they travel at a velocity between 0.87 and 0.95 times that of a shear wave. Rayleigh waves are valuable due to their high sensitivity to surface defects and features, following the curvature of a surface. Consequently, Rayleigh waves can effectively inspect areas inaccessible to other waves.

Plate waves, similar to surface waves, can only be generated in a thin, plate-like specimen, typically a few wavelengths thick. Among plate waves, Lamb waves are the most commonly utilized in NDT. Lamb waves are intricate vibrational waves that propagate parallel to the test surface throughout the material's thickness. Their propagation depends on the material's density, elastic properties, test frequency, and thickness. Lamb waves are generated at an incident angle where the parallel component of the wave's velocity in the source matches that in the test material. These waves can travel several meters in steel, making them useful for scanning plates, wires, and tubes.

With Lamb waves, various modes of particle vibration are possible, with the most common being symmetrical and asymmetrical. Symmetrical Lamb waves move symmetrically about the median plane of the plate, known as the extensional mode, as they "stretch and compress" the plate in the wave motion direction. This mode is most efficiently produced when the exciting force is parallel to the plate. The asymmetrical Lamb wave mode, known as the flexural mode, involves a significant portion of motion in a direction normal to the plate, with little motion parallel to it. In this mode, the plate's body bends as the two surfaces move in the same direction (Fig. 11.4).

Ultrasonic waves experience attenuation during propagation due to three primary mechanisms: beam spreading, absorption by the medium, and scattering by inhomogeneities. Additionally, when encountering an interface between two media with different acoustic impedances, ultrasonic waves undergo reflection, refraction, diffraction, and scattering. The behavior of elastic waves at these interfaces adheres to Snell's law and is intricate. Mode conversion, where longitudinal waves transform into transverse waves and vice versa, also occurs.

The reflection factor is contingent upon the disparity in acoustic impedance (Zi) between the two materials and the angle of incidence. In the simplest scenario of normal incidence with no mode conversion, the reflection factor can be calculated. The resulting reflected and scattered waves are commonly referred to as echoes. The time of flight of an echo is determined by the distance it travels and the velocity of the wave.

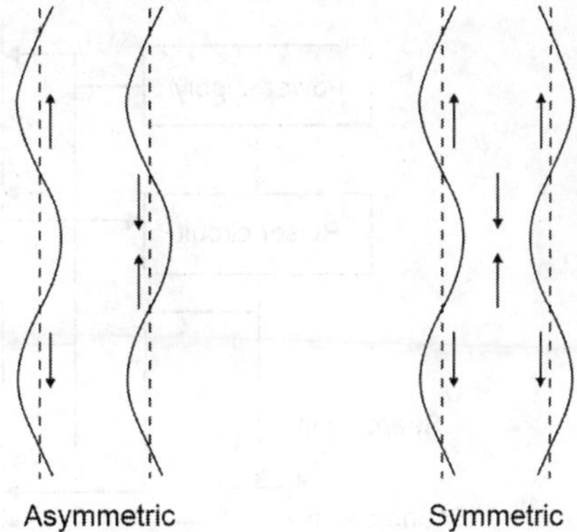

Fig. 11.4: Asymmetric and symmetric Lamb waves

Applications

UT has diverse applications including quality assurance, condition assessment, and reliability evaluation. It is capable of locating and identifying defects such as cracks, fractures, voids, and inhomogeneities. Additionally, UT can measure the thickness and size of defects, and estimate the strength of materials like concrete in various structures such as bridges, drilled shafts, slurry walls, and dams.

Flaw Detection Scanning Technique

The pulse-echo method stands as the simplest and most prevalent ultrasonic application method for flaw detection. This method employs a single piezoelectric transducer to generate an acoustic wave within the object under examination and moves around to detect internal flaws by receiving the reflected signal and utilizing an imaging technique. Three scan methods for flaw detection are commonly employed—A-scan, B-scan, and C-scan—when presenting pulse-echo data.

The A-scan, also known as an amplitude scan, involves placing a transducer directly against the solid material under examination and establishing contact between the transducer and the sample with grease. It displays the received signal in amplitude against the time base. An adjustable threshold of the amplitude level is utilized to suppress noise. Upon emission of an acoustic pulse by the transducer, the generated pulse penetrates into the specimen and is reflected by acoustic impedance discontinuities caused by flaws. The resulting echo signal is received at the transducer, amplified, and displayed as a function of time on an oscilloscope. Since the amplitude of the returned echo is influenced by the size and shape of the flaw, a rough estimate of the flaw size can be obtained by measuring the amplitude of the returned echo. Figure 11.5 illustrates the flowchart of the A-scan technique.

Due to the presence of numerous signals arising from multi-reflection and multi-scattering within the internal structure boundaries or inhomogeneities, the A-scan can be challenging to interpret and may result in loss of information, especially in civil engineering applications. An alternative display format, widely utilized in medical diagnostics, is the B-scan. In the B-scan, echoes are depicted as bright points, with brightness proportional to the echo amplitude. These points are arranged along a line, with the distance from the starting point representing the echo's time of flight. The line direction aligns with the propagation direction of the ultrasonic wave. By scanning the ultrasonic wave source along a line, a two-dimensional plot is formed, providing a longitudinal cross-sectional representation of the tested specimen. In essence, a B-scan display is derived from a set of A-scan data.

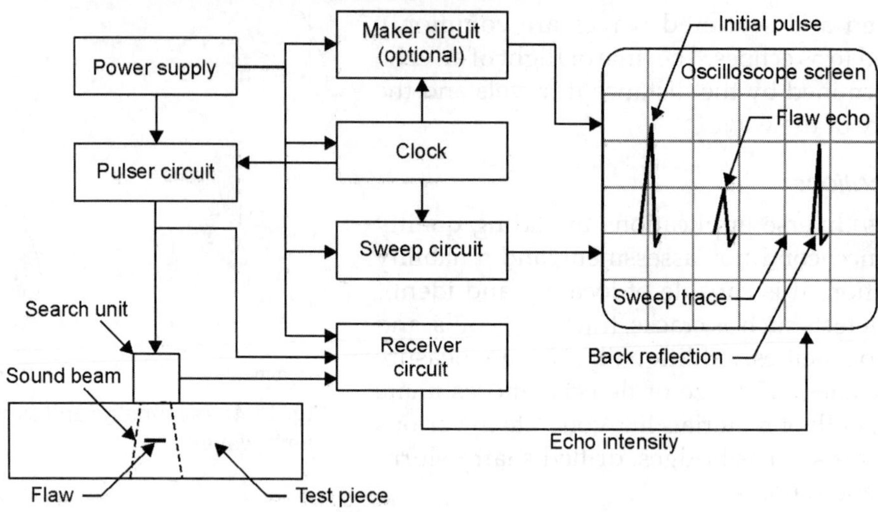

Fig. 11.5: Sketch of A-scan technique

The B-scan, also known as brightness scan, utilizes the returned echo signal to modulate the intensity of a spot on an oscilloscope. This format offers a quantitative representation of time-of-flight data acquired along a line on the test piece. The B-scan display illustrates the relative depth of reflectors and is primarily employed to ascertain the size (length in one direction), location (both position and depth), and to some extent, the shape and orientation of significant flaws. Consequently, it provides a basic depiction of the internal structure within a material, as depicted in Fig. 11.6. B-scans are widely utilized in the medical field. While the A-scan and B-scan systems share similarities, there are notable differences between the two methods. In a B-scan, echoes are represented by bright spots on the screen rather than by deflections of the

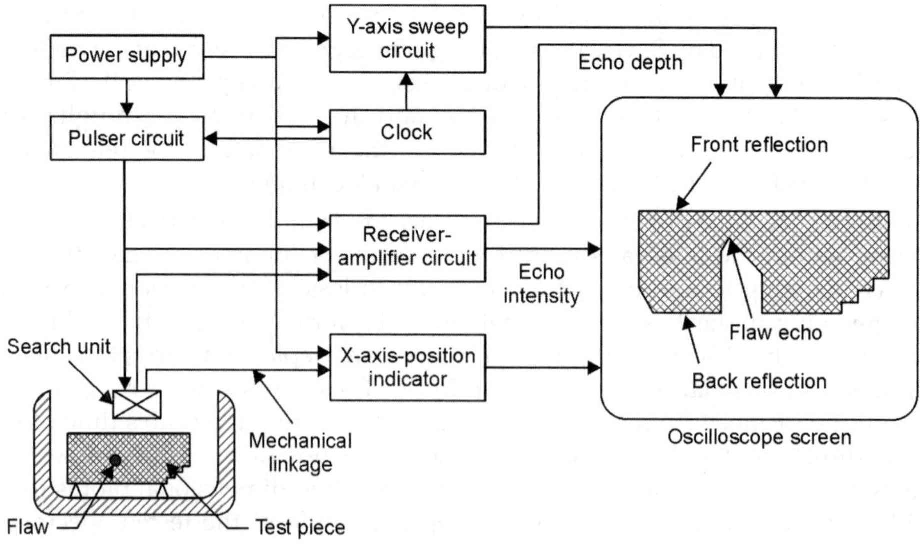

Fig. 11.6: Schematics of the B-scan technique

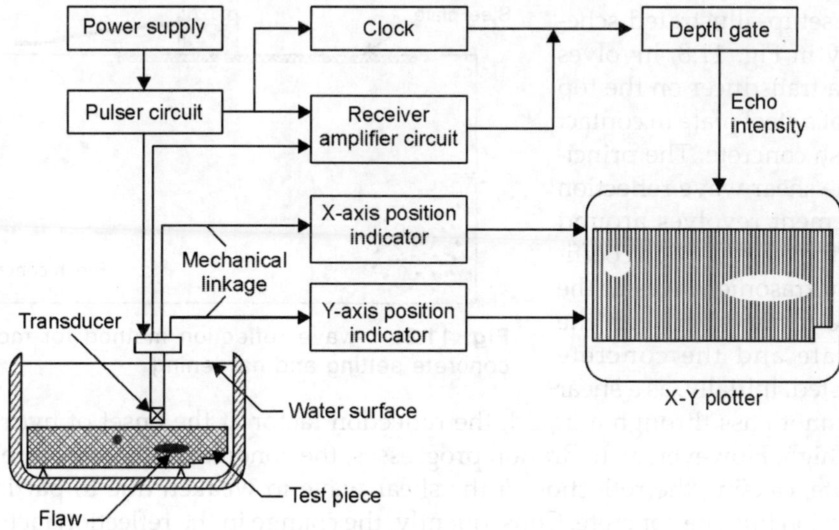

Fig. 11.7: General description of C-scan technique

time trace, allowing for visualization of an imaginary cross-section. The position of a bright spot along the axis perpendicular to the search unit position axis indicates the depth of the echo within the test piece.

Another commonly used display format is known as a C-scan. In this method, the ultrasound source is moved across a two-dimensional surface. Each source point initiates a time window at a fixed distance, wherein only the echoes within the window are depicted as bright points. The brightness of these points corresponds to the amplitude of the echo, and their coordinates match those of the source. Consequently, a lateral cross-sectional plot is generated, with the depth in the specimen corresponding to the selected time window distance.

Both B-scan and C-scan methods offer more comprehensive information compared to A-scan. Digital image processing (DIP) techniques can be applied to B-scan and C-scan data to extract further information. C-scan provides a semi-quantitative or quantitative display of signal amplitudes obtained over an area of the test piece surface. This data can be utilized to map out the positions of flaws on a plan view of the test piece, as illustrated in Fig. 11.7. Additionally, the C-scan format records time-of-flight data, which can be converted and displayed by image- processing equipment to indicate flaw depth. C-scan features an electronic depth gate that permits the reception of echo signals within a limited range, thereby excluding the display of front and back reflections.

S-wave Reflection Method for Fresh Concrete Monitoring

The ultrasonic technique has demonstrated significant effectiveness in nondestructive measurement for both fresh and hardened cementitious composites. In the 1990s, Northwestern University developed a shear wave reflection method for monitoring the hydration process of fresh concrete. This method employs high-frequency (2.25-MHz) ultrasonic waves to continuously monitor the setting and hardening of concrete.

The test setup, illustrated schematically in Fig. 11.8, involves placing a transducer on the top surface of a steel plate in contact with fresh concrete. The principle of the shear wave reflection measurement revolves around monitoring the reflection coefficient of ultrasonic waves at the interface formed between the steel plate and the concrete being tested. Initially, as a shear wave cannot pass through a liquid, the reflection factor at the onset of hydration is notably high. However, as hydration progresses, the concrete transitions into a more solid state, causing the reflection of the shear wave to weaken due to partial wave transmission into the concrete. Consequently, the change in the reflection factor at the steel-concrete interface correlates with the hydration process. The reflections of the shear waves from the steel-concrete interface are received by the transducer in the time domain. To calculate the reflection coefficient, the received signals in the time domain are transformed into the frequency domain using the Fast Fourier Transform algorithm.

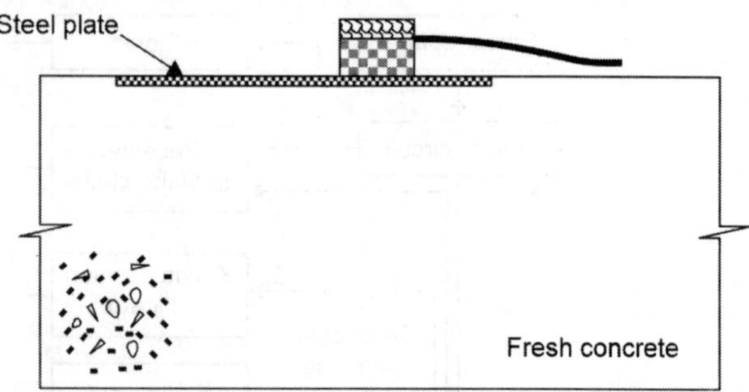

Fig. 11.8: S-wave reflection method for monitoring concrete setting and hardening

Figure 11.9 depicts a typical plot of reflection loss versus time, illustrating three distinct stages. Initially, up to point A, the reflection loss remains nearly zero, indicating nearly complete reflection of the shear wave and suggesting that the concrete is in a liquid state. Subsequently, from point A to point B, the reflection loss gradually increases, signaling a rapid hardening process of the concrete. Beyond point B, the reflection loss curve becomes relatively flat, indicating that the concrete has reached the maturity stage.

Through a meticulous calibration process, the relationship between reflection loss and both the setting time and compressive strength of the concrete can be established.

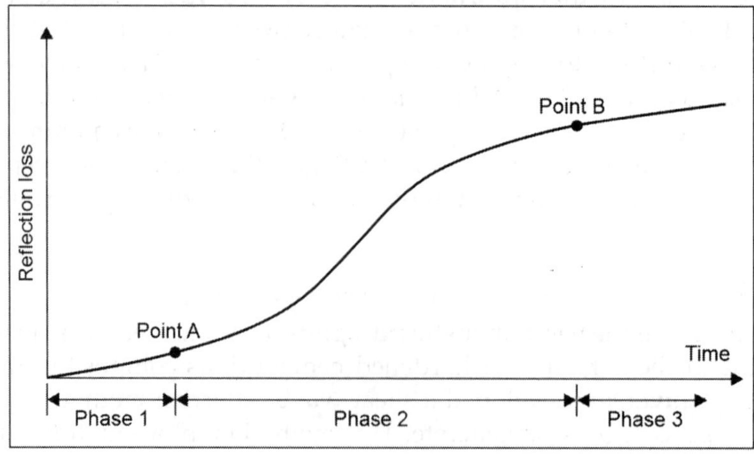

Fig. 11.9: A typical reflection loss versus time plot process

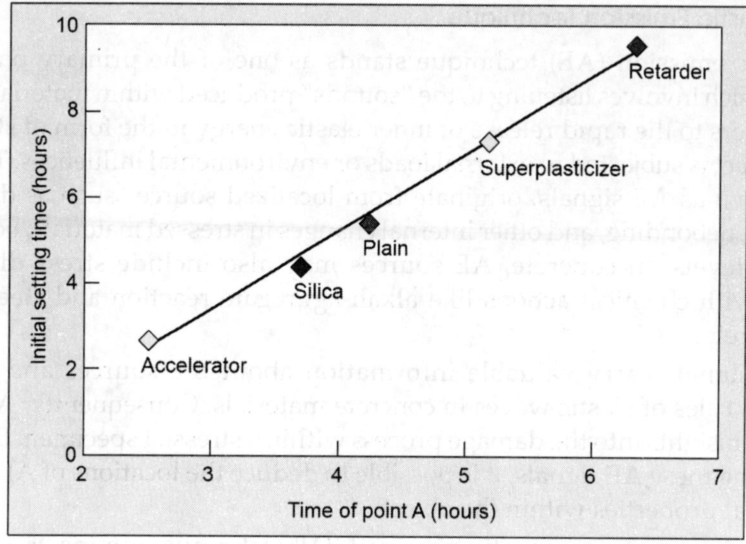

Fig. 11.10: Relationship between setting time and reflection loss

Figure 11.10 demonstrates the relationship between the setting time and the time corresponding to point A in the reflection loss curve. Notably, there exists a linear correlation between these parameters, suggesting the potential utility of point A as an index for predicting the setting time of concrete.

Figure 11.11 illustrates the relationship between compressive strength and reflection loss factors. Notably, a bilinear relationship is observed between these two parameters, with the transition point occurring between 6 and 15 hours after casting. This suggests that the compressive strength of a cement-based composite can be estimated based on the reflection loss factor of a shear wave.

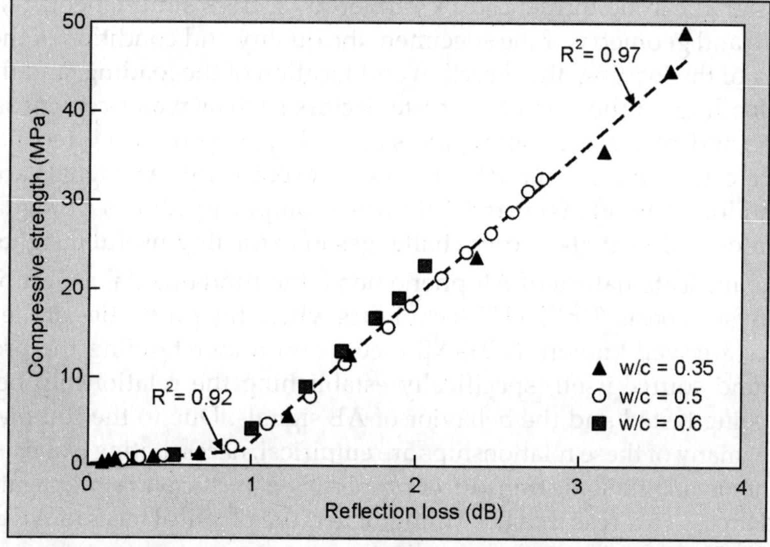

Fig. 11.11: Relationship between compressive strength and reflection loss

11.4.2 Acoustic Emission Technique

The acoustic emission (AE) technique stands as one of the primary passive NDT methods, which involves listening to the "sounds" produced within materials. Acoustic emission refers to the rapid release of inner elastic energy in the form of stress waves when an object is subjected to external loads or environmental influences. These stress waves, known as AE signals, originate from localized sources such as dislocations, microcracks, debonding, and other internal changes in stressed materials, both at micro and macro levels. In concrete, AE sources may also include stress distributions associated with chemical actions like alkali-aggregate reaction and steel corrosion within concrete.

The AE signals carry valuable information about the sources and follow the propagation rules of elastic waves in concrete materials. Consequently, AE activities can provide insights into the damage process within a stressed specimen. By receiving and analyzing these AE signals, it is possible to deduce the locations of AE events and infer material properties within the object.

NDT-AE serves as an acoustic passive NDT technique, aiming to characterize material properties and identify structural features within the test specimen or occurring inside it by analyzing received AE signals. This technique enables real-time monitoring of material condition changes and determination of the location of emission events. However, it cannot detect cracks that already exist but have not propagated. AE sources in concrete can include various mechanisms such as micro and macro crack initiation and propagation due to loading, separation of reinforcing members, mechanical rubbing of separated surfaces, corrosion of reinforced steel, debonding of different interfaces (e.g. steel bar and concrete, ceramic tile and concrete substrate), matrix cracking due to aggressive chemical products like ASR gel, fiber debonding, fracture, and pull-out in fiber-reinforced concrete, as well as damage induced by environmental factors.

The AE signal can be influenced by numerous factors simultaneously, including the structure and geometry of the specimen, the quality and condition of the material, the intensity of the loading, the direction and location of the loading, and the rate and manner of loading. In the case of concrete, factors such as water-cement ratio (w/c), cement type and properties, aggregate size and type, processing technology, and concrete age can all impact the AE process. Consequently, AE signals are typically complex, random, and often blurred. While this complexity allows AE signals to carry abundant information, it also poses challenges in extracting useful insights.

Given the intricate nature of AE phenomena, the fundamental aspect of NDT-AE lies in its physical basis. Unlike UT techniques where the properties of the ultrasonic wave source are well-known, NDT-AE focuses on understanding the properties of the ultrasound source itself, specifically establishing the relationship between the quantities being tested and the behavior of AE signals. Due to the complexity of AE phenomena, many of these relationships are empirical, necessitating extensive research on AE mechanism, ultrasonic transducer properties, acoustic wave propagation theory, and related areas. This research has strengthened the physical basis of AE techniques, leading to rapid expansion in their application.

The successful application of AE principles relies heavily on data acquisition and signal processing techniques. Predicting when and where AE events will occur can be challenging, making precise recording of AE events difficult. Unlike NDT-CE-UT, which typically involves single-channel receiving, NDT-CE-AE requires multichannel receiving techniques for characterizing AE sources. From an analytical standpoint, more channels generally lead to better insights. However, adding channels poses technical challenges due to increased interaction among channels and the associated increase in data volume and equipment costs.

Early AE testing instruments utilized analog electrical devices, which had limited capability to capture instantaneous AE events and process AE signals. Practical industrial applications of NDT-AE began in the mid-1960s in the United States, initially employed for monitoring and testing rocket shells. However, the development of NDT-AE techniques progressed slowly until the advent of numerical data acquisition AE instruments in the mid-1980s. The rapid advancement of numerical electrical techniques and computer technology, along with solid electrical circuits, high-speed analog-to-digital converters, DSP technologies, and modern computer data acquisition systems, enabled precise and synchronized capture and storage of instant AE signals, as well as the availability of fast and reliable numerical data processing methods. These advancements established a reliable hardware and software foundation for NDT-AE techniques.

After three decades of research and practice, the AE technique has made significant strides, emerging as a powerful nondestructive technique with applications expanding across various industries. When an AE event occurs within a material, stress waves propagate directly from the source to the receiver as body waves, potentially leading to surface wave generation through mode conversion. Upon reaching the receiver, the transducer responds to surface motions induced by the stress waves. AE signals exhibit a wide range of energy levels and frequencies, with modern instrumentation capable of recording AE signals in concrete ranging from 50 kHz to about 1 MHz. However, lower frequencies may be affected by background noise from test equipment, while very high frequencies suffer from severe signal attenuation.

AE signals are typically categorized into two basic types: burst type and continuous type. The former corresponds to individual emission events, whereas the latter denotes a sustained signal level resulting from rapidly occurring emission events. In AE techniques, data analysis methods play a crucial role in acquiring integrated and meaningful AE waveforms.

Various methods can be employed to characterize material behavior based on acoustic emissions, encompassing event counting, rise time analysis, spectrum analysis, AE source location (defect localization), energy analysis, signal processing, and signal duration assessment. For instance, AE activities, including event rate, accumulated event numbers, count rate, and count summation, have been utilized to predict the onset and extent of damage in concrete, correlating with the imposed stress level. Frequency components, rise time, and amplitude of AE signals have been leveraged to differentiate between different sources at varying stress levels. AE event localization can be achieved by analyzing time differences among recorded signals using an array of transducers, facilitating monitoring of microcrack localization in concrete and fiber-reinforced concrete under uniaxial tension, as well as the fracture process zone in concrete under similar conditions.

The pioneering investigation of AE in metals was conducted by Kaiser, who introduced the Kaiser effect, which denotes the absence of detectable acoustic emissions at a fixed sensitivity level until previously applied stress levels are exceeded. Concrete and fiber-reinforced concrete, being multiphase and containing numerous flaws, are ideal candidates for AE monitoring. Under load, microcracks tend to propagate along these flaws as the load increases, making them well-suited for AE monitoring. Unlike other nondestructive evaluation (NDE) techniques, AE monitoring solely indicates active flaws and cannot identify other types of flaws. It responds specifically to changes in flaw size rather than the total size, necessitating continuous monitoring to detect flaw extension whenever it occurs.

Applications

Nondestructive testing through acoustic emission (NDT-AE) finds extensive application in fracture mechanics for both metals and composite materials. In civil engineering, it is commonly employed to identify the initiation and propagation of cracks in concrete specimens under loading conditions, detect corrosion of reinforcing steel in harsh environmental settings, and monitor the debonding process of external decorations affixed to concrete structures (Figs 11.12 and 11.13).

Examples

a. Identifying crack formation in concrete subjected to uniaxial tension.
b. Detecting corrosion in reinforcing steel.
c. Monitoring the debonding of ceramic tiles from concrete surfaces (Fig. 11.14).

11.4.3 Impact-echo

Hammers are commonly employed in the assessment of piles, providing energetic impacts with prolonged contact times. While suitable for evaluating long and slender structures, they are less effective for detecting flaws in thin structures like slabs and walls. For this purpose, impact sources with shorter-duration impacts, such as small steel spheres and spring-loaded, spherically tipped impactors, have been utilized. The use of small ball bearings as impact sources marked a significant advancement in impact-echo (IE) research in the mid-1980s. This type of source produces a well-defined and mathematically simple input, resulting in waves that are conducive to easy signal interpretation. Ball bearing impactors offer ease of use, and the frequency content of the resulting stress waves can be adjusted to match the structure's size and the sizes of flaws to be detected. A data acquisition system with a sampling frequency of at least 500 kHz is recommended for optimal performance.

The optimal sampling frequency is contingent upon the thickness of the test object; however, for evaluating relatively thin members, a higher sampling rate is deemed more effective. In modern times, impact-echo (IE) testing equipment has become portable and offers a broad spectrum of applications for inspecting concrete, both in laboratory and field settings. Compared to the rebound hammer method, the impact-echo technique is noted for its precision. Studies have demonstrated the capability of the impact-echo technique to detect partial or complete discontinuities in piles, such

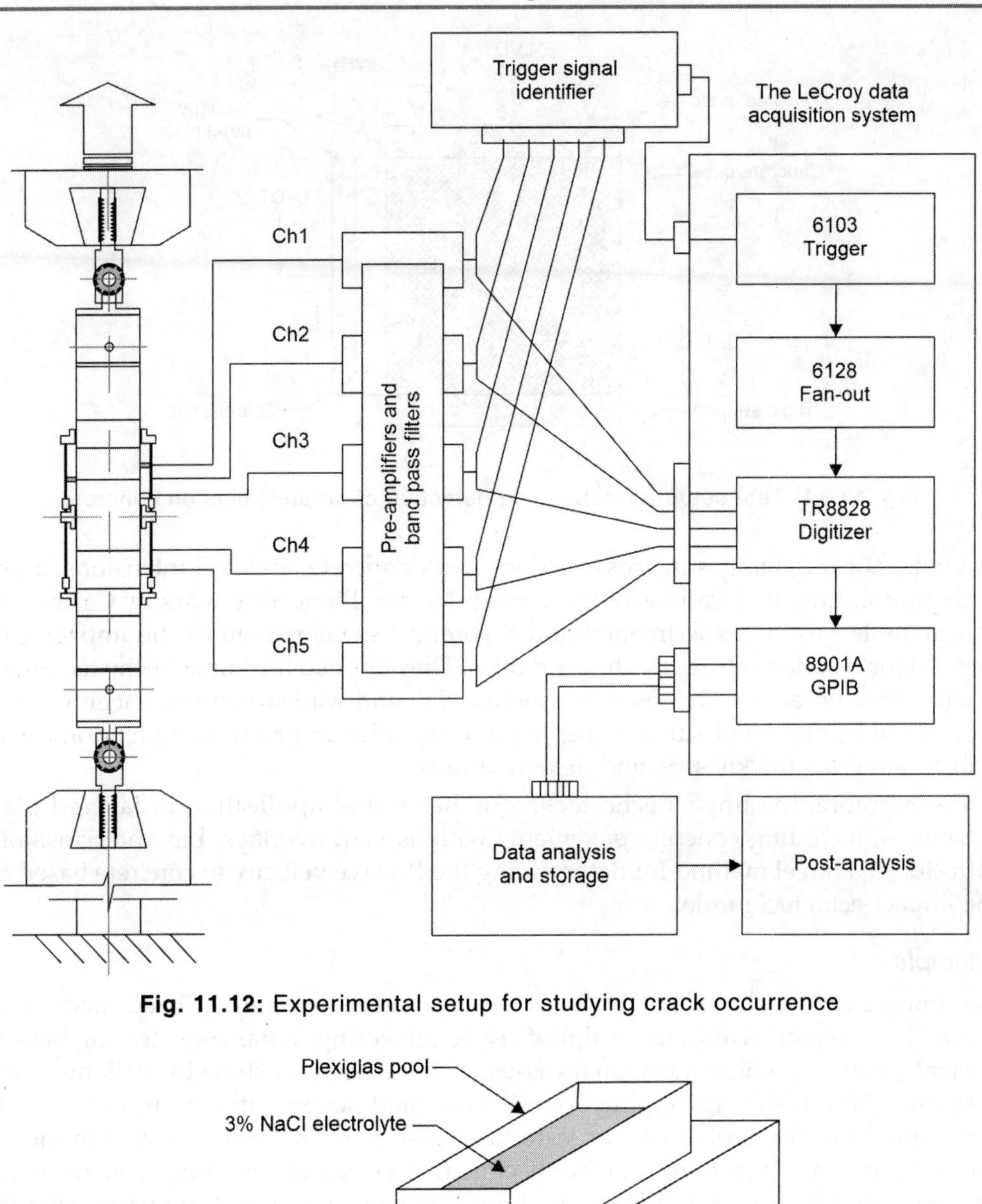

Trigger signal identifier
The LeCroy data acquisition system
Ch1
Ch2
Ch3
Ch4
Ch5
Pre-amplifiers and band pass filters
6103 Trigger
6128 Fan-out
TR8828 Digitizer
8901A GPIB
Data analysis and storage
Post-analysis

Fig. 11.12: Experimental setup for studying crack occurrence

Plexiglas pool
3% NaCl electrolyte
Rebars
Concrete
Resistor
Pre-amplifiers
AE system

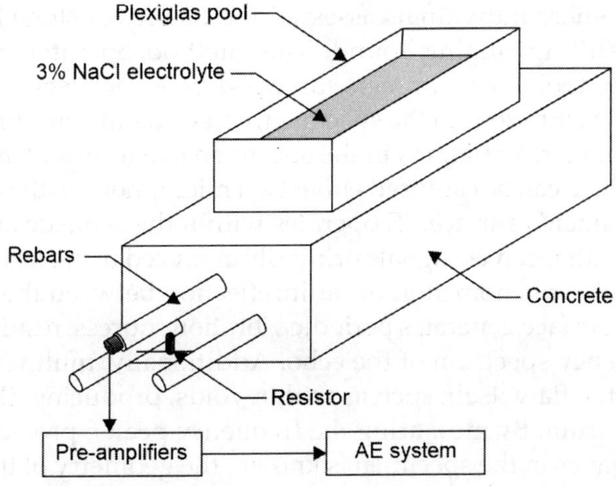

Fig. 11.13: Experimental setup for a corrosion test of reinforcement

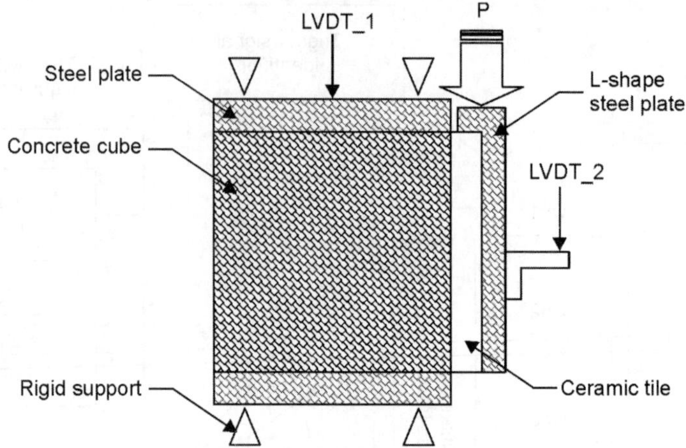

Fig. 11.14: Test setup for debonding detection of ceramic tiles on concrete

as voids, abrupt changes in cross-section, weak concrete, and soil intrusions, along with pinpointing the locations of these irregularities. Pioneering work by Carino and Sansalone led to the experimental and theoretical development of the impact-echo method for assessing structures beyond piles. They applied the impact-echo technique to identify interfaces and defects in concrete slab and wall structures, encompassing cracks, voids, depths of surface-opening cracks, voids in prestressing tendon ducts, slab and overlay thicknesses, and delaminations.

Furthermore, the impact-echo technique has found application in layered-plate structures, including concrete pavements with asphalt overlays. Lin and Sansalone introduced a novel method for determining the P-wave velocity in concrete based on the impact-echo technique.

Principle

The impact-echo technique stands as a pivotal and extensively utilized mechanical wave NDT method within the realm of civil engineering. It has roots tracing back to ancient practices, where individuals assessed the quality of stone by striking it and discerning the resulting ringing sound. This method operates as an active NDT technique, utilizing tools like hammers, dropped balls, or layered beams to induce mechanical acoustic vibrations in the specimen, consequently emitting acoustic waves into the surrounding air. Variations in the specimen's defects and anomalies alter the emitted sounds, which can be captured either by a microphone in the air or a transducer placed on the specimen's surface. IE operates within the acoustic and low ultrasonic frequency bands, with received signals primarily analyzed using fast fourier transform (FFT) techniques. The phenomenon of multireflection between the flaw surface and the specimen's top surface generates periodic vibration sources, resulting in discernible peaks in the frequency spectrum of the echo. Additionally, multireflection processes may occur within the flaw itself, such as within voids, producing distinctive peaks in the frequency spectrum. By measuring the frequency peak f, provided the velocity C of the ultrasonic waves in the specimen is known, the geometry of the flaw, including depth h, can be deduced.

An impact-echo test system typically comprises three key components: an impact source, a receiving transducer, and a digital processing oscilloscope or waveform analyzer. This setup is utilized to capture the transient output of the transducer, store digitized waveforms, and conduct signal analysis. The force-time profile of an impact often approximates a half-sine curve, with the duration of the impact representing the contact time. This contact time dictates the frequency spectrum of the stress pulse generated by the impact—shorter contact times result in broader frequency ranges within the pulse. Consequently, reducing the contact time enables the generation of higher-frequency components, facilitating the detection of smaller defects.

When utilizing the impact-echo method to locate flaws within an object, tests are conducted at regularly spaced intervals along predefined "scan" lines marked on the surface. Analyzing the amplitude spectra obtained from these scans provides insights into the depth and approximate size of any defects present. However, interpreting test data necessitates a thorough understanding of the technique. The selection of an appropriate impact source is a critical aspect of ensuring the success of an impact-echo test system.

Applications

The IE technique finds applications in detecting and pinpointing flaws, fractures, voids, and laminations in various structures such as ground decks, concrete pavements, and walls. Additionally, it enables the measurement of flaw depths and identification of non-homogeneous forms within materials. IE can also be utilized to interpret the dynamic modulus of a material.

However, developing a standard test method for flaw detection using the impact-echo technique poses challenges due to the numerous variables and conditions encountered during field testing, including the diverse types of defects and structural shapes encountered. ASTM C1383 (2004) has proposed a standard test method that utilizes the impact-echo technique to measure the thickness of plate-like concrete members. This method consists of two procedures:

1. Procedure A involves measuring the P-wave velocity in concrete by determining the travel time of the P-wave between two transducers placed at a known distance.
2. Procedure B utilizes the P-wave velocity measured in Procedure A to determine the plate thickness.

The data analysis procedure outlined in ASTM C1383 accounts for systematic errors associated with the digital nature of the data obtained from Procedures A and B.

Dynamic Modulus Measurement

The dynamic modulus of concrete can be determined using an impact-echo technique, as demonstrated by Jin and Li (2001) through the development of a specialized device. This device, illustrated schematically in Fig. 11.15, consists of a sponge box, an 8-mm steel sphere, an accelerometer, and a digitized oscilloscope equipped with a fast fourier transform function. To measure the dynamic modulus, a cylindrical specimen is inserted into the hole in the sponge box, with the accelerometer affixed to the bottom of the specimen. Subsequently, the steel ball is dropped onto the specimen's top surface.

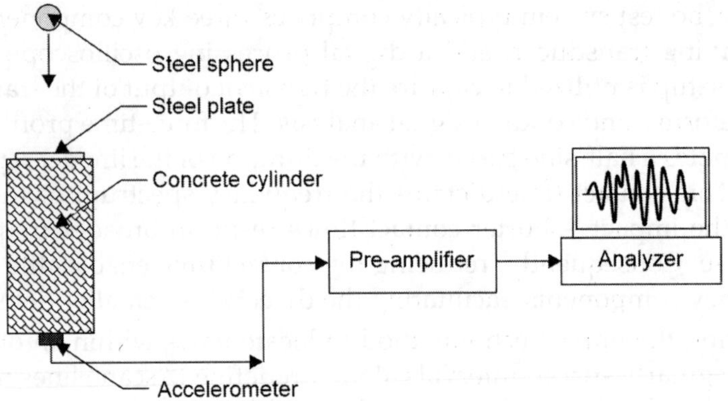

Fig. 11.15: Experimental setup for resonance measurements

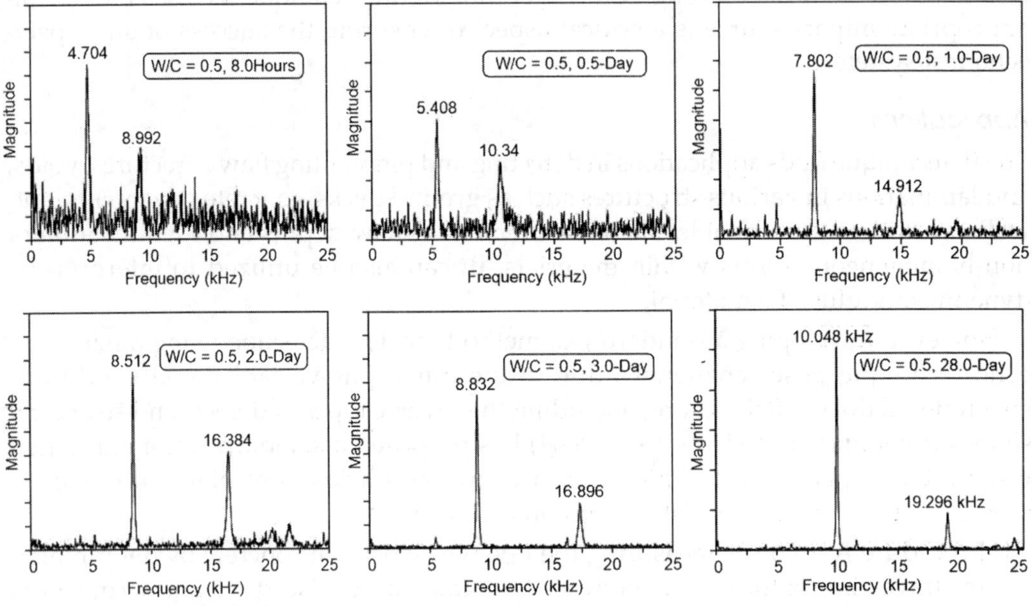

Fig. 11.16: Typical spectrum for a plain concrete (w/c = 0.5)

The resulting vibration, generated by the impact, is detected by the accelerometer and recorded by the oscilloscope. Later, the recorded waveform is transformed into a frequency spectrum to determine the dynamic modulus.

In concrete samples, dynamic modulus measurements can be conducted at various ages to study the effect of age on dynamic modulus development. To interpret the dynamic modulus of concrete, the waveforms recorded by the oscilloscope must undergo frequency spectrum transformation. Figure 11.16 depicts a typical spectrum for a concrete specimen at different ages. It is evident from Fig. 11.16 that the first two resonance frequencies consistently shift from lower to higher values with age. Thus, these resonance frequencies serve as indicators of the hydration, setting, and hardening processes.

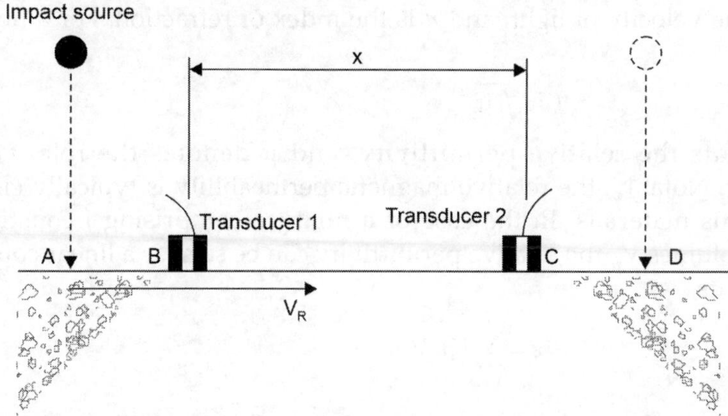

Fig. 11.17: Surface wave velocity measurement for concrete strength assessment

Surface Cracking Measurement by Impact-echo

To detect fine cracks on a concrete surface that are not easily visible to the naked eye, the impact-echo technique proves useful. Figure 11.17 illustrates the setup for surface crack measurement using the impact-echo method. This setup comprises a single impact source and two receivers. When the impact source, typically a steel ball, generates a surface wave, it propagates along the material or specimen surface. Two transducers are positioned to pick up the stress wave. If there is no crack between the transducers, their responses are nearly identical. However, if a crack is present, the response of the second transducer differs significantly from the first, indicating the presence of a crack.

The detection of surface cracks via the impact-echo method often employs self-calibration. This self-calibration technique mitigates uncertainties in parameters such as source characteristics and receiver responses. It utilizes the FFT of the captured time-domain signal (V_{AB}, V_{AC}, V_{DB}, and V_{DC}). In this context, V_{AB} and V_{AC} represent stress wave signals generated by an impact at location A and received by the nearby accelerometers at locations B and C, respectively, in the frequency domain. Similarly, V_{DC} and V_{DB} represent stress wave signals generated by an impact at location D and received by the accelerometers at locations C and B, respectively.

Typically, when an impact occurs, waves are emitted in various directions. Certain wave elements travel along the surface, while others bounce back at unbounded interfaces. By selecting a suitable timeframe, it becomes feasible to differentiate between the surface wave and the initial reflection of the P-wave from the opposite side of the sample.

11.4.4 Penetrative Radar Technique

The penetrative radar technique was developed based on the theory of electromagnetic waves. When electromagnetic waves propagate in a medium, the wave velocity v is

$$v = \frac{c}{n}$$

where c is the velocity of light, and n is the index of refraction. For a homogeneous medium,

$$n = \sqrt{\varepsilon\mu}$$

ε represents the relative permittivity, and μ denotes the relative magnetic permeability. Notably, the relative magnetic permeability is typically close to unity across various materials. In the case of a mixture comprising j constituents with respective volumes V_j, the relative permittivity can be seen as a linear combination of its constituents,

$$\varepsilon = \sum_{i=1}^{j} V_i \varepsilon_i V$$

V representing the total volume of the mixture. Consequently, it becomes feasible to infer the volume component based on the measured velocity, provided that the constituent materials are known.

In view of concrete quality assurance, water content stands out as a crucial parameter. Fortunately, water has a relative permittivity of approximately 81, contrasting sharply with the values for cement paste and typical aggregates, which hover around 5. Consequently, measurements prove highly sensitive to variations in water content. Achieving an accuracy within the range of 3–5% is attainable for standard concrete mixes. Additionally, given that air possesses a relative permittivity of 1, leveraging electromagnetic wave propagation facilitates the detection of porosity in dry concrete.

When conducting wave-based testing, the wavelength emerges as the pivotal parameter, directly influencing resolution and sensitivity. Lateral resolution primarily hinges on wavelength constraints, while depth resolution correlates with wave pocket width. Electromagnetic waves exhibit total reflection from even thin metal sheets, making it challenging to detect components within or behind metallic structures. ground penetrating radar (GPR) stands out as a potent electromagnetic tool. A fundamental radar setup includes a control unit, transmitting and receiving antennas, an oscillographic recorder, and a DC power converter. Optimal radar antennas with high resolution are preferred for concrete inspection to discern minute concrete layers. GPR proves invaluable for swiftly assessing concrete structures, determining member thickness, reinforcement spacing and depth, and pinpointing voids and defects in bare or overlaid reinforced concrete decks.

In concrete testing, short-pulse radar, akin to sonic and ultrasonic pulse-echo methods, is commonly employed. Electromagnetic pulses generated by the equipment are transmitted to the investigated member via a surface-proximate antenna. Pulse propagation velocity, dictated by electrical permittivity, determines concrete relative permittivity predominantly influenced by moisture content, typically ranging between 5 (oven-dry) and 12 (wet). Radar exploits electromagnetic waves to probe concrete materials and structures for thickness and internal defects. GPR facilitates imaging bridge pile profiles in scour investigations, where selecting a maximum frequency ten times larger than geological characteristic dimensions is recommended for clutter reduction. Frequency ranges usually span from 90 MHz to 1 GHz, with a pulse repetition frequency of 25 Hz, yielding typical results like scour depths of 1.2 m, sandy layer fillings 0.5 m deep overlying 0.8 m thick gravel, and water depths of about 1 m. The swift nature of GPR measurements makes it suitable for large area detection, such as pavement assessments covering 10,000 m^2 at airports.

Applications

Microwave NDT techniques serve multiple purposes in building inspection and quality control, detecting steel objects, moisture levels, water content, and cracks. These techniques excel in pinpointing the lateral position of rebars, metallic ducts, T-girders, and anchors within prefabricated concrete elements. They are also adept at locating plastic and metallic leads, determining cover thickness, and assessing concrete moisture content. Additionally, microwave technology reveals artificial birefringence properties in ceramics and cement, with wavelengths falling between 7.5 and 12.5 mm, akin to photoelasticity using visible light.

EMT techniques offer reliable integrity assessments, capable of locating tendons, metal ducts (with a diameter of 85 mm), and providing dimensional information. They effectively detect defects in concrete members, voids in tendon ducts, and compression faults or honeycombing in concrete structures. However, EMT techniques are not sensitive to aggregate size, with a noted example indicating a lateral position accuracy for reinforcement within ±10 mm for aggregate sizes ranging from 8 to 32 mm and a cover thickness of 340 ±10 mm.

Furthermore, microwave moisture content meters enable real-time water content monitoring in clay materials.

11.4.5 Optical Techniques

These methodologies utilize light waves as the probing mechanism and are classified as active techniques. They primarily rely on interferometry and energy transportation. A notable technique representing the former category is electronic speckle pattern interferometry. In contrast, infrared thermography stands out as a representative method for energy transportation.

Electronic Speckle Pattern Interferometry

Electronic speckle pattern interferometry (ESPI) stands as a robust laser-based measurement method, pioneered by Butter and Leendertz in 1971 with further advancements discussed by Hung and Liang in 1979. Operating on a principle akin to holographic interferometry (HI), ESPI employs video technology instead of traditional photography. It involves superimposing reflected light with a reference laser beam, capturing the resultant interference pattern via a CCD camera. These interference patterns, recorded both before and after loading, delineate displacement fields on the illuminated surface. With a phase-shift technique, ESPI can achieve a resolution on the order of 20 nm. Notably, ESPI offers non-contact, full-field measurement and monitoring of the 3D displacement field for optically diffusely scattering objects, covering surface areas exceeding 70 × 80 cm^2, contingent upon geometric configurations. However, ESPI necessitates isolation of the vibrating object from its environment due to its reliance on a reference beam, which poses a practical challenge.

Speckle pattern shearing interferometry (SPSI), also known as shearography, represents an advancement derived from ESPI, as introduced by Hung in 1982. In contrast to HI or ESPI, SPSI focuses on measuring derivatives of surface displacement directly, disregarding rigid body motions. Through a specialized set of optical elements, the light beam scattered from the object surface is split into two beams, offset by a small lateral distance, thus causing interference. This lateral displacement, or shearing, renders SPSI highly resistant to environmental vibrations, as both beams originate from the same source. An advantageous aspect of SPSI lies in its ability to directly measure surface strain, enabling operation in scenarios involving larger displacements compared to ESPI. Both ESPI and SPSI serve as effective real-time micro-crack monitors, with the phase-shifting technique facilitating quantitative fringe evaluation.

Infrared Thermography

Sunlight, an electromagnetic wave, travels at a velocity of 3×10^8 m/s in a vacuum. It can manifest as visible or invisible light depending on its wavelength. Visible light wavelengths fall within specific ranges, as outlined in Table 11.1. Ultraviolet light is characterized by wavelengths below 0.4 μm, while near-infrared light ranges from 700 to 1500 nm (0.7 μm $< \lambda <$ 1.5 μm). Mid-infrared light spans from 1,500 nm to 20,000 nm (1.5 μm $< \lambda <$ 20 μm), and far-infrared light ranges from 20,000 nm to 100,000 nm (20 μm $< \lambda <$ 100 μm).

Table 11.1: Wavelength ranges of visible light

Wavelength (nm)	*Color*
400–450	Violet
450–480	Blue
480–510	Blue-green
510–550	Green
550–570	Yellow-green
570–590	Yellow
590–630	Orange
630–700	Red

Infrared radiation, lying beyond the visible red spectrum, is invisible to the naked eye. According to physical laws, all matter with a temperature above absolute zero (–273°C) emits heat, synonymous with infrared radiation. The intensity of emitted radiation is contingent upon the object's temperature and emissivity, with higher temperatures leading to increased infrared radiation emission. When heat flows through a material body, its thermal properties and internal structure influence heat distribution, resulting in surface temperature fields. Infrared thermography leverages this principle to inspect material surface temperature fields and infer internal structural conditions.

Infrared equipment can be utilized for thermography nondestructive evaluation in two distinct ways, depending on the intended application. In a passive configuration, the infrared camera is directed at the scene, focusing on the object under inspection without applying any external thermal perturbation (Fig. 11.18). This mode is commonly employed in building inspection, where surface temperature distributions

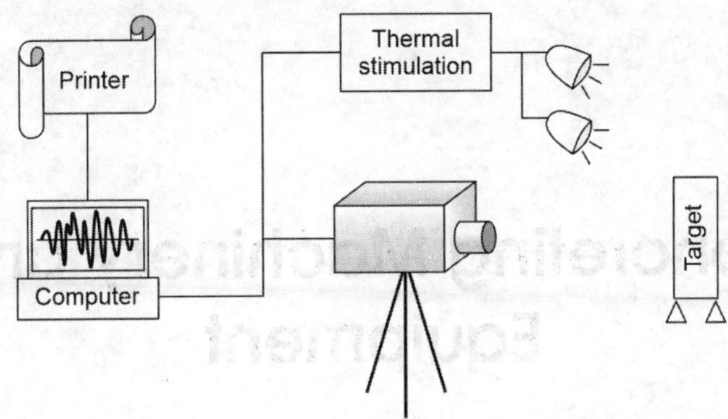

Fig. 11.18: Typical active infrared NDT experimental setup

provide valuable insights into the presence or absence of defects. Conversely, in an active configuration, an external thermal stimulus is applied to generate meaningful contrasts, facilitating the detection of subsurface abnormalities. The rate of heat dissipation through the mass of the structure varies in defect areas compared to sound areas, providing valuable information during inspection.

The first documented attempt to detect anomalies and air leaks in buildings using infrared techniques dates back to 1965. Subsequent progress between 1975 and 1985 witnessed rapid advancements in the potential of nondestructive material evaluation through infrared thermography. This progress escalated in the 1980s with the advent of commercial infrared cameras compatible with black-and-white television standards. Results were disseminated at international conferences such as SPIE's Thermosensing in the United States and remote sensing symposiums in Canada.

Significant research on infrared thermography for civil engineering applications has been conducted over the past decade, gaining widespread popularity due to its nondestructive nature, quick implementation, and safety. Buildings with surface defects like debonding mosaic tiles or delaminating render emit varying amounts of infrared radiation, detectable with modified infrared cameras. Defective areas manifest as differential transmittance of infrared radiation, revealing irregularities upon scanning. In contrast, surfaces without defects exhibit uniformity under infrared camera observation. However, interpretation challenges arise from diverse environmental conditions affecting surface temperature fields, with varying behaviors of subsurface defects in different lighting conditions and ambient environments.

Chapter

12

Concreting Machinery and Equipment

In the past, the construction industry relied heavily on manual labor. The efficiency and quality of construction were contingent upon the skills and productivity of trained workers. However, to enhance efficiency, reduce costs, and improve construction timelines, the integration of machinery became imperative. Despite the initial high investment costs associated with equipment procurement, the subsequent enhancement in construction quality and acceleration of project completion have rendered machinery indispensable in the modern era.

Infrastructure development encompasses a broad spectrum of projects, including tunneling, rock blasting, mass excavation, pipeline laying, dam construction, bridge building, and the establishment of industrial parks and towns. To meet stringent deadlines and achieve international quality benchmarks for such monumental endeavors, the adoption of advanced equipment and machinery is indispensable.

Concrete-related tasks typically involve several stages: batching and mixing, transportation, placement, and finishing. A diverse array of machinery is employed to execute these operations efficiently. Machinery isn't solely confined to concrete work but extends to associated activities in concrete construction as well. For instance, driving precast concrete piles and utilizing cranes for lifting precast concrete units are among the supplementary operations where machinery plays a pivotal role. This chapter provides an in-depth exploration of the machinery utilized for the preparation of concrete-making materials, concrete construction, and the erection of structures, elucidating their functions and applications in detail.

12.1 CONCRETE MIXERS

There are two types of concrete-mixing operations in use: (1) transit mixed and (2) central mixed. Today, unless the project is in a remote location or is relatively large, the concrete ingredients are combined at a batch plant (Fig. 12.1) and transported to the job site in transit-mix trucks, often referred to as ready-mixed concrete trucks or truck mixers (Fig. 12.2).

12.1.1 Freefall Mixers

Freefall mixers facilitate the filling and emptying of their drum through various means such as altering their rotation direction, opening them, or tilting them upwards. It is

Fig. 12.1: Concrete batch plant

Fig. 12.2: Transit-mix truck (truck mixer) placing concrete

crucial to adhere to machine-specific guidelines regarding rotation speed to ensure that the mixture's free fall is not disrupted by excessive centrifugal force. Truck mixers, which will be elaborated on later, also employ freefall mixing techniques. Among the prevalent variations of freefall mixers are tilting mixers and reversible mixers.

Tilting Mixers

Tilting mixers, typically mounted on trailers or made portable, are frequently employed as primary concrete mixing apparatus on small-scale projects or as supplementary equipment on sites serviced by ready-mix concrete facilities. These mixers feature a drum with two axes: one for rotation and another for adjusting the loading and mixing position (drum facing upwards for loading and downwards for discharge). This manual position adjustment is carried out using a dump wheel (or handle in smaller models), while the drum's rotation is powered by electricity, gasoline, or diesel. While steel drums have been conventional, polyethylene drums, known for their easier cleaning, are now available. Most mixers are of the side-dump variety, although end-dump mixers are also manufactured. Material is typically loaded manually into the drum, although some larger self-loading units are outfitted with a tilting hopper. After manual filling at ground level, the hopper is mechanically tilted upwards to deposit the material into the drum.

Reversible Mixers

Reversible mixers feature a drum rotating around a single horizontal axis. The drum has two openings, one at each end: one for adding ingredients and the other for dispensing the mixture. During mixing, the drum rotates in one direction, while for discharge, the rotation is reversed. Typically, self-loading reversible mixers are of medium to large size and are mounted on trailers with two or four wheels for mobility between sites. These mixers are outfitted with a tilting hopper similar to those occasionally found on tilting mixers, or with a hoist-like hopper that moves up and down on a short inclined rail and empties the ingredients through a bottom opening into the drum. Many models offer an optional built-in mechanical skip to aid in loading aggregates into the hopper. Most models of this type come with a water tank and meter, and optionally, larger models may include a built-in aggregates batcher.

12.1.2 Power Mixers

Power mixers, also known as paddle mixers, forced mixers, or compulsory mixers, utilize rapid rotary motion of paddles (or mixer heads) traversing centric or eccentric paths within the mixing drum to blend concrete. To prevent concrete from adhering to the sides and bottom of the drum, certain paddles continuously scrape the concrete off these surfaces and redirect it towards the center of the drum. Spring connections are employed to prevent paddle breakage due to the intense mixing action. This intensive mixing process results in significant wear on the inner surface of the drum, which is absent in freefall mixers. To withstand this wear, the drum's interior is lined with replaceable plates made from specialized abrasion-resistant material (Fig. 12.3). With their highly efficient mixing action, power mixers require shorter mixing times to achieve uniform, high-quality concrete, leading to increased productivity. The mixing output of power mixers is typically 50 to 100% higher compared to similar-sized freefall mixers. Additionally, power mixers can handle drier mixtures that freefall mixers cannot manage. Due to these advantages, power mixers are widely preferred in Europe for the ready-mixed concrete industry and dominate the precast concrete sector. Electric power mixers come in various types but are commonly classified as either pan or trough mixers.

Pan Mixers

Pan mixers feature paddles connected to a vertical shaft within a pan-shaped drum. In turbomixers, this shaft is fixed at the center of the drum. Various models exist: (1) with counter-rotating drum and paddles, (2) with a stationary drum and all paddles

Fig. 12.3: Inside view of two different types of twin-shaft trough mixers

rotating in the same direction, and (3) with a stationary drum but counter-rotating paddles. Planetary mixers have a rotary vertical shaft located eccentrically in the stationary drum, providing a double motion of the paddles akin to planets orbiting the sun. This configuration enhances mixing intensity. Counterflow mixers have a fixed vertical shaft located eccentrically in a rotating drum, where the drum and paddles move in opposite directions. Evenflow mixers are similar to counterflow mixers, but both the drum and paddles rotate in the same direction, albeit at different velocities. Various combinations of these mixers are available, such as those shown in Fig. 12.4, which features both centric and planetary paddles rotating in opposite directions. Additionally, there are double-shaft pan mixers of different types.

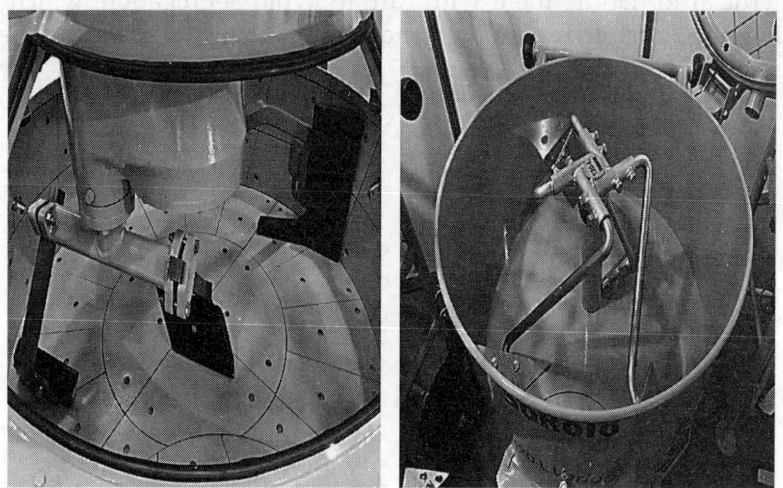

Fig. 12.4: Inside view of two different types of pan mixers

Trough Mixers

Trough mixers, categorized as power mixers, feature a drum shaped like a horizontally halved barrel. In single-shaft mixers, a horizontal shaft is utilized, with paddles arranged in a spiral formation or replaced by wave-shaped mixing arms in some models. This configuration generates both radial (rotary) and axial (horizontal) movements, creating a three-dimensional circulation path that enhances mixing intensity, resulting in reduced mixing times. Certain single-shaft mixer models are employed in central-mixing plants as climbing mixers, where the drum ascends on an inclined track during mixing, and discharge occurs by tilting the drum at the track's peak. This setup, feasible only with a single-shaft trough mixer, simplifies material conveyance as drum loading is performed at ground level. Since climbing coincides with mixing, the overall cycle time remains unaffected. Single-shaft mixers typically range from 2 to 10 cubic yards in size. Twin-shaft mixers, depicted in Fig. 12.3, are stationary machines with bottom discharge. Although their mixing principle is akin to single-shaft mixers, the twin-shaft design fosters better mixture homogeneity due to the heightened turbulence at the intersection of the two mixing circles. Moreover, the buildup of mix between the shafts leads to reduced wear compared to single-shaft or pan-type mixers.

12.2 PLACING CONCRETE

After concrete reaches the project site, it needs to be transported to its final location swiftly, ensuring there is no segregation and before it begins to set. Various methods can achieve this, depending on the distance to be covered horizontally and vertically, as well as other constraints. These methods encompass the use of buckets, buggies, and wheelbarrows, as well as chutes, drop pipes, belt conveyors, and concrete pumps.

12.2.1 Buckets

Buckets (as shown in Fig. 12.5) facilitate the placement of concrete at a suitable slump level. It is crucial to handle them with care to avoid segregation, which can occur when discharging concrete from too great a height above the surface or allowing it to

Fig. 12.5: Concrete buckets used for the placement of concrete

fall beyond obstructions like forms, especially in column construction. Gates on the buckets should be designed to allow opening and closing at any point during concrete discharge.

12.2.2 Chutes and Drop Pipes

Chutes are frequently employed for transferring concrete from higher to lower elevations. They should feature a rounded bottom and a slope steep enough to enable continuous concrete flow without segregation. Truck mixers commonly come equipped with built-in swing chutes, often extendable and hydraulically operated, allowing direct placement of concrete when the pouring location is within chute reach. Drop pipes, on the other hand, are utilized for vertical concrete transfer. The upper 6 to 8 feet of the pipe should have a diameter at least eight times the maximum aggregate size and may taper down so that the lower end is approximately six times the maximum aggregate size. Drop pipes find application when pouring concrete into walls or columns to prevent segregation caused by allowing concrete to free-fall through reinforcement. In tremie operations, a drop pipe known as a tremie pipe is used, particularly for placing concrete underwater. Tremie tubes are typically made of soft rubber to contain the concrete flow and control discharge position. The lower end of a tremie pipe remains continuously submerged in fresh, plastic concrete.

12.2.3 Belt Conveyors

Belt conveyors are categorized into three types: (1) portable or self-contained conveyors, (2) feeders or series conveyors, and (3) side-discharge or spreader conveyors. All these types facilitate the swift transportation of fresh concrete. However, it is essential to ensure that they are equipped with appropriately sized belts and operating at the correct speed to achieve the desired rate of transportation. Special care should be taken at the transition points where the concrete moves from one conveyor to another or is discharged, as segregation risks are higher at these junctures (Fig. 12.6).

Fig. 12.6: Concrete being placed by belt conveyor

12.2.4 Concrete Pumps

The utilization of concrete pumps for transporting concrete through either rigid or flexible lines has a history dating back to the initial applications in tunnel lining. German pumping technology made its way to the United States in the early 1930s, but it wasn't until the 1970s that concrete pumping became widespread in the country. The mechanism of a concrete pump is relatively straightforward: pressure exerted on a column of fresh concrete within a pipe propels the concrete along the pipeline, provided there is a lubricating inner liner and the mixture is suitably proportioned for pumping. For optimal performance, the pump requires a consistent supply of concrete with uniform workability and consistency. Plasticizer admixtures are often used to enhance the concrete's flowability through the pump and piping system. Concrete pumps are available in various sizes, capable of sustaining delivery rates ranging from 10 to over 150 cubic yards per hour. Effective pumping distances typically range from 100 to 1,300 feet horizontally or vertically. However, there have been instances where pumps have transported concrete over much longer distances, exceeding 8,000 feet horizontally and 2,000 feet vertically.

A steady supply of pumpable concrete is essential for the efficient operation of pumps. Currently, two main types of pumps are manufactured: piston pumps and peristaltic pumps. Many piston pumps incorporate two pistons, with one retracting during the forward stroke of the other to ensure a more continuous flow of concrete. Peristaltic pumps, also known as squeeze pressure pumps, utilize hydraulically powered rollers to rotate on the flexible hose within the drum, squeezing the concrete out at the top. A vacuum system maintains a consistent supply of concrete in the tube from the intake hopper. In piston-type pumps, the concrete in the hopper is fed into the pump through gravity assisted by suction, whereas in squeeze-type pumps, the concrete is fed by rotating blades in the hopper (Fig. 12.7).

Fig. 12.7: Concrete pump with separate pipeline

Concrete pumping equipment is typically available in two primary setups: (1) a pump accompanied by a separate pipeline, and (2) a pump integrated with a boom (Fig. 12.8). The latter configuration is notably efficient and cost-effective as it reduces labor requirements and eliminates the necessity for additional pipelines to transport the concrete. A third arrangement, commonly utilized in high-rise construction projects, merges the pump and pipeline with a separate boom. This boom can either be stationary and tower-mounted or a more compact, movable placing unit.

Fig. 12.8: Truck-mounted pump and boom combination

12.3 FINISHING CONCRETE

The finishing phase aims to achieve the desired final appearance and texture of the concrete surface. For unformed surfaces, screeding may suffice to contour the surface profile, while a broomed, floated, or troweled finish might be specified.

It is crucial to recognize that any manipulation of the concrete surface after consolidation can compromise its strength. Unfortunately, some concrete finishers overlook this fact and attempt to modify the surface, sometimes even adding water, to achieve a smoother, more visually appealing result. However, this practice increases the risk of scaling and surface delamination.

While an aesthetically pleasing surface may be desirable for walls and columns where surface strength is less critical, for floor slabs, sidewalks, or pavements, surface strength is paramount. Hence, only minimal finishing necessary to achieve the desired texture should be allowed. Excessive finishing can elevate surface tension, leading to localized cracking and delamination, and should be avoided. Furthermore, techniques like "jitterbugging," which involves using a steel grate tool to force coarse aggregate into the concrete, should not be permitted as they can significantly weaken the surface.

Furthermore, each stage in the finishing process, from initial floating to final troweling, should be postponed as much as possible. This timing is constrained by the need to achieve the desired grade and surface smoothness while the concrete remains workable (still in a plastic state).

12.3.1 Floating

Floating serves three main purposes:

1. Embedding aggregate particles just beneath the surface.
2. Removing minor imperfections, high spots, and low spots.
3. Compacting the concrete surface in readiness for subsequent finishing steps.

Under no circumstances should finishing commence if any free-bleed water remains on the surface. Additionally, neat cement or mixtures of sand and cement should not be applied to such surfaces to expedite drying.

12.3.2 Troweling

Power trowels (Fig. 12.9) are utilized to smooth and finish extensive concrete surfaces like floor slabs and the upper surfaces of horizontally poured precast elements. These machines are powered by gasoline engines, diesel engines, or electric motors, driving rotating blades of various sizes, numbers, and rotation speeds. Larger blade systems offer higher productivity rates in spacious areas, while smaller systems are advantageous in confined spaces, such as finishing floor slabs through doorways or around obstacles.

Fig. 12.9: Power equipment for finishing slabs

Troweling enhances the density of the upper layer of concrete and seals plastic cracks that develop between concrete placement and troweling. The quality of troweled concrete depends on both the equipment used and the quality of the concrete and placement procedures. A certain minimum time must pass between concrete placement and troweling to allow the concrete to partially dry.

The troweling process comprises two main steps:

1. Floating, which aims to remove protruding aggregate grains, level swells, fill voids, and compact the concrete surface. During this step, the power trowel blades are kept flat.

2. Troweling, which focuses on polishing, smoothing, and hardening the concrete surface. Here, the power trowel blades are slightly angled. This step may be repeated multiple times until the desired concrete finish is achieved. With each subsequent pass, the blade angle is adjusted slightly, but the raised edge should not exceed 1 inch above the concrete surface to prevent slit formation.

Due to their rounded shape, power trowels are unable to access room corners. Specialized small-radius disk trowels, vibratory trowels, or hand trowels are used for this purpose.

Power trowels can be equipped with single or double rotors, with single-rotor models typically being walk-behind types and double-rotor models being ride-on types. Both types are equipped with lifting provisions for mobility around the job site, such as lifting hooks for single-rotor trowels and lifting systems for heavier double-rotor trowels. Transport dollies are often employed to move double-rotor trowels due to their weight. Double-rotor trowels may feature overlapping or non-overlapping rotors.

Chapter 13

Future Trends in Concrete Technology

Given the distinctive benefits of concrete, it is poised to remain the predominant and extensively utilized man-made material for the foreseeable future. With a surge in global demand, particularly in developing nations and regions, the necessity arises for continuous advancements in concrete research and development. This is essential to accommodate evolving end-user requirements and tackle emerging challenges. Accurate anticipation of future trends and developments in concrete in the twenty-first century is therefore crucial. Below, pertinent issues pertaining to this subject are succinctly explored.

13.1 SUSTAINABILITY OF CONCRETE

Among the forthcoming trends in concrete development, enhancing its sustainability stands out as the paramount concern. Sustainability, defined by the Brundtland Commission Report (1987) as meeting present needs without compromising future generations', encompasses various societal facets such as civil infrastructure, energy, environment, health, and safety. Concrete, being the most extensively utilized material, consumes significant resources. Present-day concrete typically consists of approximately 16–20% cementitious materials, 6–8% mixing water, 60–70% aggregate, and 2–3% admixtures by mass. Estimating global concrete production involves determining cement output, calculating other components based on common ratios, and aggregating these figures. Based on 2020 cement production, concrete annually consumes about 4.1 billion tons of cement, 1.6 billion tons of mixing water, 16 billion tons of aggregate, and 600 million tons of chemical admixtures. This reveals concrete as a 22-billion-tons-per-year industry, the foremost consumer of natural resources worldwide. The extraction, processing, and transportation of vast aggregate quantities, along with the raw material requirements for cement manufacturing, necessitate substantial energy and adversely impact virgin land ecology, leading to significant CO_2 emissions. Such extensive resource consumption profoundly affects the environment and jeopardizes the ability of future generations to meet their needs if uncontrolled. The sustainability discourse surrounding concrete focuses on three aspects: reducing greenhouse gas emissions, notably CO_2; minimizing energy consumption; and curtailing raw material use from natural resources during concrete production, construction, and application. Strategies to attain concrete sustainability encompass reduction (e.g. CO_2 emissions, energy use), reuse (e.g. resource preservation), recycling (e.g. waste material utilization), and innovation (e.g. adopting alternative, low-carbon technologies).

A multi-stakeholder working group, spearheaded by the United Nations Environment Program Sustainable Building and Climate Initiative (UNEP-SBCI), has outlined three key avenues for enhancing the eco-efficiency of cement:

1. Increasing the utilization of CO_2^- and energy-efficient supplementary cementitious materials (SCMs).
2. Pioneering sustainable alternative cements.
3. Enhancing cement efficiency, encompassing both production and utilization aspects, such as prolonging service life, augmenting strength-to-density ratios, and reducing cement content per unit volume of concrete (United Nations et al., 2018).

Similar strategies are applicable to aggregate improvement. For these approaches to be effective, they must rely on ample raw material resources and achieve requisite performance benchmarks, ensuring market acceptance akin to regular concrete.

13.2 UTILIZING ECO-FRIENDLY RESOURCES IN A SCIENTIFIC MANNER

An effective approach to enhancing concrete sustainability involves substituting traditional raw materials (such as cement and aggregate) with low-carbon-embodied industrial wastes/by-products or natural resources. These alternative materials, often referred to as supplementary cementitious materials (SCMs), are increasingly utilized. Common SCMs include ground-granulated blast-furnace slag (GGBS), coal-combustion fly ash, limestone powders, silica fume, and metakaolin. They are readily available in substantial quantities with relatively consistent compositions. SCMs can be incorporated into cement production during the final grinding stage to reduce clinker usage, resulting in blended cements. Alternatively, they can be added to concrete mixtures during production to decrease cement content. Regardless of the method employed, integrating SCMs reduces cement usage, which is the most CO_2^- and energy-intensive element in concrete production. The manufacturing of one ton of cement consumes 4 GJ of energy and emits between 0.8 to 1 ton of CO_2 into the atmosphere.

In cement manufacture, limestone has to be decomposed as:

$$\underset{(100)}{\text{Limestone } (CaCO_3)} \ (1000°C) \rightarrow \underset{(56)}{CaO} + \underset{(44)}{CO_2}$$

On average, one ton of cement contains approximately 620 kg of CaO, and hence $CO_2 = 620 \times 44/56 = 487$ kg is produced. Additionally, fuel combustion during cement manufacturing contributes to CO_2 emissions, ranging from 320 kg to about 450 kg, depending on technological advancements in burning techniques. The global annual cement production contributes nearly 10% of anthropogenic CO_2 emissions, underscoring the potential for significant environmental mitigation through the widespread adoption of SCMs in concrete production.

Furthermore, the utilization of SCMs can positively impact concrete performance. For example, SCMs containing reactive silica (such as fly ash and silica fume) can react with calcium hydroxide (CH) generated during cement hydration, forming secondary calcium-silicate-hydrate (C–S–H) phases. This process enhances microstructural densification and improves concrete properties. Similarly, SCMs containing reactive alumina (e.g. GGBS) can enhance chloride binding capacity, thereby improving the durability of concrete structures in marine environments.

Incorporating SCMs into concrete leads to a more intricate nanometer and micrometer-level structure. Hence, in-depth research is necessary to understand the impact of SCMs on hydration product structures and subsequent macroscopic concrete properties fully. It is imperative to determine the optimal level of cement replacement with SCMs to maximize concrete performance. Through rigorous scientific investigation, the effective utilization of current SCMs can be realized.

It is important to note that many countries and regions have fully utilized their existing SCMs in concrete, leading to shortages of quality SCMs. To further decrease the reliance on Portland cement in concrete and enhance eco- efficiency, exploration of new SCM resources is imperative. These resources should include other industrial by-products containing reactive silica and/or reactive alumina, such as Pb/Zn mine tailings, phosphorus slag, coal gangue, and copper slag. These materials have the potential to yield effects similar to those of conventional SCMs.

The search for industrial waste as SCMs can extend to resources historically disregarded or deemed unreactive, hazardous, or detrimental. Examples include steel slag, air-cooled iron slag, off-specification coal ash (including bottom ash and reclaimed fly ash), and municipal solid waste incineration (MSWI) ashes. In the United States, approximately 90 million tons of cement are produced annually, with a demand for around 40 million tons of SCMs. However, the current dominant SCMs, such as GGBS and on-specification fly ash, are insufficient. Meanwhile, the US generates approximately 7 million tons of steel/air-cooled iron slags, 20 million tons of off-specification coal ashes, and 10 million tons of MSWI ashes annually, with over 2.5 billion tons of these wastes in repositories.

Similar situations may exist in other major economies like China, where cement production exceeds that of the US by more than 20 times, and underutilized waste generation is also significantly higher. However, these new waste resources often exhibit high compositional variation and contain deleterious materials (e.g. chloride, sulfate, and unburned carbon) and toxic substances (e.g. heavy metals) that could compromise concrete performance and environmental safety. Extensive research is necessary to understand their reaction mechanisms and develop effective methods to mitigate their adverse effects on concrete and the environment. Only through improved comprehension and management can these waste resources be harnessed as SCMs to promote the sustainable development of concrete.

In addition to limestone powder, natural mineral deposits offer promising resources for SCMs. These include natural pozzolans such as volcanic ash, which are readily available, and calcined clays like metakaolin—a thermally activated kaolinite-rich clay. Metakaolin exhibits similar properties to silica fume but is more cost-effective, presenting significant potential for future concrete applications.

Due to abundant natural reserves and relatively eco-friendly processing methods, limestone calcined clay cement has emerged as an eco-efficient solution for the cement and concrete industry.

Aggregate, encompassing both fine and coarse varieties, constitutes the most heavily extracted group of materials, surpassing even fossil fuels. Its utilization rate exceeds the natural renewal rate of these minerals, indicating that demand will outpace supply before 2050. To foster more sustainable resource extraction practices, certain industrial wastes can be employed as substitutes for aggregates in concrete production. These waste materials include, but are not limited to, waste glass, demolished concrete, bottom ash, and large-size slags such as steel slag and copper slag. Bottom ash and slags can typically be utilized as aggregate, partially replacing natural aggregate, provided potential deleterious substances like free lime and unburned carbon are effectively managed to prevent premature deterioration of concrete.

Figure 13.1 illustrates the use of crushed waste glass as a substitute for fine aggregate, typically ranging in size from 75 μm to 5 mm. A primary concern regarding the incorporation of glass into concrete as aggregate is the potential for alkali-silica reaction (ASR), as detailed in Chapter 5. Studies have shown that the risk of ASR diminishes as the particle size of crushed waste glass decreases. When ground into a fine powder comparable to cement, waste glass can even function as a pozzolanic material. Controlling the ASR risk associated with waste glass in concrete can also be achieved through dry-mixing (as opposed to wet-mixing) and partially replacing cement with pozzolanic SCMs.

Fig. 13.1: Recycled waste glass as an aggregate for concrete

The reuse of demolished concrete has been identified as a crucial component for the sustainable extraction of natural resources such as sand and gravel. With the aging of concrete structures, the production of demolished concrete is expected to increase. According to estimates by the US Environmental Protection Agency (EPA), concrete constituted over 70% of the 548 million tons of construction and demolition waste generated in the US in 2015—a 69% increase since 2003 (EPA, 2004; 2016). While waste concrete was historically disposed of in landfills or used as backfilling material, recycling efforts have gained momentum since the 1990s, driven by sustainability concerns. The construction and demolition recycling industry is now valued at over US$17 billion, with the volume of landfill space saved by recycling equivalent to an area of 17,401,498 m^2 (4,300 acres) at a depth of 15.24 m (50 ft) annually (CDRA, 2014).

In current practice, concrete waste is typically processed into recycled concrete aggregates (RCAs) to meet the substantial demand for aggregate. However, the majority of RCAs are utilized in road base/subbase construction and engineering fills, with only a small fraction utilized in producing new structural concrete. This limited application in primary uses is considered low-value, as the costs associated with transporting, crushing, and processing concrete waste into RCAs may surpass the sale price of conventional sub-base aggregate. Stimulating the recycling industry to produce RCAs economically necessitates their use in high-value applications, known as upcycling, such as producing high-strength, structural concrete. Despite the environmental and economic advantages, RCAs have not been widely adopted in high-value applications due to technical concerns.

The primary distinction between RCAs and natural aggregates lies in the presence of hydrated cement paste adhering to RCAs. This paste typically exhibits higher porosity and weaker mechanical properties compared to natural sand and rocks, thereby diminishing the overall quality of RCAs in comparison to natural aggregates. The increased water absorption ratio and rougher surface of RCAs necessitate a higher water demand for achieving specified workability in RCA concrete. Incorporating RCAs can have adverse effects on the compressive, tensile, and flexural strengths, as well as the modulus of elasticity of concrete, primarily due to the presence of micro-cracks, compromised interfacial transition zones (ITZ), and weaker cement paste constituents.

Drying shrinkage poses another challenge that limits the widespread use of RCAs in concrete. Their higher water absorption ratio and inferior water restraining capacities can elevate drying shrinkage. At higher replacement levels of natural aggregate, RCAs may also exacerbate chloride ion permeability, increase carbonation depth, and compromise freeze-thaw damage resistance, particularly if the parent concrete was inadequately air-entrained. In summary, incorporating RCAs tends to negatively impact concrete properties. However, there is no consensus among researchers regarding the extent of these drawbacks. The variability in experimental results can be attributed to variations in RCA properties, including differences in porosity, water absorption, mechanical properties (e.g. Los Angeles abrasion mass loss), and other factors such as chemical and organic residues in RCAs or the parent concrete. According to the US Federal Highway Administration, RCAs used in pavement applications can exhibit specific gravities ranging from 2.0 to 2.5, water absorption ratios ranging from 2% to over 10%, and Los Angeles abrasion mass losses ranging from 20% to 45%. The significant variability in properties, influenced by the quality of the parent concrete and the crushing method, complicates the design and implementation of high-value RCA concrete.

In summary, two key challenges must be addressed to enable the high-efficiency utilization of RCAs in new concrete production: (1) enhancing the properties of RCAs and (2) reducing the variability in RCA properties.

Enhancing the properties of RCAs typically involves two general strategies: removing and strengthening the adhered paste/mortar. Paste removal is commonly achieved through mechanical grinding or pre-soaking. While grinding, often aided by heating, is a straightforward method for removing mortar from coarse RCA, it can inadvertently create new cracks due to collisions. Pre-soaking in water, sometimes assisted by ultrasound, or acid solutions has been utilized to dislodge weakly adhered mortar and cement hydrates from RCA grains. However, the drawbacks of the removal strategy include high energy or chemical usage and potential damage to the resulting RCAs.

Strengthening RCAs can be accomplished through various surface treatments or impregnations, such as latexes, silane/siloxane solutions, paraffin, or pozzolan slurries containing fly ash, silica fume, or nano-silica. Carbonation, which involves RCAs absorbing CO_2 to strengthen them, has been considered a sustainable option. However, the benefits may be limited due to the relatively low amount of calcium hydroxide (CH) in the surface layer of RCAs.

In conclusion, while numerous methods may enhance RCA properties to some extent, their effectiveness could be constrained by underlying mechanisms or adverse side effects. Moreover, these methods do not address the issue of reducing RCA variability. In the future, as methodologies evolve to improve RCA and RCA concrete properties, greater emphasis may be placed on minimizing variability. After all, achieving consistent concrete properties with highly variable raw material feedstock presents a significant challenge.

13.3 LOW ENERGY AND LOW CO_2 EMISSION BINDERS

Efforts to mitigate the environmental impact of Portland cement have spurred exploration into alternative binders characterized by lower energy requirements and reduced carbon dioxide emissions. One such avenue is the development of alkali-activated cementitious materials, with geopolymer and alkali-activated slag emerging as notable examples. Geopolymer, offers a promising alternative. Activated slag employs water glass and/or other alkaline solutions to initiate a chemical reaction with slag, resulting in bond formation.

While the feasibility of alkali-activated materials has been demonstrated in laboratory settings, their widespread commercial adoption has been hindered by several factors. These include the variability in performance, particularly under varying temperature conditions, the high cost associated with the most effective alkaline activators like water glass, and the lack of robustness when utilizing cheaper activators. Additionally, alkali-activated systems typically exhibit rapid setting, rendering the use of superplasticizers ineffective. To facilitate the practical utilization of alkali-activated cementitious materials, further research is imperative.

Another system employs MgO-based binders, such as magnesium phosphate cement. However, a significant challenge in utilizing such materials on a large scale lies in controlling the setting time.

Additional systems encompass new clinker types characterized by higher levels of alumina and sulfate compared to Portland cement. These clinkers include high aluminate cement, sulfoaluminate cement, and high-belite cement (HBC). Recently, China introduced a novel high-belite cement (HBC). HBC, a belite-based Portland cement, typically comprises 45–60% C_2S, 20–30% C_3S, 3–7% C_3A, and 10–15% C_4AF. Laboratory research, industrial production, and field applications of HBC concrete have demonstrated its characteristics as a low-energy consumption and low CO_2 emission Portland cement variant, with reduced hydration heat evolution, high later-age strength, and superior performance.

For instance, the clinkering temperature of HBC is 1350°C, which is 100°C lower than that of normal PC. Consequently, the CO_2 emissions during HBC clinkering are reduced by 10% due to the lower calcium content in the clinker mineral composition and decreased coal consumption during clinker burning. HBC concrete exhibits excellent properties, including improved workability, higher mechanical strength, superior durability, exceptional thermal properties, and enhanced crack resistance. Table 13.1 provides a comparison of the energy consumption and CO_2 emissions for C_2S and C_3S, highlighting the energy savings and CO_2 emission reduction achieved by the high C_2S content in HBC.

Table 13.1: Comparison of energy consumption and CO_2 emission for C_2S and C_3S

Mineral	*Formation enthalpy (kJ/kg)*	*Formation temperature (°C)*	*CaO (%)*	*CO_2 emission coefficient per unit mass of mineral*
C_3S	1848	1450	73.7	0.578
C_2S	1336	1300	65.1	0.511

Concrete produced using HBC demonstrates superior workability compared to that made with normal Portland cement, particularly when low water-to-cement (w/c) ratios are utilized, as outlined in Table 13.2. Although concrete made from HBC exhibits slower strength development during the early stages, up to 7 days, it reaches and surpasses the strength of ordinary Portland cement concrete by 28 days and 90 days, as evidenced by the flexural, splitting, and compressive strength data provided in Table 13.3. In comparison to existing low-heat Portland cements which also contain a significant amount of belite, the new binder achieves substantially higher early-age strength levels, as illustrated in Table 13.4.

Table 13.2 Workability of HBC high-strength, high-performance concrete in comparison with OPC concrete

Concrete type	*Cement amount (kg/m^3)*	*W/B*	*Fly ash (kg/m^3)*	*Water (kg/m^3)*	*Superplasticizer (%)*	*Initial slump (cm)*	*Slump at 90 nub (cm)*
C60 HBC	414	0.32	104	165	1.0	23.2	22.5
C60 OPC	414	0.32	104	165	1.0	22.4	20.3
C80 HBC	510	0.25	90	150	1.7	24.4	20.6
C80 OPC	510	0.25	90	150	1.7	0	0

Table 13.3: Strength comparison between HBC and OPC concretes

Type	*Flexural strength (MPa)*			*Splitting strength (MPa)*			*Compressive strength (MPa)*		
	7 d	*28 d*	*90 d*	*7 d*	*28 d*	*90 d*	*7 d*	*28 d*	*90 d*
HPC-60	3.5	7.2	8.9	3.81	5.37	7.44	54.6	77.6	98.5
OPC-60	5.2	6.7	8.2	4.45	5.16	6.36	60.3	78.5	90.2
HPC-80	4.5	8.4	10.3	4.76	6.72	8.25	68.3	95.4	116.4
OPC-80	6.2	7.9	9.1	5.28	5.94	7.35	72.5	91.0	107.5

Table 13.4: Comparison of the strength requirements for low-heat Portland cement in different standards (the one in China is represented by HBC)

Standard	*Compressive, 7 days (MPa)*	*Compressive, 28 days (MPa)*
China GB 200-2003	≥13.0	≥42.5
USA ASTM C150	≥7.5	≥17.0
Japan JISA R 521	≥7.5	≥22.5

Concrete produced using the new HBC has demonstrated superior freeze-thaw resistance, reduced drying shrinkage, and lower heat release. This innovative HBC concrete has been successfully utilized in several major infrastructure projects across China, including the third phase of the Three Gorges Dam in Yichang, Zipingpu and Shenxigou dams in Sichuan Province, Beijing International Airport, and the 5th Ring Road in Beijing. Figure 13.2 depicts the application of the new HBC concrete at the Three Gorges Dam.

Fig. 13.2: Application of new HBC concrete in the three Gorges dam

Research into hydraulic alternative cements, akin to the discussion above, has been ongoing. Some recent developments include belite-ye'elimite-ferrite cements (e.g.

belite-sulfoaluminate cement) and the incorporation of a ternesite phase, which may potentially lower clinkering temperatures to approximately 1100°C. However, while these alternative cements offer some reduction in carbon emissions, the reductions are not deemed significant. As highlighted in the UNEP-SBCI report, the International Energy Agency's goal to reduce CO_2 emissions from cement manufacturing by 24% by 2050 could prove challenging to achieve with existing and emerging technologies. Furthermore, meeting the carbon-neutral targets of the US by 2050 and China by 2060 will necessitate the development of new, groundbreaking technologies such as carbon capture, utilization, and storage (CCUS) technologies, as well as innovative alternative cements that diverge fundamentally from current practices.

13.4 EFFICIENTLY UTILIZING MATERIALS: HSC AND UHSC APPLICATIONS

Enhancing material usage efficiency presents another avenue for rendering concrete more sustainable. The utilization of high-strength concrete (HSC) and ultra-high-strength concrete (UHSC), along with pre-stress techniques during design and construction, offers an effective means of optimizing concrete usage efficiency.

While it may be argued that HSC and UHSC necessitate increased cementitious materials, implying higher energy consumption and CO_2 emissions, their utilization in design and construction enables significant reduction in the cross-section of structural members such as columns and beams. Consequently, the overall material usage in a concrete structure can be diminished compared to conventional-strength concrete applications. This reduction in material volume leads to decreased cement usage, subsequently lowering energy consumption and CO_2 emissions.

Likewise, employing pre-stressing techniques enables the effective utilization of steel tendons with higher tensile strength, consequently reducing the total amount of steel required. The San Francisco Public Utilities Commission Building serves as a prime illustration of this principle. This 14-story concrete building, with one below-grade level, spanning a total area of 26,000 m^2, implements a high-strength concrete vertically post-tensioned throughout the building core. This innovative approach results in a 30% reduction in concrete and reinforcement compared to conventional-strength concrete systems.

Future advancements are poised to introduce a plethora of methodologies aimed at enhancing material utilization efficiency. In addition to innovations in materials, novel construction methods such as additive manufacturing and prefabrication will undoubtedly play significant roles in this regard.

13.5 DEEP UNDERSTANDING OF THE NATURE OF HYDRATION

A comprehensive comprehension of concrete's performance enhancement, including mechanical properties and durability, necessitates a profound understanding of the characteristics of hydration products. A longstanding requirement in cement science, as identified by Powers and Brownyard in 1948, is a quantitative grasp of C–S–H at atomic to 100 nm scales and its influence on mechanical, transport, and chemical attributes of hydrated cement paste. Computational methods are widely employed to model C–S–H structures. Despite this, the structure of C–S–H, the primary hydration product of cement, remains undisclosed. Additionally, as concrete compositions evolve with the increased utilization of admixtures and SCMs, the hydration process and resultant products become more intricate. The phase compositions originating from cement-SCM reactions may differ from pure cement hydration products. Alterations in pore structure, cohesive forces between phases, and resultant mechanical properties may occur. Embracing alternative binders like geopolymers and C-A-S-H/N-A-S-H gels adds further complexity. A thorough understanding of contemporary concrete's hydration product structure is imperative for enhancing microstructure and consequently, concrete performance.

Fortunately, recent technological advancements have provided a diverse array of experimental and computational tools for investigating the hydration of cementitious materials. Experimental techniques, including atomic force microscopy (AFM), small-angle neutron and X-ray scattering, nuclear magnetic resonance (NMR), nanoindentation, and high-resolution scanning and transmission electron microscopies, offer insights into various aspects of C–S–H at different scales. For instance, AFM allows for the examination of C–S–H aggregation shapes at the tens of nanometer scale and determination of the cohesive force nature of hydration products. Small-angle neutron and X-ray scattering techniques can be utilized to explore the "gel" porosity of C–S–H. NMR spectroscopy provides insights into the structure of C–S–H and pore structure of cementitious materials. Nanoindentation is employed for measuring the modulus of C–S–H and other hydrates. Furthermore, high-resolution scanning and transmission electron microscopies, in conjunction with chemical microanalysis, facilitate the determination of microstructural development and microchemistry of hydration phases.

The data derived from these experiments provide a partially predictive framework that spans from the atomic to the macroscopic level. However, relying solely on these experimental techniques does not fully elucidate the structure of concrete at the atomic and molecular levels. Hence, computational modeling and numerical simulations are indispensable in concrete science.

Numerical simulation methods at the atomic and molecular scale encompass approaches based on quantum chemical and molecular potentials. Quantum (first-principles) methods entail solving the Schrödinger equation under the Born-Oppenheimer approximation, mean field approximation, and periodic potential approximation, which describe the interaction of multi-particle systems. Quantum chemical methods are categorized into wave-function-based and density-functional-theory-based (DFT) methods based on the calculated quantity.

The Hartree-Fock (HF) approach serves as the theoretical foundation for wave-function-based methods, aiming to fully describe electron properties. Molecular orbitals of the electron wave function can be obtained through the self-consistent field method within the HF approach. However, this method overlooks electronic correlation effects, limiting its accuracy. Post-Hartree-Fock methods, such as configuration interaction (CI), coupled cluster (CC), Møller-Plesset perturbation (MP) theory, and quadratic configuration interaction (QCI), substantially enhance precision but escalate computational costs exponentially.

In contrast, the DFT method employs electron density as the fundamental research quantity, reducing the problem from 3N to three dimensions. The theoretical basis of the DFT method lies in the Kohn-Sham (KS) equation, which accounts for electronic exchange and correlation interactions. Nevertheless, this method includes a self-interaction effect and is less reliable for weak interaction calculations. Incorporating hybrid functionals (e.g. B3LYP and PWPB95-D3) can mitigate these drawbacks.

Potential-based methods, such as classical molecular dynamics (MD), rely on empirical or semi-empirical potentials governing interactions between atomic or molecular entities. These methods treat atoms or molecules as classical entities, computing their positions, motions, and energies as they interact under the influence of potential functions. These functions encapsulate short-range atomic repulsion, van der Waals forces, and coulombic interactions, both attractive and repulsive. MD methods track the time evolution of system structure and energy, enabling calculations of dynamic properties like vibrational spectra.

With advancements in high-performance computing, quantum (ab initio) MD (AIMD) has become increasingly accessible. AIMD generates finite-temperature dynamical trajectories by computing forces directly from electronic structure calculations performed "on the fly" during the simulation. Thus, AIMD captures bond breakage and formation and incorporates electronic polarization effects. AIMD is typically categorized into Born-Oppenheimer MD (BOMD) and Car–Parrinello MD (CPMD) (Car and Parrinello, 1985; Remler and Madden, 1990; Marx and Hutter, 2000). AIMD has found success in addressing a wide range of significant issues in physics, chemistry, biology, and is beginning to influence cement science. It unveils new physical phenomena and microscopic mechanisms inaccessible to empirical methods, even suggesting new experimental approaches and offering fresh interpretations of existing data.

Each simulation method presents its own advantages and limitations. Quantum methods typically offer greater accuracy in describing atomic positions, interaction energies, and spectroscopic properties compared to potential-based methods. However, even with the latest supercomputers, quantum methods are constrained to relatively small systems, typically a few hundred atoms. The hybrid quantum mechanics/ molecular mechanics (QM/MM) approach partially mitigates this limitation. On the other hand, MD and Monte Carlo (MC) simulations sacrifice some accuracy for the ability to model larger systems and longer reaction times, now capable of handling systems on the order of 10^6 atoms for a few nanoseconds.

Constructing a suitable model for C–S–H using simulation requires consideration of parameters and their utilization as objective functions to attain reasonable outcomes. The Ca/Si ratio stands out as a crucial criterion that simulations must adhere to. The stoichiometric equation for fully hydrated C_3S, yields a Ca/Si ratio of 1.75. Experimentally, studies summarized utilizing small-angle X-ray scattering (SAXS) and small-angle neutron scattering (SANS) have shown Ca/Si ratios ranging from 1.2 to 2.3, with a mean of 1.7–1.75.

Another crucial determinant of C–S–H structure is its density, which is contingent upon the water content within the gel. Recently, Allen et al. (2007) established a density value of 2604 kg/m^3 for C–S–H, integrating data from SANS and SAXS methodologies, factoring in combined water. This estimation is considered to better represent the intrinsic property of C–S–H gel and thus holds relevance for simulations.

The silicate connectivity also plays a vital role in understanding C–S–H structure, discernible through ^{29}Si NMR. Silicate units are based on SiO_4 tetrahedra, and the spectral peaks in ^{29}Si NMR correspond to the number of bridging oxygen atoms within a SiO_4 unit. Theoretically, ^{29}Si NMR reveals five categories of Q_n sites, each characterized by a chemical shift: Q_0 (–70 ppm), Q_1 (–80 ppm), Q_2 (–88 ppm), Q_3 (–98 ppm), and Q_4 (–110 ppm), where 'n' denotes the number of additional tetrahedra linked by sharing an oxygen atom with the base tetrahedron (Johansson, 1999). In C–S–H, Q_1 and Q_2 Si sites predominate, while Q_3 and Q_4 Si sites are typically absent. Despite conventionally being associated with surface hydroxylation of C_3S, Q_0 monomers have been observed persisting from the induction period to late hydration stages, constituting approximately 2% to 10% of the total. Hence, the role of Q_0 silicate sites must be considered in numerical simulations.

It is believed that meaningful and realistic results in numerical simulations can only be achieved by appropriately selecting a combination of Ca/Si ratio, density, and silicate connectivity as functions.

A more realistic approach to constructing a C–S–H structure at the atomic level involves understanding its formation mechanism during the hydration of C_3S. Upon encountering water, C_3S dissolves, releasing a significant quantity of Ca ions and a smaller amount of silicate groups. Subsequently, hydrolysis of surface silicate and oxygen ions occurs. Due to the hydrophobic nature and low diffusion coefficient of silicate groups, a Si-rich region forms around the C_3S surface, potentially serving as an intermediate phase for C–S–H. Synthetic C–S–H formation typically undergoes a phase transformation from metastable to thermodynamically favored structures, but whether this mechanism applies to C–S–H formed through C_3S hydration warrants further investigation.

To delve deeper into these processes, state-of-the-art simulation methods at the atomic level are indispensable for gaining insights into C_3S hydration and C–S–H formation mechanisms. Simulating the extensive hydration process, spanning significant timeframes and involving a series of chemical reactions, exceeds the capabilities of traditional MD methods due to their limited simulation timescales and high energy barriers between stable states. Addressing this challenge necessitates the implementation of enhanced sampling methods such as umbrella sampling (US), metadynamics (MetaD), and variationally enhanced sampling (VES) to explore potential reaction pathways.

For instance, the dissolution process of Ca ions from the C_3S surface has been investigated using ab initio metadynamics simulations employing collective variables CNs (the coordination number of Ca with O on the C_3S surface) and CNw (the coordination number of Ca with O from water molecules). Analysis reveals that the detachment of the last Ca-Os bond requires the absorption of six water molecules [Fig. 13.3(a)]. Subsequently, the detached Ca ion coordinates with five, six, or seven water molecules. The replacement of the previous Ca site by a water molecule and a hydron ion bonded with the O ion in the second surface layer is depicted in Fig. 13.3(b) The diffusion of water molecules into the bottom of the Ca ion necessitates relatively

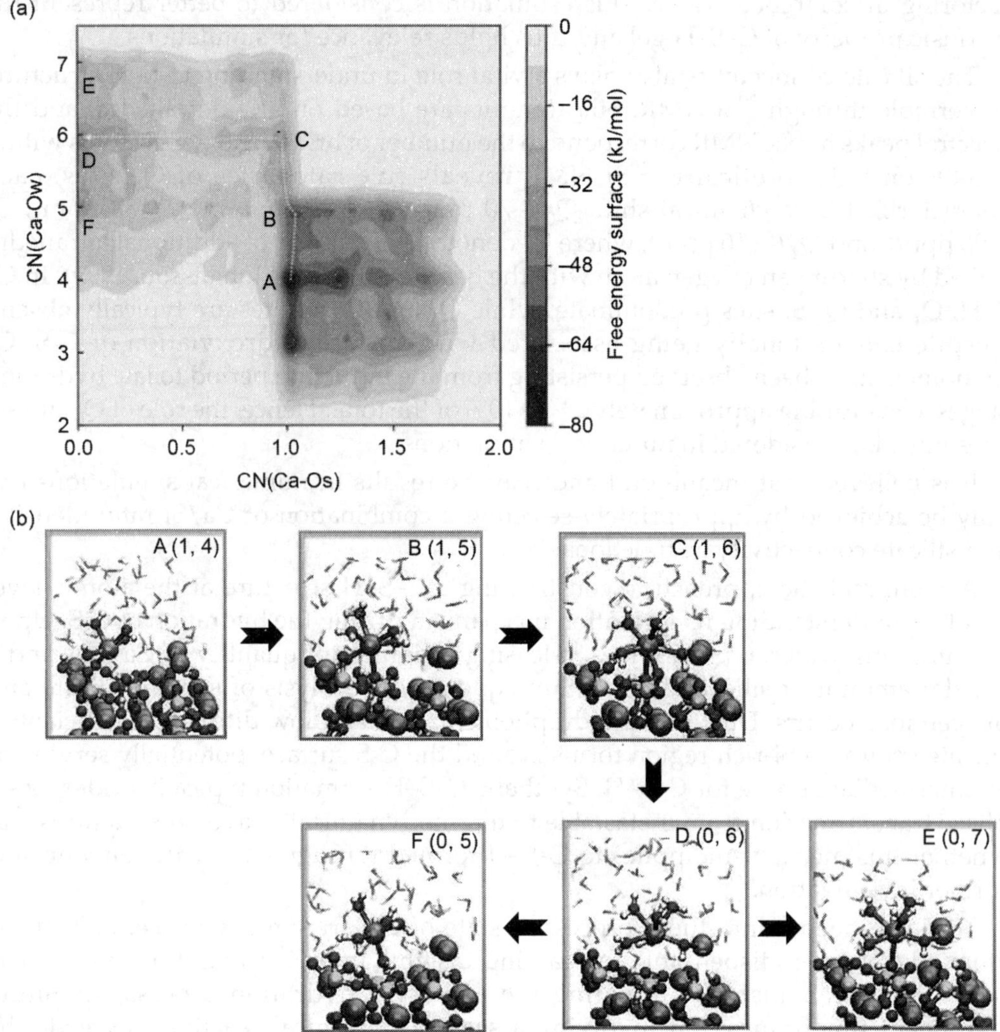

Fig. 13.3: Dissolution of the Ca ion from the C_3S surface through *ab initio* metadynamics simulations: (a) the two-dimensional free energy surface (FES) of dissolution of the Ca ion with variables of CNs (the coordination number of Ca with O on the C_3S surface) and CNw (the coordination number of Ca with O from water molecules); (b) the configurations of the free energy minimum states on the FES

high activation energy. Additionally, this water molecule exerts electrostatic repulsion on the Ca ion, promoting its vertical displacement.

In recent times, there has been a surge in the development of machine learning-based (ML) or deep learning-based (DL) interatomic potential energy surface (PES) models derived from quantum chemical methods. These models offer the capability to conduct molecular dynamics (MD) simulations for large-scale systems with quantum-level accuracy. We anticipate that this advanced technology will have a profound impact on enhancing our fundamental comprehension of cement hydration in the future.

13.6 INTEGRATED MATERIALS AND STRUCTURAL DESIGN

Design is a purposeful exploration involving decision-making and goal-oriented planning to create products, processes, and systems with desired functionalities according to specifications. In concrete engineering, structural design plays a crucial role in developing buildings and infrastructures. Integrated materials and structural design represent a design philosophy that adopts an interdisciplinary and comprehensive approach.

In many countries, structural design has increasingly embraced a performance-based philosophy, which simultaneously considers safety, durability, serviceability, and sustainability aspects of a structure. Integrated design integrates materials engineering and structural engineering during the design phase, leveraging the strengths of materials by selecting the most appropriate structural forms.

The interconnection between materials and structures is depicted in Fig. 13.4. At the base of the pyramid lies materials engineering, encompassing synthesis, microstructures/composition, properties, and performance. At the apex of the inverted pyramid are four structural engineering aspects: safety, durability, serviceability, and sustainability. It is evident that both materials and structural engineering must meet the end-use requirements and constraints of the final structure.

Integrated design encompasses two approaches as illustrated in Fig. 13.4.

1. **Bottom-up approach:** Existing materials' properties dictate potential structural forms, representing a traditional method employed by builders and engineers over centuries.
2. **Top-down approach:** Structural engineers translate targeted structural performance into desired materials properties, which may include mechanical properties, microstructure, or macrostructure. Material engineers then develop

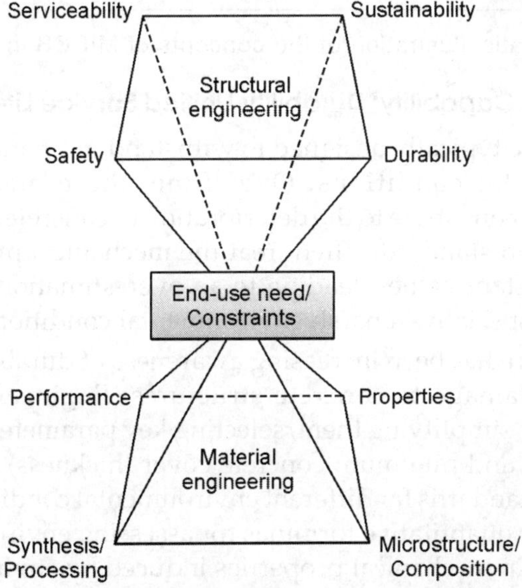

Fig. 13.4: The intertwined relationship between materials and structures

new composite materials or customize existing materials to meet these desired properties. Essentially, the performance requirements of structures drive material design and development, representing a relatively new engineering paradigm in concrete engineering facilitated by advancements in material engineering in recent decades.

Advanced design methodologies, such as the materials-oriented integrated design and construction of structures (MIDCS) method can bridge the paths between materials and structures in a top-down or bottom-up manner, as depicted in Fig. 13.5.

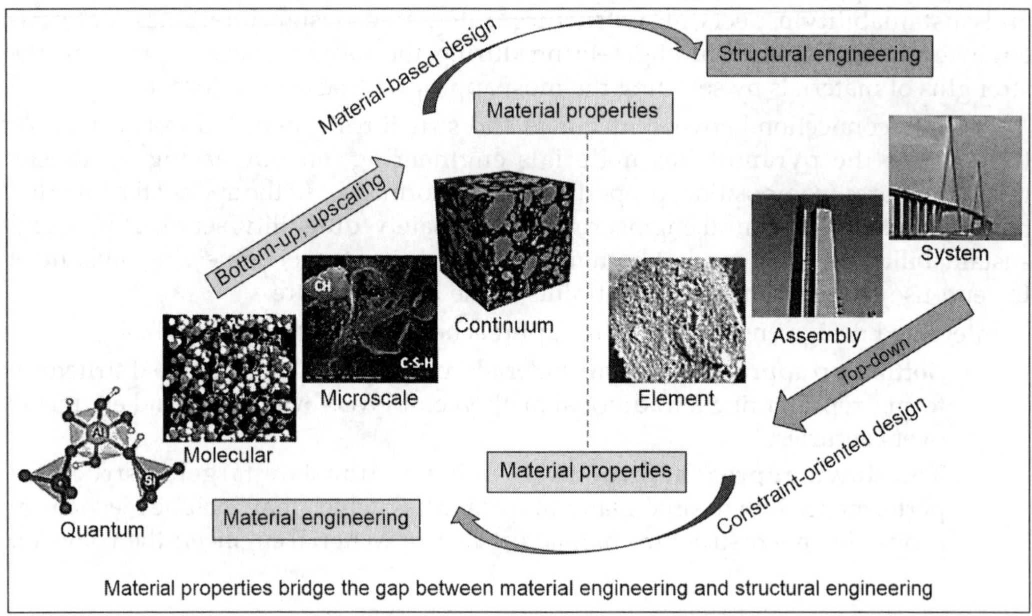

Fig. 13.5: Schematic illustration of the concepts of MIDCS in civil engineering

13.6.1 Load-carrying Capability: Durability Unified Service Life Design Theory

Concrete structures are typically designed to withstand mechanical loads and endure various environmental conditions. Over time, these mechanical loads and environmental factors contribute to the deterioration of concrete structures. However, conventional codes and standards often treat the mechanical properties of materials and structures as constant values, leading to an overestimation of the service life of concrete structures, especially in harsh environmental conditions.

Since the 1990s, there has been increasing awareness of durability issues due to the rising incidence of damage to concrete structures. Engineers currently address durability concerns by simplifying them, selecting key parameters (such as maximum water-to-cement ratio and minimum concrete cover thickness) based on established guidelines, codes, or standards for different environmental conditions. However, there is a lack of scientific or quantitative formulas for assessing environmental factors, and the dynamic changes in mechanical properties induced by environmental conditions are not accounted for in existing codes and standards.

It has long been recognized that concrete structures experience mechanical loads and exposure to various environmental conditions simultaneously, leading to property degradation. However, traditional concrete structure design has primarily focused on the structure's load-carrying capacity, disregarding the influence of environmental conditions. Although some design codes addressing concrete durability have been developed since the 1990s, they mainly provide details such as cover thickness under specific environmental conditions without offering a scientific framework to quantify environmental effects. Furthermore, these codes do not consider the dynamic changes in concrete properties and performance over time, thus failing to accurately reflect the true service conditions of concrete structures.

In a Chinese national basic research project initiated in 2009, titled "Basic Study on Environmentally Friendly Contemporary Concrete," the load-carrying capability: durability unified service life design theory was introduced for the first time. This theory proposes a novel and scientific design philosophy that integrates safety, durability, serviceability, and sustainability considerations for concrete structures in a unified manner. It aims to address two fundamental issues currently overlooked by existing codes and standards.

The first issue entails quantitatively measuring environmental factors and integrating them with mechanical loads. To tackle this, the theory has devised a viable method that converts environmental factors into equivalent stresses using thermodynamics and porous media theory. For instance, considering volume elements of cement-based materials, these elements endure mechanical loads within the cement pore solution environment (Fig 13.6). By applying thermodynamics and virtual energy calculation, the chemical reactions occurring in the pore solutions can be translated into strain or stress. Consequently, the theory quantitatively couples environmental factors with

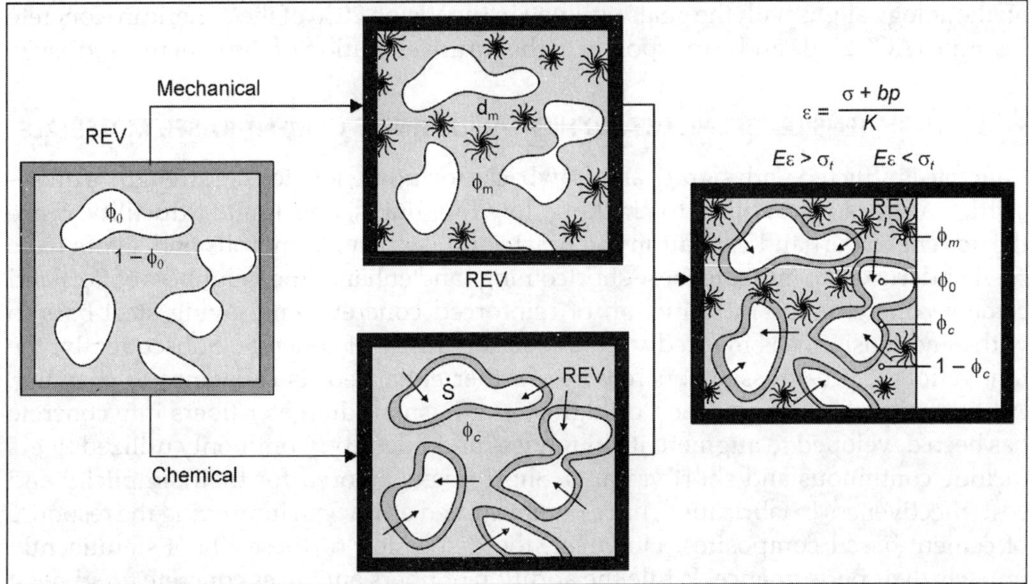

Fig. 13.6: Conversion of chemical/environmental influence to mechanical effect

mechanical loads by superimposing the two stresses, allowing the design process to adhere to existing stress analysis-based codes and standards.

The second issue involves comprehensively addressing the time-dependent properties of materials and structures. One approach is to delineate the deterioration mechanisms of materials and structures under the combined influences of environmental factors and mechanical loads, employing advanced experimental methods and/or multi-scale simulations. By elucidating these mechanisms, we can ascertain the time-dependent properties of materials and structures, enabling the prediction of concrete structure performance over time (Fig. 13.7). This predictive function facilitates the assessment of concrete structures' performance at different service periods, subsequently informing design and evaluation processes accordingly.

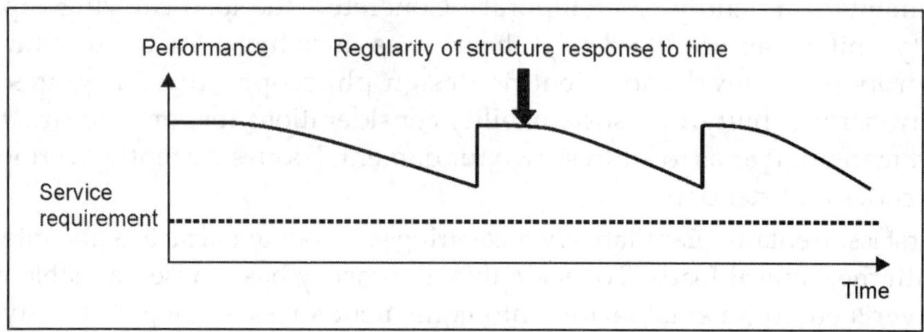

Fig. 13.7: Regularity of concrete structure performance as a function of time

This unified design method necessitates consideration of material properties and structural performance throughout the design, construction, service, and maintenance phases. It epitomizes a designer-centered, multidisciplinary, and holistic approach, encompassing the entire life cycle of buildings and civil infrastructures. Such a design methodology aligns with the goals outlined in the Vision 2030 of the American Concrete Institute (ACI, 2001) and corresponds to the future evolution of the concrete industry.

13.7 HIGH-TENSILE-STRENGTH AND HIGH-TOUGHNESS CEMENT-BASED MATERIALS

Concrete is afflicted with significant drawbacks including low tensile strength, a quasi-brittle nature, susceptibility to cracking, low toughness, and limited ductility. Since the advent of Portland cement in the nineteenth century, numerous endeavors have been undertaken to mitigate these shortcomings and enhance the toughness of Portland cement concrete. The introduction of reinforced concrete, employing steel bars to withstand tension, has markedly expanded the utility of concrete. Subsequently, the innovation of pre-stressed concrete has further enhanced its resistance to cracking. Additionally, the incorporation of high-strength, small-diameter fibers into concrete has been developed to augment its toughness and ductility. Commonly utilized fibers include continuous and short variants. Short fibers, favored for their simplicity and cost-effectiveness in fabrication, have demonstrated efficacy in improving the response of cement-based composites. However, the dispersion of these fibers significantly impacts their performance. While the addition of fibers enhances concrete toughness, limitations exist due to heightened costs and challenges associated with dispersion.

Consequently, the potential for improving the tensile strength and toughness of concrete remains constrained.

An alternative approach to enhancing toughness involves the incorporation of polymers into concrete, which is currently executed through three methods.

- Firstly, polymer concrete (PC) is produced by utilizing polymers as the binder in concrete. This method involves premixing a two-part polymer system, such as epoxy resin and hardener, and subsequently blending it with aggregate to create a hardened plastic material with aggregate acting as filler.
- Secondly, polymer impregnated concrete (PIC) involves impregnating a monomer and catalyst/initiator into hardened concrete, followed by *in situ* polymerization facilitated using steam or infrared heat.
- Lastly, polymer-modified or latex-modified concrete (LMC) is formed by dispersing a polymer, typically latex, in water and then mixing it with Portland cement and aggregate.

While PC and PIC are costly and primarily utilized for emergency or essential concreting jobs in demanding environments, LMC is more economically viable and commonly used for pavement overlay projects. Reactive latexes, such as polyacrylics, can interact with hydration products to form an organic-inorganic hybrid matrix, while inert latexes, like styrene-butadiene rubber, can result in an organic-inorganic interpenetrated structure.

Although LMC may improve tensile strength and reduce the modulus of elasticity and impermeability, it does not significantly alter the quasi-brittle nature of concrete or provide substantial enhancements in tensile strength and toughness.

There is a growing interest in academia and industry alike to develop technology aimed at enhancing the flexural strength and toughness of concrete while addressing its inherent quasi-brittle nature. Progress in this direction holds the promise of ushering in a new era of concrete technology, with recent endeavors focusing on achieving this ambitious goal.

Researchers at the Hong Kong University of Science and Technology and the University of Macau have been investigating methods to enhance flexural strength through on-site polymerization. This approach involves incorporating organic monomers, initiators, and accelerators into the mix of cement-based composites during the mixing process, allowing polymerization to occur concurrently with cement hydration.

Liang (2018) utilized acrylamide (AM) as the monomer, ammonium persulfate (APS) as the initiator, and N,N,N′,N′-tetramethyl-ethylenediamine (TEMED) as the accelerator. Through Time-of-Flight Secondary Ion Mass Spectrometry (ToF-SIMS), it was observed that a polyacrylamide (PAM) network formed within the composite, establishing strong chemical bonds between PAM and Ca^{2+} in the hydration products of cement (Fig. 13.8). This PAM network substantially improved the flexural strength of the composite. Even with a mere 1% polymer content, the flexural strength nearly tripled while maintaining compressive strength values comparable to reference specimens.

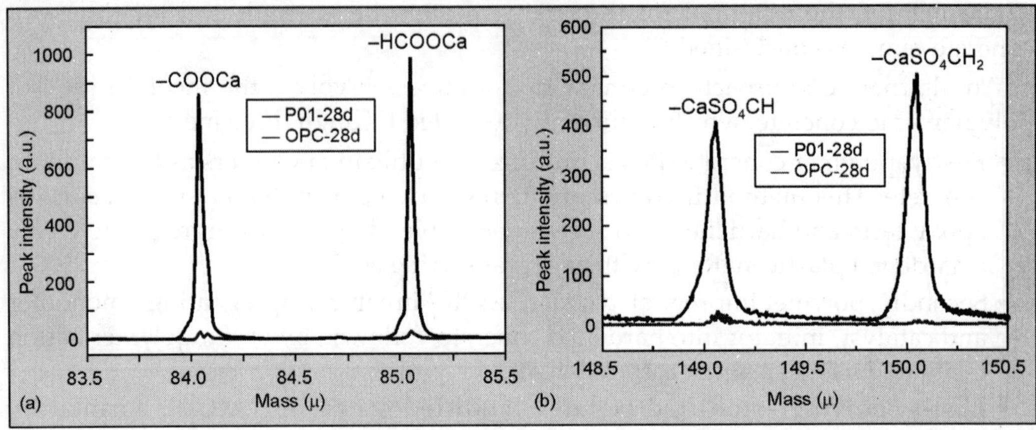

Fig. 13.8: ToF-SIMS tests of OPC and PAM/cement composite with AM/cement weight ratios of 1% (P01): (a) peaks of –COOCa (mass 84.0) and –HCOOCa (mass 85.0) appear in P01; (b) peaks of $-CaSO_4CH$ (mass 149.0) and $-CaSO_4CH_2$ (mass 150.0) appear in P01

Similarly acrylic acid (AA) and 2-acrylanmido-2-methylpropanesulfonic acid (AMPS) was employed as monomers, with sodium hydroxide serving as the neutralizer for the monomer solution. Ammonium persulfate (APS) was used as the initiator, and N,N,N′,N′- tetramethyl-ethylenediamine (TEMED) as the accelerator in the concrete mix. Experimental results demonstrated a 61.2% increase in flexural strength for concrete incorporating 7% AA-AMPS compared to reference concrete. Moreover, the toughness of the 7% AA-AMPS modified concrete exhibited a nearly threefold increase relative to the reference specimen.

In Europe, as part of the Nanocem project "Organo Mineral Composites," spearheaded by Sika (www.nanocem.org), a novel method has been proposed. This method involves the development of a mineral organic composite with dual functionality. One end of the composite is designed to chemically bond with the hydrate of Portland cement, while the other end is capable of polymerization.

The hybrid organic-inorganic polymer dispersion is created through emulsion polymerization of acrylates, urethane, or vinyl acetate, alongside siloxane molecular precursors. These hybrid particles are functionalized with siloxane molecules bearing terminal functional groups R′nSi(OR)4-n, where R′ can undergo polymerization or copolymerization. Following hydrolysis, these terminal groups form bonds with the mineral matrix of concrete, encompassing both cement and aggregates. This innovative technology is anticipated to imbue concrete with high tensile strength and exceptional ductility, representing a departure from conventional concrete materials.

In China, as part of a national key research project on concrete, a study was undertaken to enhance the toughness of concrete by introducing a novel admixture termed as a "concrete toughness enhancer." The chemical composition of this new admixture is depicted schematically in Fig. 13.9.

To evaluate the efficacy of this newly developed admixture, two sets of concrete specimens were prepared for a three-point bending fracture test. One set comprised regular concrete as a reference, while the other set incorporated the new admixture.

The test results from both sets of specimens are presented in Table 13.5. Notably, the incorporation of this admixture led to a significant increase in the fracture toughness of the modified concrete.

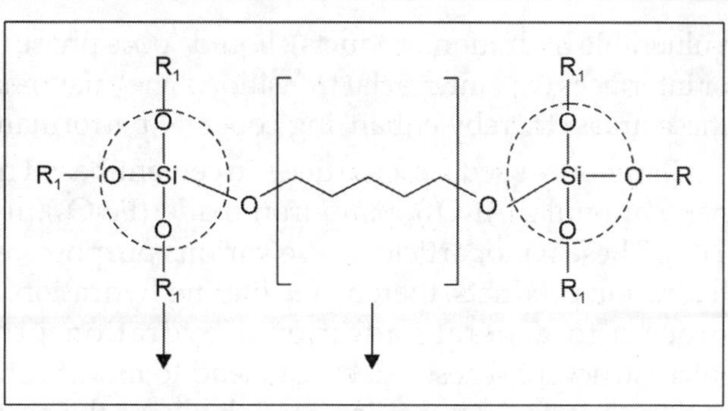

While these initial findings demonstrate promising results, achieving the ultimate goal will require considerable time and effort. Nonetheless, with a comprehensive understanding of the nature of concrete hydrates, particularly C–S–H, there exists the potential to develop methods and materials capable of reacting with C–S–H and self-polymerizing at the molecular scale. This advancement could eliminate the quasi-brittle nature of concrete, paving the way for a new era characterized by the fourth generation of concrete.

Fig. 13.9: Schematic drawing of the toughness enhancer structure

Table 13.5: Fracture test results for two types of specimens

Type (7 d)	*Dosage (%)*	P_{max} *(kN)*	K_{IC} *(MPa·m^{0.5})*	W_1 *(N·m)*	W_2 *(N·m)*	G_F *(N·m^{-1})*	*Ratio (%)*
Reference	0	4.12	1.03	0.54	0.23	91	100
Modified	1.5	5.53	1.38	0.89	0.99	220	242

13.8 APPLICATION OF NANOTECHNOLOGY IN CONCRETE

Nanotechnology typically involves the comprehension, manipulation, and restructuring of materials at a scale smaller than 100 nm, leading to the emergence of novel properties and functionalities. Two primary approaches are employed in nanotechnology: the "top-down" and the "bottom-up" methods. The former entails reducing the dimensions of larger structures to the nanoscale while retaining their original properties, albeit without atomic-level precision. Conversely, the latter approach involves the engineering of materials from atomic or molecular scales through assembly or self-assembly processes.

Although significant strides have been made in the nanoscale science of cement-based materials, including understanding cohesion and creep origins, as well as hydration and deterioration mechanisms, the practical implementation of nanotechnologies in concrete remains limited. Various nanomaterials, such as nanoparticles, nano-reinforcements, and organic molecules, have been proposed and utilized to modify cement-based materials. These materials can effectively enhance concrete properties and performance, such as mechanical strength and resistance to deterioration mechanisms, or introduce new functionalities not originally present in concrete.

Technologies employing such nanomaterials typically follow the bottom-up approach. By identifying intrinsic defects in concrete, whether in the solid phase (e.g.

vulnerable hydration products), liquid/pore phase (e.g. well-connected pore network), or interfaces (e.g. interfacial transition zone), nanomaterials can be employed to modify these areas, thereby enhancing concrete performance.

Commonly used nanoparticles in cement-based materials include nano-silica (SiO_2), nano-alumina (Al_2O_3), nano-iron oxide (Fe_2O_3), nano-clay, nano-$CaCO_3$, and nano-TiO_2. These nanoparticles serve various purposes, such as acting as nuclei for cement hydration products, thereby facilitating hydration, and participating in the hydration process to generate additional hydration products, thereby densifying the microstructure. These effects can lead to modifications in both the bulk cement paste and the interfacial transition zones between the paste and aggregate, which are critical for concrete strength and durability. Additionally, certain nanoparticles can confer unique functionalities to concrete, such as self-cleaning and pollutant removal with nano-TiO_2, and self-sensing with nano-Fe_2O_3.

In addition to incorporating nanoparticles into cement-based materials, there has been limited research on producing nano-sized cementitious materials through either a top-down approach (reducing the particle size of cement to the nano-scale through high-energy grinding, sometimes with mineral additives) or a bottom-up approach (chemically synthesizing nano-cement). Nano-sized cementitious materials have demonstrated the potential to achieve higher strength than regular Portland cement.

Since the late 1990s, carbon nanotubes (CNT), nanofibers (CNF), and graphitic nano-plates (GNP) have been utilized as nano-reinforcements in cement-based materials to enhance compressive and flexural strength, as well as the modulus of elasticity. More recently, graphene and graphene oxide (GO) have been included as nano-reinforcements. These nano-additives are often considered as 1D (e.g. CNT) or 2D (e.g. GO) reinforcements that can bridge weak hydration products, interfaces, or initial cracks, thereby improving mechanical properties, particularly tensile strength. However, it has been noted that unmodified CNT, GNP, and graphene may not interact favorably with cement hydration products. To enhance their effectiveness, surface modifications of nano-reinforcements, such as grafting functional groups (e.g. hydroxyl, carboxylate, carbonyl, and amine groups), are necessary.

Advancements in nano-science of cement during the 2000s, driven by characterization and simulation studies, have suggested that incorporating small organic groups or polymeric chains into growing C–S–H gel could potentially achieve covalent hybridization, thereby enhancing the fracture energy and strain capacity of cement-based materials. Organic substances explored for this purpose include poly(methacrylic acid) (PMA), poly(acrylic acid) (PAA), poly(vinyl sulfonic acid) (PSA), poly(vinyl alcohol) (PVA), poly(ethylene glycol) (PEG), poly(allylamine) (PAM), polysaccharides, and celluloses. These molecules were chosen due to their structural abundance of functional groups, including anionic (such as carboxyl and sulfonate) or nonionic (such as hydroxyl, alkoxy, carbonyl, and amino), which can interact with C–S–H.

Studies have revealed that these molecules can be partially intercalated into C–S–H, with the majority residing within gel pores, thereby linking C–S–H colloidal particles. Both the functional groups of polymer molecules and the characteristics of

C–S–H play pivotal roles in the interactions between polymer and C–S–H. The functional groups enhance H-bonds and electrostatic forces at the polymer/C–S–H interfaces while also filling defects in the silicate chains, potentially repairing damaged silicate chains that may occur during fracture processes by forming Si-O-C bonds. These interaction mechanisms are anticipated to modify C–S–H by increasing or maintaining a level of silicate chain polymerization, thereby influencing mechanical properties and long-term stability, such as calcium leaching and creep.

Thus far, the enhancement in compressive and flexural strengths of cement-based materials achieved by nano-particles and nano-reinforcement has typically been limited to around 30%, although improvements in the modulus of elasticity may reach up to 50%. Most studies related to organic-hybridization have focused on synthetic polymer/C–S–H composites (created through sol-gel methods) and/or molecular dynamics (MD) simulations. However, in realistic cement-based materials, the hybridization of polymeric molecules sometimes even reduces bulk mechanical properties such as indentation modulus, hardness, and strength. This ineffectiveness of nano-materials and nano-modifications in realistic cement systems could be attributed to nano-particle and reinforcement agglomeration, or hindrances posed by steric, entropic, and/or electrostatic interactions, which can impede the entry of organic molecules into C–S–H.

In the future development and application of nanotechnology in concrete, several challenges will need to be addressed, including ensuring proper dispersion, compatibility between nano-materials and cement, addressing public safety concerns, and managing costs. An ideal approach to addressing these issues could involve generating nano-materials *in situ* within fresh concrete in an economically and environmentally efficient manner. Ongoing studies at Missouri University of Science and Technology have recently demonstrated the generation of *in situ* calcium carbonate nano-particles (via carbonating calcium-bearing mixing water) and organic-inorganic nano-particles (through the chelation of metal cations using selected organic molecules), as depicted in Fig. 13.10. These advancements have been shown to significantly enhance the engineering properties of concrete.

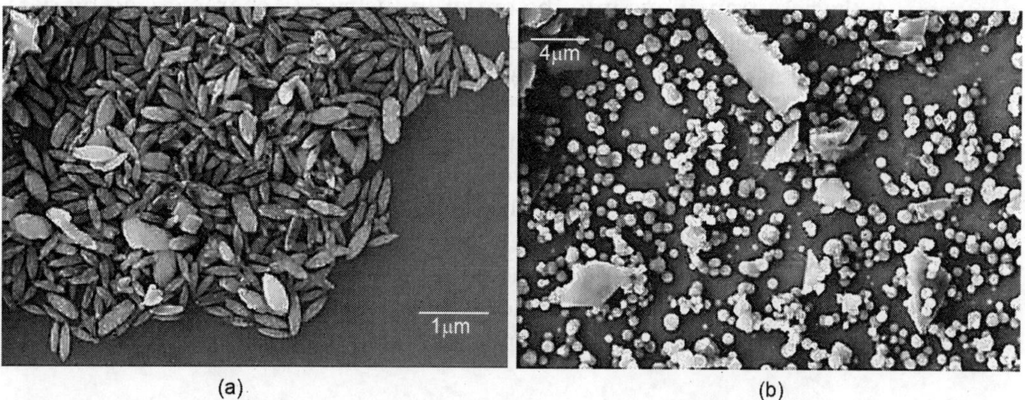

Fig. 13.10: Nano-particles formed *in situ* in fresh concrete: (a) calcium carbonate nano-particles; (b) organic-inorganic nano-particles

13.9 DATA SCIENCE AND ARTIFICIAL INTELLIGENCE IN CONCRETE TECHNOLOGY

Concrete stands out as one of the most intricate engineering materials, primarily due to the extensive diversity in the characteristics of its raw materials and service environments. The future trajectory of concrete studies may pivot on the utilization of substantial datasets, often referred to as "Big Data." The amassed data within the concrete industry presents a ripe opportunity for training artificial intelligence (AI)-based models, such as supervised machine learning algorithms, to predict properties with remarkable accuracy and reliability. These predictive models can be instrumental in designing concrete mixtures tailored to specific targets, encompassing performance, eco-efficiency, and cost considerations, as well as accounting for service environment parameters. Additionally, AI models hold promise in fully validating numerical models, such as kinetic and thermodynamic models, thereby enhancing their robustness and applicability.

Recent years have witnessed a surge in studies exploring the integration of machine learning methods within concrete technology. Much attention has been directed towards predicting the mechanical properties of concrete, including compressive strength, tensile strength, shear strength, and modulus of elasticity. The prevalent machine learning models fall under the category of supervised learning, as they leverage provided datasets to explicitly predict target values—an approach aligned with traditional engineering principles. Notable algorithms embraced in concrete technology encompass artificial neural networks (ANN), support vector machines (SVM), decision trees (e.g. random forest), and evolutionary algorithms (e.g. genetic algorithms). Ensemble learning techniques, such as random forest, have demonstrated efficacy in enhancing prediction accuracy, particularly when dealing with large datasets. Beyond mechanical properties, machine learning has found applications in forecasting hydration behaviors of novel or multi-phase cementitious materials, optimizing chemical admixture designs, and enhancing prediction accuracy of durability properties of concrete materials and structures.

In the realm of health monitoring for concrete structures, deep learning algorithms, such as convolutional neural networks, have emerged as valuable tools for crack detection. As society transitions into the era of Industry 4.0, characterized by data-driven AI and other emerging technologies, the fusion of traditional art, science, and technology—such as concrete technology—is becoming increasingly prevalent. However, cement and concrete researchers may encounter challenges in adopting data-driven AI, including the selection of suitable algorithms and the availability of sufficiently large and reliable datasets. Efforts to promote data sharing through open access protocols are encouraging, and the establishment of general protocols for screening and fusing high-fidelity datasets will be essential for harnessing the full potential of Big Data in concrete research. With the integration of machine learning methods, including physics-based machine learning and deep learning, the landscape of concrete design and evaluation stands poised for significant transformation.

Index

Symbol

3D Printable concrete 11, 12

A

Abrasion resistance 189
Absolute volume method 157, 158, 168
Accelerator 48–51
Acid attack 153–155
Acoustic emission technique 238–240
Additive manufacturing in construction 268, 269
Admixtures 6, 14, 15, 19, 40, 48–75, 77, 83–92,122, 123, 159, 161, 175
Aggregate 1, 3, 14, 93, 94, 98
  grading 121, 164, 167
  porosity 134, 136, 137
  properties 85, 89, 90
  segregation 86
  shape and texture 121
Agitation 216–217
Air content 160, 161, 165
  analysis 91
Air entrainment 123
Alkali-activated cementitious materials 265, 266
Alkali-aggregate reaction (AAR) 150, 154, 189, 197
Artificial intelligence (AI) in concrete technology 281, 282
Artificial neural network (ANN) 174, 175
A-scan, B-scan, C-scan techniques 233–235
Autogenous
  healing of concrete 111
  shrinkage 141–144
Automation and digital advancements 221, 223

B

Batch mixing 211, 214
Batch plants 93, 94
Batching of concrete 93, 94
Belt conveyors 255
Big data in concrete research 281, 282
Binder 1, 14, 17, 18, 21
Bingham model 114, 115, 124
Bleeding 81, 85–89, 91, 92
Bottom-up design approaches 272, 278
Bucket placement 103
Bucket for concrete placement 254, 255

C

Calcium-silicate-hydrate (C-S-H) 268, 275–278
Calibration and validation of NDT devices 220, 226
Capillary surface tension effect 145, 146
Carbon capture, utilization, and storage (CCUS) 261, 268
Carbonation 153, 154, 189, 198, 199
Carbon-neutral goals in construction 261, 268
Casson model 124
Cement
  content 89
  hydration 76
  storage 212, 213
Cementitious materials 157, 160
Cement-water suspension 123
Chemical admixtures 14, 15, 41, 43
Chemicals 48–75
Chloride ion penetration 153, 154
Chloride-induced corrosion 198, 199
Chute discharge 217, 218
Chutes and drop pipes 254, 255
Climbing mixers 254
Clinker alternatives 265, 266
Coarse aggregate 159, 161, 163
Cohesion in concrete 113
Cohesiveness 14, 34, 41
Cold curing 109
Compactability 83, 92, 113, 115
Compacting concrete 105, 106
Compacting concrete surfaces 258
Compacting factor test 113
Compaction 76, 77, 79–81, 83–88, 91, 92
Compound 48, 67, 68
Compressive strength 5, 10, 13, 23, 31, 32, 43, 125, 127, 129, 157, 161, 166
Computational modeling in concrete science 276, 277
Computerized batching systems 211, 214

Concrete 1–16
batch plants 251
finishing equipment 257–259
mix design 157–167
mixers 251–254
pavements 225, 243
pumps 256, 257
structure evaluation 220, 225
transportation 100–104
vibration 106, 107
Consistency 78, 81, 83, 85, 86, 89–92
Consistency and quality control 211, 215
Construction joints 103
Conveyor systems 100, 104
Corrosion detection in reinforced concrete 226, 240
Corrosion/corrosion-inhibiting 63, 64
Cost efficiency 158, 162
Crack identification in concrete 225, 241, 245
Cracking 4, 6, 9, 16, 25, 39, 44
Cracking in concrete 189, 196, 197
Creep 126, 148–150
Cube specimens 128, 129
Curing 15, 16, 23, 25, 34, 41, 67, 68
Curing compound method 109
Curing of concrete 108–110
Curing schedule 175
Cylinder specimens 128, 129

D

Data science in concrete technology 281, 282
Deep learning for crack detection 282
Defect localization 238–241
Delivery radius 217
Demec gauge 147
Demolished concrete recycling 263, 264
Diffusivity 189, 190
Digital signal processing 221, 223
Dimensional
analysis 119
stability 141–148
Double-rotor trowels 259
Drop pipes 255
Dry batched materials 211, 217
Drying shrinkage 141, 144–148
DSP concrete 11
Durability 125, 150–153, 157, 160
Durability and fatigue analysis 220, 224
Durability and permeability 113
Durability of concrete 188–190
Durability unified service life design theory 274–276
Dynamic modulus of elasticity measurement 243, 244

E

Eco-friendly cementitious materials 261–263
Efflorescence 155
Elastic strain 141
Electric trowels 110
Electromagnetic wave techniques 226, 227
Embedded items 103, 104
Energy-efficient binders 265, 266
Entrained air 123
Environmental
conditions 77, 85, 86, 88, 91
considerations 211, 215
exposure conditions 161, 178
factors 189, 197, 198
Erosion resistance 189
Expansive concrete 149

F

Fiber-reinforced concrete 10, 11
Fine aggregate 159, 163, 165
Finishing concrete surfaces 110, 111
Fire resistance 155, 156
Flexural
improvements 277–279
strength 125, 129, 130
Floating in concrete finishing 258
Flow curve 115, 119
Flow table test 77–79, 85, 91
Fly ash 5, 11, 19, 39, 40
Forced mixers 252, 253
Form vibrators 107
Formwork 9, 15, 31, 41, 103, 104
Freeze-thaw cycles 125, 150
Freeze-thaw damage 189, 205, 206
Fresh
concrete 76–81, 83–89, 91, 92
properties 112–114

G

Gas-forming 63
Gel pores 189, 205
Gel porosity 151
Geopolymers in construction 265, 266
GGBFS 56, 72–75
Graphene in concrete 279, 280
Greenhouse gas emissions in cement production 261, 262
Ground-penetrating radar (GPR) 227, 246, 247

H

Hand mixing 98
Hardening and stiffening 121
Health and safety in RMC plants 215, 216
Heat curing 108, 109
Herschel-Bulkley model 124
High strength concrete 162, 165
High-belite cement (HBC) 266, 267
High-efficiency mixing 252–253
High-performance concrete (HPC) 116, 125, 151, 267, 268
High-range water-reducing admixtures (HRWRAs) 119, 123
High-rise buildings 225
High-strength concrete (HSC) 5, 11, 267, 268
Hydration 1, 6, 15–18, 23–25, 41–44, 161, 166
Hysteresis loop 115

I

Impact-echo method 240–243
Influence of material heterogeneity 221, 224
Influence of moisture and water content 224, 226, 246
Infrared thermography 247–249
Integrated materials and structural design 272–274
Integrity assessment of large structures 220, 225
Internal friction 113, 114
IS guidelines 175–178

J

Jitterbugging effects 257

K

Kaiser effect in acoustic emissions 240
Kelly Ball test 81–83

L

Lightweight concrete 10, 11, 36, 37

M

Machine learning in concrete design 281, 282
Machine mixing 93, 94, 98
Magnetic flux leakage 228, 229
Marine environment 189, 206, 207
Material conveyance systems 255
Maximum aggregate size 121, 160, 164
Mechanical deterioration 189, 197
Micro-cracks 133, 135
Microwave moisture content measurement 227, 247
Mineral admixtures 6, 14, 39, 40
Minerals 48–75
Mix design 77, 83, 84, 86–88, 92
Mix proportioning 159, 161, 162
Mix proportions 120, 121
Mixer capacity 213, 217
Mixing blades 214, 217
Mixing concrete 93, 94, 98
Mixing methods 98
Mixing time 99
Mobile concrete plants 215
Mobility 84, 89, 113, 114
Modified Bingham model 124
Modified slump test 116–119
Modifying 59, 60
Modulus of elasticity 125, 140
Moisture adjustment 168, 182
Moisture and porosity assessment 224, 227
Mortar loss 86, 92

N

Nano-reinforcements in concrete 279, 280
Nanotechnology in cement-based materials 279–281
Nomographs for yield stress and plastic viscosity 119
Nondestructive evaluation (NDE) 220–222
Nondestructive testing (NDT) 220, 222
Nuclear magnetic resonance (NMR) 229

O

On-site mixing 216, 217

P

Pan mixers 252, 253
Performance attributes of mixed concrete 99
Peristaltic pumps 256
Permeability 189, 190
Photoelasticity with microwaves 247
Pigments 64, 65
Placing concrete 100–105
Plastic shrinkage 141–143
Plastic viscosity 114, 116–119
Plasticity 76
Plasticizer 54–58
Plasticizer admixtures 256
Plate and surface waves 232, 233
Polymeric modifications of concrete 277–279
Portland cement 1, 5, 6, 17–21, 25, 26
Power mixers 252, 253
Power trowels 258
Pozzolana 3, 5, 20, 40
Pozzolanic materials 151–153
Prestressed concrete 4, 5
Production control testing 219
Pumpability 116
Pumpable concrete 183–185
Pumping concrete 104

Q

Quality assurance 215, 219
Quality control in concrete 221, 247

R

Radiography and radiometry 230, 231
Ready-mix trucks 93, 100
Ready-mixed concrete (RMC) 210, 211
Recycled concrete aggregates (RCA) 263, 264
Reinforced concrete 4, 9
Reinforcement corrosion 153, 154, 189, 198–200
Reinforcing steel 103
Response ssurface methodology (RSM) 172, 173
Restrained shrinkage 147, 148
Retarders 51–54
Re-tempering concrete 100
Reversible mixers 252
Rheology 90
Rheology of concrete 112–114
Ribbon loading 214
Roller-compacting concrete 12

S

Salt crystallization 189, 207
Screeding techniques 257
Segregation 76, 77, 81, 83–87, 89, 91, 92
analysis 92

Segregation and bleeding 113, 114
Segregation in concrete transportation 254, 255
Self-compacting concrete 5, 6, 106
Self-leveling concrete 119, 123
Semi-empirical models 119, 124
Service life prediction for concrete structures 275, 276
Serviceability 188
Shear stress and strain rate 113–115
Shear wave reflection 236
Shotcrete 12
Shrinkage control 149, 150
Shrinkage cracking 197
Shrinkage reducers 149, 150
Signal processing in NDT 223, 239
Silica fume 5, 11, 19, 39, 40
  applications 261, 262
Single-rotor trowels 259
Site preparation 103, 104
Slag 5, 11, 19, 39, 40, 56, 72–75
Slump adjustments 217
Slump test 77, 78, 83, 85, 91, 116–119, 161, 182
  measurement 116
Smart construction materials 271, 272
Spalling 153, 156
Specific strength 9
Splitting tensile strength 131, 132
Stability 84, 85, 87–89, 113, 116
Standard curing 108
Standard deviation 177, 179
Statistical methods in mix design 172–175
Strength estimation 236, 243
Strength requirements 161, 177
Stress-strain relationship 137–140
Structural optimization 123
Structural safety assessment 225, 240
Sulfate attack 153, 154, 189, 207, 208
Superplasticizer 58–59, 151
Supplementary cementitious materials (SCMs) 261–263
Surface delamination risks 257
Sustainability in concrete production 260, 261

T

Temperature and time 90
Temperature control 109
Tensile strength 125, 129–131
Thermal properties in defect detection 248, 249
Thermal stress 197
Thickness measurement 225, 243
Tilting mixers 251, 252
Time-of-flight diffraction (TOFD) 231, 232
Tippers 218
Transition zone 133–135
Transit-mix trucks 251, 252
Transport properties 189, 190
Transportation logistics 217, 218
Transporting concrete 100–104
Tremie operations 255
Trial mixes 159, 169
Trough mixers 253
Troweling techniques 258, 259
Truck mixers 217, 218
Twin-shaft mixers 253

U

Ultra-high-performance concrete 5, 6
Ultra-high-strength concrete (UHSC) 6, 11, 267, 268
Ultrasonic pulse velocity 231–233

V

Vee-Bee test 113, 81, 83, 85
Versatility in concrete mixes 211
Vibration 76, 81, 83, 85, 86, 88
  methods 106–107
Viscosity 59–60
Volume batching method 94
Volume stability 9, 14

W

W/C ratio 5, 13, 41–44
Water content 77, 84, 87, 89
Water reducers 5, 14, 23, 43
Waterproofers/waterproofing 60–62
Water-to-cement ratio (w/c ratio) 77, 157, 160, 161, 189–190
Weigh batching method 94
Wet-leg systems 214, 218
Workability 6, 14, 15, 23, 34, 41, 43, 76–78, 81–91, 157, 161
  of Concrete 112, 113

Y

Yield stress (t_0) 114, 116–119